Meaningful Work: Viktor Frankl's Legacy for the 21st Century

Meaningful Work: Viktor Frankl's Legacy for the 21st Century

Beate von Devivere

Meaningful Work: Viktor Frankl's Legacy for the 21st Century

Springer

Beate von Devivere
bvd CONSULT
Frankfurt am Main, Hessen, Germany

ISBN 978-3-030-07859-1 ISBN 978-3-319-89791-2 (eBook)
https://doi.org/10.1007/978-3-319-89791-2

Softcover re-print of the Hardcover 1st edition 2018

Printed on acid-free paper

This Springer imprint is published by the registered company Springer International Publishing AG part of Springer Nature.
The registered company address is: Gewerbestrasse 11, 6330 Cham, Switzerland

Summary

Meaningful work has become one of the most frequently discussed and searched for issues of our times. Individuals, leaders, teams, management, organizations, research, counseling, and psychotherapy are discussing man's search for meaning in work and activities for positive change. Viktor Frankl's legacy is providing for both scientific and philosophical, pioneering approach to answering twenty-first century demands. Man's inherent search for meaning, their freedom, and their responsibility to act on it are basic components of all current meaning oriented activities. This book is discussing today's global work place challenges, presenting data on man's cry for meaning and a wide range of new approaches across diverse sectors in the international community, addressing meaning and values in work life and implementing meaningful activities. Finally, the author is suggesting integrated approach for accomplishing the Copernican turn, further promoting meaningful work.

Foreword

One rarely has the opportunity to be granted the honor of writing the opening paragraphs of a book as timely and important as the present one. *Meaningful Work* is probing, discussing, and negotiating questions tens, if not hundreds of thousands of people ask themselves day by day: Is my work meaningful? And, perhaps even more importantly: How can I navigate through my working life in such a way that my work is not a mere necessity, but a way of living up to the promise and hope of meaning, existential fulfillment, and development? What can I do to add meaning to my work, to find meaning and my calling in my work, and the work of my colleagues?

Given the fact many of us spend well more than two thirds of our adult lives at or in work, one cannot but wonder why so relatively few authors dedicated their attention to these questions, and one cannot but thank Beate von Devivere for taking up the challenge to tackle these questions, and especially for *how* she tackles them: Von Devivere brings together two research traditions which, so far, rarely have been brought together, and which, it seems, have literally been in the waiting for being brought into an engaging dialogue: management consulting and working studies on the one hand, and existential psychology in the tradition of Viktor Frankl's logotherapy and existential analysis, on the other hand.

Most readers will be familiar with the former, but perhaps not as many with the latter, and even fewer may know that Frankl's pioneering work on meaning as a psychological variable has been tested in more than 600 empirical and clinical studies (Thir and Batthyany 2016), and additionally – equally, and perhaps even more important – been tried and tested in the lives of millions of readers, clients, and patients who at times were unsettled, and perhaps even overwhelmed, by their unfulfilled or unheard quest for meaning in their everyday lives.

Yet even within the research tradition of the psychology of existential concerns, it took surprisingly long to discover the obvious: namely, that the workplace, though commonly (and perhaps stereotypically) believed by psychologists to be primarily a field of, among other things, group dynamics, collaborative decision-making, affiliation, and achievement motivation is as much an existential battleground as life beyond the workplace.

Indeed, research suggests that lack of meaning, and, at the same time, a deep seated longing for finding meaning and purpose in life and work, has become endemic. Taking this finding beyond mere epidemiology, a sizable number of studies speaks about the psychological and economic costs of ignoring the quest for meaning and purpose. A large body of studies demonstrates that the temporary or chronic frustration of the will to meaning paves the way for a range of mental disorders and indispositions or, more specifically, that even if such conditions presumably are the result of multiple factors, absence of meaning awareness significantly increases one's susceptibility to a large variety of mental health and behavioral problems.

Conversely, yet another set of studies shows that a newly found sense of meaning, together with various applications of meaning and specifically Franklian oriented interventions, described in this book is capable of initiating or promoting well-being and striving both on an individual, group, and organizational level, exert a protective effect, and, whether in isolation or in conjunction with other interventions, bring with them a significantly higher rate of health in all spheres of work life.

As the studies cited above indicate, despite the initial cautious skepticism toward Frankl's concept to put existential questions at the heart of psychology, the enterprise pioneered by Viktor Frankl of a scientifically oriented existential psychology soon bore fruit with astonishing rapidity in the late 1960s. This development is evident not least in the huge volume of research publications cited above, authored chiefly by Frankl's students in Harvard and Vienna during these early years. Today, it appears as if Frankl's logotherapy, once only one single psychiatrist's "courageous rebellion against the [...] paradigms that dominated psychological theorizing" (Baumeister & Vohs 2002), has, albeit somewhat belatedly, arrived at the research front of experimental, empirical, organizational, and social psychology.

One likely factor that may have contributed to the strong interest in the psychology of existential concerns may be the fact that, since around 1970, psychological thought in general has opened up to new ideas, especially since increasing numbers of academic psychologists have become aware of the limits of orthodox psychoanalysis (Bornstein 2001, Paris 2004). At the same time, behaviorism, which for several decades was particularly strong within experimental psychology, has likewise lost much of its original dominance. Both developments in the history of ideas of psychology took place perhaps largely due to the so-called cognitive turn in the behavioral science, which then soon spread into clinical and experimental psychology (Gardner 1986, Eysenck and Keane 1993).

This turn not only brought with it a rediscovery of the central role of internal representations of the world, which Frankl and his logotherapy had identified long before as being crucial for understanding human experience and behavior (Frankl 1958); Frankl considered much of the "old psychologies" to be disproportionately concerned with deficits and limits and held that they often tended toward a reductionist pathologism, which attempted to explain even such deeply human and existential concerns such as the need for meaning and authenticity not as expressions of human maturity, but as mere compensations for psychological defects and frustrated "lower" needs (Frankl 1961). The increased openness of psychology to less mechanistic or purely psychodynamic models also led to researchers abandoning some their earlier almost exclusive focus on deficits, and instead starting to look again at those inner resources by which real and apparent deficits can be overcome or compensated in psychologically mature and healthy ways.

In brief, for a long time, psychology was largely *deficit-based* rather than resource-oriented and thus had little use for existential concerns and the quest for meaning. For several years now, the neighboring field of positive psychology has tied in with these ideas on a broader level (Seligman and Csikszentmihalyi 2000). Still, the systematic scientific pursuit of a broad-based, resource-oriented psychology is a relatively new undertaking, and at least to logotherapists, it did not come as a surprise that research in this area would soon find that meaning is a central psychological (and existential) resource (Klingberg 2009).

Given the noticeable tendency toward a renewed interest in existential issues and their applications specifically in work life, management, and organizational development, and given the fact that the structure and nature of the working place has, at the same time, changed considerably within the past few decades, there is – or rather was – an obvious necessity to look for applications of existential concerns and specifically man's search for meaning and focused interventions in the context of the workplace. Beate von Devivere took it on herself to fill this gap: This book then, written by an accomplished practitioner active and well versed in both fields and research traditions, is truly pioneering work insofar as it does no less than opening up, and establishing, a whole new research field – current existential issues and meaning oriented approaches and interventions in the workplace, as they are coming forth on the individual, team, and organizational level.

The Endowed Viktor Frankl Chair
for Philosophy and Psychology
International Academy of Philosophy,
University in the Principality of Liechtenstei

Alexander Batthyány

References

Baumeister RF, Vohs KD (2002) The pursuit of meaningfulness in life. In: Snyder CR, Lopez SJ (eds) Handbook of positive psychology. Oxford University Press, New York, pp 608–628
Bornstein RF (2001) The impending death of psychoanalysis. Psychoanal Psychol 18:3
Eysenck MW, Keane MT (1993) Cognitive psychology. Lawrence Erlbaum, London
Frankl VE (1958) Existential analysis and logotherapy. In: Frankl VE (ed) (2010) The feeling of meaninglessness. A challenge to psychotherapy and philosophy. Marquette University Press, Milwaukee
Frankl VE (1961) Philosophical basis of psychotherapy. Philos Today 5:59–64
Klingberg H (2009) Logotherapy, Frankl, and positive psychology. In: Batthyany A, Levinson J (eds) Existential psychotherapy of meaning: handbook of logotherapy and existential analysis. Zeig, Tucker & Theisen, Phoenix
Gardner H (1986) The mind's new science : a history of the cognitive revolution. Basic Books, New York

Paris J (2004) The fall of an icon: psychoanalysis and academic psychiatry. University of Toronto Press, Toronto

Seligman ME, Csikszentmihalyi M (2000) Positive psychology: an introduction. Am Psychol 55(1):5–14

Thir M, Batthyany A (2016) The state of empirical research on logotherapy and existential analysis. In: Batthyany A (ed) Logotherapy and existential analysis. Proceedings of the Viktor Frankl Institute. Springer International Pubishing Switzerland, Vienna, pp 53–74

Acknowledgments

This book has emerged from decades of practice in consulting, coaching, and counseling. From my first, rather unexpected, encounter with Viktor Frankl's *Search for Meaning*, recommended by a fellow colleague more than 20 years ago, to over years of work with organizations, teams and individuals, with professional experts' publications and cooperation, who have been widely acknowledging Viktor Frankl's influence on their own practice and life, over my own training in Logotherapy and Existential Analysis, finding meaning in work and private life has been the guiding issue in my work: I owe my sincere thanks to my clients and their trust and their confidence in traveling together the road of finding meaning in their work for their organizations, their functions, and in their personal lives. Throughout my work in various countries, international organizations and missions around the world, in consulting, coaching, and counseling, I have found innumerable silent heroes, witnessing the greatest freedom of humans to choose their attitude to specific conditions, to rise above and to drive the Copernican turn for positive change. Their answers to life, consisting in right action and in right conduct, "taking the responsibility and to fulfill the task which life constantly sets for each individual" (Viktor Frankl) have ultimately been motivating me for editing this book and for compiling their encouraging examples for working for the greater good.

I am especially indebted to Professor Dr. Alexander Batthyány, Director of the International Association of Logotherapy and Existential Analysis and the Viktor Frankl Institute, Vienna, and to Professor Dr. Alexander Noyon (Hochschule Mannheim, Germany): Alexander Batthyány's international engagement in academic teaching, research and practice of Viktor Frankl's works and legacy, and his organizing the Biennnial International Congress "The Future of Logotherapy" have profoundly inspired me, giving me the opportunity of feeling connected with a global community of meaning searchers. Professor Alexander Noyon's research, publications and psychotherapeutic practice, and his deep understanding of Viktor Frankl's approach, putting existential analysis into practice in clients' support in their search for meaning, have been sparking and invigorating my own thinking and practice in existential consulting and counseling. My sincere appreciation and thanks!

Beate von Devivere

Contents

Chapter 1
Introduction: Man's Search for Meaning – More Current Than Ever

Meaning in work and meaning in life have become topical issues that touch on each and every individual. They have been on the agenda since ages. These questions relate deeply to all of us, up to the point of being a matter of life and death.

The meaning of work has become one of the most frequently discussed and searched for issues. Individuals, teams, organizations, scientists, and research are wondering what would make work meaningful and what difference they could make for positive change.

The human being requires meaning. To live without meaning, goals, values, or ideals, seems to provoke considerable distress. Finding meaning in work and life is defined not by asking the philosophical, general question, What is the meaning of life, but rather by individually answering the question: What is the meaning of *my* life? What is the meaning of what I am active in, what I am engaged in, of the work that I am doing? In essence, individual existence fails, unless there is some idea of what to live for.

What is work for? What type of work would I want? What is my calling? What talents do I have? Who is waiting out there for my contribution? Why was I put here? What am I responsible for? What do we live for? What do we live by? What is the meaning of life? Why do we live? What is a good life for me and the community? What is the value of my work for me, my peers, my family, the organization, society, and the global community? What is our image of humans, being the foundation and driving our activities? What sense does it all make?

Search for meaning is touching on general issues of beliefs, values, ethics, moral convictions, thinking, logic, and mind. Meaning is defined in various ways: a goal, the importance attached to an issue, the attitude toward life, and a sense of mindfulness or of self-transcendence. Above all, any definition of meaning suggests that meaning cannot be defined generally, but rather individually and in situational, concrete terms (Chap. 2).

Meaning is relative and unique: relative in terms of significance given to the various issues, and unique, since the individual person's life is a string of unique situations and, related to a specific person, unique in terms of essence and personal existence.

B. von Devivere, *Meaningful Work: Viktor Frankl's Legacy for the 21st Century*,
https://doi.org/10.1007/978-3-319-89791-2_1

Viktor E. Frankl's life, his work, his research, his lectures, and his extensive publications have had enormous impact on society, work, cultural issues in general, and the expert community in all branches of work life and various organizations, in psychology, psychotherapy, coaching, and counseling. Besides his own publications, until today, there have been boundless experts and professionals from all fields, who have in their work referred to Frankl's works on meaning. His meaning-centered approach of logotherapy and existential analysis, the so-called Third Viennese School, is more than ever relevant in the twenty-first century.

Humans are struggling with global crises and the dehumanization of an increasingly technological culture. Frankl's logotherapy and existential analysis represent a basis to rehumanize work and to benefit from this approach in consulting, coaching, and counseling. Viktor Frankl's approach provides us with a "blueprint" for a better future for humanity that is captured in this book (Chap. 3).

Because of its general holistic orientation, Frankl's approach in logotherapy and existential analysis can be applied to a wide variety of disciplines, ranging from organizational development, management, leadership concepts, training, education, staff health management, medicine, employee assistance, coaching, and counseling up to providing support in existential crisis. It can be employed in all areas of our lives so that we can fulfill our potentials. It may provide for an encouraging answer to one of the core questions that the twenty-first-century technological developments are posing: What is man?

Today, Frankl's concept provides for three roads to finding answers to the challenges and questions, which the twenty-first century is asking us: first, as an existential philosophy, Frankl's approach suggests an understanding of the "What for?," of what the individual existence is about, distinct and different from the mainstream homo economicus output-oriented management approaches. Second, Frankl intended logotherapy and existential analysis to be actively contributing to answering societal and global challenges and to being a contemporary witness of today's discussions, contributing to a good life for each and every individual. Third, logotherapy and existential analysis offer a holistic understanding of the individual person, their physical, psychosocial, and spiritual dimension, providing for a basis of understanding the human condition, for grasping the potentials of diversity of beings and unity of mankind and of the global community's yearning for meaning and the potentials that lie in man and in mankind. Fourth, Frankl's approach gives us an understanding of the current existential questions unanswered, of the sufferings and potential solutions responding to the modern cry for meaning. Frankl's legacy relating to the challenges humanity is facing, and applying it to our future in the twenty-first century, is paving the way to answering life's call upon our work and life (Chap. 4).

Today, humanity is faced with global challenges. Megatrends are shaping our very individual life. Organizations, management, work, and workplaces are actively designing and influencing the way we live. Each individual worker and employee is part of this complex world, in their various roles, being part and actively forming their environment. Freedom and responsibility rests on each person to shape and design these megatrends in a meaningful way (Chap. 5).

Searching for meaning in the twenty-first-century workplaces poses the question: What are the basic assumptions of Frankl's approach, helping us to define our road to living a more fulfilled life, including work and being productive? How do answers provided read in the twenty-first-century workplaces and in meaningful work? The philosophical, anthropological, and therapeutic considerations and empirical findings of logotherapy and existential analysis are providing for a most lucid and powerful paradigm for assessing, understanding, and maneuvering through the twenty-first century's unprecedented challenges. What is man? Viktor Frankl's three-dimensional approach, understanding the person's physical, psychological, and spiritual aspects and the space for action provided by this concept, meets with man's current search for the full potentials of humans against the reductionism of the "homo economicus." Acknowledging, understanding, and recognizing a person's inherent spiritual dimension turn out to be some of currently most discussed challenges in all spheres of life.

What is our freedom, and where is this freedom endangered to become mere arbitrariness, without being balanced by our responsibility to act on it? How do these two basic components of living a fulfilling life spell out in work, management, and in organizational development?

Work is a matter of experiencing own creative and thereby realizing one's unique mission in life. Work is the field where the unique person relates to his or her community, with this relation giving meaning and value to the individual person. This meaning and value are always related to the specific circumstances where and how this work is being delivered.

No profession or vocation has a meaning as such, or no profession has any more meaning than the other one. It is only the concrete person, delivering their own, specific service and work, that gives meaning to this work. Too many persons' natural relationship to their work as an area of potential realization of creative and experiential values and unique self-fulfillment is suffering under the current working conditions. Work has increasingly become a means of making money, establishing status, external recognition, termed as success. To a large extent, working to make a living has become the "What for," but the person's life still has no "Why" to work and live. How can we deal with this "Janus face" of work, and how can we manage work, having become the most influential part of an individual person's life, overshadowing all other spheres of existence and potential meaning in life? How does Frankl's understanding of the meaning of work translate into modern workplaces? What is meaning in work? What is the meaning of work? What is meaningful work? Is there a general definition of meaningful work (Chap. 6)?

Taking a two-dimensional approach on work, according to Frankl's lucid paradigm, offering a closer look at the diverse experiences in work, along the poles of perceived success and failure, of despair and meaning, suggests a lucid understanding of the various aspects of meaning and work (Chap. 7).

Current research andempirical findings on our inherent motivation to make sense out of what we are active in and on how to lead a fulfilling, not only strongly support Frankl's motivational concept. All relevant data on the tremendous health challenges in Western industrialized countries are backing man's frustration of their will to meaning. We are all intrinsically motivated to find meaning in our work and private life. In all spheres of life, we are confronted with the unheard cry for meaning, to be understood as existential stress, due to lack of meaning, emptiness, and a life perceived as an existential vacuum (Chap. 8).

Together with ever more sophisticated insights into human functioning, the very core of the person, the self, the forming and developing of the self, has entered the grand stage of not only scientific interest and research but is also being addressed in a wide range of management, organizational, and individual activities. All these enterprises are connected by their search for continuous self-optimization, self-actualization, and fulfillment. The unfulfilled desire for meaning in work and life has not only remained the core existential question of humanity, but it is being discussed and answered in ever more dynamic and powerful ways (Chap. 9).

What are the specific activities and measures that organizations are providing to answer this cry for meaning and to provide for preventive measures in organizational health management? Fortunately, international institutions and organizations and the international community have been connecting and linking around an impressive range of scientifically sound concepts for reacting to the greatest challenge of the Western world (World Health Organization), i.e., promoting mental health, also relating to focused workplace-related activities (Chap. 10).

The greater part of this book is relating and dedicated to one of Frankl's most influential legacies for this century: the undeniable core in every human being, the inherent core human strengths, that the twenty-first-century organizations and individuals have started to relate to in initiating the "Copernican turn" in work. Research for this book has revealed a powerful Copernican turn underway, in the ways work is understood, managed, and organized. These global activities across various business branches, fields of expertise, organizations, management levels, and diverse individuals with their distinct backgrounds and history share a guiding compass, their "true north," addressing the self's best human core (Chap. 11).

Focusing on inner rightness as guiding compass, shifting from external to internal values, the order of understanding work and organizational purpose is being reversed: We do not pursue wealth. We pursue a work and life well lived. Wisdom is aligned with rationality, honoring the complex, ambiguous, paradoxical, nonlinear nature of reality, connecting the three dimensions of our existence. These twenty-first-century pioneers and new approaches are appreciating and actually living the cognitive breakthrough, the ability to reason, transcending the "either-or" thinking pattern to the more complex "both-and" thinking, and applying it to living freedom and responsibility, relating to the self and to others in the global community. What are the crossroads, where the various approaches meet in giving answers to man's search for meaning? Where and how do logotherapy and existential analysis meet with other meaning-centered considerations, projects, and concepts of work life?

Based on Frankl's legacy, this book is dedicated to all those impressive concepts and approaches that might change the course of history, giving meaning and hope to the global community and each and every individual working: Their diverse approaches all share one commonality.

They are based on an evolutionary approach to humanity, understanding man's human potentials as they have developed throughout our millenniums of civilization, and the dark sides of humanity's present situation. Their approach draws upon the positive concept of understanding the vast unrealized capacities that lie in humanity. Their thinking has changed the paradigm from scarcity to abundance. Their activities are giving vivid examples of giving and living meaning in their work and their organizations, and they show what we need to sow in order to reap meaningful work.

This book provides for specific examples across diverse organizations from different business branches, management, activists, and research, igniting the spark for finding meaning in work and for implementing the according organizational activities. Their practices provide for powerful examples of good work, driven by values, conscience, and awareness for man's need and will to meaning in work (Chaps. 12 and 13).

Some of these activities and organizational examples are addressing the paradigm of "New Work," defining a new understanding and practice of work, appropriate for meeting the global, structural, societal, and individual challenges of the twenty-first-century work (Chap. 14).

All of these concepts, activities, and services provided for in the context of meaningful work are anchored around a strong sense of humanism, globally overarching values of humanity, of an explicit understanding of leadership around personal responsibility and, also, humility in exercising leadership not only in relation to others but also in relating to own life's challenges and potentials. All these activities are centered around a deep understanding of the human potentials and the human will to meaning that wait to be introduced and lived in work and all spheres of life (Chaps. 15 and 16).

Increasingly, recognizing and developing the core human potentials have come to the center of attention for building an overarching work culture of purpose, dignity, and abundance (Chap. 17).

The outcomes of all these activities, focused on finding meaning in work, and their effects on well-being and personal fulfillment, empirically researched and tested, are telling a persuasive story about the different meaning-oriented and existential approaches in addressing, organizing, and finding meaning in work (Chap. 18). All these findings, drawn from a wide set of current scientific approaches in humanities and natural sciences, are establishing a new understanding of the human capacity to drive positive change (Chap. 19).

Increasingly, specific services focused on the individual employee's search for a working environment and life well lived are being offered to staff. These services, ranging from business and executive coaching to counseling and employee assistance programs, are based on a shared set of ethics and values, all of which are based on a humanistic understanding of the person's best potentials, that all serve man's inherent search for meaning and, not being recognized, may lead to existential frustration. Coaching and workplace counseling refer to a variety of current therapeutic approaches, increasingly interested in the relevance and activation of the individual person's search for meaning (Chap. 20).

New approaches in finding meaning in the twenty-first-century work and in driving the "Copernican turn" are closely linked to a renaissance of philosophy and philosophic approaches. Viktor E Frankl has, until today, been the only doctor, professor, and therapist who based his approach and concept on an explicit image of humans and also on philosophical considerations, regarding human existence, which was hardly recognized in last century's discussion and activities, at least in the economic and business world. Today, a yearning for philosophy and humanity's existential foundations, their understanding of the very core of existence, going back to the ancient great thinkers' ideals and ideas about what makes us human, has entered the stage of modern work life, management, organizational development, and personal search for meaning in one's own existence. These philosophers' and engaged activists' ideas are supporting today's Copernican turn, providing insights and understanding of our potentials for driving the twenty-first-century renaissance (Chap. 21).

Being challenged not only by today's megatrends shaping our world but also haunted by the various crises around this planet, the undeniable scientific forecasts relating to climate change, depletion of our natural resources, regional conflicts, hunger, and migration, another paradigm shift can be observed: optimism in the face of adversity, for which Viktor Frankl has left us with an ever-encouraging concept of tragic optimism. An active entrepreneur has defined his own conclusion: "In case there is rescue ahead, I want to have been a part of it." This active community, driving change in their respective functions in all realms of their work, is placing hope before hopelessness, arguing that for our sake and in responsible action toward the next generations, we cannot afford to stand aside; consequently, their efforts are driven by their commitment and their conviction that a silent revolution has begun (Chap. 22).

Which answers could an integrated approach give to man's current cry for meaning? Putting together all current activities around finding meaning in work and living a fulfilled life, based on values and the best human potentials, a meaning-centered integrated approach, based on Viktor Frankl's legacy, is emerging. There is a global community, strongly aligned along the common cause of working together for making the substantial difference. We are the beings that always decide. With our capacities, each of us is the active collaborator of the individual and our common fate. With the actions described in this book, each and every individual person is writing in the book of history, not only telling about the past but with an unknown number of blank pages, which, at the end, will testify on each individual person's behalf, in whatever organization, business, work, function, and service each person is active.

It is, in Frankl's terms, up to the individual person in their respective business, expert, professional, scientific and therapeutic communities, their commitment and engagement, up to all of us, in our respective work and private communities, to turn our work into an epic, worthy of humankind. There is a strong community, encouraging and driving this change (Chap. 23).

Chapter 2
The Image of Humans in Search for Meaning

Contents

Discussing the concept of meaning in work and meaning in life implicitly presupposes some concept of being human. Although rarely being specifically clarified, searching for meaning in work is always based on a specific concept of the human being.

For more than a century, for mainstream behavioral sciences and economic theory and practices, meaning and purpose seemed minor or almost irrelevant factors for the human condition and human behavior. Although philosophers had been discussing and working on the influence of thoughts, emotions, and motives on human behavior, modern "doctors of the soul," while focusing on human drives and learning, considered issues of meaning and purpose as rather ethereal constructs with little or no relevance for healing or for giving guidance for the individual on how to live a good life, or meaning and existential beliefs were considered as mere products of underlying drives. Freud's, Adler's, and Jung's approaches as well as behavioral psychotherapy had little or no interest in existential issues, understanding them more in terms of secondary symptoms or issues to be neglected in the process of learning and potentially changing unproductive beliefs, while stressing either conscious or unconscious drives, motivating human behavior, or rationality and progress in learning, in intellectual insight and personal reflexivity.

While the abovementioned schools dramatically changed humanity's insight into our soul, our drives, the psychological triggers for our suffering, the effects of the once powerful societal restrictions, and traditional limitations for our human condition, undoubtedly leading to a liberation of thinking, breaking intolerable taboos,

B. von Devivere, *Meaningful Work: Viktor Frankl's Legacy for the 21st Century*,
https://doi.org/10.1007/978-3-319-89791-2_2

and curing the soul of many, these "schools" and approaches were based on an implicit, tacit image of humans.

Today, we live in an age of knowledge, of science, when natural sciences and technological inventions have substantially influenced the tacit image of humans.

What are the theoretical, psychological, and philosophical foundations of these approaches and practices? What is man in terms of human anthropology, studying and explaining the concept of the human person, and human ontology of being and existence?

Today, the rich foundations of the many facets of meaning, grounded in philosophical, anthropological, and ontological approaches of the human condition, have been rediscovered for a holistic understanding of meaning and its relevance for the twenty-first-century living.

We look back on the twentieth century's many decades of diverse practical approaches and practices to meaning and existential issues in medical and daily life, addressing work-related and private topics, relating to meaning and existential givens, that are implicit components of each person's life. Business coaching and consulting have taken aspects of meaning, existential issues, and human values on board of their literature and practices. Many practitioners in the field of coaching and consulting were referring in some way or the other to Viktor Frankl's concept in grand appreciation of his very own giving witness as holocaust survivor to his concept with his own life, his suffering, and his terminal conclusions on man's condition.

Together with developments in the various psychotherapeutic approaches, the new field of positive psychology emerged, putting meaning topics back on the agenda of a dynamic discussion around the very foundations of meaning and human existence, their conceptions, their importance, and influence on human's conditions, well-being, health, and dealing with life's challenges.

Today – in the age of knowledge and ever faster developments in science and technology – issues of meaning are emerging forcefully.

2.1 Meaning: Wanting or Waiting?

There are various fields of meaning-related sciences – philosophical, existential, linguistic, psychological, and semiotics – with multiple definitions of "meaning."

Meaning can be defined as sense, purpose, end, intention, a shared mental representation of possible relationships and events, and the basis of an organized network of commonly shared concepts (MacKenzie and Baumeister 2014). Meaning is also defined as cognizance of order, coherence, and purpose in one's existence, the pursuit and attainment of worthwhile goals and an accompanying sense of fulfillment, and a general perception of purpose and coherence (Mascaro 2014). Some concepts have defined a hedonic meaning, a commitment to maximize individual pleasure. This, however, does not match the common understanding of meaning.

Wong (1998) has identified seven factors that are generally viewed as characteristics of a person leading an "ideally meaningful life":

- Achievement
- Social adeptness
- Religion or spirituality
- Self-transcendence or altruism
- Self-acceptance or humility
- Emotional intimacy
- Fair treatment or justice

People are questioning:

- Does the world around us have a consistent meaning?
- Is there any purpose to existence?
- Is there a point of life?
- Does my life matter?
- How do I make a difference?

Today, we can refer to an impressing variety of scientific approaches and empirical findings referring to meaning, demonstrating substantial effort by the various dedicated schools, scientists, and research projects to conceptualize meaning. In their recent dedicated and impressive publication, Batthyany and Russo-Netzer (2014) have for the first time undertaken to present state-of-the-art scientific findings on meaning in positive and existential psychology.

Mainly three approaches have emerged, understanding meaning as:

- Motivational (defining goals and purpose)
- Cognitive (meaning making, sense of coherence)
- Various types of meaning (meaning in life, meaning of life, existential need)

MacKenzie and Baumeister (2014) defines three functions of meaning:

- To help people recognize and discern signals and patterns in the environment, to retrieve information about others, and to detect patterns of behavior
- To share information and knowledge and coordinate actions
- To regulate one's behavior and affect, consider various options, and think about long range goals

Four needs for meaning as a human motivation to find answers and explanations for life events, a desire for life to make sense of things, can be differentiated:

- Purpose
- Values
- Efficacy
- Self-worth

Looking at latest research, a holistic conceptualization of meaning begins to emerge, relating either to:

- The more functional aspects of meaning as a need for striving, achievement, intimacy, religion/spirituality, and generativity
- The more existential level, personal meaning profile, relationships, religion, service, life work, and self-transcendence

2.2 Meaning Motivation

The influence of individual meaning fulfillment on the development of or protection against mental health problems has been widely tested; Batthyany and Russo-Netzer (2014) report on more than 320 empirical studies: According to these findings, meaning can be seen as an important psychological resource "that enables people to draw strengths and insights from their positive and negative experiences, gain perspective from their present situations and point toward a worthwhile and valuable future" (Batthyany and Russo-Netzer 2014, p. 9).

- There are significant correlations between lack of meaning and a general increase in specific mental health problems, either as causative mechanism or influencing the severity of the problems.
- Poor meaning in life is itself a significant predictor of overall mental health.
- Mental health affects both positive and negative aspects of well-being.
- A renewed meaning awareness would provide crucial healing and coping resources. The presence of meaning awareness was a more significant predictor of successful aging than traditional factors such as social and cognitive resources and other demographic variables.
- An increased sense of meaning in life has a curative effect for the individual person.
- Sense of meaning highly affects individual coping capacities.
- Meaning awareness is of high significance in the processing of external stressors and life events.
- Meaning may be a source of positive experiences.

2.3 Meaning Beyond Functional Aspects

Beyond all commonly shared insights into the promising benefits of meaning awareness for individual health and well-being, nevertheless, there is a basic "meaning problem" to be acknowledged.

We are constantly confronted with findings and behaviors that do not seem to make much sense, if the only rationale of meaning motivation were the functional aspects to better cope with life events, to recover, to understand, to feel good, and to bounce back from adversity.

Everyday life alone is providing for regular examples, when bringing meaning to the individual life seems to be more than harvesting the best benefits of making meaning: All findings suggest that parenthood adds meaning to the parents' lives, but not necessarily immediate well-being, with their potential being confronted with substantial changes in all spheres of life, i.e., health, lack of sleep, economic situation, income, friends, individual spare time for hobbies, housing, etc.

In work life, we know of myriads of examples, when humans engage in actions against their individual, direct physical, or well-being benefit, because these activities appear to them more meaningful than not undertaking them and because they are understood and recognized as "good" by themselves and because they have a "value in themselves."

All volunteer work, all associations like Médecins Sans Frontières and other International Medical Aid and Crises, support activities; actually all fieldwork in international peace keeping and UN missions are based on dedication for the common good, risking personal health, well-being, and sometimes lives.

Apparently, searching for and finding meaning in life do not always relate to their functional implications and their positive benefits for the individual person in terms of empirically valid benefits. The opposite might be the case: The individual finds individual meaning beyond the tested individual short-term well-being benefits.

2.4 Ultimate Concerns

Where do we come from? What are we? Where are we going?
Paul Gauguin, Painting, Oil on Canvas, Inscription in capital letters, about 1897

Meaning and meaning awareness are central psychological and philosophical factors for understanding and for coping with the challenges of life. Still, as human beings, we are confronted with the "meaning problem": Is search and striving for meaning a means to the end of achieving well-being or comfort from anxieties and existential givens, or is search for meaning an end in itself, relating to some objective correlate "out there"?

While there are powerful motivations to strive for "meaning" to achieve subjective well-being and fulfillment, this functional approach apparently does not represent the whole spectrum of human behavior. Persons act not for their own personal or functional goals but rather according to what seems "right and good" beyond personal gains or because they find meaning and personal growth in moments of sickness, guilt, and suffering, beyond the very functional understanding of getting better, addressing, understanding, and embracing life's ultimate concerns.

The human search for meaning apparently goes beyond a mere set of diagnostic issues, it is more than a subjective tool for getting better.

The existential "entanglement of the human being" is a great and complex issue that needs to be studied further. "Is meaning wanting or waiting?" (Stephen Costello, quoted by Batthyany and Russo-Netzer 2014). There are no quick fixes, given the history of humanity, of civilization, and their making of.

Working on meaning, we are addressing no less than the full range of human conditions, emotions and concerns, and "the life worth living" as a whole.

Meaning questions are addressing the heart of humanity's ultimate concerns: Does the world around us have a consistent meaning? Is there any purpose to existence, to my existence? Is there a point to life? Does my life matter? These questions are relevant as ever: How we answer them will change our lives, not only for today, but shape our future. These are perennial questions relating to the human condition, and their answers seem to have become ever more urgent.

Throughout the greatest part of conscious civilization, the answers to these questions were given by philosophers, religions, and traditions. Together with the Enlightenment and the emerging of science, technology, and engineering, humanity is called to give their own answers to all these questions:

2.4.1 *"Where Do We Come From?"*

This query today addresses history and particularly scientific historiography. It has expanded far beyond the history of humanity as documented in written sources, drawing upon biology, paleontology, anthropology, archaeology, and a dozen other disciplines which, when integrated, give us a comprehensive overview of the origins of human beings. Human history, if extended to the origin of our species, comprises more than five million years. Answering the questions concerning humanity's origin is also about validating the goods and values that we have produced throughout our human history.

2.4.2 *"What Are We?"*

Some would claim that today's humanity is confronted with existential threats like nuclear war, bioengineered pandemic, superintelligence, nanotechnology, and unknown unknowns, perhaps discounted. Experts are observing contemporary dystopianism and the casual cynicism shown to hopeful visions of the future. Instead of asceticism, we have its antithesis, indulgence. Apparently, though, this is by far not giving a substantial answer to our search for understanding our current condition.

2.4.3 "Where Are We Going?"

We have the technology today to do much more than we are doing at present in order to mitigate existential risk, and yet too little is being done to ensure the continuity of civilization and the biosphere for the long term. Last century's countercultures of "small is beautiful" and "the limits to growth" can be understood as a perennial aspect of the human condition, searching for a better world. They were responses in an Age of Technology, first signs of a rebellion against the rationalism of the Enlightenment.

Clark (1969) wrote, that civilization requires "...confidence in the society in which one lives, belief in its philosophy, belief in its laws, and confidence in one's own mental powers" (p. 15). Today, humanity and individuals all over the world are searching for meaning, to cope with the daily impertinencies, the unforeseeable tragedies and crises, the regular yet ever-faster dynamics, and the challenges and joys of our current lives.

Together with coping with the given circumstances, humanity is called to proactively shape their own future, in defining their path in a meaningful way. With a holistic approach, the different levels of this joint effort – the individual, the community, the nation, the continent, and the global community – can hardly be differentiated in terms of addressing one level after the other or be dealt with in separated compartments. Understanding the individual as an inseparable part of the "big picture" has been one of the main drivers for all major global treaties and UN framework conventions and for their related down-to-earth-philosophies and practices of "thinking globally, acting locally" or for the approach of "many individuals taking single steps can change the global world."

Finding meaning, sense, and purpose in our activities remains an existential, continuous, and situational effort of all.

As for the individual ultimate concerns, Jurica et al. (2014) are discussing man's ultimate and existential concerns in four aspects:

- Meaning and meaninglessness
- Freedom and responsibility
- Isolation and personal relationships
- Death and suffering

Jurica et al. are concluding: We cannot mindlessly draw upon universal truths nor build the assumptions of our lives on a solid foundation of knowledge. A central challenge for each of us is to confront such realizations, acknowledge that only we have the ability to create our own identities, choices, and lives. No one can create our path for us. And, no one can truly share with us the path we choose.

2.5 Ultimate Meaning

The arts have always provided for a rich account of meanings, which cannot be verified but which have always been claimed as the ultimate source and realm of humanity's culture and developments transcending human capabilities.

The conductor Leonard Bernstein (1918–1990) once explained his highest esteem for Beethoven's music: "Beethoven is in possession of the true values, the gifts of heaven, of the power of letting us finally sense: There is something in the world, which is true and right, following its own laws, which we can blindly trust in and which will never forsake us." Being confronted with the objection that this may sound like a definition of "God," Bernstein responded: "*That is how it was meant*" (Bernstein 2006, p. 29).

Beyond all measurable and empirical findings for searching for meaning, for individual benefits, or for leaving individual benefits behind for the common good, which could still be empirically tested and verified, there is a meaning beyond human knowledge that apparently goes beyond scientific proof.

Actually, until today Viktor Frankl has been the only academic professor, doctor, psychiatrist, psychotherapist, philosopher, and author, with a multitude of professorships and honorary doctor degrees, who has actually dared to address these many facets of meaning.

2.6 Implications of the Discussion for Meaning and Work: Interim Conclusions

In Google, topics like "meaning in work" produce 803 million hits, "meaning at work" 204 million hits, "meaningful work" more than 13 million hits, etc.

The aforementioned different more existential or more positive related facets of meaning do have important implications for meaning and work. This would include that finding meaning in work-related situations does not necessarily result in instantly feeling better, working better, being more engaged, etc., with potentially powerful effects for the specific work situation.

The various approaches might differ in their understanding and concept of meaning, but they all agree on "the fundamental human yearning to make sense of the world around us, to transcend our transient existence, to discover our unique authentic calling and to leave our mark" (Batthyany and Russo-Netzer 2014, p. 12).

Experts are diagnosing ever more people, searching for "something" other "instead of success," addressing meaning issues in work-related consulting, coaching, and counseling (Schnell et al. 2013). Sometimes, overarching meaning issues are being addressed in people's religious affiliations and groups or in some type of medical-clinical contexts. But whom should people turn to with their questions, when they are not religious or feeling sick? Not finding the right counterparts for addressing and confidentially working on existential issues in personal work-related and private life can have severe and detrimental effects on personal health and well-being and lead to even deeper frustration of the search for meaning and to increased negative stress, loneliness, negative affect, hopelessness, and addiction.

Logotherapy, existential coaching, and counseling, increasingly also philosophic practitioners, are providing time and space for addressing people's existential and meaning-related issues, dealing with questions like:

What is the meaning of what I am doing?
Is there any purpose to my work?
Does my life matter at all, to whom does my existence matter?
Do I make a difference and how?
What is "my Why"?
What is "my What for"?
What is my calling?
Who out there needs me?

This search for meaning does not address any "grand meaning out there" but rather the very common, daily features and wordings of people's search for meaning in work and private life. People are searching for fulfillment, self-efficacy, contentment, inner balance, authentic living, comfort, and truth.

People word their quest for meaning accurately, clearly, and audibly:

- What is my task and role that I wish to pursue here and now?
- How do I know what is right and what is wrong?
- What do I respond to my current life's challenges?
- How can I find inner balance?
- Who actually needs me out there?
- How am I recognized in what I can do and bring to the world?

Meaning issues in work life necessarily address all spheres and aspects of meaning, functional and existential:

- Developing a personal sense of meaning
- Confirming information about existential issues
- Promoting sense of coherence
- Better coping with stress and anxieties
- Finding one's true calling
- Defining individual purpose in work
- Introducing own talents to own function and work
- Defining individual values
- Establishing a road map for leading a meaningful life
- Empowering meaningful commitment
- Strengthening resilience
- Intensifying well-being
- Coping with life events
- Supporting meaning awareness
- Living through grief and existential givens
- Coping with terminal illness

While one might argue that generally work-related issues have been addressed for a long time, in work life, there seems to be a growing gap between a merely functional and an existential understanding of search for meaning in the individual person's work life. Wong (1998) points out that a meaningful life inescapably entails transcending self-interest in order to serve a greater cause and that positive psychologists' functional approach to finding meaning in work and private life, finding happiness and well-being, seems at odds with the basic orientation of meaning, which is actually shared by the "common man on the street."

Because it is exactly business and work life shaping our present and future life in most existential ways, it may be hypothesized that every working person is sooner or later confronted with basic meaning questions, of how to make a meaningful living for themselves and their family; of following their consciousness and deep-rooted values, to following environmentally safe production regulations; of providing for resourceful relationships at work, for safe environments and working conditions, and for travelling a commonly shared road of meaning in work; or of following the road of short-term profits and shareholder values, of closing factory sites for more efficient results in other parts of the world, and of short-term individual hedonic benefits.

There are growing concerns about people's search for meaning, being abused for quick economic profits on individual employers' own terms, indirectly turning the individual search for meaning into a "cruel promise," of turning freedom from external control into internal coercion, flexibility into social insecurity, guidance and leadership provided by others into endless self-management, the potential joys of work into continuous sorrows, and excitement and creativity into fears of "never being good enough." The "gig economy" is largely marketing meaning-oriented issues and values, addressing the potentials of the younger generation, who are known for their explicit search for meaning and balance in their work and private life.

By definition alone, most of the meaning issues addressed in work life go beyond the regular coaching GROW paradigm of setting goals, assessing reality's issues and challenges, defining options and obstacles, and finally defining a way forward with reaching the initially agreed goals.

Addressing meaning in work-related contexts needs to acknowledge the two different roads to addressing meaning in work: the more positive approach with potentially clear outcomes and benefits to be reported in terms of improved self-efficacy, health, and well-being and the more existential approach addressing core aspects of the person's *being in the world*.

Communicating and dealing with people's work-related meaning issues necessarily encompass more and other "tools" and practices than regular short-term and solution-oriented consulting and coaching skills.

Communicating on existential meaning issues in work embraces an existential image of humans on the side of the coach/counselor, a meaning awareness concerning what is being presented, exchanging with the other person in a Socratic dialogue and intense communication, with unconditional acceptance.

References

Batthyany A, Russo-Netzer P (2014) Meaning in positive and existential psychology. Springer, New York, pp 3–22

Bernstein L (2006) The joy of music. Amadeus Press, Newark

Clark K (1969) Civilization: a personal view. BBC Books, London

Jurica J, Barenz J, Shim Y, Graham K, Steger MF (2014) Ultimate concerns from existential and positive psychological perspectives. In: Batthyany A, Russo-Netzer P (eds) Meaning in positive and existential psychology. Springer, New York, pp 115–128

MacKenzie MJ, Baumeister R (2014) Meaning in life: nature, needs, and myths. In: Batthyany A, Russo-Netzer P (eds) Meaning in positive and existential psychology. Springer, New York, pp 25–39

Mascaro N (2014) Meaning sensitive psychotherapy. In: Batthyany A, Russo-Netzer P (eds) Meaning in positive and existential psychology. Springer, New York, pp 269–289

Schnell T, Hoege T, Pollet E (2013) Predicting meaning in work: theory, data, implications. J Posit Psychol 8(6):543–554

Wong PTP (1998) Implicit theories of meaningful life and the development of the personal meaning profile. In: Wong PTP, Fry PS (eds) The human quest for meaning: a handbook of psychological research and clinical applications. Lawrence Erlbaum, Mahwah

Chapter 3
Searching and Finding Meaning: Viktor Frankl's Approach

Contents

What matters, therefore, is not the meaning of life in general, but rather the specific meaning of a person's life at a given moment. (V. Frankl)

Until today, Viktor Frankl, the founder of the "Third Viennese School," after Freud and Adler, has been the only doctor, psychiatrist, psychotherapist, academic professor, and author who not only put existential questions and meaning and being

B. von Devivere, *Meaningful Work: Viktor Frankl's Legacy for the 21st Century*,
https://doi.org/10.1007/978-3-319-89791-2_3

at the heart of psychology, psychotherapy, and psychiatry but who has actually pioneered in presenting a scientifically and empirically based concept of human's meaning and existence. Until today, his conception has been the basis and starting point of deeper understandings of man's condition and existence.

The logotherapeutic approach is defined by three basic assumptions, which are all closely related to defining and finding meaning in work.

3.1 Will to Meaning

Each individual is endowed with a will to meaning (Frankl 1967).

All humans are unique with an entity of body, mind, and spirit. We all go through unique situations and are constantly looking to find meaning. We are free to do this at all times in response to certain demands.

The search for meaning is the primary motivation of humans. This will cannot be demanded, commanded, or ordered. In the context of the current mainstream discussion of meaningful work, this is an important differentiation.

There is another very important differentiation: a person might be *pushed* by their physical instincts and emotional drives, but primarily they are *pulled* by their individual basic search for meaning.

The will to meaning refers to the primary motivation of seeking meaning and living a meaningful life. A person's ultimate purpose in life is not to gain pleasure or power but to find meaning and value in life. Will to meaning is essential for survival and health. The will to live is best understood as the will to meaning. A strong will to meaning enables people to endure unimaginable sufferings and to persist in pursuing their ideals.

We have inalienable freedom to find meaning.

We can find meaning in life in three different ways, termed as values by Frankl:

- By creating a work or doing a deed
- By experiencing something or encountering someone
- By the attitude we take toward circumstances we cannot change and toward unavoidable suffering

The frustration of the existential need for a meaningful life will give rise to aggression, addiction, depression, and suicidality, and it may engender or increase psychosomatic maladies and neurotic disorders.

Frankl's concept of the human will to meaning includes that each individual is motivated to discover his or her unique life calling. Calling is not only about professional pathways and approaches in coaching. It is about an assessment of the personal, unique talents and competencies to be lived and brought out into the world for serving others. This sense of calling includes a broader sense of a person's meaning in life. In the very end, it is connected to life satisfaction and a sense of fulfillment, of being in touch with the world as a greater community.

This concept also includes the general belief that one's life fits into some coherent scheme of life in general, a sense of coherence (Antonovsky 1987).

Wong (2012) points to the fact that Frankl's concept is based on the general human capacity for intrinsic motivation to personal growth and self-expansion. Each person is generally endowed with the will to fulfill their potentials and to transcend their limitations. The vast literature on sense of coherence, self-efficacy, competence, and growth mind-sets can all be integrated with the human will to meaning.

> *There is unconditional meaning in life. For, if not, then ultimately there is no meaning to survival; for a life whose meaning depends on happenstances – as whether one escapes or not – ultimately would not be worth living at all.* (V. Frankl)

3.2 Meaning of Life

Life has unconditional meaning in a person's existence as a whole and is being realized in specific, ever-changing situations.

On the grounds of their freedom and responsibility, humans are called upon to bring forth the possible best in themselves and in the world, by perceiving and realizing the meaning of the moment in each and every situation.

Every meaning is unique to each person, and each person has to discover the meaning of each particular situation for themselves.

Frankl (2014a) emphasized the discovery rather than the creation of personal meaning: "True meaning of life is to be discovered *in the world* rather than within man or his own psyche" (p. 109). Meaning can be discovered only through one's life experiences with persons and in circumstances given.

Although starting from the contrary point of defining meaninglessness as one of the basic existential givens, Yalom (1980) advocates engagement as the most important therapeutic answer to meaninglessness and points out that meaning is best pursued indirectly. "Meaning ensues from meaningful activity: the more deliberately we pursue it, the less likely are we to find it….What we must do is plunge into one of many possible meanings, particularly one with a self-transcendent basis" (p. 423).

Life has meaning under all circumstances: one cannot understand the meaning of life apart from the meaning of suffering, because suffering is an inevitable aspect and part of human existence. In today's world, which is not only offering all technical and expert competencies to finally avoid suffering, but also denying this aspect of life, Frankl's approach includes accepting the general duality of life, coping with it and integrating suffering into a philosophy of appreciation of life in all its facets. Here, Frankl's concept can be considered one of the most current aspects of his legacy in understanding suffering and in regaining dignity in shaping suffering and coping with deep fears, anxieties, and illness.

3.3 Freedom of Will and Responsibility to Act on It

Freedom, however, is not the last word. Freedom is only part of the story and half of the truth. Freedom is but the negative aspect of the whole phenomenon, whose positive aspect is responsibleness. In fact, freedom is in danger of degenerating into mere arbitrariness unless it is lived in terms of responsibleness. (V. Frankl)

The individual freedom, defined as the space of shaping one's own life within the limits of the given possibilities, derives from the spiritual/Geist dimension of the person, which is understood as the essential human realm, establishing the individual capacity to cope with all aspects of the individual life, health, and well-being and to regain a sense of control and self-determination.

Without the general capacity for freedom of will, people would not be able to choose how to respond to a given situation and decide on their own preferred life path.

Freedom of will enables people to be responsible, moral agents. There is no escape from making choices, and as generally free persons, we are accountable for the consequences of our decisions and actions.

By nature, persons can adapt, change, improve, advance, find their own purpose in life, take their own attitude, and define their own road to personal fulfillment.

Human beings, through their own consciousness, constantly create and co-create their environment, their own values, personally determine a meaning to their life, and communicate with others on the basis of these more or less conscious "givens," interpretations, and assumptions of their specific lives.

Our world is increasingly becoming socially fragmented, with the decline of organized religion and other community-based structures. Each new generation, randomly named X, Y, or Z, is more exposed to events never imagined to happen, than the previous. In this way, individuals are more "existentially attuned" (Berry-Smith 2012) than ever before. Common awareness today is articulated in a current blog posting: "Either our world is going ethical – or not at all."

With today's ever-increasing complexity and dynamics in workplaces, this basic individual freedom may be one of the most powerful drivers to lead a meaningful life amidst all the impertinences and limitations experienced in the individual life.

Self-confidence, self-awareness, and a sense of coherence are favorable prerequisites for perceiving and acting on this individual freedom.

Frankl (2000) emphasizes that freedom without responsibility would lead to chaos and nihilism. Therefore, freedom is always limited by responsibility. Fabry (1988) explains that individual responsibility is a personal response to ultimate meaning and to the meanings of the moment as they are interpreted by the unique individual.

By enlightenment and development, today, we understand ourselves as free individuals, favorably living in democratic societies, free to choose our own destiny, our place to live and to lead a good life. In this sense, we understand freedom in the sense of free from whatever circumstances and powers are inflicting on our lives. Freedom, in this sense, is a negative concept which needs a positive complement. This positive complement is responsibility. Freedom threatens to degenerate into mere arbitrariness unless it is lived in terms of responsibleness.

Responsibility has two intentional referents: It refers to (a) a meaning for whose fulfillment we are responsible and also to (b) a being or a cause for whom we are responsible. We are responsible to ourselves, to other people, to societal values, and as Fabry and Frankl (2013) explain, to the "superhuman dimension," the ultimate meaning, "an order whose laws we can violate only at our peril, regardless of whether we see the order in religious or secular terms: as God, life, nature, or the ecosystem" (Fabry 1994, p. 150).

In today's working environments, there are innumerous opportunities of freedom and responsibility to act on it in each and every situation. The activities reported in this book give but a small example of these opportunities that individuals and experts have currently introduced and implemented in their workplaces.

3.4 Values: The Human Condition

> *A thought transfixed me: for the first time in my life, I saw the truth as it is set into song by so many poets, proclaimed as the final wisdom by so many thinkers. The truth – that love is the ultimate and the highest goal to which man can aspire.* (Frankl)

There are meanings that are shared by human beings across society and throughout history. These meanings refer to the human condition as such. These shared meanings are values, meaning universals, which have developed in societies or humanity and may crystallize in specific situations. These meanings are not arbitrary but rather expressed and channeled by morals and ethical traditions, standards, and cultures. There is plenty of insight on generic virtues shared across all cultures (see character strengths, Chap. 15) and, on the other hand, on the great diversity of specific, culturally defined values.

Universal values, goodness, beauty, and truth, are given preconditions for human life, independent of the human existence. This includes the assumption that human life gains its meaning in the light of something that is more permanent and greater than human existence. Every culture displays parts of these "permanent" values, providing an opportunity for intercultural dialogue about similarities and diversity across cultures (Purjo 2014).

As Frankl explains, one may define values as those *meaning universals* which crystallize in the typical situations a society or even humanity is facing. Today, we find challenges on all levels of existence, when life is questioning us to give meaning and to traveling these value roads as defined by Frankl.

Facing today's challenges, the "possession" of ultimate values may alleviate man's search for meaning, because at least in typical situations he might be spared searching for his own ultimate values. But conflicts between various values are to be observed. Elie Wiesel (2015) suggests that in the light of the ever-disturbing fact that there are no answers, only questions, mankind should not stop searching for meaning in a situation observed or experienced.

Finally, meaning is of a transsubjective quality, beyond the individual person's arbitrary definition. Meaning cannot be invented, it can only be found.

In addition to these universal values, Frankl defines three pathways of values as pointers for meaning, giving direction and a sense of individual freedom to choose: meaning in life can be found traveling three chief groups of values – by creating a work or doing a deed, i.e., creative values; by experiencing goodness, truth, beauty, nature, and culture or encountering another unique human being, i.e., experiential values; or, deprived by these opportunities, by the very attitude which they choose to take to this predicament, i.e., attitudinal values.

In this sense, there might be meaning in every work. What opportunities do today's workplaces offer for experiencing these values? Do today's workplaces actually offer enough opportunities for creative and experiential values? What is the unheard "cry for meaning" in today's workplaces? And what type of attitudinal values can employees find in coping with today's working challenges?

3.5 Givers and Takers

Frankl explains these three pathways to finding meaning in terms of giving and taking: The first road is what man *gives* to the world in terms of his creations. The second road is what he *takes* from the world in terms of encounters and experiences. And the third road is about *the stand he* actively *takes* to his predicament in case he must face a fate he cannot change.

Today, social psychology and cognitive science are focusing again on the specific ways to find meaning by balancing giving and taking in work (Grant 2014) and exercising leadership in facilitating this balance.

3.6 Conscience: What Is "Right"? What Is "Wrong"?

Meanings are discovered by man's *conscience*. This individual conscience is, as history and everyday situations have proved over and over again, creative and some "greater power" beyond current values.

Frankl suggests that meanings are transsubjective, an intuitive capacity of man to find "what is right." If man is not to contradict his own humanness, he has to obey his conscience unconditionally, even though he is aware of his possibility of error: "The possibility of error does not dispense him from the necessity of trial" (V. Frankl). This entails humility, modesty, and tolerance on each person.

Today, we live in an era without values automatically emerging. Some go so far as to call present times a "transhuman" era approaching. Turning this potentially deeply disturbing diagnosis into a call would mean putting Frankl's conclusion into concrete action:

> *Today, education cannot afford to proceed along the lines of tradition, but must elicit the ability to make independent and authentic decisions. In an age, where the Ten Commandments seem to loose their unconditional validity, man must learn more than ever to listen to the ten thousand commandments arising from the ten thousand unique situations of which his life consists.* (Frankl 1986)

With this approach, human conscience is inseparably connected with every person's inherent humanness, specifically human being's ability to discern right from wrong. This capacity is based on the human freedom "from" restrictions and "to" his own responsibility.

The human being, in search for meaning, is challenged by their basic freedom to take an attitude toward the givens of life, the specific environment and situation. The human conscience, deeply connected with this freedom and responsibility, is hard to bear: for persons challenged by external dynamic changes, in transition, marginalized, lonely, lost, bored, uncertain, spiritually or existentially dispossessed, burdened by too much freedom, or indifferent to any values, contagious ideologies will remain tempting as quick fixes for the deep predicaments inherent to the human condition.

Conscience is based on transcendent values that come from beyond the self and something "greater than the self."

3.7 The Tragic Triad

There is no human being who has not failed, does not suffer, or will not die. These are the existential facts of life calling for meaningful attitudes toward pain, guilt, and death. Here, Frankl is explaining the very existential differences between these three existential experiences: In facing suffering, the person takes an attitude to their fate, which cannot be changed. Experiencing guilt, however, is a prerogative of being human, when each person can shape and reshape her life.

"In other words, it is a privilege of man to become guilty and his responsibility to overcome guilt" (Frankl 1988b). Prior to the following definition, in today's postmodern trans-religious world, there are, apart from the very legalistic perspective, strong reservations toward any ideas of "guilt." (p. 73)

This publication contends that each person once in their lives is facing the tragic triad. The feeling, thought, or assumption of guilt continues to be experienced by all persons as a cognitive or emotional experience, when a person realizes that he or she has compromised his or her own standards of conduct and violated a shared moral standard and feels bearing responsibility for this violation and the various effects on others in their work, private, social, or global environment.

In today's workplaces, company ethical standards, code of conduct, compliance, and leadership guidelines together with individual deeply engrained values offer plenty examples for the ethical drivers of defining these guidelines and for tragic examples of violating these defined values, when individuals deliberately broke these values, for the detriment of the greater community and the world.

With the third aspect of the tragic triad, man is constantly faced with potential or real suffering and life's transitoriness. In parallel, each person is responsible for using the transitory opportunities to actualize potentialities, to realize values.

Frankl's concept of will to meaning is of significant importance in dealing with fate and suffering.

In this world, where man is claiming to be capable of achieving almost everything, awareness needs to be raised for the positive in the negative and to the negative in the positive. The pursuit of meaning may entail personal sacrifice. Social entrepreneurs provide plenty of examples for persons committed to a cause beyond themselves and willing to sacrifice material goods and benefits. It may even mean suffering for a worthy cause. Activists for human rights and for free speech, exercising their work under extremely difficult and life-threatening situations, are giving great examples for following their cause beyond quick results.

Looking at this "tragic triad," the core question is resulting: what are today's potentialities of experiencing the tragic triad in the workplace situation that each unique individual person is facing, and what could the individual answer then be? Work in general provides for innumerous experiences of suffering, of feelings of guilt, and of various types and forms of perceived social death, be it as the individual feeling of lack of control, be it ultimately physically, be it socially in the form of feeling expelled from a community. There is an undisputable need to raise awareness for the tragic triad in the workplace, how to address it and how to give support for persons experiencing these challenges of life.

3.8 Existential Analysis

> *It has been shown repeatedly, that a return to the essential reason for human existence, being responsible as the basis of human existence, is necessary. So we will understand, that, around the pivot of logotherapy, psychotherapy must make a turn towards an existential analysis as an analysis of being human towards being responsible.* (Viktor E. Frankl)

Existential analysis was conceived by Viktor E. Frankl in the 1930s as an anthropological theory of an existential school of psychotherapy. At the same time, Frankl developed "logotherapy" as a meaning-oriented form of counseling, support, and treatment. Existential analysis is the philosophical and scientific basis of logotherapy as well as an essential practical analysis of its own.

Existential analysis is "analysis with respect to existence" or "explication of existence" (Batthyany A, Viktor Frankl Institute, Vienna Site) with consideration of a self-responsible, self-realized, and humane life.

In "general existential analysis," the pursuit of meaning is discussed and identified as a basic motivation in humans, and arguments are provided that demonstrate the fundamental possibility of finding meaning in life.

In "special existential analysis," the specific, individual life of a person is being probed. Thus the value of existential analysis lies in the elucidation of the concrete existential situation and in giving assistance in the – autonomous – search for meaning.

Existential analysis means an analysis of the conditions necessary for a life, in which values have their place and that is self-shaped and dignified (Laengle 2005). The aim of existential analysis is to develop one's perceptiveness and individual activity (capability for commitment) in one's experiences, relations, and actions. This means that existential analysis deals with the personal conditions prerequisite for a meaningful existence.

3.8.1 Unfolding the Nature of Our Personal Being

Existential analysis helps us to reflect on and clarify in order to understand the context of the problems and challenges we face as human beings, emphasizing the "unfolding" nature of our awareness of being and what it is to exist (Society for Existential Analysis):

- What does it mean to be alive?
- What are the possibilities that my life presents to me?
- What is my relationship to myself, to other people, and to the world in general?
- What are my responsibilities to myself and to other people?
- What do I value and cherish dearly?
- What is the nature of the anxiety that I experience in my life?
- What are the assumptions and attributions that underpin my thoughts and actions?
- What are the contradictions, discrepancies, and paradoxes that occur in my everyday life?
- What is my worldview – the way that I have constructed the story of my life?
- What is my true potential?
- What would it be like to choose my own way of living?

Frankl (1967) explains the core of existential analysis: "If we want to obtain an appropriate view of human reality in its full dimensionality, we must…bring in, in addition to the '*I must*' and '*I can*,' aspects of the total '*I am*' phenomenon – that dimension which can be referred to as the '*I ought*.' At the moment we bring in the '*I ought*,' we complement the subjective aspect of human existence, *being*, with its objective counterpart, *meaning*."

Frankl makes the case for an existential analysis by taking a critical perspective to commonly observed attitudes to the world and its resources. This analysis can also be understood in terms of a most up-to-date analysis of twenty-first-century humanity's challenges. He explains the starting point of human existence in time and the demands of being and responding as humans. Simultaneously, Frankl "dare says" that man never, or at least not normally and primarily, sees in the partners whom he encounters and in the causes to which he commits himself, merely a means to an end. For then he would have destroyed any authentic relationship to them, and they would have become mere tools. Consequently, the ultimate questions of human existence "are on the lips of every man."

By definition, we are continually challenged to explain our existence, and, in relating to the world in our respective functions and relations, defining the very meaning challenges of the specific situation for our own existence and in relating to those we feel responsible for, in work, in our respective professions and in giving meaning to these encounters.

An "adequate concept of the world" (Frankl) – appropriate to our education and knowledge about the world – includes:

- Taking into account the objectivity of the world around us, which alone presents a real challenge to the subject.

- Bewaring of regarding the world as a mere instrument serving purposes of our own, an instrument for the satisfaction of instinctual drives, for reestablishing an inner equilibrium, for restoring homeostasis, as a means to the end of self-actualization. This concept actually would mean degrading the world.

Existential analysis means grasping the meaning of being, or the *logos of existence*:

- Fulfilling the concrete meaning of the individual, personal existence.
- Achieving self-actualization by understanding self-actualization not as primary intention, but rather by fulfilling himself.
- The meaning in the world to be fulfilled by man is actualized through values to be realized by man.
- Man does not fulfill the meaning of his existence by his creative endeavors and experiential encounters or by working and loving.
- There are also tragic experiences in human life, existentials, that cannot be "tranquilized away." Man is willing to shoulder suffering as soon and as long as he can see meaning in it.
- This meaning cannot be grasped by merely intellectual means.
- Existential analysis is enabling the other person to see the world as it is.
- The world is to be considered assignment and challenge.
- One can only search for the concrete meaning of personal existence, a meaning which changes from man to man, from day to day, from hour to hour.
- The awareness of this concrete meaning of one's existence is not an abstract one.
- It is an immediate and implicit dedication to existential analysis.
- It can be evoked by posing questions in the frame of a maieutic dialogue in the Socratic sense.

3.8.2 Existential Analysis in Practice

Based on Frankl's concept that self-actualization is based on self-transcendence, Wong (2014, 2016) differentiates three levels of self-transcendence:

- Seeking ultimate meaning: nontheistically speaking, seeking the ultimate ideals of goodness, truth, and beauty or gaining a glimpse of the transcendental realm.
- Seeking situational meaning: to reach beyond our mental and emotional constraints. Being mindful of the present moment with an attitude of openness, curiosity, and compassion.
- Seeking one's calling: engagement and striving to achieve a concrete meaning in life, a life goal of contributing something of value to others.
- Attuning to the meaning potentials of each situation in their emotional, relational, and moral significance.
- Meaning awareness demands a rational and intellectual understanding of the situation and its associative and causal factors – and more than that.

- Appreciating the potentials of the moment.
- Developing and actualizing one's general sense of calling, being devoted to serving others and to improving oneself in order to fulfill one's potentials, entailing some sense of societal contribution beyond personal happiness and success.
- Continuing to expand our interest beyond ourselves, based on human's intrinsic motivation of self-transcendence.
- Engaging in deeds of compassion and kindness, because of our spiritual nature as human beings.
- The individual always has the freedom of choice, be it in attitude or in action.
- While a person is free to choose one's own meaning, it is only when one's choice is consistent with time-proven values that the decision or the attitude taken is meaningful.

Each of us must confront the ultimate facts of our existence. The magnitude of these concerns might lead to individuals numbing themselves to meaning, creating an enormous vacuum of meaning in modern life, leading to disengagement, apathy, depression, and addiction.

Ultimate concerns about our existence address "the bottom line truth" for which we live, die, and suffer, which lift us beyond the daily obsessions into a world that becomes increasingly vital as we accurately orient ourselves along the existential dimensions. Thus, issues of life meaning turn out to be the impetus for understanding own tasks and liberating the mind.

Existential analysis is exploring the sources of meaning in each person's individual life, relating to interpersonal relations, spiritual life, and career experienced as a calling and altruism or self-transcendence. All these categories are considered as ends in itself, intrinsically motivated activities and development of the ability to connect with the intrinsic value of everyday experiences.

Mascaro (2014) explains the importance of existential analysis: Nonacceptance of the givens of existence, especially suffering and transience of our existence, involves not only denial of reality, resulting in an inadequate meaning framework, that cannot productively manage experiences, but it also involves continuous efforts that pull attention away from defining meaningful behaviors and attitudes. "Meaning comes to those who allow it to emerge."

Practical approaches to dealing with distress in life suggest exercises of acceptance of distress while pursuing ends that are irrelevant to the distress, yet meaningful. This might also include activities that might be considered self-transcendent, such as altruistic service, and interacting with the world in a mindful cognition.

Jurica et al. (2014) explain existential analysis along the ultimate concerns of humans:

- Meaning vs. meaninglessness: Supporting the ability of each person to establish meaning and create meaning for their own lives and to cope with feelings of meaninglessness.
- Freedom and responsibility: Because we are free to transcend the limitations of our existence and determine our essence, the responsibility to be who we are rests on us alone. Individuals are called to accept, embrace, and utilize the free-

dom. Realizing that this freedom excludes acting as a puppet or feeling victimized or blaming others, this anticipated weight of freedom might lead to anxieties, avoidance of responsibility, and denial of individual freedom. Existential analysis is supporting the person to identify this potential fear of responsibility and help to exercise individual freedom
- Isolation and personal relationships: Each act of self-creation implies accepting the individual uniqueness, separate and different from every other person. Existential analysis helps the individual person to understand their identity, their environment and societal influences, and their beliefs and influences. This understanding is co-created by interacting with others and by building relationships with others. Positive social interaction with others can bring meaning to a person's life. The authentic human relationship between the two persons working with each other is a core element in the process of existential analysis.
- At the core of existence is fragility, suffering and accepting life's transience. Individuals can, under all circumstances, craft lives of personal meaningfulness.

Existential analysis does not give the answer to life's questions but rather encourages the person to find their own meaning in dealing with the tragic triad of suffering, guilt, and death.

Existential analysis is not a narrow-minded, urgent search for meaning, but actually it is about highlighting the specific meaning potentials of a concrete situation and the according behaviors, attitudes, and values to be actualized by the free and responsible person.

While the logotherapeutic consulting, coaching, and counseling approach is fully aware of the importance of the quality of the encounter between the two persons – I and Thou – (Martin Buber 1971), this encounter between human beings is one in which one is not only concerned with the other person's *ontos* (*being*) but also confronts the other with the potential *logos* (*meaning*) of their lives. Here, the logotherapeutic approach is basically neutral relating to the specific meanings in a person's life but dedicated to the idea of man as outlined here.

This publication suggests that all situations in working and private life assume some basic understanding of life, mostly not defined or explained. Many approaches reported in this book are based on a positive image of humans, understanding each individual as inherently good, endowed with creativity, free will, and positive human potential. Frankl's approach focuses on man's basic need to fulfill meaning, applying all their given, humanistic potentials.

3.9 The Three Dimensions of Human Existence

Frankl coined his approach, logotherapy, from the Greek word *logos*, which can mean study, word, spirit, God, or meaning.

Frankl uses the division between the physical, psychical, and the "noetic," defined as his *dimensional ontology* concept.

In doing so, his concept integrates a medical, psychotherapeutic, and philosophical understanding of the human existence with substantial implications for all topics of human existence.

According to Frankl's dimensional differentiation, a dimensional approach is required to explain human existence and to actually liberate the human potentials.

A human being is a somatic, psychological, and noological or spiritual entity, an ontic totality (Frankl 1988a, b). Actually, one cannot separate them.

The spiritual dimension is the most extensive, pervading the totality and uniqueness of the human being. Thus, in diagnostic and therapeutic situations, one should remember that life is not an "either-or" and "yes-or-no" choice. Frankl emphasizes in Latin: *tertium datur* (the third answer/way is given). By this he means that *life* is a complex web. The relationships between the separate aspects of a person emerge out of experience.

Frankl also uses the Greek word *noos*, which means mind or spirit. In traditional psychology, he suggests, we focus on "psychodynamics," which sees people as trying to reduce psychological tension. Instead, or in addition, Frankl says we should pay attention to *noodynamics*.

In all his works, Frankl was concerned with the danger of reductionism, medical schools reducing all phenomena to physiology, psychiatry, and psychology, promoting reductionism by denying the spiritual dimension. Frankl concludes the importance of this three-dimensional approach:

> The de-neuroticization of humanity requires a re-humanization of psychotherapy. (Frankl 1975, p. 104)

3.10 The Spiritual Dimension

According to Frankl, the spiritual dimension can liberate a person from attachments to somatic and psychophysical issues: one can discover despair despite success and fulfillment despite failure.

"Man is more than psyche. Man is spirit" (Frankl 1967). The person has a psychophysical overlay, whereas the person "is spiritual" (Frankl 2000). "We would only have to imagine that the personal core – the spiritual center that is encompassed by the peripheral somatic and psychic layers – is prolonged so that we would have to conceive it as an axis. In other words, we have put together the two-dimensional models and made them into a three-dimensional model that more accurately depicts the human reality" (Frankl 2000, p. 35).

> *Logotherapy and existential analysis, as a secular theory and practice, must restrict itself to factual statements, leaving to the person the decision as to how to understand his own being responsible, whether along the lines of religious beliefs or agnostic convictions.* (Viktor Frankl)

Since the late 1990s and together with the events around 9/11 and the various global crises at the beginning of the twenty-first century, observers have noted a "spiritual movement" in organizations and business institutions.

While innumerous and diverse programs in the workplace are addressing employees' "spiritual needs" with various definitions of spirituality, this movement shows the outstanding relevance of Frankl's legacy relating to the "spiritual dimension," today addressed also in workplace programs.

Viktor E. Frankl's approach provides for two basic human needs: to understand life and to provide for direction in each individual life. It is an approach, which not only recognizes man's spirit but actually starts from it.... In this connection, *logos* is intended to signify "the spiritual" and beyond that "the meaning" (Frankl 1986). Frankl links "being human" to an individual person's freedom and responsibility and living up to these givens in a "new dimension," which he defines as the noological dimension. Also, he is clearly distancing logotherapy from any misunderstandings regarding "spiritual" or "religious." Frankl explains his anthropological approach:

"...A person is free to shape his own character, and man is responsible for what he may have made of himself. What matters is not the features of our character or the drives and instincts per se, but rather the stand we take toward them. And the capacity to take such a stand is what makes us human being. Taking a stand toward somatic and psychic phenomena implies rising above their level and opening a new dimension, the dimension of noetic phenomena, or the noological dimension – in contradistinction to the biological and psychological ones. It is that dimension in which the uniquely human phenomena are located. It could be defined as the spiritual dimension as well. However, since in English "spiritual" has a religious connotation, *this term must be avoided as much as possible.* For what we understand by the noological dimension is the anthropological rather than the theological dimension. This also holds for "logos" in the context with "logotherapy". In addition to being defined as "meaning," "logos" here means "spirit" – but again without any primarily religious connotation. Here "logos" means the humanness of the human being – plus the meaning of being human (Frankl 2014b, pp 142–151).

Frankl continues in explaining how a person specifically lives the noological dimension, whenever he:

- Is reflecting upon himself – or, if need be, rejecting himself.
- Is making himself an object – or making objections to himself.
- Displays his being conscious of himself – or whenever he exhibits his being conscientious. In fact, being conscientious presupposes the uniquely human capacity to rise above oneself, to judge, and evaluate one's own deeds in moral and ethical terms.

Viktor Frankl's legacy, as a secular theory, must – by definition – restrict itself to factual statements, leaving to the other person the decision about how to understand their own being, responsibility, and meaning: whether along the line of religious beliefs or agnostic conviction. Logotherapy and existential analysis must remain available to everyone. Capitalizing on responsibleness to this extent, logotherapy cannot spare each person their own decision for what, to what, or to whom they are responsible.

A person "has" a psyche and body, and a person "is" a spiritual being.

"Inasmuch as logotherapy makes man aware of the hidden logos of his existence, it is an analytical process" (Frankl 1986) explains on defining each person's very own purpose in life.

Human existence is essentially self-transcendent. This quality renders man "a being reaching out beyond himself."

The individual human spirit, the *Geistige Person*, is each person's core. This "noetic" (nous or spirit) dimension of the human spirit is the "medicine chest" (Fabry 1994) of logotherapeutic approaches, containing such various inner resources as love, the will to meaning, purpose in life, hope, dignity, creativity, conscience, and the capacity for choice.

Existential analysis of the individual life focuses on activating the noetic dimension in each individual person.

This human spirit may be conceptualized as the human basic yearning and capacity for meaning and spirituality. The human spirit, the "Geistige Person," remains "under all circumstances" an "indestructible part of a person and his dignity." It may be blocked by biological or psychological sickness, but it does remain the core of a person; the spirit cannot get sick, even when the psychobiological organism is injured. Keeping in mind and following this approach makes one of the most fundamental differences in relating to a person in work or private life, especially in situations of emotional distress and sickness and also during recovery or reintegration in the workplace.

To remove the blockages and free the human spirit to fulfill its tasks is the main objective of existential analysis. We all have within us the spiritual need to seek self-transcendence, in search for engagements beyond ourselves and for leaving a legacy, connecting with others, reaching beyond the self toward causes to serve or people to love, for serving a higher purpose for the greater good.

Mostly though, the search for spiritual guidance is defined directly or indirectly as a type of personal mastery rather than a person's given in his three-dimensional quality.

Going back to the Greek meaning of spirituality, we would find Frankl's very definition of nous, spirit, Geist

Logotherapy, as a secular theory and medical practice, must restrict itself to factual statements, leaving to the person the decision as to how to understand his own being responsible, whether along the lines of religious beliefs or agnostic convictions.

"To sum up: Spiritual phenomena may be unconscious or conscious… the spiritual basis of human existence is ultimately unconscious…. Precisely at the place of its origin, the retina of the eye has a 'blind spot', where the optic nerve enters the eyeball. Likewise, the spirit is 'blind' precisely at its origin – precisely there, no self-observation, no mirroring of itself is possible." (Frankl 1967, pp. 37–38)

"Meaning must not coincide with being; meaning must be ahead of being. Meaning sets the pace for being. Existence falters unless it is lived in terms of transcendence towards something beyond itself." Frankl 2000, p. 29)

Frankl never ceased to emphasize that the spiritual, noetic dimension of human existence differs from the psychological, mental dimension no less than the latter differs from the bodily, material dimension (Leontiev 2016).

The human noetic or spiritual core contains such qualities as:

- Will to meaning
- Ideas and ideals
- Creativity
- Imagination
- Faith
- Love
- Conscience
- Commitment
- Responsibility

There are two main features that characterize and constitute human existence: The first is self-transcendence – the fact that man is always reaching beyond himself, reaching out for meaning to fulfill, for other beings to encounter. The second is self-detachment, the intrinsically human capacity to rise above the level of somatic and psychic data (Viktor Frankl in Batthyany and Russo-Netzer 2014).

3.10.1 A Matter of Clean Language: Definitions of Religion, Religiousness, Spirituality, Mind, and Existential

Literature and research are providing various terms, concepts, and approaches on the complex topics of spirituality, religion, "Geist," spirit, and transcendence and how these are reflected in human nature and specifically in well-being and life satisfaction.

3.10.1.1 Geist, Mind, Spirit, and Spirituality

Until today, different cultures have a different understanding of "mind." These various concepts have been discussed for ages. Until today, philosophy, science, psychology, and various religious concepts are defining the mind, understanding it in terms of perception, thinking, judgment, intelligence, memory, subjective awareness, and intentionality, responding to stimuli, consciousness of feelings, emotions, thoughts, and cognitive understanding that form basic attributes of the mind.

Different religions have a different understanding of "mind." Body/mind concepts are continually being discussed with various approaches relating to their respective influence on human behavior.

Digital intelligence is searching for technical means to artificially recreate intelligence as a mere material function of the brain, as the current discussion around

Harari's *Deus* (Harari 2017) may show. Geist and mind still remain a "hard problem."

Frankl's dimensional ontology refers to the *Geistige Person* as the human core, providing the undeniable freedom of will (Batthyany: Viktor Frankl Institute Vienna Website): "This freedom is grounded in the spiritual dimension of man, which, in addition to body and psyche, makes up his own personality and dignity. As a spiritual person, man is no longer merely a reaction or a reaction, but an acting, shaping being."

Addressing spirit and spirituality has become – for good or bad – a fashionable issue. Until today, definitions are blurred.

C. G. Jung (1926) remarked on the complex issue of spirit: *"The connection between spirit and life is one of those problems involving factors of such complexity that we have to be on our guard lest we ourselves get caught in the net of words in which we seek to ensnare these great enigmas... 'Spirit' and 'Life' are familiar enough words to us, very old acquaintances in fact, pawns that for thousands of years have been pushed back and forth on the thinker's chessboard...."*

Equally, the professional community around researchers, psychotherapists, and counselors, has – since the turn of the century – been engaged to make the various definitions, approaches, and effects of addressing and/or including spiritual needs transparently and open the discussion for continued research.

Also driven by positive psychology, the American Psychological Association (APA 2013) has issued more than ten handbooks around religion and psychology, and scientific journals (e.g., journals *Psychology of Religion and Spirituality and Spirituality in Clinical Practice*) are publishing current research findings.

Relating this complex term to recent discussions and publications, the following concepts of "spirit" are being discussed:

- Unlike the incorporeal concept of soul, the human spirit grows as an integral part of a living being.
- A unified concept of a greater spirit, a unified consciousness.
- A metaphor for loyalty and the feeling of inclusion.
- A term to describe God.
- A meaning closely related to what is being discussed, like "in the spirit of...."
- Related to current thinking, i.e., *Zeitgeist*.
- In the workplace: a term for a demonstrated positive behavior fostering cooperation and well-being, e.g., *team spirit*.

The VIA Institute on Character defines the character strength "spirituality":

Spirituality is believed to describe both the private, intimate relationship between humans and the divine and the range of virtues that result from the relationships. Spirituality is universal. Although the specific content of spiritual beliefs varies, all cultures have a concept of an ultimate, transcendent, sacred force. Spirituality falls under the overarching virtue category of transcendence. Transcendence describes strengths that provide a broad sense of connection to something higher in meaning and purpose than ourselves.

The World Health Organization has included the spiritual dimension by defining health as "...a state of physical, mental, spiritual and social well-being." In 1984, the World Health Assembly declared:

> *The spiritual dimension is understood to imply a phenomenon that is not material in nature, but belongs to the realm of ideas, beliefs, values and ethics that have arisen in the minds and conscience of human beings, particularly ennobling ideas. Ennobling ideas have given rise to health ideals, which have led to a practical strategy for Health for All that aims at attaining a goal that has both a material and non-material component. If the material component of the strategy can be provided to people, the non-material or spiritual one is something that has to arise within people and communities in keeping with their social and cultural patterns. The spiritual dimension plays a great role in motivating people's achievement in all aspects of life.* (World Health Organization 1991)

While the biopsychosocial approach (Dziegielewski 2013) is the foundation in social services and health care, experts (Rankin et al. 1996) have been introducing a fourth area specifically addressing the spiritual needs of the person, focusing "attention on the being of the individual, the role of the transcendent in a person's life and the spiritual qualities of the belief system a person holds" (p. 516), because addressing all four dimensions is offering a much broader concept of the individual person's potentials.

3.10.1.2 Existential

How does human nature, the individual person in their diverse environments, traditions, and cultures, with their complex values and orientations in time and space, reflect on basic issues of their respective lives, and how do these complex factors influence their mind-set, their health, their well-being, and their life satisfaction?

Existential issues that human beings are dealing with throughout their life cycle are globally defined as issues:

- Relating to the individual existence
- Bringing to life
- General givens in life, independent of individual choices
- Extreme, critical situations

Each person and experts from all fields and the scientific community have been engaged in searching insight and extract best approaches to alleviate and enhance the lives of individuals and to introduce knowledge and best approaches in the face of these existential givens, according to their relevant cultural and social backgrounds and environments they live in.

3.10.1.3 Religion

Religion has become one of the core issues of twenty-first century in research, health care, and societal and social life, discussing its influence on well-being and meaning in life.

The term encompasses:

- A community, sharing
- Specific traditions, rituals, and texts (Christianity, Judaism, Islam, Buddhism, Hinduism a. o.)

Religiousness
- Institutional religious affiliation and beyond that
- Individual lifestyle integrating the respective religion into everyday life

The Virtues in Action Signature Strengths define "religiousness" as "*having coherent beliefs about the higher purpose and meaning of the universe and knowing where one fits within the larger scheme.*" The German language VIA test combines various terms in their definition: "*Religiosität & Spiritualität (Gläubigkeit, Sinn): Religiöse bzw. Spirituelle Menschen haben starke und kohärente Überzeugungen über den Sinn und Zweck des Universums. Ihre religiösen Überzeugungen beeinflussen ihre Handlungen und sind eine Quelle des Trostes und der Kraft*" (Translation by author BvD: "Religiosity and Spirituality: Religious and spiritual people have strong and coherent beliefs about the meaning and purpose of the universe. Their religious beliefs influence their actions and are a source of consolation and strength.") In addition to the English definition, the German language definition is including the terms of "faith" and "meaning" in the definition of "religiousness." These differences may hint to diverse culturally defined meanings of religiousness.

3.10.2 International Guidelines Regarding Experts' Dealing with Spiritual Issues

As of today, organizations in the United States and in some European countries have issued guidelines on dealing with spiritual issues in their professions. The table below is not exhaustive but rather intends to demonstrate the substantial variations in addressing religion and spirituality in a professional context.

These guidelines show legal, professional, and cultural differences between the various countries. Taking these guidelines into account and respecting them in the experts' daily practice is more than a legal and professional issue that experts need to observe. These guidelines also demonstrate the engagement and – ever since psychotherapy's successful establishment of defining and offering psychotherapy independent from religion – continuing struggle for a clear distinction between secular, evidence-based counseling and spiritual/religious approaches (Table 3.1).

The author BvD suggests to closely observe these guidelines in the various workplace settings with their different cultural backgrounds and history of professional discussions. Frankl (1988a, b) has always stressed and engaged for logotherapy and existential analysis, scientifically established on the grounds of research, based on (1) tests, (2) statistics, and (3) experiments. In today's intercultural, diverse, and global world, Frankl's three-dimensional approach offers a most valid concept of

Table 3.1 International guidelines regarding experts' dealing with spiritual issues

Organization	Year	Title
(APA) American Psychological Association	1990 (first)	Guidelines
		Spiritual and religious competencies for psychologists
Great Britain	2011	Guidelines
Royal College of Psychiatrists		
Austria	2012	Bundesministerium für Gesundheit
	2014	"Esoterik-Richtlinie"
Germany	2016	Empfehlungen zum Umgang mit Religiosität und Spiritualität in Psychiatrie und Psychotherapie, Psychosomatik und Nervenheilkunde
DGPP		
Deutsche Gesellschaft für Psychiatrie und Psychotherapie, Psychosomatik und Nervenheilkunde		

understanding and supporting individuals, respecting their very individual spiritual and religious affiliations.

3.11 Addressing Religion: The Pivotal Question

Religious psychotherapy is inconceivable. (V. Frankl)

Asked about the difference between religion and spirit – Is there a place for religion in your theory? – Frankl summarized: "Fusion of psychotherapy and religion necessarily results in confusion, for such a fusion confounds two different dimensions, the dimension of anthropology and theology" (Frankl in Batthyany 2016 p. 8).

Frankl continued, and as his explanations hold true for his theory in general, not only in terms of psychiatric or psychotherapeutic interventions, "patient" and "doctor" can easily be replaced with "each individual person" (italic terms by the author BvD): "There cannot be a place for religion in any psychiatric school or theory, precisely *because of the difference of dimension.* The only thing that can be demanded of a psychiatric approach is that it be *left open toward a higher dimension...*(and)...must remain open *so that the religious patient is not done injustice.* I am compelled by the Hippocratic oath...(and) – guarantee that *Logotherapy be available for each and every* patient, *including the agnostic* patient and usable by each and every doctor including the *atheistically oriented* doctor" (Frankl in Batthyany 2016 p. 11).

Frankl understands a "religious psychotherapy" as inconceivable. He points to the "essential difference" between psychotherapy and religion, which is a dimensional difference: To begin with, the aims of the two are different. Psychotherapy aims at mental health, i.e., Seelenheil/healing of the soul. Religion aims at salvation, i.e., Seelenheil.

How can one approach be differentiated from the other? This differentiation is a matter of the mutually agreed goals in the encounter. Accordingly, the interventions provided by the counselor are either scientifically based, according to the clients' health-related needs, or they are spiritually based, addressing clients' religious and spiritual beliefs.

"Logotherapy does not cross the boundary between psychotherapy and religion. But it leaves the door to religion open, and it leaves it to the patient whether or not to pass the door. It is the patient who has to decide whether he interprets responsibleness in terms of being responsible to humanity, society, conscience, or God. It is up to him to decide to what, to whom, and for what he is responsible." (Frankl 1988a, p. 143)

Referring to the many traumatic events and crisis that humanity has been facing since the turn of the century, and the observed rise of spiritual issues and current practices in companies, here is Frankl's approach, when being questioned, if man can overcome despair "without a personal God": "...Logotherapy seeks to know, not to believe. The ultimate decision for or against a religious Weltanschauung or philosophy of life is up to the patient, not the doctor. Logotherapy does not have the answers, but Logotherapy is *education toward responsibility* and thus the Logotherapist is least in danger, of all schools, of taking responsibility for such a decision from the shoulders of the patient. He will *try to enable the patient* to make a decision of his own" (Frankl in Batthyany 2016 p. 9).

Frankl lucidly observed the trend moving "toward a profoundly personalized religion," so that "every man will arrive at a language of his own, find the words of his own, when addressing himself to the ultimate being," and he would define these values and beliefs as "the personal style" of the individual; he continues with the question, if in this context, organizations and institutions in the field of religion will therefore disappear? By no means, because there are symbols commonly shared, and a common store of symbols always will remain (Frankl 1988a, b, p. 153 ff).

"Let me conclude: You do not give meanings, attribute meanings, ascribe meanings, attach meanings to things or happenings.... We cannot give meaning in an arbitrary way.... Reality is no neutral screen upon which you project your wishful thinking.... Each situation in life implies a question, a call...to be answered in an existential way by making decisions. These decisions cannot be made arbitrarily, they must be made responsibly. Our answer has to be an existential, responsible action." (Frankl in Batthyany 2016, p. 11)

Today, the discussion around the issue of spirituality acknowledges man's search for existential meaning and transcendence and, at the same time, seems to be somewhat lost in various spiritual approaches and religious terms and is losing sight in search for addressing man's basic search for transcending his very self.

3.11.1 Religion and Spirituality

Initially closely linked to each other, in the late twentieth century, spirituality and religion became disconnected from each other. Together with declining membership in religious institutions, spirituality became more and more oriented on subjective experience of developing the "true self," potentially in combination with reference to Eastern spiritual knowledge.

This trend is still ongoing. While some concepts of spirituality rather refer to the humanistic ideas of a "moral character," others embrace transcendental ideas.

These are some of the currently most relevant definitions and practical roads of spirituality:

- A postmodern term replacing religiousness.
- Living humanistic ideas of tolerance, patience, forgiveness, and contentment.
- The deepest values and meanings by which people live.
- Psychological practices fostering self-awareness, character, and inner peace.
- Connecting to a "greater reality" beyond the self.
- Meditation practices supporting mindfulness.
- An inner path to discover the essence of the own being.
- A practice to overcome the ego.
- A holistic understanding of the world.
- Practices supporting compassion for others.
- Inspired, selfless action, the path of one's work, where diligent practical work becomes in itself a spiritual practice, and work in daily life is perfected as a form of spiritual liberation and not for its material rewards.
- Basic practice in self-help movement, developing working for others, and self-sacrifice.
- Spiritual care (Puchalski et al. 2014), defined as "*...a dynamic and intrinsic aspect of humanity through which persons seek ultimate meaning, purpose, and transcendence, and experience relationship to self, family, others, community, society, nature, and the significant or sacred. Spirituality is expressed through beliefs, values, traditions, and practices....*"

According to a 2005 poll, about 24% of the US population identified itself as "spiritual" but not religious.

A recent representative study "Generation What?" among European young persons aged 18–34 years, with 1 million participants from 35 European countries, showed that 58% of all young European citizens, irrespective of their level of education, have "no trust" in religious institutions; 85% of all participants believe that they can be happy without believing in God (EBU 2016).

3.11.2 What Kind of "Ministry": Frankl's Approach on Religion

In one of his major works, Frankl (2000) elaborated on meaning and content of "ministry," challenging the reductionism of the mainstream therapeutic professions regarding values. Again, his considerations for medical professions can well be extended to coaching and training services in the workplace: "That aspect of logotherapy which I call medical ministry must not be confounded with pastoral ministry." Frankl is pointing to the major differences between theology and psychiatry and arguing that "psychiatrists should resist the temptation to dabble in the field of theology.... They should not flirt with grace.... Let us ask ourselves whether or not medical ministry is medical at all. Does it in truth belong to the responsibilities of the medical profession to comfort the patient? This is the way that every good doctor has understood his responsibilities of the medical profession, to comfort the patient.... It is the patient who has to decide whether he interprets responsibleness in terms of being responsible to humanity, society, conscience or God. It is up to him to decide to what, to whom and for what he is responsible" (p. 131 ff).

Religion and spirituality are "anthropological universals," addressing the specific essence of the human being and of being human. The specific content and circumstances, in which these universals are presented to the professional expert, are left to each individual person. It is the expert's responsibility to respond to their clients' needs with empathy, recognition, and respect. Here, the individual person's search for meaning and purpose and the existential givens are empirical facts, individually rendered in the specific context of the encounter between two persons.

3.11.3 "A World Void of Intrinsic Meaning..."

In 1985, Viktor Frankl had been awarded the Oskar Pfister Prize (Frankl 2000) for important contributions in the field of religion and psychiatry. In 2000, the American Psychiatric Association awarded their Oskar Pfister Prize to psychiatrist and psychotherapist Irvin Yalom. In his acceptance speech, Yalom (2000) reports on the initial dialogue with the chairman, Dr. Harding (italics by the author BvD):

"...Religion? Me? There must be a mistake....You know, I regard myself as a practicing atheist...." Dr. Harding: "We believe that you have dedicated yourself to *religious questions*." Yalom continues with a comparison between his approach in existential psychotherapy and religious consolation: "I believe these two approaches have a complex, strained relationship. In a sense, they are cousins with the same ancestors and concerns: they share the *common mission of ministering to the intrinsic despair* of the human condition. Sometimes they share *common methods* – the one to one relationship, the mode of confession, of inner scrutiny, of forgiveness of others and self.... And yet, it is true that the core beliefs and basic practical approaches of psychotherapy and religious consolation are *often antipodal*.... I grew to believe that the religious and the scientific world view were incompatible... .I felt sympathetic with Schopenhauer predicting that once the light of scientific insight dispelled the darkness of ignorance, religions would shrivel.... My college education was science based...and in my psychiatric training, the eclecticism of the psychiatric residency curriculum...suited me well...but I felt dissatisfied with the rigid and impersonal posture of the analyst and felt dissatisfied, too, with the then narrowed and reductionist analytic belief system – at times analytic doctrine felt to me uncomfortably similar to a religious fundamentalist venue.... I learned early on that a therapist cannot easily address raw existential issues…. Consequently, I began to concentrate my clinical practice on those patients, who, for one reason or other, were forced to confront fundamental issues of life and death…." Yalom (2000) continues to explain any human being's four ultimate concerns: death, isolation, meaning in life, and freedom and a counselor's role in supporting their clients (Yalom 2000, pp. 6–11):

> "Everyone – therapists as well as patients included – is destined to experience not only the exhilaration of life, but also its inevitable darkness: disillusionment, ageing, illness, isolation, loss, meaninglessness, painful choices, and death: When I speak of the ultimate concerns, I am obviously veering close to the domain which is the stuff of every religious tradition…. It is indisputable that religious belief and practice has been ubiquitous throughout the ages…and religion emerges as humankind's basic attempt to quell existence anxiety…. Religion provides powerful forms of connectivity. A religious person is offered the consolation of a personal eternally observing deity, who is not only aware of his/her existence, but also promises ultimate reunion – with lost loved ones, with the universal life force. And of course, it is readily apparent that organized religion provides connectivity through community…. My task is to be of help and that means to be as empathic as possible to patient's belief systems…." (Yalom 2000, p. 12)

As for any person's search for meaning and purpose in life and how this search is connected with self-transcendence, Yalom (2000) concludes:

> "We humans appear to be meaning-seeking creatures…Our ongoing search for substantial purpose in life often throws us into a crisis…It seems evident to me that life-purpose projects take on a deeper, more powerful significance if they are self-transcendent – that, is, directed to something or someone outside themselves – the love of a cause, the creative process, the love of others or divine essence…I find that purpose-in-life is best approached obliquely – it is best not to pursue purpose explicitly but to allow it to ensue from meaningful and authentic engagement, from lunging into an enlarging, fulfilling, self-transcending endeavor…." (Yalom 2000, p. 12).

In Europe, due to Sigmund Freud, who addressed the potential dark sides of religious beliefs, finally criticizing religious beliefs as signs of neurosis and religious orientations as obsessive-compulsive individual fixations, until recently, there have been, for good reasons, persistent and strong reservations, especially in the scientific and professional scene, against potential benefits of religion and spirituality and their integration in counseling.

Nevertheless, individual psychotherapists have recognized and started to include potential clients' spiritual and religious needs and/or spiritually based practices in their support for those in need, one of their most outstanding European representatives, especially in the field of trauma therapy, being Luise Reddemann (2011).

As of today, there are still substantial differences in the discussion around religion and spirituality and their influences on work and workplaces in the United States and in Europe. Only slowly the European scientific community is taking on board the professional discussion around integrating clients' beliefs into their own professional approaches. Therapeutic experts publishing findings and recommendations for an integrated approach (Utsch et al. 2014), bringing existential, meaning, spirituality, and religious issues "into the light," are still pioneers in their field.

Beyond all differences in addressing, communicating, and dealing with existential issues, existential analysis' approaches and the benefits the experts in this field are offering to human beings in today's world may provide substantial support to persons around the globe confronted with ever more substantial questions on their very core of existence, a support, whose benefits are still much underestimated, especially in the light of the existential questions that humanity needs to answer.

3.11.4 *Religion and Well-Being: Some Research Data*

Research on any links between religious orientation and well-being noted that there needs to be a basic differentiation between:

(i) Agnostic persons, (ii) spiritually oriented persons with no religious affiliation, (iii) nonreligiously affiliated persons, (iv) persons religiously affiliated who practice their religion, and (v) persons religiously affiliated who do not practice their religion. Assuming that living one's character strengths and virtues might positively influence well-being, the data do not support any direct links between religious orientation and well-being, because the issue is much more complex, taking other influencing factors of well-being into account.

Practicing the character strengths of gratitude, kindness, and forgiveness – as a part of most religious exercises – has proved to be directly related to increased satisfaction with life. Extrinsic religiousness, e.g., has no influence on satisfaction in life.

Studies show that satisfaction with life was higher with individuals who report to practice their religion (Koenig 2012). Engaging in religious practices seems to be beneficial in the development of several strengths: 16 of the 24 character strengths – gratitude, kindness, forgiveness, curiosity, love of learning, persistence, zest, teamwork, leadership, modesty, prudence, and self-regulation – were increased with individuals carrying out individual practices. On the direct influence of religious practices on life satisfaction, the authors (Bertholt and Ruch 2014) conclude: it is possible that religious practices have an indirect influence on life satisfaction.

Their findings also showed that pleasure was lower, whereas meaning was higher in individuals engaging in religious practices compared to those which did not practice their religion and the nonreligious participants. These findings support the findings of previous studies that reported a negative relationship between religiousness and orientation to pleasure and a positive relationship between religiousness and orientation to meaning. The authors note that their study was carried out in European countries with declining religious affiliation.

Especially since 9/11, research and practitioners in various fields have given increased attention to the resources that spirituality may provide in coping with difficult life events (Utsch 2016). Spirituality is understood as the person's competence to detach from their ego self (self transcendence) and connect with some power greater than themselves. Spirituality is understood as counterbalancing our performance and consumer-oriented societies. In this respect, spirituality is understood as the attitude and competence of dealing with existential issues.

A recent survey among 1000 psychotherapists in Germany showed that more than 50% of the participants believe in a higher, caring power (Utsch et al. 2014, p. 866) and 25% of the practitioners are interested in training about "religion in psychotherapy."

Concluding the research data: there is much to explore with the connection between well-being and religiousness and/or spirituality.

3.12 Addressing Spirituality in the Workplace

In the very end, Viktor Frankl is providing for a very factual approach for defining the three dimensions inherent to each individual in their quest for spirituality. Frankl's approach is putting this quest on its feet by defining a person's spirituality as a matter of *Sein*, independent of whatever specific approaches.

Until today, all discussions and research findings around spirituality and focused programs in the workplace are supporting Frankl's secular approach to the human spirit and the search for meaning in every individual being.

Reflecting the current sometimes fashionable spirituality programs implemented in workplaces, the findings are making an ever-stronger case for Frankl's three-dimensional approach of human existence and his strong reservations against any easy combination or confusion of existential issues and search for meaning with religious affiliation.

In recent years, taking hypothetical human "spiritual needs" into consideration in workplace settings, the topic of spirituality has gained increased attention (Litzey 2003).

Ever since the "spiritual turn" in last century's late 1960s, observers have recognized a "spirituality movement" in organizations and management practices, seeking to create a sense of meaning and purpose for all. Since large global companies like Ford, Nike, Boeing, and AT&T have been introducing "spiritual" practices in the workplace, this movement has taken considerable influence on all spheres of life. Ken Wilber (2000) introduced the "transpersonal and integral" approach, which has had great influence on business, consulting, and coaching, and religious psychology and Buddhism-related mindfulness exercises have gained much influence in all spheres of life.

Since the late 1990s and with increasing breadth, intensity, and dynamics, organizations have been creative in offering various types of "spiritual" programs to their employees. Spiritual practices in the workplace may be demonstrated on two levels: the organizational and the personal levels.

Some companies claim to foster a "spirited workplace"; others are offering "soul at work" programs. As of today, a complex and confusing market of services and programs touching on some type of spirituality can be observed:

- College and universities' MBA programs.
- Management academies are offering programs on spirituality in the workplace.

- Business coaches provide coaching in "spiritual leadership."
- Church institutions with specific religious approaches are offering management trainings with a clear religiously oriented – mainly Christian denomination – approach.
- In large US corporations, there are 10,000 prayer groups being offered at lunch time.
- Companies are inviting their employees for individual personality development programs.
- Bringing "their entire self" to work.
- Developing mindfulness programs.
- Consulting firms have been active in developing and implementing according strategies for addressing spirituality and tapping into the "unconscious."
- Companies are offering MBSR and stress management programs.
- Yoga classes are being provided.

Some claim the human need for addressing spirituality issues in the workplace and the good reasons for offering services in this direction. Harrington et al. (2001) note: "…Spirituality at work is not about religious beliefs. Rather, it is about people who perceive themselves as spirited beings, whose spirit needs energizing at work. It is about experiencing real purpose and meaning in their work beyond paychecks and task performance. Spirituality is really about people sharing and experiencing some common attachment, attraction, and togetherness with each other within their work unit and the organization as a whole."

Others refer to data suggesting employees' explicit request for some type of spiritual programs. Providers of spiritual practices in the workplace distinguish between spiritual and religious practices in the workplace, seeing spiritual practices referring to the individual internal self, while religious practices are connected to external norms and defined practices. Earlier, Mitroff and Denton (1999) reported that employees would find "religion" a highly inappropriate topic in the workplace; they would equally assess spirituality as a highly appropriate topic to be discussed in the workplace.

Introducing spirituality in the workplace, advertising and investing budgets in offering this type of support services to staff, claims to hold many promises, for all stakeholders, higher profits, higher morale, less absenteeism, less stress.

Litzey (2003) finds: "*There is the widespread belief that for companies to survive in the 21st century in the face of economical downturn and global competition, it would be helpful to seek inspiration from above (God/heaven) and tap into employees' spiritual resources*" (p. 2).

The California-based Institute for Management Excellence is differentiating between finding "*Your Self*" (capital "S" as "the greater energy of the Universe that connects all of us") and "*Your self (small s)* – the person you are here on this planet," suggesting to link the two selves with according practice.

In his anthology on the spiritual dimension in coaching and consulting, German business coach M. Haensel (2012) reports that clients have been increasingly raising questions and concerns relating to issues beyond their functional aspects in their professional life and respective roles. They are moved by questions about the meaning of their work, matching of their professional life with their broader life goals, and overarching, general concerns about their purpose and calling in life. Subsequently, more and more persons are connecting their work with their search for meaning – all of these, as Haensel suggests, being existential and spiritual issues. As a business coach, he foresees growing demand for mutually discussing these issues beyond mere coaching for short-term business solutions, defining the extended role of the business coach as a "*companion*" in the joint reflection of meaning, identity, and life balance. Irvin Yalom described his relationship with his patients as "fellow travelers." Haensel concludes spirituality in organizations to be something "greater beyond the very organization itself, a greater good, a driving energy and power to follow a purpose transcending self-interest."

Business coach F. Asslaender (2012) is describing the dynamics of taking meaning, spiritual and religious issues, as introduced by the client, into coaching considerations, concluding (translation by the author BvD): "As coaches we then act rather as pastors than as coaches. Als Coach agieren wir dann eher als Seesorger."

3.12.1 Spirituality Cannot Be Bought or Implemented

Lately, the author BvD received short greetings from a client who had, following friends' recommendations and his own desire to "go to a retreat," chosen to turn into a very expensive Ayurveda spa clinic for a 2-week stay, near his German place of living – since he was medically not fit to travel all the way to India. The client's note was reading: "*There is no place to feel more unhappy and be hungry all the time than this Ayurveda clinic.*"

Together with the rise of "spiritual" concepts and practices in the workplace and the promises they claim to hold, there are growing concerns about the misuse of the human search for transcendence.

Yalom (2000) diagnosed: "We are everywhere surrounded by not only a variety of religious beliefs with many of them existing upon the uniqueness of one particular set of beliefs, but we are also surrounded by the presences of less thoughtful and more patently psychic surgery, ghosts, witches, astrology, TM levitation, astral traveling, dowsers, crystals, palm reading, astrology, aura reading, psychokinesis, poltergeists, exorcism, Tarot cards, precognition, synchronicity, and I am sure each of you could add to this list…. Such extraordinary claims demand extraordinary proof and no such extraordinary proof has ever been posited…. There are times when I feel (but keep to myself) sorrow as I consider the amount of an individual's life that can be spent on excessive preoccupation with ritualistic practice. What is lost is some part of human freedom, creativity and growth." (Yalom 2000, p. 12)

All research studies on organizational performance and development and human needs to be met in the workplace conclude that organizations can be successful only when they link their goals and purpose to the individual employees' search for purpose and meaning in their work. Persons wish to experience their working and private lives as complete, holistic persons.

3.12.2 Critical Considerations

This is the space, where critical considerations are expressed by the author:

- The human search for meaning and purpose in life is in danger of being exploited.
- Haensel (2012) is arguing that spirituality "cannot be bought or sold." And he is also warning about the potential ego-inflation of developing nothing but the self-capacities and meditation competencies.
- Introducing the topic of spirituality in the workplace is, for reasons of effectiveness, focused on the individual employee in their function and work.
- Employees are searching for a reason, a meaning of what they are active in.
- Companies and managers are traveling two roads: They are, both on an organizational level and as individual executives, seeking purpose and inspiration and – at the same time – a scientifically based approach, giving evidence to the material outcomes of specific interventions, according to their performance goals, their KPIs, their balanced scorecard, etc.
- It is in this space, where spiritual business with trainings, in house exercises, etc., is growing, directly linking mindfulness with material financial outcomes for the organization.
- Especially human resource departments and their staff are advertising specific programs to their employees in general or to individual persons, supposedly in need to work on their stress management or life balance or in the context of health-related performance issues, expecting positive outcomes of this intervention for all stakeholders.
- Mindfulness and awareness-raising trainings are claiming to change the "deep-rooted mind-sets" and are frankly addressing and tapping into the "unconscious," employees' both conscious and unconscious thoughts and feelings, and the "below-the-surface factors," including the fears and threats to their identity.
- Focused programs are advertising their competencies for "new mindsets to be instilled" (global consulting firm).

Experts are questioning:

- Is the individual person's informed consent guaranteed?
- How are the unconscious, "below-the-surface factors" being assessed?
- How would employees feel being addressed on their "*small* selves," with the goal of developing "appropriate mind-sets"?
- Spiritual training does not necessarily lead to a better personality. The ego tends to subordinate these newly acquired tools.
- There is the danger of "ego-inflation" through knowledge about fashionable trainings.
- Participants of trainings offered to find the "true self" report higher levels of stress, because they find they are not "successful" in calming down.
- There are strong reservations against the spirituality business, serving the ego-inflation.

- Humanity has reached the highest level of conscience and awareness about what makes us humans and about our core, issues around spirituality kept being highly discussed.
- Wong and Page (2003) notes that "spirituality" needs to be integrated into the "corporate culture": if this would be a desirable objective, how could it be assured that "spirituality" in the workplace is not a means but rather an end?

3.13 Implications of Frankl's Three-Dimensional Approach for Today's Workplaces

The spiritual core of a person is seen as a potential source of health and strength. This core is incorruptible and irreducible and has its own dignity beyond assessment, judgment, and interpretation by others.

Today's human resource experts are investigating the motives and drivers of the younger "Generation Why?", their aspirations toward work and life, and their hopes and fears relating to their personal and family well-being. Here again, Frankl is making a strong case for their search, assessing it as an "achievement," for truly listening to them, including their potential feelings of void and being lost and for actually taking all this as a driver for positive change in organizations.

"What is to be done for a young man, for instance, who cannot see any meaning in life, at least not immediately? He should be made aware that his condition, which is called existential vacuum, is no neurotic symptom" (Frankl 1988a, b). Rather than being something to be ashamed of, it is, in Frankl's terms, "something to be proud of":

- It is a human achievement. It is, above all, a prerogative of young people.
- Not to take for granted that there is meaning inherent in human existence.
- To try, to venture, to question, and to challenge the problem of meaning of existence.

Purjo (2014) defines some major characteristics of Frankl's conception of the human being and specifically their being a spiritual person that can well be reflected for today's workplaces:

- Knowing and conceptualizing
- Awareness of values: discovering values and purposes, respecting human worth and worth of life in general, and making decisions based on highest values
- Responsibility for oneself, fellow-men, nature, and even cosmic harmony
- Consciousness and actualization of self-development tasks: enliven one's potentials for personal growth, sensitizing of experiencing love and other highest values
- Growing to an authentic personality with the goal of self-guidedness in one's life, criticality to mass behavior, and independent creativity within personal possibilities

- Being socialized, fulfilling ethical principles in one's life, enhancing the good of others, and constructive civil activism

The author (BvD) would suggest that those professional and ethical standards defined for counselors, psychotherapists, and doctors in discussing existential issues with their clients (Noyon and Heidenreich, 2012) would also hold true for any spiritual practice and programs being offered in the workplace. It is suggested that the providers as persons (trainers, coaches, counselors) may assure their certified professionalism in the following areas:

- Understanding of own existential issues
- Empathy and a reflected self
- Reflected neutrality: knowing own values, beliefs, and world views so that these would not interfere with the other person's reflections and issues
- Engagement: supporting the other person in finding their own world view and their own viable values
- Refraining from own judgments as fundamental attitude
- Exploration of the world view of the other
- Role clarity, especially relating to corporate in-house trainers and coaches
- Continuous training of the self

Ethical guidelines defined for coaching practitioners in the global community (AC, Association for Coaching; EMCC, European Mentoring and Coaching Council; ICF, International Coach Federation) are widely accepted in business and may also serve as a globally shared basis for professional ethics in dealing with spiritual and religious issues.

Frankl's anthropological approach holds myriads of resources for discovering, addressing, and living health, well-being, ethics, values, and meanings in workplace settings.

The three dimensions of human existence provide for an outstanding understanding of current, dramatic, global challenges relating to spiritual quests and religious orientations. Workplaces and their staff are "going global" beyond their potential religious affiliations. The "spiritual" roads they travel cannot be a matter of competencies or discussions in workplaces. Workplaces cannot claim to cover up or fulfill any alleged spiritual needs of their staff. Here, Frankl's anthropological secular and factual approach is providing for a secular, science-based approach, without reducing the person to their evidence-based levels. Frankl's approach is indeed rehumanizing the person, exploring on their undivided and singular dignity "under all circumstances."

In the context of global challenges regarding migration and persons' potential religious orientations as a source of resilience, hope, and meaning, Frankl's approach provides for most relevant considerations in living diversity and tolerance (Mitteramskogler 2015).

References

Antonovsky A (1987) Unraveling the mystery of health. Jossey-Bass Inc., San Francisco
APA American Psychological Association (2013) Handbook of psychology, religion and spirituality. American Psychological Association, Washington, DC
Asslaender F (2012) Vom Coach zum Seelsorger. Mein eigener Weg. In: Haensel M (ed) Die spirituelle Dimension in Coaching und Beratung. Vandenhoeck & Ruprecht, Goettingen
Batthyany A (ed) (2016) Logotherapy and existential analysis. Springer, Cham
Batthyany A, Russo-Netzer P (eds) (2014) Meaning in positive and existential psychology. Springer, New York
Berry-Smith St (2012) Death, freedom, isolation and meaninglessness. The Existential Psychotherapy of Irvin D. Yalom. A literature review. Dissertation submitted to Auckland University of Technology in fulfillment of the requirements for the degree of Master of Health Sciences (MHSc), Auckland, NZ
Bertholt A, Ruch W (2014) Satisfaction with life and character strengths of non religious and religious people. It is practicing the religions that makes the difference. Front Psychol 5:876. Published online 2014 Aug 14. Prepublished online 2014 July 14. https://doi.org/10.3389/fpsyg.2014.00876
Buber M (1971) I and Thou. Touchstone, New York
Dziegielewski S (2013) The changing face of health care social work. Opportunities and challenges for professional practice. Springer, New York
EBU (2016) Generation what? Young people and optimism, a pan-European view. National reports. Geneva, Switzerland
Fabry J (1988) Guideposts to meaning. Discovering what really matters. New Harbinger, Oakland
Fabry J (1994) The pursuit of meaning. Institute of Logotherapy Press, Abilene
Fabry JB Frankl VE (foreword) (2013) The pursuit of meaning. Purpose Research, Birmingham
Frankl VE (1960) The will to meaning. Foundations and applications of logotherapy. Meridian, New York
Frankl VE (1966) Questions and answers. In: Batthyany A (ed) (2016). Logotherapy and existential analysis. Proceedings of the Viktor Frankl Institute Vienna, vol 1. Springer, Switzerland, pp 7–12
Frankl VE (1967) Psychotherapy and existentialism. Penguin, Harmondsworth
Frankl VE (1973) Psychotherapy and existentialism. Selected papers on logotherapy. Penguin Books, New York
Frankl VE (1975) The unconscious god: psychotherapy and theology. Simon and Schuster, New York
Frankl VE (1986) The doctor and the soul: from psychotherapy to logotherapy. Random House, New York
Frankl VE (1988a) The will to meaning. Foundations and applications of logotherapy, Expanded edn. Meridian, New York
Frankl VE (1988b) Medical ministry. In: The will to meaning. Foundations and applications of logotherapy. Penguin Books, New York
Frankl VE (1995) Ärztliche Seelsorge.Grundlagen der Logotherapie und Existenzanalyse. Fischer Taschenbuch Verlag, Frankfurt am Main
Frankl VE (2000) Man's search for ultimate meaning. Basic Books, New York
Frankl VE (2014a) Man's search for meaning (Rev & updated edn). Beacon Press, Boston
Frankl VE (2014b) The will to meaning. Foundations and applications of logotherapy. Plume, New York
Grant A (2014) Give and take. Penguin Books, New York
Haensel M (2012) Die spirituelle Dimension in Coaching und Beratung. Vandenhoeck & Ruprecht, Goettingen
Harari NY (2017) Homo deus. A brief history of tomorrow. Harvill Secker, London

Harrington WJ, Preziosi RC, Gooden DJ (2001) Perceptions of workplace spirituality among professionals and executives. Empl Responsib Rights J 13(30):155–163
Jung CG (1926) Nature and spirit. Lecture delivered to the literary society of Augsburg. In: Hull RFC (1960) The collected works of C. G. Jung vol 8, Pantheon Books, New York, pp 319–320
Jurica J, Barenz J, Shim J, Graham K, Steger M (2014) Ultimate concerns from existential and positive psychological perspectives. In: Batthyany A, Russo-Netzer P (eds) Meaning in positive and existential psychology. Springer, New York, pp 115–128
Koenig HG (2012) Religions, spirituality and health: the research and clinical implications. In: ISRN psychiatry 2012, Published online 2012 Dec 16. https://doi.org/10.5402/2012/278730
Laengle A (2005) The search for meaning in life and the existential fundamental motivations. Existent Anal 16(1):2–14
Leontiev D (2016) Logotherapy beyond psychotherapy: dealing with the spiritual dimension. In: Batthyany A (ed) Logotherapy and existential analysis. Springer, Cham, pp 277–290
Litzsey Ch (2003) Spirituality in the workplace and the implications for employees and organizations. Research paper, Southern Illinois University, Carbondale. http://www.academia.edu. Accessed 30 Oct 2017
Mascaro N (2014) Meaning sensitive psychotherapy: binding clinical, existential and positive psychological perspectives. In: Batthyany A, Russo-Netzer P (eds) Meaning in positive and existential psychology. Springer, New York, pp 269–289
Mitroff I, Denton E (1999) A study of spirituality in the workplace. Sloan Manag Rev 40(4):83–92
Mitteramskogler M (2015) Logotherapie und Spiritualität. Die Gretchenfrage in der Logotherapie. Masterthesis Department für Psychotherapie und Biopsychosoziale Gesundheit. Donau Universität, Krems
Noyon A Heidenreich T (2012) Existenzielle Themen in Psychotherapie und Beratung. Beltz Verlag, Weinheim
Psychology of religion and spirituality in clinical practice. Journal edited by American Psychological Association, Washington, DC
Puchalski C, Vitillo R, Hull Sharon S, Relle N (2014) Spiritual dimensions of whole person care: reaching national and international consensus. J Palliat Med 17(6):642–656
Purjo T (2014) Logotheory as philosophical anthropology. In: Presentation at the future of logotherapy, 2nd international congress on logotherapy and existential analysis, Vienna
Rankin SHD, Stallings K, Lonndon F (1996) Patient education in health and illness. Lippincott Williams & Wilkins, Philadelphia
Reddemann L (2011) Psychodynamisch Imaginative Traumatherapie PITT-Das Manual. Ein resilienzorientierter Ansatz in der Psychotraumatologie. Klett-Cotta, Stuttgart
Society for Existential Analysis (2017) London, UK. Official Website: http://existentialanalysis.org.uk. Accessed 10 Oct 2017
Utsch M (2016) Ressourcen der Religion und Spiritualität. In: Verhaltenstherapie und Psychosoziale Praxis 04/2016
Utsch M, Bonelli RM, Pfeifer S (2014) Psychotherapie und Spiritualität: Mit existenziellen Konflikten und Transzendenzfragen professionell umgehen. Springer, Berlin/Heidelberg
Wiesel E (2015) Open heart. Schocken, New York
Wilber K (2000) Integral psychology. Shambala Publishing, Boston
Wong PTP (2012) The human quest for meaning. Theories, research and applications. Routledge, New York
Wong PTP (2014) Viktor Frankl's meaning seeking model and positive psychology. In: Batthyany A, Russo-Netzer P (eds) Meaning in positive and existential psychology. Springer, New York, pp 149–184
Wong PTP (2016) Meaning-seeking, self-transcendence and well-being. In: Batthyany A (ed) Logotherapy and existential analysis. Springer, Cham, pp 311–322
Wong PTP, Page D (2003) Servant leadership: an opponent-process model and the revised servant leadership profile. Address presented at the Servant Leadership Roundtable. School of Global Leadership and Entrepreneurship, Regent University, Virginia Beach, VA

World Health Organization Publications (1991) Issue 9290211407. Chapter 4: the spiritual dimension in the global strategy for health. Geneva
Yalom I (1980) Existential psychotherapy. Basic Books, New York
Yalom I (2000) Religion and psychiatry, Acceptance Speech, delivered at the American Psychiatric Association Annuel Meeting, New Orleans. In: Am J Psychother 3/2002

Chapter 4
What Is Man?

Contents

> The specifically human capacity to 'will' remains empty as long as it has not yet been complemented by its objective counterpart, to will what I 'ought'. What I ought, however, is the actualization of values, the fulfillment of the concrete meaning of my personal existence…Values are necessarily more than a mere self-expression of one's inner life…If meanings and values were just something emerging from the subject himself – that is to say, if they were not something that stems from a sphere beyond and above man – they would instantly lose their demand quality (V. Frankl)

Ethics, values, and meaning have long been grounded in philosophy.

Together with all other related medical and therapeutic professions, professional associations supporting other persons in their pursuit of a fulfilling and good life, such as psychologists, psychotherapists, counselors, and coaches, have been continually engaged in defining their ethical standards, their core values, and their image of humans, to give best guidance to their clients, themselves, and the greater community.

B. von Devivere, *Meaningful Work: Viktor Frankl's Legacy for the 21st Century*,
https://doi.org/10.1007/978-3-319-89791-2_4

Until today, all therapeutic and medical professions are related and have been referring to a deeply humanistic image of humans, which is being amended according to current issues. In their Ethics Code, the American Psychological Association is explicitly referring to science, other materials, and guidelines that have been adopted or endorsed by scientific and professional psychological organizations *and the dictates of their own conscience.* Each and every therapeutic profession has formulated their image of humans, because this is the basis of their therapeutic profession. Today, it is exactly this "Menschenbild" (image of humans) that is being challenged by twenty-first century's new deterministic image of humans, reducing the person to their neurological processes and denying the human free will, which is actually the basis of all therapeutic encounters and healing processes.

Therapeutic professions cannot shy away from these challenges and have not concealed the potential dilemmas between their humanistic approach and attempts to artificially replace humans by allegedly improved cyber beings. Ethics are describing norms, what is ideally considered to be right or wrong. Normative ethics and standards describe a moral course of action, how one ought to act.

All professionals are bound by ethical standards in exercising their profession, legally defined by their respective professional associations. These legal regulations reflect centuries of good practice, e.g., the Hippocratic Oath, and their ethical standards can be well understood in terms of overarching values of humanity (see also VIA character strengths).

4.1 Neutrality Is Not Indifference

Preserving absolute religious and ideological neutrality in any counseling, coaching, and consulting practice is a matter of professional and ethical standards. A neutral stance does not mean indifference but would rather include taking a professional, active attitude toward the client's individual needs, individual goals, and individual potentials to draw from:

- Refraining from siding with any of the client's potentially conflicting drives
- Supporting the client in their own self reflection
- Understanding their conflicts and motives
- Getting access to own resources
- Strengthening their autonomy
- Assuring their individual freedom
- Finding potential options for their own way forward
- Empowering their own confidence in taking action

4.2 Ethical Standards Relating to Coaching and Counseling Experts' Activities

The following examples of Code of Ethics are highlighting the links between ethics and values:

The APA American Psychological Association defines in its Ethical Principles for Psychologists and Code of Conduct (2010) five general principles, covering, but not being limited to, the clinical, counseling, and school practice of psychology and research, teaching, supervision of trainees, public service, policy development, social intervention, development of assessment instruments, conducting assessments, educational counseling, organizational consulting, forensic activities, and program design and evaluation and administration.

The APA Ethics Code applies to these activities across a variety of contexts, such as in person, postal, telephone, Internet, and other electronic transmissions, and understands itself to give guidance toward the highest ideals of psychology. The APA General Principles defined are:

- Beneficence and nonmaleficence
- Fidelity and responsibility
- Integrity
- Justice
- Respect for people's rights and dignity

The APA Ethics Code further covers ethical standards relating to resolving ethical issues, competence, human relations, privacy and confidentiality, advertising and other public statements, record keeping and fees, education and training, research and publication, and assessment and therapy.

DVP German Association for Psychotherapy In their ethical guidelines, DVP refers to their professionals' respecting the dignity of each person and pursuing, maintaining, and protecting basic human rights.

The EAPA International Employee Assistance Association Their Code of Ethics (2017) intends to provide guidance for employee assistance professionals for the benefit of their clients, both individual employees and employer organizations. The guidelines are covering the following ethical principles for rendering best employee assistance:

- Service – professional, competent, and impartial
- Beneficence
- Fidelity – trusting relationships
- Integrity
- Respect for client's rights
- Competence

Their further guidelines are exclusively emphasizing and elaborating on "responsibility" to colleagues and other professionals, employees and clients, employers or work organizations, vendors and providers, the employee assistance profession, and broader society, in conducting research.

The ICF International Coach Federation Code of Ethics The ICF International Coach Federation is the only global coaching association. Their standards and their Code of Ethics (2017) are designed to provide guidelines, accountability, and enforceable standards of conduct for their members, covering topics of professional standards of qualification, conflicts of interest, and confidentiality and privacy, being committed to:

- Reliability
- Accountability
- Openness
- Acceptance
- Congruence

ICF clearly differentiates between its core values and its code of ethics, defining their ICF core values as:

- Integrity
- Collaboration
- Respect

4.3 Humanism

Humanist thinkers convinced us that it was the individual person who can make the right decision and that our free will is the highest authority of all. According to this humanistic approach, each individual has the inherent drive toward self-discovery, seeking truth and possessing the communicative competence, with reason and autonomy being the basic aspects of human existence.

Explicitly referring to these humanistic ideals, the German psychotherapeutic clinic sysTelios Klinik is binding their in-house therapists and external cooperating professionals to overarching principles (translation by the author):

- Human dignity is impeachable.
- Everyone has the same right to freedom and life, as well as to determine all the decisions affecting and influencing his life.
- Every person is fundamentally good. Each one has an independent and intrinsically valuable personality.
- The uniqueness and diversity of each person must be respected, as well as his individual expression, even if it may seem incomprehensible to others. For the person concerned, it is fundamentally meaningful.

- Each person is capable and able to make their own decisions and to determine his life on a moral and ethical level. From our point of view, it is directed toward self-actualization and growth.

4.4 Taking Responsibility

During the past years, there has been a lot of attention paid to ethics, frequently triggered by violation of ethical standards not observed.

Organizational ethics express the values and principles of an organization. The organizational code of ethics is a set of principles that is used to guide the organization in its decisions, programs, and policies. An ethical organizational culture consists of leaders and employees adhering to these ethics.

Responding to the question "What is right, what is wrong?" might be this century's greatest challenge. Considering the impact that mega technologies have on this and future generations' lives has been occupying corporations, executives, the society as a whole, and individuals to an unprecedented extent. Some would even observe a generation divide, with the younger ones challenging "the capitalist system" as a whole, withdrawing from the many seductions, consumer and lifestyle opportunities presented to them, more or less actively claiming new ways of organizing work and private life, actualizing a lifestyle of sharing, rather than spending, of waiving status symbols they would find inappropriate for fulfilling their needs along a conscious life, rejecting their parents' – mostly fathers – endless striving for career advancements, while they were sacrificing family life for their companies' benefit, witnessing that these individual sacrifices were null in the light of economic and financial crisis, shareholder value-oriented management decisions, restructuring. This younger generation has witnessed the vanishing of their parents' once culturally paramount professions (e.g., composers, printers, bookbinders, and other members of the letterpress craft work). They observed individuals with little or no professional expertise demonstrating their rigorous will to rise and exercise their highest possible global impact, experiencing momentary pleasure as "masters of the universe" (name of a film made by a former investment banker about his work and influence), ultimately triggering global crisis.

It was in this context that today's "younger generation" coined as "Generation Y/ pronounced as Why?" was raised. Until today, they developed and built their identity on the grounds of what they observed, what they were taught, how their families have coped with their complex issues in work and private life. Many of these experiences were traumatic to their parents; many of them are still struggling to make a decent living, trying to manage the many changes they are confronted with, sometimes lacking the resources or competencies to adapt to these ever faster changing market demands, or being left behind for structural reasons (age, level of education, previous profession, local or national economic environments, and conditions). Now their children are today's and tomorrow's potentials, who will shape the world.

They are confronted with unprecedented challenges, not only economically and technically but mostly relating to ethical questions, of finding meaning in their work and exercising values and right judgment.

4.5 Unprecedented Ethical Challenges

In the past four decades, technology has fundamentally altered our lives:

The debates on stem cells and embryo research – genetically modified organisms, genome-editing technologies, artificial intelligence and robotics, development and operation of drones, neuro-inspired computers with their own brain, building neuro-morphic chips, the integration of smart machines and materials in manufacturing – are influencing all spheres of production.

Together with the dynamics of these technologies "radical disruptions will occur…. These technologies are demonstrations of human excellence, yet computers that think could be devastating for our species:" Al-Rhodan (2015), philosopher and Honorary Fellow at the University of Oxford, concludes: The ethical consequences of such developments must be thoroughly thought through. Sometimes, immediate "ethical red flags" are emerging. Dangerous forms of dependences on machines and new understandings of humanity and our emotions are emerging. The new technologies are already redefining our concepts of biology, nature, and the material world around us.

Al-Rhodan emphasizes that we must welcome innovation and the benefit it brings us, but we must also remain committed to the issues of human dignity and the equality of individuals.

Perhaps it is exactly this "must" of appreciating the technologic discoveries and willingly benefiting from all their potentials and promises that is endangering humankind. Maybe the discoveries in life sciences are different from all previous discoveries that humankind had "managed somehow," attending to the warnings that we are somehow, but not fully, acting "like gods." Philosophers are observing a loss in confidence that we can manage what we invented – that the technologies invented in artificial intelligence will rather replace all forms of humankind. What if humankind is putting themselves with their technology above all gods? Could those who have all the insights and are implementing biotechnology and artificial intelligence rule human mankind?

Humanism is now facing an existential challenge and the idea of "free will" is under threat.

Scientists with their insights into the way our brains and bodies work suggest that our feelings are not some uniquely human spiritual quality. Rather, they define them as biochemical mechanisms that all mammals and birds use. Human physical sensations, feelings, and emotions are, to their understanding, nothing but neurological processes, wired together and firing together. The living brains, of animals or humans likewise, can be understood in terms of algorithms. According to their understanding, all behaviors of these beings are based on "decisions" driven by brainy instincts.

4.6 Homo Deus? An Existential Crisis of Humankind

This is the core conclusion in historian Yuval Noah Harari's latest, world best seller publication with the title *Homo Deus. A Brief History of Tomorrow* (2016a), spanning human history from the evolution of homo sapiens (title of Harari's previous book 2014): "Modernity is a deal…The entire contract can be summarized in a single phrase: Humans agree to give up meaning in exchange for power" (p. 17).

Harari (2016a, b) is suggesting that Silicon Valley and other technological powers on the edge of their technological knowledge have the access to all the biochemical algorithms, allegedly governing human behavior, and can calculate the data. "Dataism" is taking over. According to Dataism, Beethoven's Fifth Symphony, a stock exchange bubble, and the flu virus are just three patterns of data flow.

Harari (2016a, b) warns: "Every day millions of people decide to grant their smartphone a bit more control over their lives or try a new and more effective antidepressant drug. In pursuit of health, happiness and power, humans will gradually change first one of their features and then another, and another, until they will no longer be human" (p. 26).

4.6.1 Homo Deus or Free Will

With these stunning conclusions and their empirical facts presented, Harari and other researchers' findings and views are not only challenging "some mysterious free will"; Harari (2017) is explicitly denying human free will: "There is no free will." Harari tells the history of modernity as a constant struggle between religion and science, with science prevailing. Harari argues: "The modern world promised us unprecedented power. The promise has been kept. Now, what about the price? In exchange for power, *the modern deal expects us to give up on meaning.*" Until today, beauty, art, creativity, morality, and compassion have "survived" but will disappear. Technology and artificial intelligence will, according to Harari, undermine the foundations, on which humanism once was built: "The free individual is just a fictional tale, concocted by an assembly of biochemical algorithms…People's once acclaimed freedom to choose is limited to a few alternatives suggested to them by external algorithms." The same would, in Harari's world view, apply to human conscience, in his terms being defined as a reflection of mostly unconscious links between physical and emotional processes driving some behavior.

Until today, humanists have been shaping our modern understanding of humans as free human beings, who claimed their free will to be the highest authority of all. Today, Harari explains, high-tech gurus and Silicon Valley are creating a new universal narrative, legitimizing the authority of algorithms and big data, finally, "becoming the source of all meaning of mankind". When big data algorithms "know me better than I know myself, authority will shift from humans to algorithms."

Here, Harari finally "ventures into dystopian territory, as previously defined by Aldous Huxley" (Naughton 2016). We definitely need to take all the desires, decisiveness, the dangers, as well as the potentials and paradisiac promises of dataism into close consideration.

4.6.2 New Sciences: "Nothing but Algorithms" – Twenty-First Century's Reductionism

The man on the street, he has always understood what I am saying. He sees that something is missing. He realizes that he is more than his id, more than his drives. (Viktor Frankl)

Harari brilliantly observes the promises that the new sciences with biotechnology and the emerging dataism are offering:

For scholars and intellectuals, Dataism promises to provide the scientific Holy Grail…a single overarching theory that unifies all the scientific disciplines from musicology through economics, all the way to biology…(equally understood as) data flow that can be analyzed using the same basic concepts and tools. This idea is extremely attractive. It gives all scientists a common language, builds bridges over academic rifts and easily exports insights across disciplinary borders…. (Harari, Financial Times)

Actually, Harari is making an ever stronger case of intensifying the public dialogue and "reasoning" about the philosophical and anthropological assumptions, the ethics, ethical standards, and specific borderlines in all sciences, with his warnings (Harari 2016b): "Of course, like previous all-encompassing dogmas, Dataism, too, may be founded on a misunderstanding of life. But even if Dataism is wrong about life, it may still conquer the world...Dataism has especially good prospects, because it is currently spreading across all scientific disciplines. A unified scientific paradigm may easily become an unassailable dogma."

How to deal with dataism, "21st century's dogma"? There are various lines of critical approaches to Harari's hypothesis that dataism is already now successfully taking a hold of "all other scientific disciplines." In fact, issues, directions, and advancements in sciences are strongly influenced by their cultural and sociological environments, in which they work. It is in this framework that their ethical, material, economic, and legal boundaries are defined. Some examples: Until today, there are substantial variations in the public discussion, topics, and limitations defined in five major scientific fields of the potentially emerging dataism in Germany and the United States:

- Biosciences and GMOs' genetically modified organisms, especially their benefits and dangers in agriculture as opposed to the increased development of sustainable, biodynamic agriculture.
- Strong legal regulations for human genetics and embryo stem cells research.
- Ethical, societal, and ethical implications of immunotherapy and their accessibility in the light of citizen equality and basic constitutional rights.

- Researchers are identifying considerable risks of addiction to the use of smart devices and are engaging in awareness raising of the potential health risks for children and youngsters.
- The social media business is being challenged for their abuse by criminal activities and technologically organized attack on democratic regimes and their reported lack of data protection for the individual. In Europe, a critical mass of people observing the detrimental effects of Big Data is emerging.

Discussions and specific regulations around bioscience are a convincing example of (Rolf 2010) "how biologically ambiguous facts in their ethical judgements are interpreted quite differently, as the scientific and ethical discussion around embryo research might show." Rolf (2010) argues:

From a biological point of view, the human embryo, once a new genome has been formed with the fusion of the pre-nucleus, is a human being that is continually developing to birth and further development. Now this fact is ethically necessary because it does not yet make normative statements on the handling of embryos.

Scientific research and their limitations are also defined referring to basic values, like human dignity, as specifically defined by constitutional human rights, which, in turn, reflect the public discussion of what the respective societies would understand by this term today, also taking their history and desired future into considerations.

"Human dignity," in turn, is, by today, a human right, defined and laid down not only in the Declaration of Human Rights but has also become an explicit part of many national constitutions. Until today, ethics and basic values cannot be "seen," "discovered," or translated into algorithms, because they are part of human conscience and deliberate thinking, based on detached reflection and thought. They remain part of the human "third dimension," the "Geistige Person."

Markus Gabriel (2017), Professor of Philosophy, concludes that delegating decisions to other experts or processes outside the human self might seem comfortable and attractive: "If I succeed in telling me that I am that brainy thing under my cranium, then I am relieved from the arduous work of constantly making a decision, who I actually will be. Then I am relieved from all the moral questions that life is constantly posing to us. Because, if I am that brainy thing, then there could be an expert for my being self, who could take an external perspective, give a much better opinion on me than I could ever give myself" (Translation by BvD).

4.7 Human Reasoning

> The I can be understood as a social construction, but that does not make it an illusion (Juergen Habermas).

Until today, scientific research and practices in humanities and their related fields of philosophy, psychotherapy, counseling, and coaching have been relating to humanism's concept of the person, their freedom, and responsibility to shape their own personality and their environments.

Neurobiology, supposing that it is the "brain," not my "self," that thinks and acts, is intuitively incontestable with the ordinary self-concept of acting subjects. According to neuroscience, freedom of the will is an illusion, understood rather as mental causation.

Actually, the debate around brain research and the determinist standpoint might evoke feelings of being transported back into the nineteenth century, but life sciences' current claims are giving even higher relevance to a highly important philosophical debate about human's free will.

If we were "…nothing but" individuals, why do we ever have to demand justifications from one another? Could this process of conscious rationality and communication ever be shrugged off by post hoc commentaries on neurologically caused behavior? And who would ever go into this kind of trouble, after the responsibility had been taken off the individual person's shoulders?

Juergen Habermas is one of today's internationally most outstanding philosophers to defend the concept of human free will. In his Kyoto speech (2004), he elaborated on the current debate on man's free will, rejecting the deterministic approach, and, by doing so, also addressed ever more current issues of individual accountability and responsibility. Reflecting on his approach and contrasting it with the current powerful denial of any free will throws a dazzling light on the dangers and challenges humankind is actually facing, with two roads diverging: Either rationally nourishing the idea of human free will or of generally denying it with ultimately no difference between human beings and primates.

Habermas is pointing to a mere everyday observation of our understanding of ourselves: supposing that it is "the brain," not my "self," that thinks and acts cannot seriously challenge our intuitively anchored and pragmatically sustained understanding of ourselves as accountable agents. Relating to the neurobiological determinist approach, Habermas elicits the preconditions for understanding human reasoning and according actions based on thinking:

- There is no diminution of freedom when the agent lets himself be "determined"… he experiences his subjective nature as a source of capabilities.
- Being determined provides constitutive support for self-determination.
- Looking back in time, it remains puzzling, why the extravagance of a space of reason's eve emerged in the first place.
- Human's existence and development integrated learning and cognitive development through communicative socialization, perceiving and understanding members of the same species as intentionally acting beings that separate home sapiens from its closest relatives.
- Cultural development.
- Experiencing a relationship with another person is constitutive for the distancing stand on the world and on oneself.
- Human beings learn by instruction and cooperation. They share and exchange on cultural background knowledge.

- The same holds true for the character that we develop in the course of our individual lives: The author is in each case the unique person one has become or the irreplaceable (unvertretbare) individual that one understands oneself to be.
- Motivation by reasons requires not merely an agent for whom reasons count but *who lets himself be determined by insight.* Consequently, the authorship and accountability needs to be defined other than through neurobiological preconditioning.
- Responsible authorship involves taking the initiative, for reasons, and attributing the initiative to oneself.

4.7.1 Taking an Attitude

Habermas concludes: "The actor won't reach a decisive practical judgment on how to act without weighing alternative courses of action. These alternatives do, of course, present themselves within a field of possibilities that is limited by capacities, character, and circumstances…In this sense, he is not *unconditionally* free to act one way or another. In the course of his reflections, the actor reaches a rationally motivated position that is not arbitrary." Habermas claims nothing less than the undeniable human capacity of being the actor of history for all times.

4.7.2 The Hybris of Dataism

Dataism's claim to develop an improved cyber being, cyborgs, is a double discard: It denies all concepts of human beings' transcendent dimension and disowns basic existential givens like beginning and end of life. It is this realistic claim and ethical hybris that could eventually bring with it the end of this powerful industry. Then, dataism would not attract all sciences with their promises, but their dogmatic reductionism would rather limit their influence or repel substantial parts of the scientific community.

Which direction will humanity and global sciences facing these challenges take?

Hoping that today's most influential and powerful tech companies might collapse from the inside does not seem to be a conscious and viable option for shaping the "history of tomorrow."

Observers like John Naugthon are arguing that "dataism" might "collapse under the weight of its own absurdity," referring to their direct allusions to creating robots better than any living human beings, their denial of existential givens, of beginning and end of life, of conscience, their promises to endless optimization of life, while, at the same time, their distinct failures to deliver on these false promises, together with mankind's increasing unhappiness and inadequacies in dealing with today's technological achievements, become ever more apparent.

4.8 The Ontological Differences and the Anthropological Unity of Man

Viktor Frankl (1988) made the science-based case for the anthropological unity of the person, arguing against all types of reductionism: "How is it possible to preserve the oneness of man in the face of the pluralism of sciences, when the pluralism of sciences is the nourishing soil on which the reductionism is growing." Frankl has been challenging this reductionism, coming in diverse forms of man's being "nothing but…" and thereby "disregarding the essential openness of human existence."

The present discussion touches on the philosophical, ethical, and anthropological foundations of what humanity considers as "human." Again, like centuries ago, it is a discussion around the image of humans and empirical findings, Frankl (1988) explains: "I would define man as unity in spite of multiplicity. Conceiving of man in terms of bodily, mental and spiritual strata of layers means dealing with him as if his somatic, psychic and noetic modes of being could be separated from each other. I myself have tried to do justice to the ontological differences and the anthropological unity of man."

Reading and listening to Harari's lucid description of past and potential human history and carefully going into his publications and interviews, one would finally find Harari himself suggesting a stunningly hopeful option for humanity:

4.9 What Makes Us Human?

> If you want to stay beyond the reach of the algorithms, there is probably just one piece of advice to give you, the oldest in the book: know thyself. In the end, it's a simple empirical question. As long as you have greater insight and self-knowledge than the algorithms, your choices will still be superior and you will keep at least some authority in your hands. If the algorithms nevertheless seem poised to take over, it is mainly because most human beings hardly know themselves at all. (Harari 2016b)

Others argue that it is the almost forgotten domain of awareness, where we experience values like truth, goodness, beauty, love, and compassion and also intuition, creativity, insight, and focused attention.

In his testimony, Frankl is a witness of the reasonable, detached observer describing the radical evil around him, radical absurdity, stripped of everything, except, literally, naked existence.

His approach has come to be a very philosophical and extremely practical one, an approach that is pointing rather to the common needs and shared responsibilities in shaping the world for the common good, an approach that could serve as a guiding question for today's challenges: "We need to stop asking ourselves about the meaning of life, and instead to think of ourselves as those who were being questioned by life, daily and hourly" (Frankl).

4.10 Three Human Conditions

For the past centuries, philosophical anthropology has defined understandings of the human condition that touch on the current issues and discussions about the meaning of work, its effects and counter effects, and the stand to take in the future. Three human conditions have been defined, which may well describe man's actual situation.

4.10.1 Animal Laborans or Homo Faber?

In the human condition, the great philosopher Hannah Arendt (1998) describes the "vita activa," differentiating between labor, work, and activity. In her approach, coined as political existentialism, Arendt emphasizes the individual free will and the limitations to human freedom set by the respective environments.

According to Arendt's differentiation, labor concerns itself with the absolute necessities of life, perpetually producing goods to make a living, just as all animals are providing for their life and their survival. The activity of labor is commanded by strict necessity. This mindset of being forced to work to make a living does generally contradict the realm of human freedom as the basis of the human condition. According to Arendt, today's capitalist working environment, together with the prioritization of the economy influencing all spheres of live, is destroying all creative aspects of work and the creation of a public understanding of the common good.

In Arendt's understanding and as described in Max Frisch's novel *Homo Faber* (1969), for the "homo faber," work is a distinctly human activity, consciously creating our common world and collective existence. Homo faber's typical functions are the builder, the architect, the craftsperson, the artist, and the legislator, building the world both physically and institutionally by constructing buildings and making laws. In this understanding (Arendt 1998), homo faber transforms his environment according to the plans and needs of humans, making his activities and creations a distinctly human (i.e., non-animal) activity. This world is governed by human ends and intentions; it is under humans' sovereignty and control, thereby exhibiting a certain quality of freedom, unlike "labor." Thirdly, whereas "labor" is concerned with satisfying the individual's life needs and so remains essentially a private affair, work is inherently *public*; it creates an objective and common world. "This common world of institutions and spaces, which "work" creates, furnishes the arena in which citizens may come together as members of that shared world to engage in political activity." (Arendt, p. 36)

In Arendt's critique of industrial modernity, the world as created by *homo faber* is threatened with extinction, by the rise of *animal laborans* over *homo faber*.

Because "labor" applies to managing pure necessities, be it by animals or human beings, Arendt describes the "inhuman" aspects of "labor": "What man shares with all other animals, was not considered as human 'labor', was understood as generally contrary to human freedom." (Arendt, p. 294)

Individual freedom can only be realized through according activities: In this sense, man does (and does not) possess freedom, as a matter of his being human, but this freedom needs to be realized by him actualizing his freedom in the world as a matter of his givens. Freedom comes into existence only by being actually demonstrated.

Here, Arendt's approach meets with those concepts, defining freedom as choosing one's attitude, being the last of all freedoms (Viktor Frankl), an existential given (Yalom), a process rather than a given (Carl Rogers), and a precondition for human existence and exercising personal will and building community (Habermas).

Although homo faber is realizing "creative values" and thereby bringing meaning to his life (Viktor Frankl), these experiences and things created by him could, in the end, well be a matter of self-actualization only, regardless of the public domain, and being limited to leading the personally best individual life, irrespective of the effects this "work" might have on the greater community.[1]

Thus, homo faber is the only "human" condition of work: he is still limited by the conditions around him, making even his most creative works a matter of necessity – and be it for contributing to some defined public needs like social welfare budgets, etc. – and thus limiting individual freedom.

Today, the common working life seems to move between the two poles of labor and work. Trapped between these two poles, for individual employees and organizations as well, work seems to be organized around performance, best performance, or underperformance. Individuals are measured and appraised against their colleagues. For too many, work seems to be exactly a matter of necessity for making a living, void of creativity, and meaning.

The organization of modern workplaces, their terms and tools, from understanding human beings as a quantity and budget, and managing "human resources" up to ever intensified digitalization of work, might suggest that this concept generally holds true and that, over a defined period of time, there are measurable differences in their performance between individual employees. KPIs, balanced scorecard, ROI, and others have been following this mind-set. Individual staff members and organizations have actually moved and delivered along this understanding of the working person for the past more than 50 years. This dimension of measured success and failure, though, provides for plenty of misunderstandings, demotivation, conflicts, suffering, and costs on the individual, team, and organizational level of organizations.

[1] Examples of famous architects' planning public preschools with a substantial budget might illustrate the potential dilemmas between individual creativity and public interest: A golden rooftop, which was – on the one side – argued to count as the architect's absolute personal imprint but could – on the other side – not be afforded by the town, with the architect unsuccessfully bringing his alleged needs to court or a lofty, glass covered entrance hall, where children and educators could hardly acoustically manage, due to the high volume immediately created by lively children, interacting with each other, sometimes wishing to whisper.

4.10.2 Homo Amans

With finding meaning in "experiential values," we experience something in the world – such as goodness, truth, beauty, or the other person – and we bring ourselves into relationship with that outside and beyond our very selves. Frankl understood these common, everyday experiences as an important building block for finding personal meaning:

The goodness, truth, and beauty that we see around us become a physical and emotional part of us. We are engaged with them, and they are engaged with us in their own way. In being aware of these givens, an individual is actively defining and shaping the meaning of a concrete situation.

All approaches and exercises suggested for leading a good life, for getting into touch and building relationships, for balancing work and private life, and for ultimately supporting individual health and well-being are based on a positive relationship with the environment and, above all, the persons and individual is relating to.

Appreciating the moment, being aware of the givens around us and appreciating their existence as such in a positive, loving way, letting go of all achievement-oriented thoughts or intentions in favor of the natural givens around us, of the what is rather than what needs to be, is a substantial building block of all modern approaches in coaching and therapy and especially of all meditation practices.

In modern life, when work has become the most important area in life for people and is taking its toll on well-being, consciously realizing experiential values has become an ever more important part of leading a "good life."

Especially in circumstances, when – due to sickness or unemployment – creative values cannot be realized, experiential values are available. In a medium- and longer-term perspective, experiential values of living and building relationships, of becoming aware and appreciating the talents of others, of taking care of others, and of supporting others might be the most important building block of creating meaning. The current demands and answers, especially rich societies give to the global refugees' displacement, are testing industrialized, rich states' experiential meaning potentials, understanding the Other as a vital part of Me, both being part of the global community.

According to Frankl (2006), *e*xperiencing love is the ultimate meaning a person can find, experiencing self-transcendence.

The concept of "homo amans" and his experiential values may not be confused with the sensual and cognitive characteristics that can be "experienced" through consumption and that modern marketing and customer relations are continually triggering, arousing emotions of craving, of affection, desire, euphoria, of greed, of pleasure, and of pride – just to name those that product marketing is referring to and which have become one of the main fields of digitalized product placement.[2]

[2] See common examples, like Internet shopping platforms, suggesting other articles to the customer, relating to their personal consumer profile ,similar to others' (triggering affection and curiosity) or the digital dating services, suggesting the "perfect match" for allegedly finding true love. For other examples, see Harari Y.N. (2016).

The system thinking approach would also contrast the concept of homo faber by claiming: Only love expands intelligence. To live in love is to accept the other and the conditions of his existence as a source of richness, not as opposition, restriction, or limitation. Love is the grounding of our existence as humans and is the basic emotion in our systemic identity as human beings (Maturana Römerin and Verden-Zoeller 2009).

The pursuit of meaning may entail personal sacrifice. Social entrepreneurs provide plenty of examples for persons committed to a cause beyond themselves and willing to sacrifice material goods and benefits for the love of humanity.

4.10.3 Homo Patiens

The pain we feel is the pain of something old that is dying, while something new is waiting to be born. F. Laloux

In contrast to the competent, mindful, and conscious man, finding meaning in creative (homo faber) or experiential values (homo amans), the homo patiens is a witness of mankind's general humanness in itself: capable of rising above and taking a stand to his suffering. With this, the individual moves to a different dimension than the initial poles of success and failure and of achieving.

Frankl repeatedly explained that suffering in this context is relating to unavoidable and inescapable suffering, when the individual is called upon to take an attitude to this given or existential situation.

Today's workplaces and performance-oriented careers offer plenty of examples of man's striving to avoid this human condition of holding on to their creative and experiential values. Simultaneously, the condition of the "homo patiens" has become an almost everyday situation for an ever-growing part of the global workforce: Personally destructive feedback, shareholder value-driven restructuring of companies, layoffs, devastating work relationships among colleagues or with managers, dysfunctional working environments, or market dynamics leading to falling stock prices, unethical management practices, all of these are creating a substantial work force experiencing suffering and trauma. Some of them have no means of bearing this condition, due to their deep felt despair and their self-concept. They deny or violently end their situation that they would find unbearable.[3] Schnell (2016) and others are suggesting that these tragedies might show a significant lack of understanding and indifference toward the existential meaning of life under all circumstances.

Fortunately, communicating own emotions and bringing own despair to another person's attention have become less of a taboo and an individual competence of persons, who are approaching coaches, counselors, and employee assistance professionals with their existential despair, questioning how they could cope with their situation and find their wax "back to life."

[3] See the series of suicides among bank managers following the financial crisis in 2008.

Consequently, it would be even more important to "spread the information" about the undeniable human dignity and value of a person under all circumstances and of the (potentially) highest achievement of all, that of taking an attitude to things that cannot be changed. Although the term "achievement" here might sound as being related to workplace performance, homo patiens is gaining unprecedented dignity, the moment he can "turn his tragedy into a triumph" by deliberately taking an attitude to given circumstances he cannot change.

Also, in this world, where man is claiming to be capable of achieving almost everything, of constantly advancing, and of successfully overcoming the negative, awareness needs to be raised for the positive in the negative and to the negative in the positive (Kashdan & Biswas-Diener 2014). Facing adversity courageously is in itself an absolute, unquestionable achievement that is challenging all concepts of obvious success and failure, measured by industrial advancement.

Gabriel (2017), Professor of Philosophy at the University of Bonn, finds suffering a basic competency and component of human consciousness:

> When we speak of consciousness as human beings, we refer to states of experience of suffering beings. If we could build robots that are externally not distinguishable from humans, screaming with pain, this does not mean that they actually feel pain. I am convinced that our experiencing pain just as all other sensations are built on a million-years evolution, a prerequisite for our viability. This evolution is constitutive for our human consciousness.

Homo patiens may even mean suffering for a greater cause.[4] Activists for human rights and for free speech, exercising their work under extremely difficult, sometimes life-threatening situations, are giving great examples for following this cause.

This concept of homo patiens may not be misunderstood as a motive of its own; this, actually, would be a fundamental misapprehension of this notion. While Viktor Frankl in his roles and functions as a doctor and university professor has continually pointed to the fact that suffering must be avoided under all circumstances, there do remain areas and issues in life, when suffering is apparently addressing and touching other dimensions of human existence:

health and well-being, giving professional support to those persons, who are confronted with unavoidable suffering. Until today, Frankl's concept of 'medical ministry' is hardly explicitly exercised in doctors' practices, intensely taught to students in medical schools and systematically researched in its effects on persons' and patients' wellbeing. Only in palliative care, the concept of homo patiens has been widely accepted and implemented in all types of services and support.

Existential givens: Finally, it is the concept of homo patiens that is touching on existential givens and emotions of potential despair, dread, and meaninglessness. Neither the theoretical concept of existentials, which we are all faced with, nor the implications of this concept for everyday life are part of mainstream thinking and practice, which is occupied with finding solutions for problems, with offering all types of "anti" products, pills, and services for issues that each individual is facing in their lives, be it illness, aches, aging, sadness, grief, fear, or, terminally, death.

[4]As Mahatma Gandhi or Martin Luther King and all the unknown heroes of today working in peace missions have been giving witness

In a recent study (Schnell 2009), researchers have defined a substantial part (one third) of a cross-national German-speaking group as "existentially indifferent," i.e., persons who would find their lives neither meaningful nor suffering from a perceived lack of meaning. These persons' profiles also show comparatively low levels of self-awareness, spirituality, religiosity, and generativity. Schnell suggests to focus more attention on this group and their levels of well-being and resources for dealing with the "givens" of life, once they might be confronted with suffering.

Other scientists and researchers suggest to proactively approach and embrace the existential givens in life by offering educational programs on meaning, purpose in life, happiness, and fulfillment, already starting at middle school. Eliciting and further developing a person's own potentials and learning to get access to them in dealing with challenges, difficult times, and potential crises has become an effective objective of these classes; Fritz Schubert and Prof. Axel Burow (Germany) and Philip Streit (Austria) have become leaders of this positive pedagogics approach (see www.akjf.at and others).

4.11 Conclusions

The logotherapeutic concept does not disregard the physical and psychological conditions, our drives, and the importance of childhood, environment, and upbringing. But these influences are supplemented by the assumption of another dimension, which replaces the deterministic and nihilistic concept that we are "nothing but" an evolved animal, a product of chance, with the positive idea that we are "essentially more than" and that it is exactly this dimension that makes us "human."

In the end, human beings are human beings only together with and relating to other human beings.

Today, more and more scientists, consultants, coaches, and counseling experts are relating to each other in the public "space of reasons" (Habermas), where they, as socialized individuals, take a stand and act deliberately and thus freely, as the responsible authors of their own actions. They are creating new concepts of how to best bring the free will forward again, exercising freedom and responsibility and bring to life, "what makes us human." Their concepts are presented in this book.

References

Al-Rhodan N (2015) The many ethical implications of emerging technologies. Scientific American, 13 Mar 2015

APA American Psychological Association (2010) Ethical principles of psychologists and code of conduct. http://www.apa.org/ethics/code/ethics-code-2017.pdf. Accessed Oct 2017

Arendt H (1998) The human condition. The University of Chicago Press, Chicago

EAPA Code of Ethics (2017) Official website. www.eapassn.org

Frankl VE (1988) The will to meaning. Foundations and applications of logotherapy. Penguin Books, New York

Frankl VE (2006) Man' search for meaning. Beacon Press, Boston

Frisch M (1969) Homo Faber. A report, Edition Suhrkamp. Frankfurt am Main

Gabriel M (2017) Ist das Leben ein Traum – oder doch eher eine Orange? Psychologie Heute 05/2017

Habermas J (2004) Freedom and determinism. Kyoto Prize Address, 10 Nov 2004

Harari YN (2014) Sapiens. A brief history of humankind. Harvill Secker, London

Harari YN (2016a) Homo Deus: a brief history of tomorrow. Harvill Secker, London

Harari YN (2016b) Interview. Financial Times. 26 August 2016

Harari YN (2017) Ein Historiker erzählt die Geschichte von morgen: Interview with Y. N. Harari. In: srf Kultur, 14 April 2017

ICF International Coach Federation. Code of ethics. Official Website. https://www.coachfederation.org/about/ethics. Accessed 3 Nov 2017

Kashdan T, Biswas-Diener R (2014) The power of negative emotion. Oneworld Publications, London

Maturana Römerin H, Verden-Zoeller G (2009) The origin of humanness in the biology of love. Imprint Academic, Charlottesville

Naughton J (2016) Forget ideology. Liberal democracy's threats come from technology and bioscience. Guardian, 28 Aug 2016

Rolf S (2010) Embryonenforschung. Über den Umgang mit menschlichem Leben. Deutsches Ärzteblatt 107(10):A-438/B-384/C-376

Schnell T (2009) The Sources of Meaning and Meaning in Life Questionnaire (SoMe): relations to demographics and well-being. J Posit Psychol 4(6):483–499

Schnell T (2016) Psychologie des Lebenssinns. Springer, Heidelberg

sysTelios Klinik., Siedelsbrunn/Germany. Official Website http://www.systelios.de/klinik/konzept/visiomission.html

Chapter 5
Twenty-First-Century Meaning Challenges of Work

Contents

The ideas of our clients are shaped by the spirit of the age and change with it. (Frankl)

5.1 Megatrends Shaping our Future

Today's global developments are defined by megatrends (Tse and Esposito 2017), which have developed and which are shaping our present and our future. These inventions, policies, and ideas have not only produced massive shifts during the past decades, but they will significantly transform the global landscape over the next decade and beyond.

We are witnessing and are amid the so-called 4th industrial revolution: Internet-based, digital worlds are being created and are influencing our ways of living, our cultures, our traditions of communicating with each other, and our very human existence on all physical, emotional, and mind levels in yet hardly understood ways. Flexible, fluid workplaces are being created, making local and physical times and places secondary.

5.2 Global Societal Challenges

Individuals, businesses, and societies around the world are confronted directly or indirectly with the implications of these megatrends. Smart factories, infrastructure, urbanization, mobility, and new business models are but a few examples. Their

B. von Devivere, *Meaningful Work: Viktor Frankl's Legacy for the 21st Century*,
https://doi.org/10.1007/978-3-319-89791-2_5

negative effects can be observed: worldwide migration, exhaustion of resources, education gaps, lack of trust in governments to deal with these challenges, poor leadership, rise of new super powers, gender disparity, breakdown of traditional social structures, and right-wing populism.

5.3 Work Life in a VUCA World

Observers describe our world being defined by volatility, uncertainty, complexity, and ambiguity with ever-growing demands of "distinct types of responses" in work: Living conditions, specific situations, and change drivers are volatile (unexpected, unknown, unstable), uncertain (lack of cause and systemic information), complex (many hidden interconnected parts and variables), and ambiguous (unclear causal relationships, unknown unknowns). The strategies, attitudes, and behaviors suggested to the individual person and management add to the vast expectations for self-improvement and are challenging the individual basic needs: Staying curious, getting out of the individual comfort zone, taking risks, and creating islands of certainty amid uncertainty. In the end, observers conclude that there are too many elements beyond the control of traditional centers of power and authority.

Diagnosing this state of the world's state and challenges adds to the actuality of Viktor Frankl's meaning-centered approach.

5.4 Four Western World Challenges

The above-described living conditions in today's western world can be characterized by four challenges questioning the meaning we want to give to today's situations:

- We live in an age of crumbling and vanishing traditions. Never before our freedom of will to choose was more obvious and irrefutable than today.
- We live in an age of affluence and depletion of natural resources.
- We have all the information that would be necessary to take action in the right direction. We are questioned by life and we can only respond by being responsible.
- We live in an age where unprecedented technical means to shape our individual lives are being offered. We are called to choose, i.e., to make decisions on what means and techniques we want to benefit from and which ones would be detrimental to human lives and individual well-being and to humanity as a whole.

There are different levels of challenges we are confronted with. All levels interact with each other, and the change we as individuals may introduce on one level will influence all other levels, directly or indirectly. We cannot dismiss ourselves from none of these levels. On the contrary, life is questioning us individually, and we respond to these challenges, individually and with all freedom to choose the right approach. This is the factual and the mindful reason to differentiate between the various levels, leading to different activities and results:

- Individual challenges: The type of individual activity will depend on the respective most productive level to introduce substantial change. Here, the belief that the individual person can introduce powerful change has been a guiding principle for humanity throughout history. Trust in individual action to change the own destiny has been the strongest motive for introducing substantial change in a person's individual life; throughout history, it has inspired the greatest substantial change processes. In this context, the concept of character strengths and virtues (Peters and Seligman) refers to general human capacities, which, beyond all specific differences, would define human resources, deeply engrained in individuals all over the world, forming humanity as a whole and individually enabling the person to shape these global trends, while they are emerging.
- Workplace community challenges: The needs of a community, a team, and an organization are comprised of being aware of and balancing various individual needs to create an understanding and strive for the common good. All organizational conflicts and recent crashes of organizations have been based on denying the common good for short-term, egoistic, and materialistic aims of making profit without adhering to customers' needs or guiding values and principles.

This responsibility, to define the best common good also, refers to the other two levels:

- Societal challenges: Each nation and specific society is challenged by their specific history, background, culture, ideas, traditions, convictions, politics, etc. to be defined, discussed, balanced in a public dialogue, and implemented in today's global world in a transcultural approach, based on respect, dignity, and acknowledgment of diversity.
- Humanity's challenges: Today, all humans are faced with global challenges, facing and dealing with the megatrends, that are globally defining life for all and that will shape our future for the next years.

5.5 Diagnosing the Twenty-First-Century Gap

In his groundbreaking historical analysis of human development, and his empirical examples for "Reinventing organizations," Frederic Laloux (2014) is presenting a lucid diagnosis of human history and development during the past 10,000 years. From this analysis, he finds plenty of resources for human development, meeting the unprecedented challenges humankind is facing today:

- In less than two centuries, modernity has brought unprecedented wealth and well-being not only to the Western world but around the globe, where millions of people in India, China, and Africa are lifting themselves out of poverty.

- In medicine, a dense network of organizations, research centers, pharmaceutical companies, hospitals, medical schools, health insurance companies, and medical services have provided for a highly sophisticated medical system that would have been unthinkable a 100 years ago. Age-old scourges like polio, leprosy, smallpox, and tuberculosis are mostly part of history, even in the poorest countries of the world.
- In education: A network of schools – kindergartens, elementary and high schools, colleges, and graduate schools – have brought education that was once the privilege of the very few. The high degrees of literacy that we now take for granted are unprecedented in history.
- In people's engagement: An ever-increasing number of people donate time, energy, and money in pursuit of purposes that matter to them and to the world.

And yet, many people sense that the current way we run organizations has been stretched to its limits. Economically, a model of ever more growth with finite resources "is bound to hit the wall" (Laloux, p. 3):

- Surveys consistently report that work is dread and drudgery, not passion and purpose.
- Even professions of calling are not immune to organizational disillusionment and burn out.
- Hospitals have turned into bureaucratic institutions that dispossess doctors and nurses of their capacity to care from the heart.
- Behind the façade and the bravado, the lives of leaders and workers are ones of quiet suffering.
- Our way of conducting business has outgrown our planet.
- Our organizations contribute on a massive scale to depleting natural resources, destroying ecosystems, changing the climate, and exhausting water reserves and precious soils.
- The very survival of many species, ecosystems, and perhaps the human race itself hinges on our ability to collaborate in new ways to heal our relationships with the world.

From this diagnosis, which Laloux describes as "the unmistakable signs of change ahead," he is presenting a brilliant model of the conscious organization for answering the twenty-first-century needs. He describes the structure and processes of this new model, by drawing on the human potentials that have developed over thousands of years. This type of organization could well be the paradigm for twenty-first-century general cooperation in diverse institutions, where organizations around the world work for meeting the needs of those they are called to serve, and thereby living the "breakthrough," that people and organizations around the globe are yearning for in their search for substantially making or initiating a positive change, to their contributing to making this world a better place.

Lately, Steven Pinker (2018) , Professor of Psychology in Harvard, also made his strong case for putting reason, science, humanity, and their values back on the agenda of global world development. His publication, *Enlightenment Now: The*

Case for Reason, Science, Humanism, and Progress, provides for a most encouraging insight into our potential future. He shows that the bleak assessment of mankind's past, present, and future is "wrong" and that the ideals of the enlightenment have never been more relevant than they are today.

References

Laloux F (2014) Reinventing organizations. Nelson Parker, Brussels

Pinker S (2018) Enlightenment now: the case for reason, science, humanism, and progress. Penguin Random House, New York

Tse TCM, Esposito M (2017) Understanding how the future unfolds. Lioncrest Publishing, Austin

Chapter 6
Meaning in the Twenty-First-Century Workplaces

Contents

6.1 Work: A Potential Source of Meaning

Today, meaningful work is used as a synonym for decent work, non-alienated work, socially and ecologically responsible work, work that people can identify themselves with, or work that is useful for the organization or for the society, work design, the social perception of the work, and subjective approaches to meaningful work. Hardering (2015a, b) suggests meaningful work as "a rich concept of subjectivity, which divides between the experience of meaningfulness, ascriptions of meaning and practices of meaning-making" for its broad understanding.

In work, persons are forming close relationships with their colleagues. Work can touch and fulfill basic human needs of bonding, feeling connected, self-assurance, competence, and coherence.

Work can be a source of creative, experiential, and attitudinal values (Frankl 2014).

At its best, work and workplaces are fulfilling basic human needs (Rosenberg 2003) of connection, autonomy, and coherence. They can provide for well-being and promote mental health. They can provide for a meaningful life (Frankl 1986) for the individual person by offering:

- Creative values, i.e., contributing good work and results to a team or an organization and influencing and guiding others.
- Experiential values, i.e., being valued at work; enjoying relationships, communication, and appreciation with and by other persons; joining in for joint activities; and finding pleasure and joy in others. Also, work places can provide a supportive environment and productive learning opportunities for modeling individual coping skills and for rewarding personal development.

B. von Devivere, *Meaningful Work: Viktor Frankl's Legacy for the 21st Century*,
https://doi.org/10.1007/978-3-319-89791-2_6

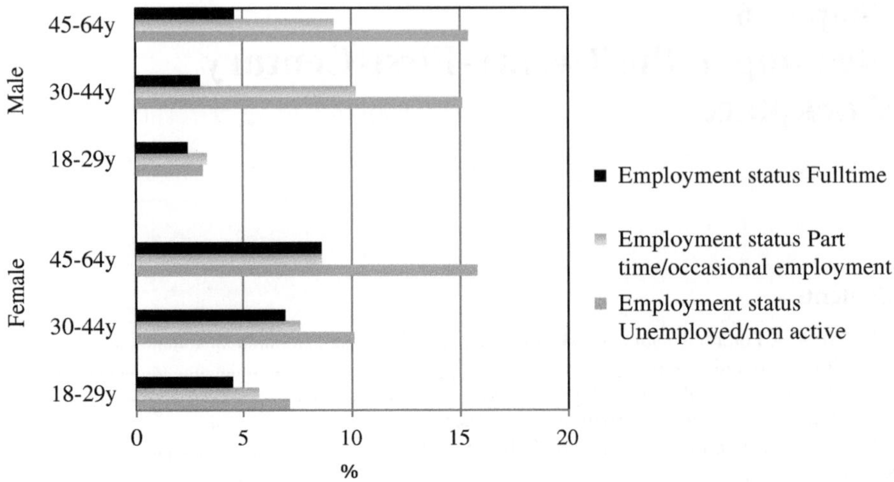

Fig. 6.1 Diagnosed depression in Germany by age and status of employment 2009/2010 (Robert Koch Institut, GBE kompakt 2/2013)

- Attitudinal values, i.e., developing own skills in finding the best way to deal with situations, persons, circumstances, frameworks, and structures that are given and cannot be changed.

"Only when the emotions work in terms of values can the individual feel pure joy" (Frankl 1986). Individuals are motivated by their search for meaning in their personal lives, be it by giving their competencies and contributing through their work, including volunteering; by receiving, experiencing, and appreciating what they are surrounded by and what they would see, hear, feel, taste, or smell; or by taking an attitude and responding to whatever fate, destiny, and environment is confronting them with that could not be changed by their own action.

6.2 Employed and Unemployed

In that respect, persons of working age are – in general, as statistics (Robert Koch Institute 2013) indicate – less affected by mental disorders than unemployed persons for whom mental disorders significantly rise with the duration of unemployment (Fig. 6.1).

6.3 The Janus Face of Today's Workplaces

Work life is flooding actual life (V. E. Frankl)

Yet, this picture of potentially meaningful work is incomplete without taking a closer look at the quality and challenges of today's workplaces in our Western hemisphere.

Western and industrialized societies are attributing ever-rising status and importance to work and money. All areas of life are overshadowed by economic standards, restraints, and reflections referring to success, performance, money, and economic status.

While these symptoms are true for the twenty-first century just like for the last decades, we observe that work and workplaces have more and more become the most important part of peoples' lives in general, be it day or night; be it on-site or off-site; be it personal or virtual; be it for singles or dual-career partners, with or without children; and be it for good or for bad.

The significance of work and the value attributed to work in our modern societies are holding individuals from the outside and within, extensively defining, regulating, and influencing their lives as never before. On a large scale, people's health and well-being are at stake, not for natural causes or fate but for "man-made" reasons.

Today, economic standards of effectiveness and efficiency have taken hold of all spheres of life, be it considerations about founding a family and raising children; be it social work, education, health organizations, clinics, NGOs, and NPOs; and be it all types of available personal, private, or company management tools.

"The economy" seems to have seized power over the individual, organizations, and societies with tragic effects for all: greed, search for ultimate pleasure, addiction, fear of falling out of the system, exhaustion, suffering, and despair.

Today's working environments offer plenty of triggers for frustration of man's will to meaning, for suffering and despair, for languishing, and for illnesses.

Torn between the promising opportunities of a global and virtual world and the unprecedented challenge to constantly improve, optimize, and shape his life more efficiently, man finds himself lost in the harsh reality of life, "the absurd madness of the everyday world" (David Foster Wallace 2006) with the consequence that everybody revolves around himself, increasingly exhausted by the dynamics of change, the expectations for his performance at work, his search for distractions from his search for meaning, and his getting trapped in infinite jest (Wallace 2006) with hopelessness, addiction, and despair waiting for him on that road.

This frustrated will to meaning would show in all the feelings addressed to workplace social counseling: employees feel afraid, annoyed, vulnerable, tense, disconnected, sad, irritable, panicked, worried, and depressed. While this workforce is growing substantially, with their values frustrated, needs not met, and unproductive feelings experienced, these symptoms being of a complex nature, the specific arrangements at work, play an ever-increasingly important role for individuals' well-being and health.

6.4 Homo Economicus: Powerful Reductionism

Today's economy is ruled not ruled by the value-driven menschenbild but by a completely opposite concept of man, i.e., the homo economicus, regarding a person's only desire to maximize their individual needs. Such an individual is described as a supposedly *nothing but* rational actor, who desires wealth above anything else and would build his relationships with others on only utilitarian aspects of his own desires. In spite of all scientific findings on the nature of man, reassuring the individual's complex physical, rational, emotional, and behavioral being in the world and as recently discussed by behavioral economics' studies on the high influence of individual impressions and beliefs on their decision-making, the concept of homo economicus still has the helm in economic sciences, in universities, and in the business world. The ruling concept of man considers persons' decision-making according to mathematical equations.

By now, the scientific discussion is powerfully challenging this concept, which is reducing the human kind to selfish individuals. Currently, neuroscientist T. Singer (2015) is opening up a completely new area of research and training for compassion, built on the insights into the complex nature of the human being and their potentials, to make this world a better place.

6.5 Self-Actualization, Pleasure, and Self-Optimization

Man initially does not seek pleasure or happiness, but rather that which causes these effects. Only when and to the extent that this search for meaningful living becomes frustrated, the will for pleasure, adventure, and extreme and peak experiences comes in. With this assumption, the logotherapeutic and existential approach has by definition a fundamentally different approach to human existence and an individual's search of meaning in life.

Again, today's workplaces offer plenty of examples about fundamental man's search for purpose and meaning over pleasure, peak experiences, and material success in terms of bonus and rewards for competitive outperformance against their peers.

> It is my contention that in the final analysis, the pleasure principle is self defeating. The more one aims at pleasure, the more this aim is missed. In other words, the very "pursuit of happiness, is, what thwarts it…Hyper intention and hyper reflection…are likely to create neurotic patterns of behavior. Normally, pleasure is never the goal of human strivings, but rather is, and must remain, an effect, more specifically, the side effect of attaining a goal… In other word, happiness ensues…one cannot pursue it. (Frankl 1988)

In that context, *self-actualization* is always an *effect* of meaning fulfillment. Only to the extent to which man fulfills a meaning out there in the world does he fulfill himself. All these phenomena cannot be pursued, but rather they ensue.

References

Frankl VE (1986) The doctor and the soul: from psychotherapy to logotherapy. Random House, New York

Frankl VE (1988) The will to meaning. Foundations and applications of logotherapy. Meridian, New York

Frankl VE (2014) Man's search for meaning (Rev & updated ed.). Beacon Press, Boston

Hardering F (2015a) Sinn und Arbeit – sinnvolle Arbeit zwischen Sinnkrise und Sinnerleben. Goethe Universität, Frankfurt

Hardering F (2015b) Meaningful Work: Sinnvolle Arbeit zwischen Subjektivität, Arbeitsgestaltung und gesellschaftlichem Nutzen. Oesterreichische Zeitschrift für Soziologie 40:391–410

Robert Koch-Institut Diagnose Depression (2013) Unterschiede bei Frauen und Männern, GBE Kompakt (2/2013)

Rosenberg MB (2003) Nonviolent Communication. Puddledancer Press, Chicago

Singer T, Ricard M (2015) Caring economics. Conversations between scientists, economists and the Dalai Lama. Picador, New York

Wallace DF (2006) Infinite jest. Back Bay Books, New York

Chapter 7
A Two-Dimensional Approach

Contents

Frankl's diagram of life (Frankl 1960) is more current than ever: It provides for a sound basis of understanding the challenges and traps of modern work life and for proactively seeking meaning in one's own work and for coping with the direct demands in work life.

Translating the poles of this paradigm into modern workplace terms, the diagram may read like this (Fig. 7.1):

7.1 Reconciling Two Dimensions in the Human Being

With this concept, Frankl's paradigm may suggest a highly inspiring and comprehensive framework for understanding and developing meaningful work in today's world.

Of course, man strives for success but, if need be, does not depend on feelings and experience of failure or being confronted with his fate, which does or does not allow for success. A human being, by the very attitude he takes, is capable for finding and fulfilling meaning, under all circumstances and even in "hopeless" situations. Leaving the seemingly inescapable paradigm of success versus failure, the individual may change to another dimension, providing for unconditional meaning. There is an empirical truth alone, to introducing another dimension.

Apparently, we find despair despite success, when this apparently productive state meets with anguish, assessed as an "existential vacuum," when no factual indicators and criteria of success would count for the individual in despair. Also, we would experience failure that can, by definition, in any circumstances, be turned into fulfillment and meaning, changing from despair to triumph.

B. von Devivere, *Meaningful Work: Viktor Frankl's Legacy for the 21st Century*,
https://doi.org/10.1007/978-3-319-89791-2_7

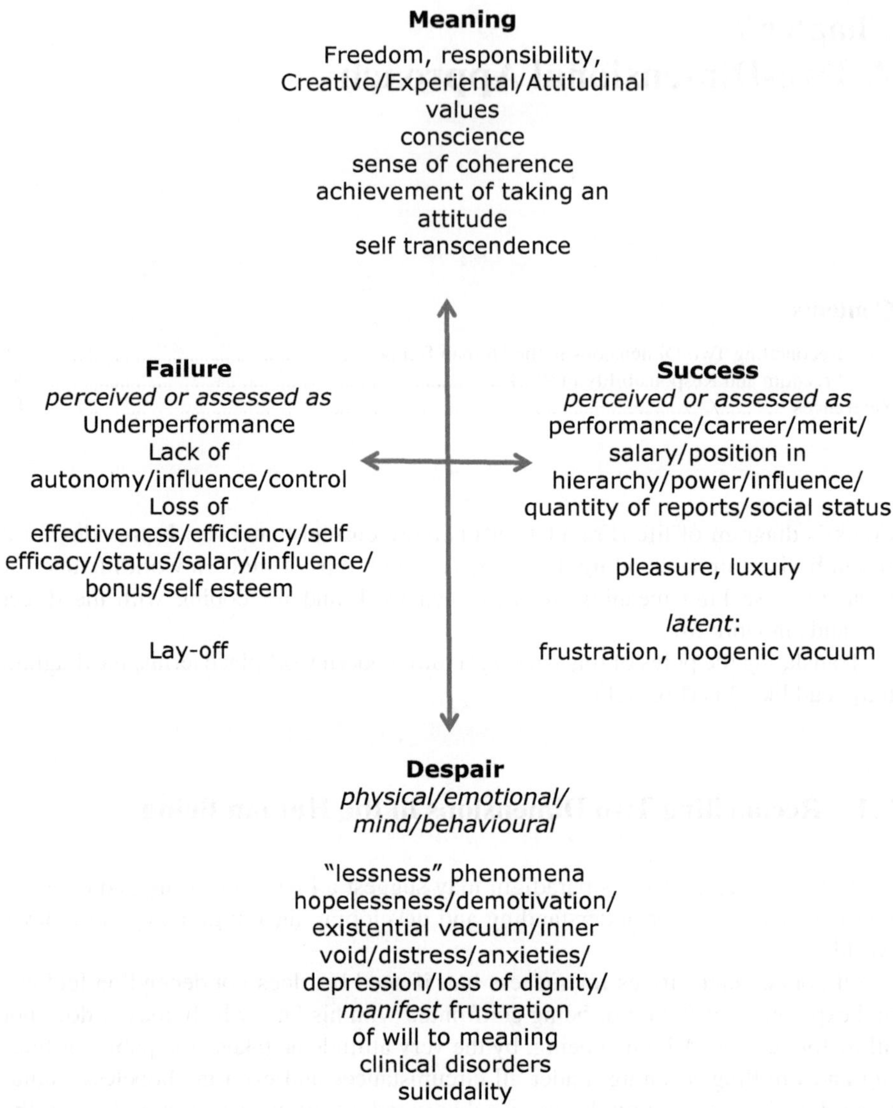

Fig. 7.1 A two-dimensional approach to workplaces

7.2 Freedom and Responsibility in Work

In this world of matters, deliverables, and tangible and intangible goods, freedom, according to Hannah Arendt (Arendt 1998), is to be found in the *vita activa*. The fundamental defining quality of this *vita activa* is its inalienable freedom, its status as an end in itself.

Arendt has argued that it is a mistake to take freedom to be primarily an inner, contemplative, or private phenomenon, for it is in fact active, worldly, and public. Our sense of an inner freedom is derived from first having experienced "a condition of being free" as a reality. "We first become aware of freedom or its opposite in our relationship with others, not in the intercourse with ourselves."

Action would be meaningless unless there were others present to see it and so give meaning to it. The meaning of the action and the identity of the actor can only be established in the context of human plurality, in the presence of others, both to understand and recognize the uniqueness of ourselves and our acts in encountering others.

Work is about fulfilling basic human needs. Earning money, though, has never been a basic human need but rather a means to fulfill human needs. "Happiness is inversely related to income at higher levels of income because of the declining marginal utility of getting richer" (Layard 2006).

And finally, since work as such can never directly contribute to a meaningful life, and since values inherent in all humans are not automatically activated through work, human needs are not understood and met, and there is a rising frustration of the existential need for meaningful goals in work and life.

References

Arendt H (1998) The human condition. The University of Chicago Press, Chicago
Frankl VE (1960) The will to meaning. Foundations and applications of Logotherapy. Meridian, New York
Layard R (2006) Happiness. Penguin Books, London

Chapter 8
The Twenty-First Century Cry for Meaning

Contents

Existential frustration is not manifest, but latent and masked:

Afraid of his inner void, man runs away into work, pleasure, will to power or will to money. I consider the speed, the haste of our times, to be rather an attempt – albeit an unsuccessful one – to cure ourselves from existential frustration, to drown the existential vacuum. (V. E. Frankl)

B. von Devivere, *Meaningful Work: Viktor Frankl's Legacy for the 21st Century*,
https://doi.org/10.1007/978-3-319-89791-2_8

8.1 Mental Health in the Workplace: The Greatest Challenge of the Twenty-First Century

In today's population of working age, mental health disorders are on the rise. Apparently, this is the toll that Western, industrialized societies and their people are presently paying for their technological advancement beyond measures.

Challenging and questioning this situation, fighting the triggers and underlying causes of this extremely disturbing assessment, and promoting better living are, according to World Health Organization (2017), the "greatest challenge of the twenty-first century."

What do we know about the triggers and causes of today's persons' distress in the workplace? What action can we take?

> Those who suffer do so not because they lack something but because they have something: conscience, human capacity for pain – often regret over the plight of others – and heart. (Wilkerson 2012).

8.2 Facing the Existential Vacuum of Our Times

Today, as Frankl explains, no drives or instincts tell man what he *must* do. Second, no conventions or traditions tell him what he should do. And often, he does not even know what he wants to do. The evolving *existential vacuum* is more current and empirically verified than ever before. The frustrated will to meaning shows in boredom, apathy, demotivation, exhaustion, hopelessness, cynicism, and incapacity to take initiative and to define and find meaning in the actual personal life.

The will to pleasure and the will to power are mere derivate of the will to meaning. Pleasure is actually the effect of meaning fulfillment. And power is actually nothing but the means to an end. Only if one's original concern with meaning fulfillment is frustrated is one content with exercising power or experiencing pleasure.

Today's frustration of man's will to meaning, creating an existential vacuum, is of primary and steadily increasing importance, as is widely observed in all research. This meaning frustration can be called the collective vacuum or the "general poverty syndrome" (Batthyány 2016) of our times in the Western world.

Two stages exist in the syndrome of meaninglessness (Frankl 2010). The first stage is the existential vacuum, which is characterized by a subjective state of boredom, apathy, and emptiness. Persons feel cynical, a lack of direction, questioning the point of life. One may have free time, but there is nothing one feels compelled to do. The second stage can be named existential disorder with symptomatic manifestations such as alcoholism, depression, and delinquency, rushing in to fill the vacuum.

People are confronted with an "inner void," a desperate feeling of emptiness. This existential vacuum, in whatever states and behaviors it may show, does not represent a mental disease as such. Doubting whether one's life has a meaning is an existential despair and, as such, a normal reaction to a world denying meaning. The search for a meaning for one's existence is a spiritual distress, not a mental disease. It is the experience of a total lack or loss of a meaning to one's existence that would make life worthwhile. Frankl has preferred to speak of noetic (nous, spirit) rather than psychic phenomena in the context of this vacuum.

This vacuum, feeling the inner void and emptiness, shows in many ways.

Idleness, Sunday boredom, lack of motivation, fatigue, and exhaustion, being afraid of experiencing this existential vacuum – man runs away into various kinds of compensation: work, pleasure, power, money, sex, alcohol, and drugs. The inner void is literally drugged and compensated.

Specific situations in a person's work life, when the will to meaning is knocking at the individual person's door, provide for feeling the existential vacuum: negative appraisal, conflicts in the workplace, company reorganizations and restructuring up to loss of functions and status, layoffs, and unemployment.

All these symptoms, however, are by no means pathological as such. They rather are normal reactions of a human being. Experiencing the existential vacuum is no neurosis or to be diagnosed as a clinical disorder, and if there would be significant symptoms, it is a sociogenic disorder, caused by a spiritual problem.

Other adverse behaviors rush into this vacuum, this "horror vacui," further intensifying this desperate state: alcohol, all kinds of substance, and drug abuse, going for "ultimate experiences" with substantial risks for life and health, eating disorders, unhealthy lifestyles, and sexual delusions. All these behaviors intensify the risk of potential disorders, such as, emerging addiction, depression, anxieties, and suicide.

8.3 The Four Collective Maladies of Our Times

Common behavioral reactions to today's crisis of meaning are conformity (doing what others do), submission to totalitarianism (doing what others wish or say), or scapegoating and ventilating own feelings of inferiority or lack of control to others in uncontrolled forms up to hatred and false accusations: experts and scientists are diagnosing specific states of mind and approaches, sometimes showing in moods, in views expressed, and in perspectives actively taken that Frankl (1973) diagnosed and described in lucid terms and tested these maladies by parallel questions to his clients; all of these attitudes can be observed in today's employees in their workplaces.

8.3.1 An Ephemeral Attitude Toward Life

Do you consider it worthwhile to act, since after all, we never know what tomorrow will be like, what the executives will decide, where my job will be in a couple of years, what partner I will have, what family I could afford, what my life will be like tomorrow?

Too many persons have given up the idea of planning far ahead or of organizing their lives around a definite purpose, defined by no one else but themselves. Together with the ever faster dynamics of our times and the changes attached to that, persons are living provisionally.

Their answers would be negative, where at the same time they are suffering from the lack of control and influence they perceive in defining their work, their functions, their influence, and their efficacy.

8.3.2 A Fatalist Attitude Toward Life

Do you believe that man is a product and match ball of outer and inner forces and powers influencing and determining your health and well being, your work and beyond that your private life, your family and their well being, their education and their future?

He considers himself a victim of external circumstances or internal conditions, a product of some influences beyond himself, misinterpreting himself and his behaviors as the mere result of external drivers and influences.

8.3.3 Conformist or Collectivist Thinking

Do you think it is best to make yourself small, to not speak up for your individual rights, to do as all others are doing, to remain as inconspicuous as possible, in order to get a good appraisal, a bonus, your boss' acceptance, to stay in the company career pipeline, to remain part of the team, the staff, the neighborhood, your peer group?

Persons denying their own personality and the freedom of the individual other. Today's right wing movements with their propagated hatred against individual freedom and dignity and a person's unalienable right to live their own lives with all their diversity fit into this ever-rising phenomenon of our times.

8.3.4 Fanaticism

Do you believe that anyone is justified in using any means he considers appropriate to achieve his goals, according to the saying that the end justifies the means?

The person who suffers from fanaticism denies the personality of others. No one else may prevail. No opinion other than his own can expect a hearing. This person has no opinion of his own, but rather has an opinion shared in his community. Fanaticism politicizes humans – while politics actually should be humanized. Current fanatic developments and emerging right wing movements in the Western hemisphere are more than a most disturbing writing on the wall of this existential void being exploited by reckless persons, who currently give the words and language and "have hatred exercised by others" (Emcke 2016). Running on nationalist and often racist platforms, far-right parties have gone from the streets into government, enjoying renewed popularity on local and national levels throughout Europe, while far-right violence against migrants and refugee camps booms all over Europe. The rage, hatred, and hostility are not just being expressed verbally anymore. Persons from all spheres of the community, who would express their own opinion, are berated and physically attacked.

All these afflictions derive from fear of and flight from the ultimate human condition of freedom and responsibility, denying his spiritual condition and general meaning of life. It is an expression of "spiritual poverty" (Batthyány 2016).

The Copernican turn, currently to be observed, is addressing these unfulfilled needs and turning them into potential solutions and ways forward.

8.4 Continuous Stress

> Human life is based on a certain degree of tension, the tension between what one has already achieved and what one still ought to accomplish, or the gap between what one is and what one should become. Such a tension is inherent in the human being… What a person actually needs is not a tensionless state but rather the striving and struggling for a worthwhile goal, a freely chosen task. What they need is not the discharge of tension, but a potential meaning waiting to be fulfilled by them. (Frankl 2006)

Any acute stress reaction is an evolutionary routine of human reaction to unexpected challenges. Today's workplaces, though, are defined by continuous chronic stress levels. Humans switch to their autopilot system, automatically assessing and responding to the situation not freely choosing and blocking potential alternative options of reaction.

8.4.1 Different Types of Stress

It is the individual's evaluation of their situation that is initially important.

In line with the increased attention to the individual person and their self-management and self-improvement, some researchers have given increased attention to this initial appraisal of the situation by the individual person. In her book *The*

Upside of Stress, McGonigal (2016) presents seven studies that show "how stress can do your mind and body good," explaining that the findings presented are about "acute," "short-term," or "moderate" stress – the kind that is short-lived and related to something specific. The effects of chronic stress, triggered by office environments, technology, and intensive work, are being addressed by research and practitioners only recently (e.g., Compernolle).

8.4.1.1 Negative Stress

Staff members may experience stress, "when they perceive that there is an imbalance between the demands made of them and the resources they have available to cope with those demands. Although the experience of stress is psychological, stress also has physical health effects" (European Agency for Safety and Health at Work).

Negative stress generally becomes a risk to safety and health and to workplace performance when it is protracted.

8.4.1.2 Chronic Stress

It relates to a substantial, individually perceived, and assessed gap between demands and control/influence or an imbalance of effort and rewards in the working situation.

Increasingly organizations are caught in the "company acceleration trap," because they almost unthinkingly keep starting major change initiatives without finding time for consolidation and regeneration." Indirect consequences and costs for society, the organization, and the individual staff member include superficiality and mediocrity, lack of motivation, resignation, exhaustion, burnout syndrome, disengagement, and demotivation.

8.4.2 Health Effects of Stress

Work-related stress is assessed to be one of the biggest health and safety challenges in Europe. Nearly one in four workers is affected by it, and studies suggest that between 50% and 60% of all lost working days are related to it. This represents a huge cost in terms of both human distress and impaired economic performance.

According to the latest EU survey, 22% of employees in the EU reported that they felt affected by stress. An ever-increasing amount of working days is reported to be lost due to work-related stress. Continuous stress is closely related to decreasing job satisfaction and is often an underlying factor which triggers secondary health problems. Stress is one of the most important reasons for sick leave from work, and stress-related causes of absence are increasing. In Germany, early retirement due to psychosocial diagnosis is increasing with an ever lower age: almost

50% of all cases of early retirement were related to mental diseases with an average age of 49 years (Deutsches Aerzteblatt 2014).

In 2002, the European Commission reported that the yearly cost of work-related stress in the EU15 was EUR 20.000 million each year:

- France: the cost to society of occupational stress is somewhere between EUR 830 and EUR 1.656 million, the equivalent of between 10% and 20% of all expenditure by the Occupational Accident and Disease branch of the Social Security System.
- Netherlands: most of the costs to society of poor working conditions come from work-related absence and disability, which are mainly caused by musculoskeletal disorders (43% of the all diagnoses) and psychological diseases (40%).
- United Kingdom: in 2005/2006 work-related stress, depression, and anxiety cost Great Britain in excess of £530 million.

8.4.3 *Prevalence of Stress, Anxiety, and Irritability in EU 27 States by Sector*

In 2005, stress was the most prevalent in the education and health sectors (Fig. 8.1).

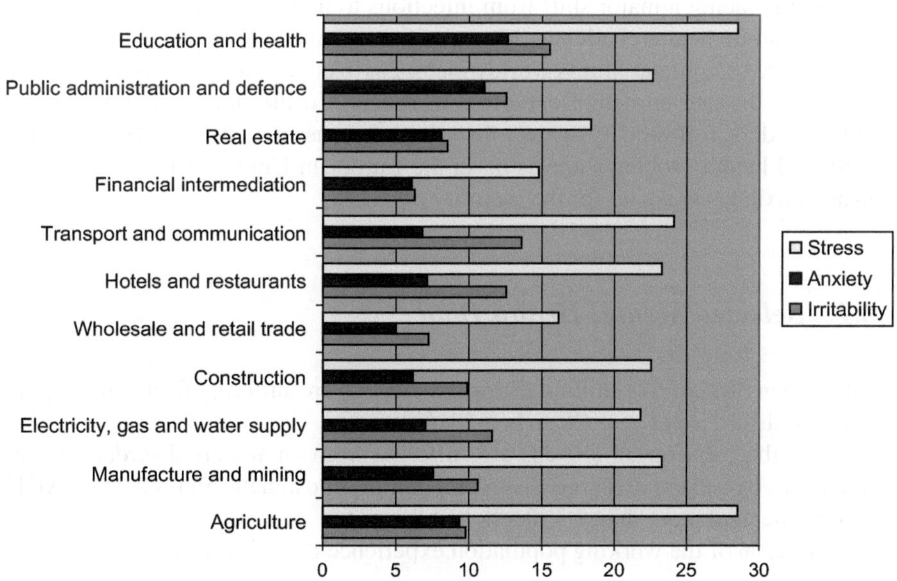

Fig. 8.1 Prevalence of stress, anxiety, and irritability in EU 27 States by sector (European Foundation for the Improvement of Living and Working Conditions. Fourth European Working Conditions Survey, 2005)

8.5 Emerging Risks

These are the main emerging psychosocial risks identified in the forecasts (EU-OSHA – European Agency for Safety and Health at Work, 2005–2007):

- New forms of employment contracts and job insecurity
- (the use of more precarious contracts together with the trend toward lean production and outsourcing)
- Special risks for the aging workforce
- Work intensification – high workload and work pressure
- High emotional demands at work, violence, and harassment
- Poor life balance
- Combined exposure to psychosocial and physical risks

There is an ethical, a legal, and a business case for addressing stress in the workplace.

Employers have an obligation to manage work-related stress.

Work-related stress is preventable.

8.6 Undeniable Suffering

The world is facing a major shift from infectious to noncommunicable diseases as the major public health challenge. Mental disorders and substance abuse were the leading cause of nonfatal illness worldwide in 2010, contributing nearly 23% of the total global disease burden. Depressive disorders are the most common mental health disorders, followed by anxiety disorders, drug use disorders, and schizophrenia. Mental health problems are rising in the European Union. Diagnosed depression and anxieties make up for the majority of cases.

8.6.1 Selected Mental Health Data

- More than 38% of 514 million European citizens are suffering from a neuropsychiatric disorder per year (Wittchen 2016).
- 14% of these European citizens are suffering from an anxiety disorder, mostly phobias, 7% severe sleeping disorders, 5% psychosomatic illnesses and ADH syndrome, and more than 3% alcohol addiction.
- Nearly 25% of the working population experience depression each year.

- One in four of those living with a mental illness receive care of treatment. Nearly a third of all people with long-term physical conditions have comorbid mental health problems like depression and anxiety.
- Ischemic heart disease and depression are on track to become the leading source of work years lost through premature death and disability.
- Mental illnesses have an increasingly young face. The average age of onset of depression in the United States is 26 and in Canada 21.
- The average age of onset of anxiety disorders in the United States is 15 and in Canada 12. Depression and anxiety disorders are growing faster as a component of the global burden of disease than cardiovascular disease.
- Depression can no longer be described as only a brain disorder; it is a series of changes spanning the brain, genes, and the body.
- Within the past 15 years, diagnosed mental health disorders have more than doubled, according to the study of the German Bundespsychotherapeutenkammer (2014): depression (plus 96%), personality and behavioral disorders (plus 74%), and substance abuse (plus 49%).
- Diagnosed depression rates are increasing, particularly among the young population.
- Within 15 years (2001–2016), depression diagnosis has increased by 96%.
- In any given year, 9% of the EU population suffers from depressive disorders.
- This corresponds to 20.8 million women and men suffering from depression each year.
- It is generally underrecognized and undertreated in health-care systems.
- In all countries treatment rates are low. At best about 50% of depression cases receive any professional attention.
- There is a substantial lack of access to in-time treatment: In Germany, an average waiting time of 7 months is being reported.
- Within 10 years, sick leave days due to depression have nearly doubled, with an average employee reporting sick from work due to psychological issues for 34 days per year.
- Depression ranks as number 1 among the most disabling diseases.
- On average, due to depression a person's life span of being engaged and living a productive life is being curtailed by one third of their potentials.
- 70% of adults diagnosed with depression have lived with their symptoms since childhood.
- According to the recent Global Burden of Disease Study (GBD), globally, the total number of people with depression was estimated to exceed 300 million in 2015. Nearly that number again suffers from a range of anxiety disorders. Since many people experience both conditions simultaneously (comorbidity), it is inappropriate to simply add these two figures together to arrive at a total for common mental disorders.

The consequences of these disorders in terms of lost health are huge. Depression is ranked by WHO as the single largest contributor to global depression and is also the major contributor to suicide deaths, which number is close to 800,000 per year.

There is a massive direct and indirect burden (World Health Organization Global Burden of Disease Studies) of these disorders on all:

- *Individual* (e.g., high distress, disrupts social roles, work productivity, sickness days, disability, premature mortality)
- *Family* (e.g., high emotional distress, economic consequences, malignant effects on dependent family members, friends, and colleagues)
- *Society* (direct and indirect health and social costs)

8.6.2 Suicide

> Although suicides may not be undertaken out of a feeling of meaninglessness, the desperate ones might have overcome the impulse to commit suicide, if those individuals had had a vision of a meaning to their lives. (V. Frankl)

- Suicide is now the leading cause of violent death in the world.
- In the United States, more lives are lost to suicide each year than in the entire Vietnam War.
- Across North America and Europe, 76,000 persons are committing suicide each year.
- In Canada, suicide is the second leading cause of death among children aged 11–14, and suicides exceed the number of deaths due to traffic accidents, AIDS, influenza, and murder.
- About one third of all depression cases have attempted or will attempt suicide.
- More than 90% of all suicides have had a depression history. From 1950 to 1995, the global rates of suicide have increased by 60%.
- In 2000, suicide claimed an estimated 815,000 lives worldwide.
- Suicide rates among adolescents and young adults have increased considerably over the last few decades in a number of industrialized countries.
- The magnitude of the problem is even more significant when the number of attempted but uncompleted suicides – 20 times more common – is included. Registered suicides are equivalent in magnitude to deaths from road traffic accidents.
- In Germany, deaths by suicide exceed deaths by traffic accidents, homicide, and AIDS together.
- In a 10-year period, over 630,000 people will die by suicide in EU 27. This is the equivalent to the extinction of the entire population of Frankfurt, Germany.
- Premature death from suicide is a significant cause of mortality in EU 27.
- The rate of actual suicides may often be double than official suicide rates.
- On average, there were 9.4 deaths per 100,000 inhabitants resulting from suicide in the EU 27 in 2010. Each year 63,000 people die by suicide in EU 27.

- The rate of hidden suicides is considerably higher.
- Since 1995, suicide rates have decreased in many countries.
- Some countries have experienced a noticeable rise in suicide rates in young male subjects. Suicide has become a leading cause of death in the young, and in some countries (e.g., Sweden), it is now the most common cause of death in 15–24-year-olds.
- A continuous dramatic rise of suicides is being reported in Greece connected to the economic crisis: from 677 reported suicides in 2009 to 830 cases in 2010, 927 cases in 2011 and above 1000 cases until 2014.
- Suicide is heavily stigmatized and only a portion of actual suicides are recorded as such.

We believe we could save 31,000 lives from suicide over the next 10 years through the convergence of medical-, economic-, social-, community-, and school-based activities (Bill Wilkerson 2012).

Our global community is confronted with unimaginable pain (von Devivere 2016) in acknowledging this tragedy and dealing with the effects: As human beings, we all perceive losses in our communities, questioning our individual reason for living, the values we live by individually, in our working lives, in our team, and in the organization. Each person is dealing with this loss differently, managing their own distress, grief, and sadness and potentially seeking support and safe places and/or counseling for recovery.

The data point to a stunning question: in general, work and workplaces do:

- Offer support
- Give purpose
- Help to sustain
- Provide social connection

It also holds true: most people who die by suicide around the globe are of working age. What is the global communities' answer to this cry for meaning?

8.7 Brain-Based Economy

8.7.1 The Five Brain Chains

Lack of mindful management of digital devices and abuse of technological knowledge and electronic communication devices have led to what Theo Compernolle (2014) defines as the "five brain chains": always being connected, multitasking, a continuous level of negative stress ruining the brain, lack of breaks and sleep, and brain hostile open space offices. He argues that it is not us who could generally deny this megatrend that is factually influencing today's world and our global future but rather that this technology is questioning us, and we must give the answer of how to deal with the challenges with this "genie out of the bottle." "It is not the technology, it is about us" (Compernolle 2014).

8.7.2 The Great Convergence

There is a clear link between today's economy and the rise of mental health issues: we now live and work in a "brain-based" economy emphasizing cerebral skills over manual skills. In this world, there is a constant rise of "brain-based" critical conditions and mental disorders for two powerful trends converging (Wilkerson 2012):

the largely brain-based economy and their functions putting more emphasis on cerebral skills over manual skills and the apparent rise of the critical conditions relating to thinking, beliefs, and existential issues. In today's workplaces, persons are expected to continually think, be creative, and be innovative: the minds, not the backs of employees, are now doing the heavy lifting (CEO of a steel company).

8.7.3 Giving Brainy Answers

In this brain-based, global economy, cognition is termed to be the ignition of productivity. Here, cognition is related to emotional intelligence, resilience, and managing employee health. In Frankl's terms, these issues are addressing man's search for meaning and finding meaning by living the creative, experimental, and attitudinal values, which are inherent in every situation and challenge given. With all we know, our intellectual and emotional intelligence given, our insight, our knowledge, and the human capacity of deciding about the direction we want to take, we can seek understanding through thought, experience, reasoning, and judgment. The brain-based economy, biotechnology, and artificial intelligence are made by humans and served by humans. All concepts of homo deus, lifting himself up and beyond his human creator, have been demystified by their own activities and ignited powerful drivers for the Copernican turn, sparking new roads for powerful questions about meaningful work and about the ways to understand and organize good living on this planet for all, based on a mutual understanding of the diverse needs of humans. Understanding the existential issues we are all challenged by, organizing the right platforms and places for communicating this "state of the art," and taking action with freedom and responsibility lie within the scope of humanity's capacity. According to the dramatic challenges given, this effort needs to be most powerfully intensified and nourished.

References

Batthyány A (2016) Lecture. Future of logotherapy. Third World Congress of Logotherapy, Vienna

Commission of the European Communities (2002) Guidance on work related stress. Office for Official Publications of the European Communities, Bruxelles, Luxembourg

Compernolle T (2014) Brain chains: your thinking brain explained in simple terms. Compublications, Brussels, Belgium

Deutsches Aerzteblatt Fast jede zweite neue Fruehverrentung ist psychisch bedingt (2014, January)
Emcke C (2016) Acceptance speech of peace price of German booksellers, Frankfurt am Main
Frankl VE (1973) Psychotherapy and existentialism. Selected papers on logotherapy. Penguin Books, New York
Frankl VE (2006) Man's search for meaning. Beacon Press, Boston
Frankl VE (2010) The feeling of meaninglessness (ed Batthyany A). Marquette University Press, Milwaukee
McGonigal K (2016) The upside of stress: why stress is good for you, and how to get good at it. Avery, New York
von Devivere B (2016) Unimaginable pain. Dealing with suicide in the workplace. In: Batthyány A (ed) Logotherapy and existential analysis. Proceedings of the Viktor Frankl Institute Vienna, vol 1. Springer, Cham
WHO (2017) World Health Organization GBD Global Burden of Disease Studies. Anniversary. www.who.int
Wilkerson B (2012) Text of speech. The annual conference of the International Society of Certified Employee Benefit Specialists. San Francisco, CA
Wittchen HU (2016) European Mental Health Data. In: European Neuropsychopharmacology, Bd. 21. p 655

Chapter 9
Man, as He Is

Contents

> *People can initiate and live with change because and if there is a changeless core inside them. The key to the ability to change is a changeless sense of who you are, what you are about and what you value.* (Covey S)

What is this "core"? Since ages, philosophy, anthropology, psychology, religion, and, until today, neuroscience, consulting and coaching have been occupied with defining the self and this changeless core of human beings.

B. von Devivere, *Meaningful Work: Viktor Frankl's Legacy for the 21st Century*,
https://doi.org/10.1007/978-3-319-89791-2_9

9.1 The Self

The concepts discussed here are all centered around the individual self, with all her potentials and limitations. They are addressing "man, as he is" and "man, as he could be", relating to man's inherent motivational search for meaning.

Our self develops in a "cloud" and we perceive ourselves in a mirror:

Mental–cognitive processes are not purely psychophysical processes; they take place as part of a person's brain–body–world–identity–forming process. We perceive ourselves on the three levels of me, we, and them.

We experience ourselves with the respective cognitive, emotional, spiritual, and social layers, forming the self.

As humans, we are the only living beings that can take a third perspective on their individual being and on the human condition as such. As such, we are capable of looking back on ourselves, of detaching from the very moment and of taking a third perspective on ourselves, taking the role of the "observing self," the "witness," or understanding the various "ego states" of our very own biography.

We perceive ourselves as forming our identity as unique, singular, and unparalleled individual persons and, also, as forming humanity, their values, and their condition. From this, ultimate questions about human existence, where we come from and what meaning life has, have made for the rich history of philosophic and existential approaches and literature.

Our self is a construct, formed in time and space, complex, and ever changing relating to the environment, the cultures, the beliefs and values, and the roles and attributions being offered from external influences that are processed by the self and which this self is constantly cocreating in relating to their environments and recreating.

The self is the center of consciousness, of will. It represents the self-concept, the individual identity. It is the I and the me. The self can be lived in the form of the *ego*, the superficial premature self, or the *true self* in its wholesome capacity, integrating various layers and states.

Current concepts strongly relate to the individual person, the self, the individual person's search for happiness, autonomy, self-determination, self-efficacy, mastery, and fulfillment.

The human striving for autonomy, though, necessarily entails responsibility as the counterpart. Here, issues of sustainability and also of sensing, factually being and exercising responsible for the effects of own actions in the global community, form one of the most potent drivers for changes in today's workplaces and organizations. Because human beings are relational and spiritual, they can be intrinsically motivated for a greater cause beyond themselves and caring for others is an expression of humanity.

9.1.1 Self-Detachment and Self-Awareness

It is self-awareness with self-detachment as its basis that has established one of the fundamental ideas of Viktor Frankl's approach to unconditional meaning of life and the human meaning-seeking and meaning-making:

> To detach oneself from even the worst conditions is a uniquely human capability. By detaching himself from the very situation, man remains capable, under all circumstances, to preserve his dignity, to turn personal tragedy into triumph. (Frankl 1992)

Individuals become conscious of themselves through the development of their self-awareness. Starting with infancy over early childhood and adolescence, a person develops her own awareness as an individual with own thoughts, beliefs, emotions, and behaviors. Based on this self-awareness, reflective practice is based on the individual person's capacity to reconsider one's emotions, actions, and behaviors in a process of continuous relating to the world around us, consciously reflecting own motives, attitudes, values, feelings, emotions, and actions.

Some would differentiate between reflection and reflexivity.

> Reflection is a means to monitor oneself as life unfolds. You sense, comprehend and process the events in a millisecond. It is systematic, even habitual in education. I mull over my thoughts, I reflect on my actions. The instant I speak or move; these actions are followed by feedback from my senses. My muscles deliver kinesthetic information and my evaluative thoughts of myself are weighed immediately. I hear myself speak and judge my word choice and tone. The feedback loops are numerous and if you attend to each you are in a position to make adjustments… (Ryan T 2005)

Reflexivity is relating to the introspection of the self. Ryan explains:

> What I discovered is that I was actually being personally reflexive which is quite different from being reflective. The reflexive process involves introspection. A deep inward gaze into every interaction whether it be in teaching or any other interaction in life. Interactive introspection was the tool I used to improve my interactions and study my thoughts, feelings and behavior. I considered my mental state, my emotional being, thoughts and motives within a context.

9.1.2 Self-Acceptance

Self-acceptance (Ryff et al. 2008) includes the awareness of one's strengths and weaknesses, a generally positive self-attitude and belief in one's general value, awareness about one's identity, the realistic appraisal of one's talents and capabilities, and feelings of satisfaction with one's self, despite deficiencies and regardless of past behaviors and choices.

9.1.3 Self-Efficacy

Self-efficacy describes a person's belief in own abilities to complete tasks and reach objectives. This "feeling" reflects an individual's understanding of what skills this person has, to cope with situations and experiencing creative values for themselves and what this person can offer to the community.

Both concepts, self-efficacy and self-acceptance, refer to a person's self, with all the competencies and limitations of the individual being.

9.1.4 Self-Esteem

Self-esteem reflects a person's own evaluation of his or her own worth. It encompasses beliefs about oneself and emotional states of the actual self. Health and well-being is not possible unless the essential core of the person is fundamentally accepted, loved, and respected by this very person. Albert Ellis (2005) rejected the concept of self-esteem as misleading and misguiding to evaluation and degrading of the individual, suggesting to replace this concept with *unconditional self-acceptance and unconditional other-acceptance.*

Along with this critical approach, Fontane (2017) reflects on coaching programs claiming to develop "the best possible self" or improving the self, which may be easily interpreted by the employee as being "not good enough," more or less directly relating to the person's sense or rather lack of self-acceptance. These training programs might suggest a "desired self" to be achieved. This might unintentionally decrease well-being. Therefore, the authors suggest that it is crucial to carefully address and discuss with the coaching client what their motives for change are and why and what they actually want to change. Eventually it is only with unconditional self-acceptance and positive evaluation of one's self and one's past that well-being and sustainable change can be achieved.

9.1.5 Self-Determination and Autonomy

Deci and Ryan (2000) and Deci et al. (2004) focus on people's growth tendencies and innate psychological needs that are the basis for their self-motivation, as well as for the conditions that foster those positive processes.

Central to their self-determination theory is the concept of basic psychological needs that are assumed to be innate and universal. According to the theory, these three basic needs must be ongoing satisfied for people to develop and function in healthy or optimal ways (Deci and Ryan 2000).

Many of the propositions of this self-determination theory derive from the postulate of fundamental psychological needs, and the concept has been proven essential for making meaningful interpretations of a wide range of empirically isolated phenomena.

The Basic Psychological Needs Scale (La Guardia et al. 2000) is a family of scales: one that addresses need satisfaction in general in one's life and others that address need satisfaction in specific domains. The Basic Need Satisfaction at Work Scale (Deci and Ryan 2000) has been used most often. It captures a person's sense of autonomy, relatedness, and competence at work.

9.1.6 Self-Actualization

> *Being human always points, and is directed, to something, or someone, other than oneself – be it meaning to fulfill or another human being to encounter. The more one forgets himself – by giving himself to a cause to serve or another person to love – the more human he is and the more he actualizes himself. ... What is called self-actualization is not an attainable aim at all, for the simple reason that the more one would strive for it, the more he would miss it. In other words, self-actualization is possible only as a side-effect of self-transcendence.* (Frankl 1984 p. 133)

Until today, MBA programs and trainers across the world teach Abraham Maslow's hierarchy of needs to be fulfilled, with the "highest need" of self-actualization, fulfillment, and "being values" lived, with the prior basic needs (physical, emotional, security, belonging, etc.) to be met.

Maslow (1966), in his correspondence with Frankl, revised his concept of "peak" experiences, agreeing with Frankl that man's highest concern was his will to meaning, which seeks to be actualized in this world through experiencing values.

In Frankl's understanding, self-actualization is a by-product of fulfilling the human calling to serve the greater good as a terminal value.

In positive psychology, the pursuit of self-actualization is instrumental to experiencing happiness, a concept fundamentally different from Frankl's approach.

It is exactly this self-transcendental prime motivation, in contrast to promises of achieving some benefits along with serving this greater good, that two globally recognized management consultants have recently been recognizing as the major difference between conventional and pioneer, new thinking.

In his groundbreaking analysis *Reinventing Organizations*, Frédéric Laloux (2014, 2016) is serious about the prime motive of pioneer organizations, first and mainly striving for the common good.

Also, Fredmund Malik (2005), professor at the University of St. Gallen and founder of a globally active management consultancy, has adopted Frankl's approach as the one management concept for meeting current and future management challenges and making the right decisions in recruiting the right executives. Realizing creative values, contributing to a greater cause, is the only and apt basis for exercising "right, good, and effective management" according to the St. Gallen International Management approach.

9.1.7 *The Limitations of the Self-Concept*

All three concepts discussed here – self-efficacy, self-acceptance, and building resilience – refer to the self with all the promises and limitations given in the individual person. Research is recently discussing these limitations of self-reference and self-relating activities, being focused on evaluating this self in never-ending self-optimization cycles, following an endless "bamboo strategy" of unlimited bouncing back from adversity but encountering the same structural and systemic challenges as before – an endless cycle feeding low self-esteem, increased efforts of self-amelioration, followed by exhaustion, a feeling of personal failure, in the best case recovery, and starting this cycle again. This "weariness of the self" (Alain Ehrenberg 2009) is a phenomenon of our times.

In parallel, experts are discussing ways and tools on how to bring more attention to human's interdependence and relatedness and how to bring this relatedness into the focus of organizational and work life awareness and organizational concepts, oriented toward flourishing of the individual, the society, and the global community (Rosa 2016).

9.1.8 *The Self-Focus of Increased Management Attention*

Companies are investigating the drivers for employee peak performance, for high employee engagement, and for reducing health costs. The employee's self has entered mainstream management attention: self-esteem, self-optimization, self-awareness, self-management, self- and social awareness of the self, social skills of the self, and finally self-actualization and an innumerous variety of concepts and trainings being offered are on the market.

9.2 Sense of Coherence

Focusing on factors that support health and well-being, Aaron Antonovsky (1979, 1987) coined the term "salutogenesis." Human flourishing and well-being require that persons experience themselves as having a sense of coherence.

The sense of coherence is comprised of three factors:

- *Comprehensibility*: a belief that things happen in an orderly and predictable fashion and a sense that you can understand events in your life and reasonably predict what will happen in the future.
- *Manageability*: a belief that you have the skills or ability, the support, the help, or the resources necessary to take care of things and that things are manageable and within your control.

- *Meaningfulness*: a belief that things in life are interesting and a source of satisfaction that things are really worthwhile and that there is good reason or purpose to care about what happens.

According to Antonovsky, the third element is the most important:

If you don't comprehend, what's going on, but you know you can handle it, that's not such a problem. If you understand things but can't deal with them, at least you know where you stand and you'll probably be able to get through it by reaching out and managing the process. If you don't understand matters and you don't know how to deal with the matter, you can still hold out hope that things will get better and that there is a reason to hold on.

If a person believes there is no reason to persist and survive and confront challenges, if they have no sense of meaning, then they will have no motivation to comprehend and manage events. His essential argument is that "salutogenesis" depends on experiencing a strong "sense of coherence." His research demonstrated that the sense of coherence predicts positive health outcomes.

Meaningfulness is considered to be related to the feeling of participation and motivation and to a perceived meaning of the work.

The meaningfulness component has also been linked with job control and with task significance. Job control implies that employees have more authority to make decisions concerning their work and the working process. Task significance involves the experience of congruence between personal values and work activities, which is accompanied by strong feelings of identification with the attitudes, values, or goals of the working tasks and feelings of motivation and involvement" (Bauer et al. p. 81).

The *manageability* component is considered to be linked to job control as well as to access to resources. It has also been considered to be linked with social skills and trust. Social relations relate also to the *meaningfulness* component.

Together with the various global challenges and crisis and feelings of lacking personal understanding, individual control, and influence on overarching issues of life and well-being, Antonovsky's approach and the sense of coherence with his strong emphasis on meaningfulness have gained increased attention for the workplace (Bengel et al. 1999).

9.3 Self-Care

The maintenance of one's personal well-being and health, though extremely important especially in all health-related occupations and functions, has long been underestimated and overlooked. It was either devalued as self-indulgence and egotism, neglected due to lack of time, or overlooked due to internal beliefs about the self and others. Back to the doctor Michael Balint, who, in the late 1950s, invented the Balint groups, until all current health professional groups coming together to exchange their individual sources for well-being and health, to recover and for stress relief until recent positive psychology interventions of cultivating the positive in a person's life, and up to practicing mindfulness meditation, there are many diverse ways to practice self-care. Self-care again is strongly related to unconditional self-acceptance and is the basis of effective care for others.

Ljubomirsky (2008) suggests these strategies to exercise self-care:

Counting your blessings
Cultivating optimism
Avoiding overthinking and social comparison
Practicing small acts of kindness
Nurturing relationships
Doing more activities to engage in
Replaying and savoring life's joy
Learning to forgive
Practicing religion and spirituality
Taking care of your body

Researchers (Lyobomirsky and Layous 2013) have identified several conditions under which positive activities most effectively enhance well-being. The specific features of the positive activities and the individual person's attributes (preferences, beliefs, etc.) are important variables moderating the effects of positive exercises on happiness and well-being.

9.4 Competence, Calling, and Autonomy in the Workplace

Ryan and Deci (2000) defined three basic psychological needs, their degree of fulfillment, and their effects on well-being and satisfaction in life. These nutriments in life are essential for positive motivation in all realms of life. The fulfillment of these basic psychological needs is of great influence for human's intrinsic motivation to seek novelty and development and to experience vitality, creativity, and enjoyment. Yet, this intrinsic motivation needs external supportive conditions in order to flourish and be lived.

- Autonomy – making our own choices
- Competence – experiencing accomplishment and fulfillment in what we do
- Relatedness – being close to other people

As human beings, we are related and dependent on community with other beings from the moment of our birth. Wong (2014) points to the fact that self-transcendence is, by definition, intrinsically relational, transcending ego-concern and self-interest by being directed at others. "It is intrinsically compassionate and altruistic. In self-transcendence, other people matter in their own right, because of their intrinsic valued…We engage in deeds of compassion and kindness because we are simply expressing our spiritual nature."

These basic needs, when satisfied, yield enhanced self-motivation and health and when thwarted lead to diminished motivation and well-being. Ryan et al. (2008)

refined their model by defining self-determination as autonomous and self-determined action directed at goals that are intrinsically valued and have prosocial consequences.

9.4.1 The Sense of Calling

Frankl's motivational concept understands a person's talents and vocational education of one's life-long calling to serve others. This calling may be understood as a general sense and search for contributing one's best talents to the community and to develop and improve the individual competencies in order to fulfill one's potential. In line with this, a person's calling is always related to the broader community and is definitely a notion beyond personal success, status, and happiness.

In referring to human's "nature" of meaning-seeking and meaning-making individuals, Wong (2016) refers to Frankl's anthropological and theoretical framework, attributing self-transcendence to the "spiritual nature of human beings." Referring to Frankl's anthropological and motivational conceptual framework, Wong describes three levels of practicing self-transcendence, one of them defined as a sense of seeking one's calling: to reach beyond self-actualization and pursue a higher purpose for a greater good. This involves engagement and striving to achieve a concrete meaning in life, "a life goal of contributing something of value to others" (Wong 2016, p. 313). Wong explains this "calling" as an individual sense for a mission, consistent with one's values or passion, or a vocation, of not only being aware of one's strengths, the need of the hour, or the opportunities offered but also having a sense of responsibility to serve the common good.

Finding one's calling needs to start from "discovering a life role, that makes use of one's unique talents, temperament and experiences" *and also* holding other-oriented values and goals as primary motivation (Wong 2016, p. 315).

Finding one's unique talents as an integral part of the own self-concept and bringing these talents to work have produced a vast field of career advice services in publishing, consulting, and coaching. It has been well addressed by Edgar Schein's *Career Anchors* (2013) concept. At their best, these concepts are supporting the individual grown-up person to reliably define their strengths and talents. Many of these concepts directly or indirectly hold the promise that the individual would find their role if only they knew their talents well enough and could present themselves in such a way that they would be the one making the pitch on the external recruitment market, against their competitors, prevailing for a limited period of time on the external companies, "war for talents," after they successfully participated in trainings on "Branding Yourself" and learned to understand themselves as brands and things that come and go like fashion and that would need continuous marketing in order to stay attractive on the market of buying and selling goods.

Today, all of these concepts can be seen as one side of the coin of finding one's calling; the other side of the individual person's sense of values and meaning-seeking needs to be "elicited" (Frankl) to personally define what makes a life meaningful and to give meaning to one's own individual life.

This sense of calling is an integral part of one's self-identity; this self-knowledge and self-identity – knowing who one is and what one's life is all about – is necessary for one's sense of meaningful living.

This inherent sense of "calling" stretches from young students in their identity formation, wondering what to do in life, what to engage with in life, what to bring to life – in short, what their "place in life" is all about – what life is expecting from them, and what their life's purpose is actually all about. It goes all the way to those who have found their calling and are giving their best talents to a greater good beyond themselves. Their names are unknown, in best cases except for those they are serving. Global news media bring their images and spread their contributions from the poorest hut in a suburban slum to any excellently furnished living room in the wealthy hemisphere. Exercising their calling ranges from their being part of a peace mission around the globe, of technical crisis relief support teams, to doctors dedicating their knowledge and skills to the most disadvantaged and burdened.

9.4.2 The Path to Purpose

> *What exactly do I mean by a "life purpose"? A purpose is an "ultimate concern". It is the final answer to the question "Why"? Why are you doing this? Why does it matter to you?...A purpose is an end in itself. (It) can organize an entire life, imparting not only meaning, but also inspiration and motivation for ongoing learning and achievement.* (William Damon)

In his lucid research on young people, finding their calling, William Damon (2008) reports on Stanford University's extensive studies on the American youth. The findings reveal "a society in which purposefulness among young people is the exception rather than the rule" (Damon 2008, p. 8). Damon diagnoses a "directionless drift" in "finding their own ways in making their own contributions to their families and eventually to the world beyond themselves." Their identity formation is being characterized by indecision toward any "wholehearted dedication to an activity or interest that stems from a serious purpose, a purpose that can give meaning and direction to life" (Damon 2008, p. 7). Only a step away from falling – or jumping – off the track, many of these young students are aware that something is missing. Lacking a sense of what they want to do with their lives, they express their inner void by anxiety, cynicism, or apathy, until some external situation, event, or crisis finally brings their frustration to light.

Because this transitory period of identity formation is so important not only for the individual young person, seeking their role, but also for the well-being of society as a whole, Damon suggests for all those educating, supporting, and accompanying the younger generation:

- Listen closely for the spark, then fan the flames.
- Convey your own sense of purpose and the meaning you derive from work.
- Instill in children a feeling of agency, linked to responsibility.

9.4.3 Living the Calling

Everyone has his own specific vocation or mission in life; everyone must carry out a concrete assignment that demands fulfillment. Therein he cannot be replaced, nor can his life be repeated, thus, everyone's task is unique as his specific opportunity to implement it. (Viktor Frankl)

The doctors being active in "Médecins sans Frontières" or similar organizations around the world provide an ever-convincing example: Risking their lives and their health and working in devastating environments with barely any of the tools they are used to from their well-organized and technically excellently equipped hospitals at home, they are repeatedly verifying their strong sense of highest fulfillment and experience of self-transcendence in relating to the poorest and most unfortunate humans, suffering, fleeing, migrating, and searching for shelter and protection.

9.5 Motivation

I consider it a dangerous misconception to assume that what man needs in the first place is equilibrium, or, as it is called in biology, homeostasis, i.e. a tensionless state. What man actually needs, is not a tensionless state, but rather the striving an struggling for a worthwhile goal, a freely chosen task. (Viktor Frankl)

9.5.1 Intrinsic Motivation: The Inherent Given

Deci and Ryan (2000) found intrinsic motivation as the most convincing, inherent given for the positive potentials of human nature: From the time of birth, children are active, inquisitive, curious, and playful, all in the absence of specific rewards. They examined the conditions that elicit and sustain, versus subdue and diminish, this innate potential.

They found that all expected tangible rewards made contingent on task performance do reliably undermine intrinsic motivation. Also, not only tangible rewards but also threats, deadlines, directives, pressured evaluations, and imposed goals diminish intrinsic motivation because they conduce toward an external perceived locus of causality. In contrast, choice, acknowledgment of feelings, and opportunities for self-direction were found to enhance intrinsic motivation, because they allow people a greater feeling of autonomy.

Deci and Ryan refer to the many situations in work, when external expectations are defined toward the individual employee. In order to integrate these external expectations with their own personality and engagement, persons will need to relate to these potential meanings and synthesize these with respect to their other goals and values. Such deep, holistic processing is facilitated by a sense of choice, volition, and freedom from excessive external pressure toward behaving or thinking in a certain way. In this sense, support for autonomy allows individuals to actively transform information into their own work and define their own behaviors as a matter of acknowledging the expectations and taking an attitude.

Intrinsic motivation, then, is man's inherent tendency to seek out novelty and challenges, to extend and exercise one's capacities, to explore, and to learn. It describes man's natural inclination toward assimilation, mastery, spontaneous interest, and exploration, that is so essential to cognitive and social development and that represents a principal source of enjoyment and vitality throughout life. The maintenance and enhancement of this inherent disposition requires supportive conditions and can be disrupted by various nonsupportive conditions.

9.5.2 *We Are All Intrinsically Motivated*

> *One cannot lead a life that is truly excellent without feeling that one belongs to something greater and more permanent than oneself. People who are very high in extrinsic goals for wealth are more likely to attain that wealth, but they're still unhappy. Satisfaction depends on not merely having goals, but on having the right goals – goals that are greater than their own self-interest.* (Pink 2011, p. 6)

Based on studies done at MIT and other universities, in his paradigm-changing book *Drive*, Daniel Pink (2011) explains that, until today, most businesses have not caught up with the research based on up-to-date understanding of what actually motivates us. Businesses and organizations still operate with an outdated, last century understanding of human motivation. Accordingly, organizations and employees suffer from three compatibility problems:

- Many new business models actually feel that easy-at-hand practices are outdated, and they are in search of organizing themselves around ideas and approaches in line with intrinsic motivation.
- Humans are – by nature – intrinsically motivated purpose maximizers, not profit maximizers.
- For a growing number of businesses and employees, work and tasks are (or are expected to be) interesting, creative, self-directed rather than routine, boring, and other-directed.
- Twenty-first-century work and organizations will need to be organized around the intrinsic motivation drivers for the sake of fulfilling their purpose and their mission.

From this analysis, Pink describes three drivers for motivation:

- Autonomy – Our desire to be self-directed. It increases engagement over compliance.
- Mastery – The urge to get better skills.
- Purpose – The desire to do something that has meaning and is important.

In his publication, Pink defines motivational considerations apt for the twenty-first-century creative and complex tasks in organizations and workplaces as "motivation 3.0."

Pink explains why, with complex tasks and questions to be answered in today's workplaces and organizations, extrinsic motivation and "carrots and sticks" management have definitely reached its turning point: Rewards can transform an interesting task into a punishment. They can turn play into work and foster short-term thinking. Traditional "if-then" rewards can extinguish intrinsic motivation; diminish performance; crush creativity; expel good behavior, encourage cheating, shortcuts, and unethical behavior; and become addictive. Extrinsic rewards delude the individual employee to take the quickest road there, even if it means "taking the low road" (type X motivation). Type I behavior is intrinsically motivated. It is a constantly renewable resource, based on autonomy, mastery, and purpose.

In contrast, when the reward is the activity itself, deepening learning, delighting customers, and doing one's best – this is "the high road". Pink reports a threshold of research findings, showing:

- Intrinsic motivation, type I behavior concerns itself less with the external rewards an activity brings and more with the inherent satisfaction of the activity itself. Type I's almost always outperform type X's in the long run.
- Intrinsically motivated people usually achieve more than their reward-seeking counterparts.
- Type I behavior promotes greater physical and mental well-being. They have higher self-esteem, better interpersonal relationships, and greater general well-being than those who are extrinsically motivated.

Pink describes that, for professional success and personal fulfillment, there is an undeniable need to move from motivation type X to type I and calls for a "default setting" in business, i.e., to be autonomous and self-directed.

Finally, Pink suggests a new purpose motive for the twenty-first century: to "*accompany* profit maximization with purpose maximization," by defining organizational goals that use profits to reach purpose, by emphasizing *something more than self-interest*, and by allowing people "to pursue purpose on their own terms."

With this approach, Pink does not go all the way, supposing to actually travel two roads in parallel and taking the elevator at the same time. Bottom line, his far-reaching suggestions, directed at twenty-first century needs, seem like an attempt to square the circle in search for harmonization of basically contradictory motives.

9.5.3 Suggesting a Reconciliation of Two Motivational Theories

Life can be pulled by goals just as surely as it can be pushed by drives. (Viktor Frankl)

According to Frankl, man's inherent search for meaning is a motive different from the suggested "purpose motive": It is about an expanded discovery beyond rational purpose. Frankl's approach is more about being *(Da-sein)* than about doing. While the above-described approaches by Deci and Pink are aimed at reconciling search for individual purpose and meaning in life with purpose in work and organizations, Frankl's concept of the individual person's search for meaning is, by definition, including innate tensions between the individual's own goals and also with the organization's objectives.

Frankl is presupposing: When one is faced with a potential meaning to be fulfilled, a person's dormant will to meaning will drive him to fulfill the meaning. There is an essential aspect of our being, whose nature is not to shirk from the unexplored, taking refuge in homeostatic security, but to engage in it, so that it may continue to grow, develop, and become.

There are some human drives and goals that need to be acknowledged irrespective of the value of their drives and motives and circumstances and which cannot be assessed by someone else with respect to their self-centeredness or intentionality to something or someone beyond the self: "Self care, self confidence, self awareness, unconditional self acceptance and trusting in own self worth in each and every moment are preconditions for living a meaningful life. Lack of self confidence and self doubts are limiting personal decisiveness and might lead to existential frustration" (Huss 2017).

Ever since Frankl's late exchange with Maslow, with the latter acknowledging self-transcendence beyond self-actualization, the discussion of these two motivational theories goes in two directions: In many trainings and leadership seminars, Maslow's needs pyramid is still being quoted and taught as the most recent and relevant basis of human's needs orientation. Logotherapy and existential analysis practitioners and research claim that Maslow finally agreed with Frankl, and they hold on to Frankl's approach of man's primary will to meaning, being directed to something or someone beyond the self.

Riedel et al. (2008) have been suggesting an extension or resolution of Frankl's self-transcendent and Maslow's self-centered motivational theories, reconciling and integrating their respective focus – for the sake and benefit of accepting persons' and clients' both self-centered and self-transcendent motives, acknowledging both of these motives as valid considerations for supporting clients' health and well-being: defining a continuum between the two "poles" of "self-centeredness" (fulfilling basic needs of living and taking care of own health) and "intentionality" (being directed toward someone or something beyond the self). Riedel et al. are describing the benefits of this approach for the other person: If one would observe or assume an excessive or dissociated orientation toward one of the poles, the dedicated partner could offer his observations as a potential additional resource for the client in search for finding what is "right" for him. Arguing from this continuum would accept the human person in all his dimensions: a person's basic needs, whose fulfillment is "fundamentally good and right" for leading a good and fulfilled life (Riedel et al., p. 393), and his will to meaning, also touching on existential issues.

9.6 Building Resilience

When we are no longer able to change a situation – we are challenged to change ourselves. (Frankl)

Interestingly enough, the term "resilience," initially being defined and applied in natural sciences and in trauma treatment and – during the late twentieth century literature – being overlooked or regarded as rather irrelevant for organizational concepts and workplaces, has been given increasing attention: "To bounce back from adversity" has become an issue for both individuals in their workplaces and in organizations.

One may wonder about the workplace application and rise of a once psychotherapeutic concept for treating a serious condition, relating to a man-made trauma event or to a natural disaster.

It seems that linear thinking and relating to physics and natural sciences have attracted corporate decision-makers in their search for the right health management approach with no further consideration of the previously specifically trauma-related background of this concept.

The concept of resilience is relating to the individual person's inalienable freedom to take an attitude. Being applied in workplaces and organizations, it can provide a powerful resource for coping with the potential loss of creative and experimental values and for restoring personal dignity and hope for the future.

Referring to trauma, we need to remember that traumatic events in workplaces are mostly referring to "man-made" traumatic incidents, which are much more difficult to cope with than trauma events caused by natural events. Which events would eventually be perceived as traumatic is depending on the individual staff member; it may be a critical feedback discussion with the manager, potentially indicating layoff, and it can be an incident of mistrust or perceived unfair treatment in the workplace up to critical incidents in the workplace, when health and well-being of the individual or a fellow staff member is sustainably damaged.

Today, resilience is conceptualized in terms of protective factors within the individual and in the culture or environment. Such factors not only prevent persons from getting sick but enable them to bounce back from illness or trauma. Resilience depends on having sufficient inner and external resources to cope with difficult life events. Resilience also depends on learning effective coping strategies and skills to manage different kinds of troubles and threats. This learning process requires cultural knowledge and the ability to differentiate between adaptive and maladaptive coping processes.

Resilience is a two-dimensional construct, referring to:

- Exposure to adversity/crisis/external resistance
- The positive adjustment, i.e., positive outcomes

Resilience relates to the processes that protect individuals and organizations against the overwhelming influence of risk factors. Developmental (vs. trait given) and the individuals' and organizations' capacity:

- To navigate their way to psychological, social, cultural, and physical resources that may sustain their functioning, performance, well-being, etc.
- To negotiate for these resources to be provided and experienced

9.6.1 Inner Strengths Comprising Resilience

Seven critical factors, or inner strengths, that comprise resilience have been isolated:

- *Emotion regulation* – The ability to stay calm under pressure. Resilient people can control their emotions, especially in the face of a challenge or adversity, in order to stay goal focused. This factor is important for succeeding at work, forming intimate relationships and maintaining physical health.
- *Impulse control* – The ability to rein in own behavior under pressure (closely links to emotional regulation).
- *Self-efficacy* – Own sense of competence and mastery in the world. This resiliency factor represents our belief that we can solve problems we may experience and our faith in our ability to succeed.
- *Realistic optimism* – A belief that things can change for the better, that there is hope for the future, and that you can control the direction of your life.
- *Empathy* – How well a person is able to read other people's cues to their psychological and emotional states.
- *Reaching out* – The ability to seek out new opportunities, challenges, and relationships.

Developing resilience is a personal journey. People do not all react the same way to traumatic and stressful life events. An approach to building resilience that works for one person might not work for another. Some variations may reflect cultural differences. A person's culture might have an impact on how he or she communicates feelings and deals with adversity.

9.6.2 Resiliency Strategies

The following most helpful strategies to cope with adversity are centered around the individual person. They describe the individual achievement of taking an attitude (Frankl) to an event that cannot be changed, and they relate to an organizational climate facilitating these strategies through displaying unconditional recognition and respect for the individual person and for offering services for social counseling in the workplace.

Making Connections
Good relationships with others are important. Accepting help and support from those who care and will listen strengthens resilience.

Avoiding Seeing Crises as Insurmountable Problems
We can't change the fact that highly stressful events happen, but we can change how we interpret and respond to these events. Looking beyond the present to how future circumstances may be a little better, noting any subtle ways in which one might already feel somewhat better.

Accepting that Change Is a Part of Living
Certain goals may no longer be attainable as a result of adverse situations. Accepting circumstances that cannot be changed can help focus on circumstances that can be altered.

Moving Toward Goals
Developing some realistic goals. Doing something regularly – even if it seems like a small accomplishment – that enables to move toward forward.

Taking Actions
Acting on adverse situations as much as one can take actions, rather than detaching completely from problems.

Looking for Opportunities for Self-Discovery
People often learn something about themselves and may find that they have grown in some respect as a result of their struggle with loss. Many people who have experienced tragedies and hardship have reported better relationships, greater sense of strength even while feeling vulnerable, increased sense of self-worth, a more developed spirituality, and heightened appreciation for life.

Nurturing a Positive View of Oneself
Developing confidence in own ability to solve problems and trusting own instincts help build resilience.

Taking Care of Oneself
Paying attention to own needs and feelings. Engaging in activities that one enjoys and finds relaxing.

Additional Ways of Strengthening Resilience
For example, some people write about their deepest thoughts and feelings related to trauma or other stressful events in their life. Meditation and spiritual practices help some people build connections and restore hope.

9.7 Empathy and Compassion

Since Daniel Goleman's publications on emotions and what emotions awareness would mean for workplaces, organizations, management, and each and every individual (Goleman 1998), insights into our emotional system have gained much attention. Goleman coined the term "emotional intelligence," with this term referring to the one-sided ruling rational approach of the homo economicus in business and workplaces. Today, insight into our "fast" and "slow" thinking (Kahnemann) has reached global attention.

9.7.1 Empathy

Emotional intelligence (EI) is the ability:

- To monitor one's own and other people's emotions
- To discriminate between different emotions and name them appropriately
- To use emotional information to guide thinking and behavior

Daniel Goleman (1998) defines four components of emotional intelligence, influencing selfs, social awareness, recognition, and regulation:

- Self-awareness: emotional self-awareness, self-assessment, self confidence
- Social awareness: empathy, organizational awareness, service orientation
- Self-management: self-control, adaptability, initiative
- Relationship management: inspirational leadership, developing others, change catalyst, influencing others, building bonds

9.7.2 Compassion

So, what is the difference between the three basically positively defined notions?

Empathy is the ability to mutually experience the thoughts, emotions, and direct experience of others.

Sympathy is feelings of care and understanding for the "feelings" of others.

Compassion can best be described as the emotion that one feels in response to the suffering of others, that motivates a desire to help and to relief the pains of another person. Recently, feeling compassion has been researched in the context of neurosciences and mirror neurons, suggesting that it needs a deliberate awareness of the specific state of consciousness.

Together with mindfulness and the significance of mirror neurons, research is focusing on the substantial difference between showing empathy and compassion. Research by Rilling and Berns, neuroscientists at Emory University, shows how acting on compassion induces a positive feeling in people and how humans are innately wired to want to help the suffering.

It is, for sometimes realistic reasons, for the individual person to decide whether they want to express their empathy or their compassion. Consequently, the person may take a conscious attitude to rather distance herself from the very situation or event, because feeling empathy without being capable of initiating any change to the suffering observed and exercising true compassion might produce an overload of emotional involvement. A human resources manager once explained "I am not sure whether I really want to go into the compassion mode," because he realized that his influence on changing the situation in favor of the other person was too limited; he rather preferred to stay in the mode of exercising empathy and transparently explaining to the member of staff that he understands how the other feels, suggesting to connect to other support available.

9.8 Self-Transcendence

Especially in business contexts, it might seem somewhat hard to grasp the essence of Viktor Frankl's understanding of self-transcendence, its implications, and potential effect on work.

> *By declaring that man is responsible and must actualize the potential meaning of his life, I wish to stress that the true meaning of life is to be discovered in the world rather than within man or his own psyche, as though it were a closed system. I have termed this constitutive characteristic 'the self-transcendence of human existence.' It denotes the fact that being human always points, and is directed, to something or someone, other than oneself – be it a meaning to fulfill or another human being to encounter. The more one forgets himself – by giving himself to a cause to serve or another person to love – the more human he is and the more he actualizes himself. What is called self-actualization is not an attainable aim at all, for the simple reason that the more one would strive for it, the more he would miss it. In other words, self-actualization is possible only as a side-effect of self-transcendence.*
> (Viktor Frankl)

In this concept, self-transcendence has several implications (italics by the author BvD):

- "Being human profoundly means to be *open to the world, a world, that is, which is replete with other beings* to encounter and with meanings to fulfill" (Frankl 1966, p. 97).

- To Frankl, self-transcendence is the essential condition for human existence. Without self-transcending, the person falls into an existential vacuum or existential frustration, missing the essence of life.
- Finding one's identity happens in the process of *dedication and devotion beyond the self.*
- Frankl (1966, 1992) emphasizes that pleasure is only a by-product of the pursuit of meaning, rather than its motivating power, and fulfilling life is achieved by following the direction of meaning, even if this process involves effort and suffering.

Self-transcendence involves being motivated by meaning, which can only be found, experienced, or created in the process of *active interaction with the world.* The perception of meaning "boils down to becoming aware of a possibility against the background of reality... '*becoming aware of what can be done about a given situation*'" (Frankl 1992). This cognitive restructuring of a situation happens due to the activity of conscience that evaluates each situation. The perception of the possibility of meaning is only a first step toward creating meaning in life, which emerges as a result of *active doing*, *experiencing*, *or position taking*.

Today, there are several empirical approaches to self-transcendence (ST). ST has been empirically operationalized, for work and various areas in life, in terms of:

- Self-forgetful vs. self-conscious experience, transpersonal identification vs. self-differentiation, and spiritual acceptance vs. rational materialism
- The ability to expand the boundaries of the self and to experience intrapersonal, interpersonal, and transpersonal connectedness
- Shift of focus from centeredness on self and material interests toward a cosmic and transcendent view of life
- Meaning is understood as the possible relationship with the world, which is perceived, a direction which motivates the individual to act. However, in order for an experience of a meaningful life (existential fulfillment) to emerge, continuous action guided by meaning is essential.

In applying Frankl's concept to today's search for meaning in work life, these are some of the conclusions based on applications of logotherapy in business consulting, coaching, and counseling experience:

- The term "self-transcendence" might spontaneously seem somewhat misleading, especially in today's business world, for two reasons: firstly, clarity and transparency would definitely suggest to explain what is meant by Frankl's concept; secondly the current mindfulness trainings made available in the business world might suggest some type of focused transcendental meditation or spiritual contemplation practices.
- Literature and research referring to Frankl's concept of ST tend to reduce self-transcending business and work as well as according practices to specific areas of work, e.g., health-care services, to supporting the suffering, to spiritual care, or explicitly working for the common good, when reaching beyond the self or delivering services to others seem all too obvious.

- Also, Frankl's concept of self-transcendence is frequently being associated with "loosing oneself," lack of relevant resources, or suffering through the most demanding, extreme, and sad experiences in life, with being murdered and final execution. Here is a small collection of terms, being associated with self-transcendence in research and publications on Frankl's concept of ST: austerity, self-denial, cheerlessness, moral musts, confronting, confrontational, challenging, relating to gerotranscendence, processing existential life events of life and death, and making suffering more meaningful. ST is explained, because humans are "hardwired to spirituality and a Higher Power or to love God, the ST concept being a 'hard sell' in this selfish world, other interpretations of ST suggest a general" willingness to lose everything", giving examples of Nobel Prize Winners like Mahatma Ghandi, Mother Teresa, Martin Luther King and Nelson Mandela. ST-oriented persons are described as working tirelessly and cheerfully, because they love what they do, being constantly *inspired by their selfless devotion* and *believing* that their work is consistent with their respective *end value and purpose in life*. All this is substantiated with introducing Frankl's life as a witness of man's inherent search for meaning and survivor of four concentration camps. All these ST concepts are rather hard to translate into today's modern work place environments and challenges.

With these words in mind, the lay person, so often quoted by Frankl as the most understanding person around, is either encouraged to give meaning to his suffering or to take an attitude to life's questions and give his own answer. Or, in some ordinary situation in work and life, he might be left stunned, overloaded, discouraged, confronted with his supposed ego or "smaller self," exhausted, afraid of potentially being challenged by some tragic life event around the corner, actually "loosing himself" before "finding himself," unable to ever realistically match with these personalities, who have dedicated their lives to these great causes of humanity, comparing their historic achievements, forever stored in the collective memory of civilization, with his work in a small automotive supply factory assembly hall in Munich, his dreary life in some forgotten apartment in a small village in the Northern American "rust belt," or a family mother's life in a hut in some settlement for the homeless in the outskirts of Bukarest, Nairobi, Manila, Kalkutta or Caracas. This concept of self-transcendence would truly be "hard sell" for all of them.

In addition, some of Frankl's wording might invite to this interpretation of self-transcending, while Frankl has been crystal clear about self-transcendence being lived by each and every person in their daily lives:

- Self-transcendence is an existential feature of all human beings and a way of living. It is being lived and demonstrated each day and in the most diverse situations, whenever a person "rises above," whatever the circumstances with lacking resources, the external "invitations" to quick wins, the insinuations, the unworthy treatment, the negativity, the hopelessness around, the powerful mainstream approaches, the materialist thinking, and their nudging temptations might be. Whenever a person acts from an understanding of human abundance, appreciation, and resourceful understanding of the Thou and whenever a person takes an attitude of human *ethos* amidst chaos, of humility amidst all options of power available, of hope amidst undeniable reasons for hopelessness, and for courage amidst silent followers, this person is demonstrating the human potential for self-transcendence, leaving their footprint in their environment, and living and giving their example of the human potential of initiating true change.

- Many of these examples lived by individuals in their daily challenges, exercising their functions on various organizational levels, are engraved in the history of their fellow employees, their teams, their company, and their organization as "life changing," "supporting," "encouraging to carry through," "giving an example," "acting as a role model," etc. It does not need exceptional situations or special workplaces to exemplify man's inherent motivational search for meaning with self-transcendence as the pathway of becoming who we are, in private and in work life: to encounter another human being in a truly appreciative dialogue as a matter of careful leadership, to truly serve clients' needs in banking as a matter of honorable business, to reject inappropriate behavior without retaliation, to believe in the human potential for peace in a world of war, to practice personal responsibility in management (example of Fredmund Malik and others), and to engage in transitioning organizations to meet the forward-looking minds of people for the twenty-first century. It definitely needs "meaning awareness" not only, but substantially by leaders, to carefully observe these "meaning wakeup calls" in every situations and to sensitively acknowledge those new thinkers and activists, ready to collaborate für humanity's best potentials.
- The capacity for self-transcendence is being demonstrated in "silent heroism" by uncounted individuals, who are living up to their best potentials in all those situations, when life is questioning them to give their individual answer, wherever they work and live: in organizations by not tiring to demonstrate ethical behaviors and to take a personal attitude for positive change and in the community by safeguarding the dignity of all and engaging in activities for the common good.

All of these are but a few examples of the human potential for self-transcendence, being continuously demonstrated around the globe and of which this book is about.

Together with the rather limited empirical research on applications of existential analysis and search for meaning in work, the author BvD is suggesting a concept of self-transcendence in the workplace along these areas of finding meaning in work:

- Creative values: Where and how is the individual person striving to give her creative talents to the specific context of work?
- Experiential values: What does the individual person experience in the world around her, in her environment, and in the team? What parts and competencies in others does this person experience? What behaviors of others is this person appreciating? What is it in the working environment and relating to the organization's purpose that this person values, experiencing some type of inner fulfillment?
- Attitudinal values: What are the person's general beliefs about human beings, about her specific partners in work, and about the organization's/company's purpose?
- Is this person in a difficult conflict situation or crisis, searching for a meaning in the specific work situation, suffering from a lack of resources or support, and

feeling lost and void? How can the potentials for detachment and distancing be activated in this person in order to recover from deep frustration, hopelessness, and victimization to reestablishing a state of freedom to choose and to take an attitude to the very circumstances?

- Reassuring the person's undeniable dignity and freedom to take an attitude, under all circumstances
- Defining taking an attitude as a most powerful achievement, potentially an act of "heroism," that is being acknowledged and stored in the past under all circumstances, witnessing this person's achievement beyond the void terms of success

References

Antonovsky A (1979) Health, stress and coping. Jossey-Bass, San Francisco
Antonovsky A (1987) Unraveling the mystery of health. Jossey-Bass, San Francisco
Bengel J, Strittmatter R, Willmann H (1999) What keeps people healthy? The current state of discussion and the relevance of Antonovsky's Salutogenetic Model of Health. BZgA, Cologne
Damon W (2008) The path to purpose. How young people find their calling in life. Simon & Schuster, New York
Deci EL, Ryan RM (2000) The "what" and "why" of goal pursuits: human needs and the self-determination of behavior. Psychol Inq 11:227–268
Deci EL, Ryan RM (eds) (2004) Handbook of self determination theory. Rochester, New York
Deci EL, Ryan RM, Baard PP (2004) Intrinsic need satisfaction. A motivational basis of performance and well-being in two work settings. J Appl Soc Psychol 2004:2045–2068
Ehrenberg A (2009) The weariness of the self: diagnosing the history of depression in the contemporary age. McGill-Queens University Press, Montreal
Ellis A (2005) The myth of self esteem. Prometheus Books, Amherst
Fontane S (2017) 8 positive psychology coaching skills to put on your resume in 2017. positivepsychologyprogram.com
Frankl VE (1966) Self-transcendence as a human phenomenon. J Humanist Psychol 6:97–106
Frankl VE (1984) Man's search for meaning. Beacon Press, Boston
Goleman E (1998) Working with emotional intelligence. Bloomsbury, London
Huss G (2017) Unconditional saying Yes zu the self. Strengthening self confidence. Establishing Basic Trust, Presentation. Viktor Frankl Museum, Vienna October
La Guardia JG, Ryan RM, Couchman CE, Deci EL (2000) Within-person variation in security of attachment: a self-determination theory perspective on attachment, need fulfillment, and well-being. J Pers Soc Psychol 79:367–384
Laloux F (2014) Reinventing organizations. A guide to creating organizations inspired by the next stage of human consciousness. Nelson Parker, Bruxelles
Laloux F (2016) Reinventing organizations. An illustrated invitation. Nelson Parker, Bruxelles
Ljubomirsky S (2008) The how of happiness: a scientific approach to getting the life you want. Penguin Press, New York
Lyobomirsky S, Layous K (2013) How do simple positive activities increase well-being? Association for Psychological Science. Curr Dir Psychol Sci 22(1):57–62
Malik F (2005) Sinn – wenn die Motivation aufgebraucht ist. In: Malik Management Letter 12/2005. St. Gallen, Switzerland
Maslow A (1966) Comments on Dr. Frankl's paper. J Humanist Psychol 6:107
Pink D (2011) Drive. The surprising truth about what motivates us. Riverhead Books/Penguin, New York

Riedel C, Deckart R, Noyon A (2008) Existenzanalyse und Logotherapie. Ein Handbuch für Studium und Praxis. Wissenschaftliche Buchgesellschaft, Darmstadt. Germany
Rosa H (2016) Resonanz. Eine Soziologie der Weltbeziehung. Suhrkamp, Berlin
Ryan T (2005) When you reflect are you also being reflexive? Faculty of Education at Nipissing University, North Bay, Ontario, http://oar.nipissingu.ca/PDFS/V812E.pdf. Accessed 1 Nov 2017
Ryan RM, Deci EL (2000) Self-determination theory and the facilitation of intrinsic motivation, social development, and well-being. Am Psychol 55:68–78
Ryan RM, Huta V, Deci EL (2008) Living well: a self-determination theory perspective on Eudaimonia. J Happiness Stud 9:139–170
Schein E (2013) Career anchors. The changing nature of careers. Self assessment. Wiley, San Francisco
Wong PTP (2014) Viktor Frankl's meaning seeking model and positive psychology. In: Battyany A, Russo-Netzer P (eds) Meaning in positive and existential psychology. Springer, New York, pp 161–184
Wong PTP (2016) Meaning seeking, self transcendence and well being. In: Batthyany A (ed) Logotherapy and existential analysis. Proceedings of the Viktor Frankl Institute Vienna, vol 1. Springer, Cham

Chapter 10
The Inherent Demand Quality of Present Work Life

Contents

It is not us who are questioning life – life is questioning us and we give the answer. Every time has their own topics and needs their own answers. (V. Frankl)

Health and well-being encompass the abilities to develop emotionally, psychologically, intellectually, socially, and spiritually. It includes concepts such as resilience, a sense of mastery and control, optimism and hope, as well as the ability to initiate and sustain relationships and to play a part in our social world. Communities, organizations, and societies benefit socially and economically where people have good mental health, and this is therefore a desirable condition to foster.

Health issues are touching on all areas of life with responsibilities shared by the various stakeholders.

The World Health Organization has defined positive health in various terms:

- As *a state* of well-being: This "state" is characterized by feeling well, having fulfilling relationships, as well as having the ability to cope with the normal stresses of life. Perceived well-being strengthens resilience and self-esteem.

B. von Devivere, *Meaningful Work: Viktor Frankl's Legacy for the 21st Century*,
https://doi.org/10.1007/978-3-319-89791-2_10

- The individually perceived states can also be described as points on a constantly changing, dynamic continuum of individual health and well-being.

Individual human behavior is complex and no singular aspects could be separated. Due to the urgency of joint efforts in the field of promoting health and well-being and treating and preventing depression and suicide, European institutions, bodies, and agencies have set up various expert activities with impressing positive results. All of them are linked to potential workplace activities in disseminating information, raising awareness, training, and primary prevention.

In their latest research, EU health experts (PREVENT Report 2014) conclude: Mental health and mental illness have often been described as points on a continuum. However, research suggests that there are two continuums to be considered: The absence of mental illness may not always be reflective of genuine mental health. And secondly, even in the absence of complete mental health, a person may be flourishing.

Mental health issues are highly stigmatized in society and especially in workplaces where best performance, fully functioning effectively and efficiently, are expected at all times.

What is the call for action? What can we do?

In research in different fields, in people management, resilience programs, workplace counseling, and psychotherapy, meaning-centered approaches are celebrating an impressing and outstanding "comeback" of interest and focus. Viktor E. Frankl's matrix of the modern individual in search for meaning being trapped between "success" and "failure" in modern workplaces has never been more acute than today.

All activities taken are challenging the described mind-sets of success or failure, the pitfalls of stigma and denial, to improve health and well-being in the interest of all stakeholders.

10.1 Intermediate Bottom Line

> *The constantly changing demands of modern life are developmentally inappropriate for us as adults. We should …learn how to support development – and have the patience to wait for it to come…* (Kegan 1994, p 5)

Big ideas have failed us. Truth does not exist. Beliefs are ideology.

Questions keep pounding at the doors of our workplaces:Who are the leaders? What should I do when the leaders disagree? Where would I find guidance in these challenging times? Who am I? What do I believe in? How would I know? Should I refer to self-help? Should I consult an expert? Who is out there to give me guidance?

Research (Keyes 2002) suggests that there are two continuums to be considered: the vertical continuum of "flourishing and languishing" and the horizontal continuum of "mental health and mental illness," establishing four quadrants of ever-changing states of health and well-being (Table 10.1).

Table 10.1 The dynamics of personal health on two continuums

Flourishing			
Mental illness	Psychological and social functioning and well-being, moderate/high Some mental health problems present	Positive emotions Psychological well-being Social well-being Complete mental health	Mental health
	Negative emotions Relative absence of psychological and social determinants of well-being, mental health problems present	Negative emotions Relative absence of psychological and social determinants of well-being, moderate mental health	
Languishing			

These two continuums provide for four quadrants, establishing various perceived states of health and well-being: This multidimensional approach allows for a holistic understanding of a person, who may be flourishing even in the absence of complete mental health.

Especially in the context of providing health services in workplaces, it needs to be differentiated between mental health issues and "disorders," as assessed according to the DSM and ICD.

There are a variety of individual as well as work-related factors, relevant for staff health and well-being in their workplace situation:

Workplace-Related Factors Influencing Health and Well-Being
Research has consistently shown that work, which has positive features, can boost and protect health. Features of working life that are known to promote health and well-being include, besides the material support:

- Being valued at work
- Having meaningful work
- Being able to make decisions on issues that affect the individual employee
- Being adequately trained for the specific work
- Having the adequate resources
- Having a job that is well designed
- Experiencing social relations and social support
- Social interaction in the workplace which can directly or indirectly provide opportunities to learn effective coping skills
- Work function
- Role in the organization
- Work content
- Workload and pace
- Work schedule
- Control
- Personal and career development
- Environment and equipment
- Interpersonal relationships at work

- Structural aspects
- Management style
- Organizational culture

Personal Factors Influencing Health and Well-Being
General health condition
Resources
Coping skills
Previous work and life experiences
Individual and family background
Family status and children
Traumatic incidents
Life events
Social support

All these factors are closely interlinked with each other; they interact with each other in a dynamic process with no distinct cause-effect relation. Being aware of the multidimensional aspects of health may help to take advantage of the positive factors for prevention or mitigation of negative factors, in order to deescalate toward resolution and well-being rather than amplifying the situation from problems to illness- and disorder-related conditions.

10.2 Making the Case for Promoting Well-Being and Health in the Workplace

There are, altogether, three "cases for promoting health in the workplace": a business case, a legal case, and an ethical case.

The mental health and well-being of the workforce are increasingly recognized as being an important issue for all stakeholders.

- Business, organizations, management, consultants, coaches and counselors, and professionals on all levels are impacted by these issues – from health care to occupational health and safety to HR professionals and others – mental health issues pose special challenges to their practice which physical health issues rarely do. Processes concerning taboos, lack of awareness, discrimination, and stigma operate in ways that are much more significant for mental health issues than for physical health.
- For employers, it is increasingly clear that there are costs involved – these may be expressed in terms of absenteeism, presenteeism, and lost productivity. In addition, there are difficult issues concerning how mental health and well-being are handled – how may risk be mitigated, how may mental health and well-being be promoted, how can return-to-work processes be managed, and how may recruitment processes for people with mental health problems be handled.
- For employees, there are also costs in terms of health care, loss of wages, and the health and social impacts of mental health breakdown. In addition, there are

issues concerning stigma, recovery, and reintegration into employment which take on special significance in the case of mental health breakdown.
- There are costs to society at large – the health-care and social insurance systems bear real financial costs, while individuals, families, and communities also carry health and social costs.

Besides these tangible costs, there is a broad variety of intangible effects and costs of poor staff well-being, such as increased level of individually perceived stress, anxiety and fear, anger, negative reputation, deteriorated organizational climate, lack of trust, increasing level and severity of workplace conflicts rising risks of serious incidents, unreleased potentials of creativity, frustration, silent resignation, etc.

Today, researchers agree that finding meaning and purpose in life by living creative, experiental, and attitudinal values to the best of an individual person's potentials is a major protective factor for the individual person's well-being.

A proactive, primary prevention approach is aimed at strengthening the individual protective factors supporting individual resilience in work.

- Strong connections to family, friends and communities, and colleagues in the workplace
- Ongoing individual medical and health care
- Support for help-seeking approach in situations of need and crisis
- Individual belief in resolution
- Effective access to and professional care for individual psychosocial issues

There are various positive impacts of work on mental health: Work, on the average, is good for both mental and physical health. Research has consistently shown that good-quality work (i.e., work which has positive features) can boost and protect health. Features of working life that are known to promote mental health and well-being include:

- Being valued at work
- Having meaningful work
- Being able to make decisions on issues that affect you
- Being adequately trained for the work that you do
- Having the resources you need to do the work
- Having a job that is well designed, i.e., not overloaded
- Having work that is well organized in terms of work schedules and time off

The social aspects of the workplace can also provide a supportive environment for mental health and well-being. For example, it can provide:

- Social support – Workmates can help individuals cope with and overcome personal problems.
- Coping skills – Social interaction in the workplace can directly or indirectly provide opportunities to learn effective coping skills.
- Material support – Workplaces provide resources in terms of monetary income. They can also provide direct material support to help solve problems from work colleagues.

10.3 Three Levels of Health Interventions

The specific types of relevant interventions in workplace staff health and well-being relate to the three levels of health management activities, focused primarily on:

Primary interventions, addressing preventive activities in all areas of occupational safety and health. Primary prevention addresses general issues relating to health and well-being in organizations that can be managed proactively on the higher levels of decision-making in organizations and human resources management taking a forward-looking approach to provide for additional resources to actively manage potential risks (like shift work) and to reduce and mitigate these risks.

In 2014, the EU has adopted a Strategic Framework Agreement to better protect the more than 217 million workers in the EU from work-related accidents and diseases; the European Commission has adopted a Strategic Framework on Health and Safety at Work 2014–2020, which identifies key challenges and strategic objectives for health and safety at work, presents key actions, and identifies instruments to address these. This framework is focusing on strategic objectives, which may be interpreted as guiding objectives of all work-related preventive activities: Further consolidating national health and safety strategies through, for example, policy coordination and mutual learning, the Strategic Framework identifies three major health and safety at work challenges to improve the prevention of work-related diseases by tackling new and emerging risks without neglecting existing risks.

Secondary interventions are concerned with changing the way that employees manage problems and with improving their ability to cope with them. It often involves training and awareness raising among employees and is one of the most common types of intervention.

Tertiary interventions are focused on problems and health conditions that have occurred in the past. Here, psychological symptoms such as negative stress reactions, burnout, depression, or anxieties are addressed that need further specific action (referral, treatment, etc.) Tertiary interventions also refer to reintegration and are therefore closely tied in with all return-to-work processes and the according stakeholders in the specific organization.

10.3.1 First-Level Prevention

Mental health issues should be addressed as an equally important area of workplace health management like physical health. Workplaces are ideal venues to disseminate knowledge and skills and to change cultural approaches and mind-sets. Here, proactive, appreciative, and supportive management of staff is of vital importance.

10.3.1.1 Individual Protective and Risk Factors

The following risk and protective factors are assessed as leading factors for positive health and well-being at work or are, if not observed, being associated with critical individual situations and needs.

10.3.1.2 Protective Factors for Staff Health and Well-Being

There are complex factors influencing mental health and well-being. The European PREVENT Report (2008) collects the following workplace or work-related factors influencing personal health and well-being:

- Job content
- Workload and work pace
- Work schedule
- Control
- Environment and equipment
- Organizational culture and function
- Interpersonal relationships at work
- Role in the organization
- Career development
- The economy and labor market
- Threat of and state of unemployment
- Type of job work contract
- Job security
- Income

10.3.1.3 Individual Risk Factors

- Biopsychosocial risk factors (individual history, family history) are largely unknown and not disclosed in the workplace.
- Personal risk factors, e.g., hopelessness, isolation, vulnerability, unproductive beliefs, and stigma associated with seeking help.
- Substance abuse.
- Environmental risk factors, e.g., stressful life events.
- Lack of information or factual lack of access to professional support.
- Perceived workplace-related stress is reportedly a major trigger for individual depression and anxieties.

10.3.2 Second-Level Prevention

Applying intervention strategies and awareness raising for positive and critical factors to be observed in workplace settings mainly occur when critical behaviors have already emerged and individual persons may need focused care and referral to professionals. General awareness for staff health and individual situations is key just as respecting the general rule: no diagnosing in the workplace.

Breaking the silence about mental health issues, linking all activities to social counseling support, defining organizational guidelines and policies on appropriately addressing and managing staff health issues with an integrated approach of involving all business areas and levels of the organization and managing data with the shared objective of improving healthy workplace environments, and proactively advertising information on off-site expert support for mental health issues are effective activities for secondary prevention.

10.3.3 Third-Level Prevention

Persons in acute danger might either withdraw or reach out to others – sometimes directly and sometimes indirectly. Rarely persons immediately pass the information about their potential despair and hopelessness. They might rather exhibit some of the following warning signs in their behavior:

- Severe problems with eating or sleeping
- Visible loss of weight
- Withdrawing from family, friends, and/or colleagues
- Intense distress or agitation
- Expressing hopelessness by saying “I just can’t take it anymore. I am done. I have had it.”
- Sudden mood change

10.4 Awareness Raising and Training in the Workplace

Best organizational health management practices suggest to:

- Extend primary prevention activities in the field of promoting organizational culture and visible leadership.
- Regularly assess organizational risk factors and follow up on prevention activities.
- Offer training on workplace health issues and how to deal with the challenges to the various management levels and staff.

- Allow for a trustful exchange of individual experiences and open questions in a non-blaming safe environment.
- Broadly advertise on-site social counseling and medical support services.
- Disseminate information on depression and treatment experts in the closer vicinity of the organization with the objective to get better access to early expert support and treatment.

10.5 Integrated Health Management Approaches

Well-being and health influence how people think, communicate, learn, and grow.

Positive mental health provides for all types of resources for successful involvement in professional life, in the community, in society, and in relationships.

Physical and mental health and well-being are closely interrelated with each other. Problem situations in one area may trigger a great variety of problems in other areas of health and well-being. Any situation affects a person in all their aspects and is realized on all levels of being, conscious and unconscious, automatic and intellectually, and being aware or unaware. State-of-the-art knowledge accepts that a person's health is a complex state, being influenced by all spheres of the individual person's life.

By today, there are many existing guidelines in the area of mental health and work. The commonalities of these guidelines cover taking an integrated perspective on health management in the workplace, addressing all stakeholders in the organization on the various levels – individual, team/division, management and broader community services – and taking a positive health management approach, i.e., from assessment over planning to outcomes evaluation and learning.

Some major workplace networks and guidance reports, focusing on joint activities in actively addressing health promotion in workplaces, are as follows:

10.5.1 European Council Directives

In 2014, the Nottingham University Work Research Centre issued a Guidance Document based on the European Council Directive 89/391/EEC of 12 June 1989) on the introduction of measures to encourage improvements in the safety and health of workers at work. This directive (known as the Framework Directive) is the first of the EU's legislative initiatives on health and safety and presents an overall approach to how health and safety at work should be managed.

10.5.2 The Luxembourg Declaration on Workplace Health Promotion

Founded more than 20 years ago in 1997, this initiative has spread to many branches and member organizations. Their members agree on the following areas of action:

Company codes of conduct and guidelines that view employees not only as cost factors but as important success factors are addressing these issues:

- Company culture and management policies that include the participation of the employees and encourage them to assume responsibility
- Work organization that enables employees to balance the demands made by the job with their own personal skills and to control their own work and social support
- Personnel policies that incorporate health targets into all other areas of the company
- Integrated occupational health and safety services
- Inclusion of employees in health issues at all levels (participation)
- Systematic implementation of all measures and programs (project management)

10.5.3 European Network for Workplace Health Promotion (ENWHP)

The European Network for Workplace Health Promotion (ENWHP) started an initiative to help promote mental health in workplaces. Within the framework of the campaign, three guidelines were developed:

The business case for mental health – This brochure is designed to assist corporate stakeholders to gain more insight into the economic and general aspects of psychosocial issues in the workplace (stress, violence, harassment, burnout, etc.).

Employers Resource – A guide to promoting mental health in the workplace.

Employees Resource – A guide to creating a mentally healthy workplace.

10.5.4 The ProMenPol Project

This initiative aims to support the practices and policies of mental health promotion. The website provides a toolkit with practical instruments. The ProMenPol toolkit provides a. o. for a Manual for Implementing Mental Health Projects in Workplaces with multiple tools.

10.5.5 *Standards Council of Canada*

This standard offers a comprehensive approach to managing psychological stress as it arises in the workplace. It outlines principles of approach, the planning and implementation of a hazard control system, and it points to how to manage some of the major sources of occupational stress. It also provides support for implementation in terms of resources, implementation models, audit tools, and related documents.

10.6 Conclusions

Leadership, responsible and sensitive communication, an atmosphere of trust, and basic knowledge about the individual protective and work-related health risks factors, and also about potential warning signs for the individual person, form the basis of sensitively dealing with first warning signs of lack of health and well-being of the individual employee.

Combining proactive and focused prevention activities on all levels and in all business areas is the most effective approach to improving staff health and well-being.

Well-being is a continuous process, not a state. An integrated organizational health management approach is about constantly asking:

- What factors maintain and promote health and well-being?
- What are healthy activities?

Today, the World Health Organization is defining health in a way that holds true for individuals as well as organizations:

Positively contributing to the community
Realizing own potentials
Coping with the stressors
Working productively
Experiencing fulfillment and purpose

References

ENMHP European Network on Mental Health Promotion in the Workplace. http://www.mentalhealthpromotion.net. Accessed July 2017

ENWHP European Network for Workplace Health Promotion. http://www.enwhp.org/enwhp-initiatives/8th-initiative-work-in-tune-with-life.html. Accessed April 2017

EU Occupational Safety and Health (OSH) Strategic Framework 2014–2020 (2014) http://ec.europa.eu/social/main.jsp?catId=151. Accessed 20 Sept 2017

Kegan R (1994) In over our heads. The mental demands of modern life. Harvard University Press, Cambridge

Keyes C (2002) The mental health continuum: from languishing to flourishing in life. J Health Soc Behav 43:207–222

PREVENT: Promoting mental health in the workplace: guidance to implementing a comprehensive approach, Draft guidance document, Work Research Center, June 2014

The Luxembourg Declaration on Workplace Health Promotion in the European Union (version of 2007) http://www.enwhp.org/fileadmin/rs-dokumente/dateien/Luxembourg_Declaration.pdf. Accessed July 2017

Work Research Centre Prevent (2014) Guidance report. Promoting mental health in the workplace: guidance to implementing a comprehensive approach. Draft guidance document. Nottingham University, Nottingham

Chapter 11
Initiating the Copernican Turn: Answering the "What for"

Contents

Where danger abounds, grows what saves. (Friedrich Hoelderlin)

Whatever our role and function, we all share some basic beliefs and convictions about humanity and human beings. Living up to these convictions in modern workplaces may connect all stakeholders and create the common basis for taking according twenty-first-century action.

Awareness and action fostering humanity's ideals based on enlightenment, humanism, learning, and advancement may support meeting the challenges of the twenty-first century and reduce the unimaginable pain that we all are called to act on.

Putting the sufferings, the crisis, the positive and the devastating, and the unanswered questions in a type of Copernican turn on their feet, today's world and people from all around the globe are searching for their answers, putting meaning and the common good first. They have long started rediscovering and actively following deeply engrained values (Fig. 11.1).

11.1 The What for: The Meaning of It All

Ultimate meaning necessarily exceeds and surpasses the finite intellectual capacities of man... What is demanded of man is not, as some existential philosophers teach, to endure the meaninglessness of life, but rather to bear his incapacity to grasp its unconditional meaningfulness in rational terms. Logos is deeper than logic. (Viktor Frankl)

B. von Devivere, *Meaningful Work: Viktor Frankl's Legacy for the 21st Century*, https://doi.org/10.1007/978-3-319-89791-2_11

Fig. 11.1 "What would life be without hope?" Remembering Friedrich Hoelderlin's residence and work in Frankfurt am Main, Germany. (Photo 2018: Beate von Devivere)

Frankl's term of ultimate meaning is addressing issues as the meaning of the individual existence, the meaning of work, the meaning of suffering, and the meaning of life. This search is an ongoing process.

Discovering the meaning potentials of the very moment relates to widespread research on the positive effects of mindfulness and awareness raising for the quality of the moment. Being attuned to meaning potential of the moment relates to leadership concepts of living by example, showing responsible behaviors in the various work life situations and encouraging a meaning mind-set in each individual employee.

Viktor Frankl's positive message is restoring hope and purpose to all those who are struggling in the negative territories of life. The nature of his approach differs from positive psychology because Frankl embraced both the bright and dark sides of human existence and believed that inevitable human suffering could contribute to human achievement and meaning in life.

Viktor Frankl's recognition of freedom of will and the human spirit reflects his philosophical position that human beings, unlike animals or machines, have the capacity to rise above the macro social forces and freely pursue their own interests and dreams in order to endow their lives with significance and purpose (Wong 2012a, b).

Employees in today's workplaces are seeking answers to their basic questions: What am I here for? What influence do I have? What is the common good? How can I make a good living for me and my family? Where is the what for? What is the meaning of it all? Indeed, we are meaning-seekers and meaning-makers.

In work life, this ultimate meaning might be questioned in existential situations of personally being confronted with existential questions about the general direction of one's own life, in the light of circumstances that cannot be influenced by the individual person, e.g., the closing of a company site with lay-offs, decisions on the basis of profit seeking as the only business objective, exclusive shareholder value thinking, hastened retirement against the person's will or as a seemingly preferred "last-exit" option, greed, ego-centered behaviors, and exercising power over virtue. Here, individuals are faced with questions of ultimate meaning of life and their personal identity.

Ultimately, we need to arrive at some kind of general theory of meaning that integrates all current approaches in search of a purposeful live, supporting all those in search for a better living around the globe.

11.2 Meaningful Work

There is no doubt that meaning must be found and cannot be given...to try to give meaning would amount to moralizing. (Frankl)

Today, researchers and practitioners agree that work is one means by which we might pursue and achieve the "good life" or, as some might claim, "eudaimonia."

Meaningful work has an objective dimension (working conditions) and a subjective dimension (individuals' perceptions).

The terms meaningful work, meaning of work, and meaning in work may be further differentiated:

Meaningful work is the comprehensive term for all meaning-centered approaches and best practices in contemporary management and research.

Also, the term is used for any work being generally defined by societies as meaningful, because of the benefit that these professions might generally provide for the larger community. Here, human history offers many admirable stories of evidently meaningful work achievements that have arisen from dire conditions (e.g., military peacekeepers and civil rights workers often work in dangerous and materially deprived conditions). Also, we might find persons actively engaged in functions defined as meaningful work, who would still find themselves in a desperate situation, perceived as totally meaningless.

Meaning *in* work cannot be given; it must be found by the individual member of staff. Managers and organizations cannot be morally obligated to provide meaningful work, fully acknowledging that such expectations rather point to the potential dark sides of meaning management, when meaning might become a form of normative control.

Meaning *at* work refers to all organizational and leadership approaches aimed at providing some of the most supportive structures and policies for facilitating the individual person's search for meaning.

Michaelson et al. (2014) summarize the current vivid discussion and literature on meaning in work and organizations' obligations to promote this meaning: "Meaningful work might matter more now than ever in a world coming to terms with a new economic order and changing ethical values that may determine the form of employee participation and the content and conditions of work for future generations to come… Meaningful work can be an important catalyst to preserve and promote a just society that supports meaningful lives for its citizens. We are optimistic about the potential for meaningful work to yield cross-cultural dialogue on the conditions of work for the powerless and the values of work shaped by the powerful."

The next decades will be a test for mankind's courage and character. (Al Gore)

11.3 Meaning in Work: A Means or an End

Against the inherent tendencies of organizations to dehumanize, the topic of "meaningful work" has entered the mainstream of organizational and business ethics studies:

> The current situation of irresponsibility, of compromised work, is worrisome, whether or not it is unprecedented. I like to recall the words of former Federal Reserve chairman Alan Greenspan: "It is not that humans have become any more greedy than in generations past. It is that the avenues to express greed had grown so enormously." No doubt we are dealing with a human proclivity toward crossing ethical lines – the question is whether, and to what extent, that proclivity can be curbed, and an ethical sense can be cultivated instead. (Gardner 2008)

11.3.1 Meaning as an End

What leaders can give, is an example of personal commitment to the search for truth…No one can show to someone else what in a given situation, the meaning is...As a matter of fact, the answer to the question, What is the meaning of life' can only be given out of one's whole being – one's life is itself the answer...Humanness of man is grounded in his responsibility… Being human means responding to life's situations, replying to the questions they ask. Being human means answering these calls – but who is calling? To whom is man responding? To his life. (Frankl)

This radical "abstinence from value judgments" leaves it to the individual person to decide what is right. Albeit difficult, research is ever strengthening this individual approach as the only sustainable approach to leading a meaningful life in these times of global challenges:

> *The current financial meltdown with its catastrophic consequences for the entire global economy will cause more and more people to rethink the way in which some companies have been led and governed in the past, and make them want to embrace a different approach to life and work in the future. If that happens, even this crisis will have done some good.* (Gardner 2015)

Empirical evidence are defining three components that would comprise meaningful work:

- Experiencing
- Autonomy
- Mastery and purpose

defined by Frankl as the basic human need for freedom of will, search for meaning, and self-transcendence.

11.3.2 Meaning as a Means: The Potential Dark Sides of Man's Search for Meaning

Before going into detail of the ever-encouraging concepts in research, in science, and in the business world to support meaningful work, there needs a caveat to be expressed:

Unsurprisingly, there is still a "missing link" in search of meaningful work:

Management, consultants, research, and literature have lately been concentrating on the topic of meaningful workplaces, focusing on the alleged business effects and potential profits to be gained from meaning orientation.

Cranston and Teller (2013) have studied management's and organizations' search for meaning for pushing their employees' peak performance: "While IQ and EQ are absolutely necessary to create the conditions for peak performance, they are far from sufficient. The longest list of words we have compiled from executives' answers to our peak-performance question over the last ten years has little to do with either of these categories… We describe this third category as the meaning quotient (MQ) of work… when we ask executives to locate the bottlenecks to peak performance in their organizations, more than 90 percent choose MQ-related issues…"

Here, meaning is discussed as a means of expanded business results: Of the three Qs that characterize a workplace likely to generate flow and inspire peak performance, business leaders would find the meaning quotient (MQ) is "the hardest to get right."

The language of this approach is telling, when meaning is discussed in terms of "engineering," "manufacturing," "arranging," "systemizing," and "implementing meaning tools."

Cranston and Teller (2013) report: "When we ask leaders about the ingredient they think is most often missing for them and for their colleagues they almost invariably signal the same thing: a strong sense of meaning. By 'meaning' they imply a feeling that what's happening really matters, that what's being done has not been done before or that it will make a difference to others…."

Quoting this immediate business interest in meaningful work, these are three main roads of understanding meaning as a means for – potentially – making more profits, which are being seriously discussed in management:

- When we choose for ourselves, we are far more committed to the outcome – by a factor of at least five to one.
- The sheer number of flow experiences, particularly in the business environment, can be engineered much higher (management feedback to experiencing flow at work).
- If employees working in a high-IQ, high-EQ, and high-MQ environment are five times more productive at their peak than they are on average, how persuasive, what even a relatively modest 20-percentage-point increase in peak time would yield in overall workplace productivity – it would almost double.
- A manager reports that, in his daily management practices, he is constantly questioning whether this and that employee is *adequately linked to meaning*, in terms of his commitment to our business and engagement in his specific function.

Cranston and Teller (2013) conclude: The MQ describes the peak-performance experience….

This search for promising or implementing meaning by applying specific "meaning toolkits" must fail. Executives being asked to locate the issues leading to peak performance in their organizations point out that much of the "IQ toolkit" is readily observable and central to what's taught in business schools. The "EQ toolkit" is now relatively well understood – the bottleneck to peak performance is related to meaning.

Consequently, on the basis of having defined and successfully implemented the IQ and the EQ, research has increasingly focused on defining a "meaning quotient," addressing business executives as potential "meaning-makers," and encouraging managers to ask their employees "testing questions" about their potential "meaning alignment" with the organization. According to this concept, executives are advised to "tell their employees meaning stories" about the impact of their work for the society, customer, team, and their employees' selves.

Ultimately, the "meaning toolkit" is suggesting a road that cannot work because of any person's inherent individual will to meaning that cannot be defined by external authors. Meaning cannot be given, demanded, or assessed, but only found, with individual responsibility and freedom.

11.4 The Human Need for Freedom

As if the authors would understand that "telling stories" about meaning cannot work, they are also suggesting another strategy: giving way to the individual search for meaning, freedom, and responsibility by letting employees "write their own story."

Indeed, this is the only management strategy that can work: Referring to Nobel Prize winner Daniel Kahneman's research findings (Kahneman 2011) on human decision-making, one basic component of meaningful work is referring to be conscious about the individual freedom in work. Kahneman's work, who created the field of behavioral economics and has revolutionized large parts of cognitive psychology and social psychology, is giving a powerful message, namely, that human reason is apt to engage in a number of fallacies and systematic errors and that we need to distance ourselves from the immediate concern for ourselves, transcending our automatically generated thoughts, feelings, and potential behaviors. With his great insights into human nature and psychology, Kahneman has been challenging the homo economicus rational image of man. He explains the two systems that drive the way we think. System 1 is fast, intuitive, and emotional; System 2 is slower, more deliberative, and more logical. Kahneman exposes the extraordinary capabilities – and also the faults and biases – of fast thinking and reveals the pervasive influence of intuitive impressions on our thoughts and behavior. He points at the potential impact of loss aversion and overconfidence on corporate strategies, the difficulties of predicting what will make us happy in the future, the challenges of properly framing risks at work and at home, and the profound effect of cognitive biases on everything in our work and private life – each of these can be understood only by knowing how the "two systems" work together to shape our judgments and decisions.

Kahneman also shows that we have the means to overcome some of our limitations, through education, through institutions, and through enlightenment.

In line with this, best practices and research for meaningful work are increasingly focusing on the inherent human need for autonomy and freedom to make decisions beyond intuitive thinking, which is driven by our psychophysical impulses and self-interest.

In Frankl's terms, we need to distance ourselves from what our fast or slow thinking might suggest. We need to take a third perspective attitude to come to responsible decisions.

What are the best practices approaches on this road we are traveling?

References

Cranston S Teller M (2013) Increasing the 'meaning quotient' of work. McKinsey Quarterly, January

Gardner H (2008) Tanner lectures on human values. University of Utah

Gardner H (2015) Good work. The Focus Magazine, Egon Zehnder, Frankfurt am Main

Kahneman D (2011) Thinking fast and slow. Farrar, Straus and Giroux, New York

Michaelson C, Pratt MG, Grant AM, Dunn CP (2014) Meaningful work: connecting business ethics and organization studies. J Bus Ethics 121:77–90

Wong PTP (ed) (2012a) The human quest for meaning: theories, research, and applications (personality and clinical psychology). Routledge, New York

Wong PTP (2012b) From logotherapy to meaning-centered counseling and therapy. In: Wong PTP (ed) The human quest for meaning. Routledge, New York

Chapter 12
Toward a Meaningful, Integrated Approach: We Reap What We Sow

Contents

> *If we take a man as he is, we make him worse, but if we take man as he could be, we make him capable of becoming what he can be…This is the most apt maxime: If you presuppose, there must be a spark of search for meaning, let us recognize it, let us presuppose it, then you will elicit it from man and make him capable of becoming what he can be.* (V. Frankl)

In practice, various approaches have been addressing man's meaning-seeking, the individual road to meaning-making, and living one's own life at its best.

All these practices from a wide range of the most different fields – business, science, research, consulting, counseling, and psychotherapy – are providing important insights, information, and resources to not only cope with the global challenges but to make a true difference on how to address and develop the best in each individual person and to make this world a better place.

These approaches, all together, actually might represent and create something like a "critical mass" for sustainable change. They suggest living and giving examples to nourish the best potentials in humans and thereby create a true alternative.

Which specific "real realist" (Frankl) approaches have currently been defined in search for meaningful work?

12.1 Appreciative Inquiry

Appreciative inquiry (AI) is a model, initially developed by David Cooperrider et al. (2008), that seeks to engage stakeholders in self-determined change. They felt that focusing on the problems of organizations hampered any kind of social improvement, and what was needed were new methods of inquiry that would help generate and encourage new ideas and models for how to organize. Their approach is based on the assumption that the questions asked will focus attention in a particular

B. von Devivere, *Meaningful Work: Viktor Frankl's Legacy for the 21st Century*,
https://doi.org/10.1007/978-3-319-89791-2_12

direction, that organizations evolve in the direction of the questions they most persistently and passionately ask. Appreciative inquiry was the first serious managerial method to refocus attention on what works, the positive core, and on what people really care about, and until today, this approach is directed toward bringing out the best in organizations.

AI is focused around three basic activities:

- Appreciating and valuing the best of what is
- Envisioning of what might be
- Dialoguing what should be

This approach utilizes four processes for bringing out the best in individuals, teams, and organizations: discover, dream, design, and deploy.

Until today, appreciative inquiry has inspired an ever-growing global community and has been applied by innumerous organizations for their search for transformational change, reaching from the Dalai Lama Center for Peace and Education to businesses, health-care bodies, social nonprofit organizations, educational institutions, and government and public service.

12.2 Positive Psychology and Finding Meaning in Work

Since psychology's increased attention to what makes an individual healthy and flourishing besides focusing on the detrimental signs and influencing factors for diseases, research has turned to the role of meaning and its stabilizing influence on individual health and well-being. This research has connected meaning to life satisfaction and positive affect as well as other measures and indicators of well-being and mental health. The importance of individual meaning for stress reduction and existential coping strategies was examined and meaning's influence on recovery from post-traumatic stress.

Positive psychology has put great emphasis on meaning. Seligman's theory of authentic happiness (Seligman 2002) includes meaning as a basic component of well-being and flourishing. His PERMA model is comprising five factors for well-being and improving personal health:

- Positive emotions
- Engagement
- Relationship
- Meaning
- Accomplishment

In this model, meaning remains a part of well-being and the pursuit of meaning can clash with the pursuit of happiness.

Peterson (2006) considers meaningful work, love, play, and service the major domains of a good life.

Wong (2012) and other meaning-centered experts rightly claim that, ultimately, meaning cannot equally be a means and end in an individual person's life and that from finding meaning, flourishing can – in Frankl's terms – only ensue, but never been pursued.

Serving something bigger than oneself implies that a meaningful life and meaningful work entail transcending self-interest and self-actualization in order to serve a greater cause. Search for meaning here is a terminal value, not an instrumental one. This differentiation seems important in the context of meaning as a means or meaning as an end. The former would consider finding meaning as a matter of defining meaning in order to achieve a specific goal.

Finding meaning in work as a terminal goal is referring to taking another perspective beyond the very own interests, i.e., those of the team, the organization, the clients, the customer, and the greater good, linking these needs to the self and taking responsibility to act on the conclusions.

12.3 The Concept of Good Business

Csikszentmihalyi (2014) argues "The search for a life that has 'relevance or meaning'…is the primary concern of the soul. This is the need that motivates us to become part of something greater or more permanent."

Following his groundbreaking publication on "flow," in his book *Good Business*, Csikszentmihalyi (2003) has taken a closer look at modern times work, stating that this is an age in which business and work have replaced religion and politics as central forces in contemporary life.

Csikszentmihalyi (1996) confirms the central role of creative values in work: "Creativity is a central source of meaning in our lives…most of the things that are interesting, important, and human are the results of creativity…when we are involved in it, we feel that we are living more fully than during the rest of life" (p 1).

Csikszentmihalyi reveals how business leaders, managers, and employees can contribute to a just and evolving society. He identifies the factors crucial to the operation of a "good business": trust, the commitment to fostering the personal growth of employees, and the dedication to "creating a product that truly helps mankind."

12.4 Unchaining the Brain Chains: The Attitude Taken

Compernolle (2014) is taking the three levels of workplaces – me, we, and they – into due account. He argues that it is not the technology; it is rather the attitude taken that can lead to substantial positive change. Compernolle defines the three levels in a working environment where, by taking the right attitude and actions, today's "five brain chains" may be unchained:

"Me" level:

- Dare to disconnect several times a day.
- Become a right-taker: ruthlessly and radically reduce the switches.
- Let your brain idle between tasks and get enough sleep.
- Manage your stress well.
- Save a brain and a life, maybe your own: never ever use your phone or other ICT (Internet communication technology) while driving.
- Get support: turn bad habits into good habits.

"We" level:

- Respect and support people who regularly disconnect.
- Collaborate to enhance each other's right-tasking.
- Fight Franken mail together.
- Convince people of the dangers of phoning while driving.
- Give as much social support as you can – for your own benefit.
- Band together against badly designed open offices.

"They" level (all the above):

- Stimulate your professionals to regularly disconnect and do the same.
- Prevent multitasking and task-switching, including on the shop floor.
- Drastically reduce e-mail while improving its use.
- Fight at all levels to ban the use of phones while driving.
- Drastically eliminate ICT from meetings and eliminate back-to-back meetings.
- Build brainwork-friendly offices, resolving the focus-contact dilemma.
- Manage their stress well.

References

Compernolle T (2014) Brain chains: your thinking brain explained in simple terms. Compublications, Brussels

Cooperrider DL, Whitney D, Stavros JM (2008) Appreciative inquiry handbook. Berrett-Koehler Publishers Inc., San Francisco

Csikszentmihalyi M (2014) Creativity: flow and the psychology of discovery and invention. Harper Collins, New York

Csikszentmihalyi M (2003) Good business. Leadership, flow, and the making of meaning. Penguin Group, New York

Csikszentmihalyi M (1996) Flow. Harper Collins, New York

Peterson C (2006) A primer in positive psychology. Oxford University Press, Washington, DC

Seligman M (2002) Authentic happiness. Free Press, New York

Wong PTP (ed) (2012) The human quest for meaning: theories, research, and applications. Routledge, New York

Chapter 13
Igniting the Spark in Every Person

Contents

Otto Scharmer and Adam Grant have been introducing two inspiring examples on how to integrate the three levels of individual, organizational, and societal challenges and change for creating a new way of implementing responsibility in work.

13.1 Theory U

With his research on Theory U and his publications, Otto (Scharmer and Senge 2005, 2016) introduced a fresh perspective on how to individually perceive, think, and act on the challenges of today's life and workplaces:

What we pay attention to, and how we pay attention, is the key to what we create. What often prevents us from "being present" is what Scharmer calls our blind spot, the inner place from which each of us operates. Becoming aware of our blind spot is critical to bringing forth the profound systemic changes so much needed in business and society today.

First introduced in his book Presence (Scharmer et al. 2004), the Theory U methodology of leading profound change is expanded and deepened in Theory U. By moving through the "U" process, we learn to connect to our essential self in the

B. von Devivere, *Meaningful Work: Viktor Frankl's Legacy for the 21st Century*,
https://doi.org/10.1007/978-3-319-89791-2_13

realm of "presencing" – a term coined by Scharmer. When "presencing" we are able to see our own blind spot and pay attention in a way that allows us to experience the opening of our minds, our hearts, and our wills. Through this process we are able to shift our awareness to allow us to connect with our best future possibility – and to realize it.

Scharmer proposes a new model for understanding and conducting profound change and deep learning. Instead of analyzing and referring to old patterns of the past which are often inadequate in addressing the current challenges of our time and which might be even part of the problem itself, his new focus rather is on learning from and bringing into life the best of all future possibilities – a process that he calls presencing.

Scharmer was called a "scientist who dares to incorporate spirituality in his findings." Discussing the prerequisites for individual and institutional change, Theory U has apparently answered a need for transformational change on all levels of the workplace; his Theory U has entered leadership and organizational thinking across cultures around the globe, where institutions are in search for how to contribute to the greater good.

The "U" comprises one process and five moments. It is traveling together a road to the source from which leaders actually operate, beyond the common thinking about the how's and the when's. This joint journey is about moving down the left side of the "U" (connecting to the world outside the organizational "bubble") to the bottom of the "U" (emerging to the world from within) and moving up the right side of the "U" (bringing forth the new into the world). This journey encompasses five moments:

- Co-initiating: Building common intent
- Co-sensing: Observing, observing, observing
- Presencing: Connecting to the source of inspiration and will
- Co-creating: Prototyping the new in living examples
- Coevolving: Embodying the new in ecosystems that facilitate seeing and acting from the whole

Theory U develops essential leadership capacities and encourages all stakeholders engaged in this process to actually step into their defined new future, kindling and encouraging social change and practical innovations.

13.2 Givers and Takers

Adam Grant, Professor at Wharton school, has been recognized as one of the world's most influential management thinkers. His (Grant 2013) research findings "Give and Take" draw together many years of his and others' research on reciprocity in human interaction and prosocial motivation. With his research, he takes up Frankl's initial definition of man's innate potentialities of giving or taking.

Grant suggests that corporate cultures sit on a continuum with "giver cultures" and "taker cultures" at the extremes and matcher cultures around the midpoint.

Givers are guided by prosocial motivation, "the desire to help others, independent of easily foreseeable payback." Givers "add value without keeping score"; they do not expect immediate gain. The most successful givers care highly for others but also have some self-interest, such as attending to their work and other needs. They give in ways that reinforce social ties. They set boundaries to ensure giving has maximum impact and joy, without burning out or compromising their work commitments. They are cautious about giving to takers. Givers are motivated by a sense of service and contribution and are more productive when they think of helping others. Grant found, however, that givers are not successful if they lack assertiveness, become subordinates, or burn out by excessively giving.

Takers ask for help, but give little or nothing in return. They tend to claim personal credit for success, for example, saying "me" and "I," rather than "we" and "us." They tend to "kiss up and kick down" and seek to come out ahead.

Matchers help others but expect an equal amount of help in return. They give to people who they think will help them in return.

Unfortunately today's working environment, employees receive little encouragement for acting in the interests of others. As economists and experts observe, many employees are subject to organizational reward systems that feel zero-sum: In promotion decisions, only one person advances, while the rest are left behind. In forced-ranking performance evaluations, employees are expected to rate their own performance against their fellow team members and, finally, for every employee who earns a five, another must be given a one. In competitive bonus pools, more money to "stars" means less for the rest. These situations put employees against one another, encouraging them to undercut rather than support their colleagues' efforts.

"Giver" behaviors result in these organizational improvements:

- Group effectiveness, cohesion, coordination
- Interpersonal networks
- Sales performance, revenues
- Productivity
- Client satisfaction
- Creativity
- Quality
- Problem-solving
- Staff retention, job satisfaction, sense of belonging, pride
- Personal success

Grant concludes that in the long run, the greatest success – and the richest meaning – will come to those who, instead of cutting other people down, pursue their personal ambitions in ways that lift others up. From a manager's perspective, it would be wise to clear the path for more givers to succeed, "so that they can bring others along as they climb to the top."

13.3 The Diamond in the Rough

When asked how to identify those persons, who have the potential to do great things as they go forward, Grant (2013) points to a stunning fact:

Most people might assume that a manager has enormous potentials and "a great eye for talent" and that he's immediately able to spot the quantitative savants and then basically work with them. It is the exact opposite. Be it a good teacher, be it an excellent manager: They see every person who walks in as a diamond in the rough, waiting to be polished. Then he tries to make his own activities as interesting as possible to bring out the best in those persons. Now, of course, it doesn't work with every person. But what he finds over time is, by making his material interesting, he does shift some people toward becoming what they are and can be.

Grant (2014) suggests that people in leadership positions can promote givers in their organization by the following activities:

- Encourage reciprocity.
- Help givers to set boundaries.
- Guide giving behavior in the direction of best impact: helping others while protecting one's own work commitments.
- Emphasize the intrinsic motivation which occurs when being a giver.
- Help staff to match their own expertise and resources to others' needs.
- Implement reward and recognition systems which favor givers.
- Role model giving behaviors.
- Design jobs to connect the individual role directly to the recipient and client and to a sense of purpose.
- Screen out takers; minimize the number of take employees.
- Pass on the links to the articles and books to our clients to know that increasing peoples' giving behaviors can bring a range of organizational improvements.
- Clients who are natural "givers" can be affirmed and supported by this research. We could help these clients to set boundaries or to re-craft their jobs to suit their strengths.
- Help leaders introduce transformational change.

13.4 Reinventing Organizations

Life is not asking us to become anything, that is not already seeded in us. (Frederique Laloux)

Assessing the industrial world, how organizations are currently doing business and managing people and organizations, the consultant Frederic Laloux concluded that something is broken in today's organizations, which have stretched beyond their limits. According to this assessment, we are at a crucial moment in history, when we have all the capacities and knowledge to create a new way of managing businesses, schools, and hospitals, to stop trying to fix the old model, but rather make a fundamental leap in the way we work and cooperate. In his groundbreaking publication *Reinventing Organizations*, Frederic Laloux (2014) is suggesting and empirically reporting on nothing less than an organizational model and according practices that are better suited to respond to the factual complexity of the world and its challenges as well as their dynamics and to also answer the cry for meaning, the yearnings of the human soul.

Laloux' central research questions focuses on these topics: "Could we invent a more powerful, more soulful, more meaningful way to work together? We yearn for more, for radically better ways to be in organizations. If it turns out that it is possible to create organizations that draw out more of our human potential, then what do these organizations look like? How do we bring them to life?" (Laloux 2014, p. 2).

Laloux' approach has gained global recognition and ignited a spark around the globe, encouraging organizations, leaders, and individuals to take a new attitude to their existence and to bringing their talents to the world.

It is Laloux' historical perspective on humanity's development during the past centuries, his appreciation of the respective stages of human consciousness at their respective time and phases, which makes his insights appealing and encouraging to go forward to the next stage of working and living together. Laloux' approach differs fundamentally from Harari's rather gloomy conclusions on human history.

13.4.1 An Evolutionary Approach to Humanity

Laloux draws on the human potential as it has developed over time and evolution, arguing that "life is not asking us to become anything, that is not already seeded in us" (Laloux 2014, 2016), under the humanist premise, that, as human beings, "we are not problems to be solved, but potentials to unfold."

Laloux' concept and insights are based on a variety of humanist thinking and ideas that make his approach so deeply significant for our times. As if to give additional evidence to his evolutionary approach, Laloux is aligning his organizational psychology related approach with the evolution of the human individual from birth to the complex state of consciousness – considering the best case of human development.

What are the core components of this evolutionary approach?

- Taking the evolutionary perspective on human development involves a "mindset" different from the previous models of how humankind has come to where we are today.
- It means appreciating the cognitive, psychological, structural, and societal reinventions that people went through in history to adapt to their environments and get work done. It means understanding at which point in history the respective world views, the organizational paradigms lived by, and the level of consciousness did

no longer meet the needs of humankind in the specific historical context, initiating breakthroughs into the next stage of development.

- An evolutionary approach means understanding and taking into account that human societies, like individuals, don't grow in linear fashion, but in stages of increasing maturity, consciousness, and complexity.
- Accordingly, human development in its various stages cannot be evaluated or judged by their shortcomings only, but rather by taking a closer look at their reasons, their why's, their world views, and their achievements for inventing and structuring their organizations the way they did. Today, humankind lives from our predecessors. Every new stage includes and transcends previous stages, with all their lights and shadows.
- Any person's consciousness is complex, multidimensional, evolving over time with various layers: cognitive, moral, psychological, social, and spiritual. It is exactly this insight into individual persons' diversity that makes the way for a positive understanding of what binds humanity together, rather than defining an individual state as "better than" or "worse than" any other.
- The evolutionary approach also includes a systemic understanding of all the complexity of humans and their environments, with regard to their physical, cognitive, moral, psychological, and spiritual dimensions and needs in their living context.
- Taking an evolutionary perspective on the past, present, and future of organizations finds that with every stage in human consciousness came a breakthrough in mankind's ability to cooperate, taking a new attitude to the challenges that the respective environments were posing to previous societies.

13.4.2 From Scarcity to Abundance

Where all the previous stages of human development (almost until the turn of this millennium) had operated out of a sense of lack and scarcity and deficiency, this new level acted out of a sense of radical abundance, as if it were overflowing with goodness, truth and beauty. (F. Laloux)

The postmodern era already showed characteristics that were unprecedented in human history and which Graves called "a monumental leap in meaning."

Since then, philosophers, historians, organizational scientists, psychologists, and – most important – organizations and their employees in all business branches and areas of life have been searching for ways to live a new paradigm of what humans consider to be best for humanity. "Evolutionary" organizations are emerging around the globe. Their new paradigm as living organisms is built on self-management and a deep sense of purpose, according to which "the most exciting breakthroughs of the twenty-first century will not occur because of technology, but because of an expanding concept of what it means to be human" (John Naisbitt, quoted by Laloux).

Laloux' insight and findings are resulting from an exceptionally humanistic and psychological approach, which – as he indicates – had largely been overlooked by historians, in favor of rather observing the given world views of organizations with all their dark sides and failures. Until today, enlightenment and reasoning have left their imprints on our thinking, on our culture, and on the way we are cooperating together. Humankind, today, is searching for what has been lost in the course of this phase. Laloux' perspective is an integrative one:

According to Laloux' assessment of the evolution of human conscience over the past 100,000 years until today, consciousness is accelerating faster and faster, understanding the unlimited complexity of human existence.

13.4.3 Five Stages of Human Development: Breakthroughs in Human Consciousness

According to Laloux' assessment, there have been five distinct organizational paradigms in human history.

Every transition to a new stage of consciousness has embraced a whole new era in human history. At every crossroad, everything changed: the society (going from family bands to tribes to empires to nation-states), the economy (from foraging to horticulture, agriculture, and industrialization), the power structures, and the role of religion. Each of these phases was born in the context of their historic environments and challenges, with their guiding "metaphors," in which they coped, developing their own specific cultures, rules, and processes.

Each of these five stages was characterized by key breakthroughs. Until today, the various organizational models once developed by powerful groups are – on the grounds of their respective world views – still in practice. Here, Laloux shows his extraordinary approach of connecting our current life and challenges with our history as human beings. His message: There is no future without understanding, acknowledging, and appreciating our past. We cannot dismiss our past, but we can appreciate and integrate it into our best future.

It is in this approach that the author BvD would again retrieve Viktor Frankl's approach of unconditional acceptance of the potentials in every human being to rise above his limitations by his own will.

With every new stage in human consciousness came a breakthrough in human ability to collaborate, bringing about a new organizational model. Organizations as we know them today are – by large – the expression of our current world view, our current stage of development.

- The earliest developmental stage of humanity spans from around 100,00 to 50,000 BC, when we lived in small bands of family kinships. Foraging is the basis of subsistence. Conscience of the self is not developed.

- 15,000 years ago, the magical stage began. From small family bands to tribes, the universe is full of magic; ritualistic behaviors prevail, with some extremely limited task differentiation.
- 10,000 years ago, the first chiefdoms and proto-empires evolved. The world is seen as a dangerous place. One's needs being met depends on being strong. The guiding metaphor is the "wolf pack," the key breakthrough division of labor.
- 4000 BC the *conformist phase* started with a command–control structure. A collective "us or them" is developed with strict organizational hierarchies and structures, formal hierarchies, guaranteeing stability, planning, titles, ranks, uniforms for role clarity, and security against "others." The according organizational paradigm can be observed with the first large industrial age organizations and until today in all organizations with strong and rigid hierarchies, guaranteeing safety and predictability.
- In 1350 AC, with the Renaissance and the Age of Enlightenment, the *achievement-oriented organizational paradigm* started – involving a fundamental breakthrough in knowledge and cognitive understanding of the world in all its complexity. Scientific investigation, innovation, and entrepreneurship brought unprecedented insight and prosperity to mankind. The corresponding world view is "solidly" materialistic – denying whatever cannot be empirically be proven or observed and denying any other Geist or spiritual human dimensions, based on fundamental suspicion against the influence of powers beyond knowledge and proof. Laloux is strong in concluding: "Our ego reaches the peak of its dominance at this stage, as we invest our ego with all our hopes of achievement and success" (p. 25).
- Starting around the late 1960s, *pluralistic organizations* were developed with some fundamental breakthroughs: Fundamentally rejecting all hierarchy, these organizations were built around shared leading purpose of what was offered to the community, values, paramount leadership humility demonstrated, and a broad stakeholder perspective with social responsibility as a core element.

Starting with the Renaissance and the Enlightenment, the age of reason and revolution changed the world in every detail: Representative democracy replaced monarchy, freedom replaced slavery, and "modern sciences" replaced mythic religions. Geology, physics, chemistry, biology, psychology, and sociology made their triumphant way. These sciences were so successful, that the other major domains of human existence and knowledge (from arts to ethics and moral) were either pushed back and deemed less relevant; science became the only and only paradigm, resulting in "the disenchanted universe" (Max Weber). Until the late 1960s, past 300 years were seen as a mixture of great advance and stunning discoveries, accompanied with a reductionism and scientific materialism. Then, all of these past accomplishments were attacked as the ails of "modernism" and its general reign of materialism. Postmodernism claimed to challenge modernity's reductionism with a fresh perspective on cultures, with pluralism of thinking and tolerance. Still though, this approach divided humanity's choices with a type of binary thinking into two major ones – before and after modernity, either–or.

Depending on the various organizations' needs and especially those of their leaders, it is left to their freedom of decision, if they would strive to organize around a new paradigm. Change cannot be enforced, and it would be a great misunderstanding of Laloux' approach to divide between allegedly "apt" and "outdated" organizational paradigms as such.

It is more or less these last three hundred centuries, a glimpse in the eye of human history, that we anticipate today with all their achievements and sufferings.

13.5 Core Human Strengths

Until today, there is a coexistence of various organizational paradigms. In their development, they all drew from basic human strengths. Answering the question, what the next paradigm in human history will be about, Laloux is reminding the reader of the undeniable core in every human being. These are some of the core human strengths that twenty-first-century organizations can relate to in initiating the "Copernican turn":

- Inner rightness as guiding compass, shifting from external to internal values, questioning *Does this decision seem right? Am I being true to myself? Is this in line with whom I sense I am called to become? Am I being of service to the world?* In contrast to outdated organizations and their individuals working there, the order is reversed: We do not pursue recognition, success, wealth, and belonging to live a good life. We pursue a life well lived.
- Wisdom beyond rationality, honoring the complex, ambiguous, paradoxical, nonlinear nature of reality, unconsciously connecting patterns that our rational mind cannot.
- Appreciating and actually living the cognitive breakthrough, the ability to reason, transcending the either–or to the more complex both–and thinking, and applying it to living freedom and responsibility, relating to the self and to others.

There are some explicit assumptions about the human capacity in reinventing organizations; these assumptions build on the humanist understanding of who we are and what makes us human:

- People are systematically considered to be good (reliable, self-motivated, trustworthy, intelligent).
- There is no work-related "performance" without happiness and personal fulfillment.
- To be happy, we need to be motivated. To be motivated, we need to be responsible. To be responsible, we must understand why and for whom we work and be free to decide how.

13.6 A Leap in Meaningful Work

Laloux is making a strong case, theoretically and empirically, for the next stage of human consciousness, that – with all the examples provided – has already started and that might answer man's search for meaning and purpose in twenty-first century and further fuel the dynamics of the Copernican turn. This new paradigm described in his book translates into concrete structures, processes, and cultures, i.e., a specific concept of "pioneer organizations," with specific characteristics of the next developmental stage, lived by in these organizations. After his theoretical work, he found plenty of organizations with their employees living this new paradigm.

13.6.1 Success Ensues

In this new type of organizations, profits are necessary and investors get a fair return, but the objective is purpose, not profit. Profits are a by-product of a job well done. Laloux explicitly refers to Viktor Frankl's approach: Success, like happiness, cannot be pursued; it must ensue, and it only does so as the unintended side effect of one's personal dedication to a cause greater than oneself.

What might look like a great paradox, actually, turns out to be the application of a general psychological insight into bringing out human potential: By focusing on purpose rather than profits, profits tend to roll in more plentifully, this being said with precautions against any false instrumental concept of driving purpose for quick wins. Here, success is being defined as a matter of achieving the organization's meaningful purposes and ends.

In such an organization, each individual is contributing to the organization's purpose via three human and organizational breakthroughs:

- Self-management: Value is created by each and everyone on the "shop floor," with almost no hierarchy to delegate to or to blame. With freedom comes responsibility for knowing the self and own development.
- Wholeness: To live from within, without hiding nonwork-related roles from the organization and bringing own needs and feelings to the attention of others for expanding their potentials in supporting their fellow colleagues.
- Evolutionary purpose: Answering the questions in search of meaning: Does the organization's purpose resonate with me? Is this a place I feel called to work? Will this place allow me to grow and develop?

Since last century's late decades, a new stage has begun: The emergence of "being values" can be observed with organizations and individuals around the globe. Their thinking is inclusive and systemic, acknowledging that all of the previous stages of humanity were important and true, embracing them as part of the common past of humankind.

13.6.2 Structures, Practices, and Cultures of Pioneer Organizations

All of the abovementioned breakthroughs need to be consciously implemented and developed in these "pioneer" organizations' structures and processes. Here, HR may play a vital role in encouraging and empowering the pioneer organization through recruitment, training, performance management, feedback, encouragement, and organizing daily life. Laloux is giving vivid and convincing examples of pioneering organizations in various branches and across their in-house tasks from product development, financing, sales, marketing to service management, exemplifying how the profit or not-for-profit organizations managed to transform their work to a new stage.

Leadership plays a vital role in this process. There is no formal hierarchy. Leadership is understood as taking and exercising individual responsibility in the context of self-organizing teams.

All in all, Laloux' research findings are witness to the three dimensions of human existence, physical, psychosocial, and mind. Also, they provide for a practical account of how meaningful work can be organized and of why "happiness" cannot be pursued, but rather ensues by building on the fundamentals of human capacities in all their dimensions.

References

Grant A (2013) Givers vs takers: The surprising truth about who gets ahead. Wharton University, Lecture

Grant A (2014) Give and take. A revolutionary approach to success. Penguin Random House Books, New York

Laloux F (2014) Reinventing organizations. A guide to creating organizations inspired by the next stage of human consciousness. Nelson Parker, Bruxelles

Laloux F (2016) Reinventing organizations. An illustrated invitation. Nelson Parker, Bruxelles

Scharmer CO, Senge P (2005) Presence: human purpose and the field of the future. Society for Organizational Learning, Crown Publishing Group, New York

Scharmer CO, Senge P (2016) Theory U. Berrett-Koehler, New York

Scharmer O, Senge P, Jaworski J, Flowers BS (2004) Presence. Human purpose and the field of the future. SoLPress, Cambridge, MA

Chapter 14
New Work: New Culture

Contents

As a philosopher and existentialist, Frithjof Bergmann has engaged in research on freedom and self since many decades. After his publication on *The Experience of Values,* he published his book *On Being Free* (Bergmann 1977). In this book, Bergmann argues against the standard views of freedom *from* external limitations or as an irrational act that rejects all order. Both of these would leave us, as Bergmann argues, with nothing substantial for a self at all, and thus, he suggests, constitute virtually a *reductio ad absurdum* of modern ideals of education, society, and the family. Instead, he argues that the primary prerequisite of freedom is a self, searching for something that wants to be acted out.

In 1984, Bergmann founded an organization called "New Work" with a special focus on the goods and perils of modern technology.

He defines New Work integrating three relevant modern society issues: technology, individual freedom, and the human search for a global community of the common good: "New Work represents the effort to redirect the use of technology so that it isn't used simply to speed up the work and in the process to ruin the world – turning rivers into sewers and rain into acid" (Bergmann 2012).

Frithjof Bergmann's concept is addressing basic issues of today's challenges in shaping the megatrends and specifically the digitally defined fourth industrial revolution.

Bergmann has given the "briefest possible summary" of his New Work concept, naming today's current challenges of:

- Managing innovative technologies

B. von Devivere, *Meaningful Work: Viktor Frankl's Legacy for the 21st Century*,
https://doi.org/10.1007/978-3-319-89791-2_14

- Producing goods in a transformative way
- Creating a new system of work
- Meeting community needs
- Organizing work in communities
- Acknowledging the greater good of others
- Finding work that persons really want to do

By this concept, New Work is understood as an ascent, an uprising through the intelligent and imaginative use of a spate of startlingly innovative technologies. These technologies have in common that they are all "small-scale and small-space." They no longer require gigantic factories with long lines of enormous machines that necessitate boatloads of capital. Instead, they can be grouped together in a neighborhood or village or community center. In short, one half of New Work is the transformation from industrial to "Community Production." The result, in this concept, will be the creation of new enterprises but also progressively the increasing local production of food, housing, and energy, and equally of furniture, appliances, and clothing, and beyond that of still more of what is needed for a pleasurable, modern, and fulfilling life.

The creation of this new economy is the base on which a new system of work and eventually a new lifestyle and culture can be emerging. Instead of being restricted to one ever more problematic mode of work, a growing number of people would be engaged in Community Production about 10 h per week. For another 10 h, they would work in one of the new enterprises that utilize the radically innovative "small-scale and small-space" technologies that are replacing the industrial technologies of the past. And in the third place, they will be doing the genuinely "New Work" that has been the capstone and goal all along: work that people deeply and seriously want to do and work that, according to Bergmann's vision, gives people strength and meaning and the conviction of a truly lived life.

The goals of this New Work concept are:

- The alleviation and eventual eradication of poverty in all countries, everywhere. This cannot be achieved through the ever more desperate efforts to just create "more jobs." But it can be attained through the further development and the slow global spread of the new economy of Community Production.
- A decisive reduction in the amount of body- and spirit-crippling work and an enormous increase in body-strengthening, mind-developing, and spirit-enhancing seriously chosen work.
- The undoing of the "seven tsunamis." The "Financial," the Economic, and the "Desert People" vs. "Oasis People" guerilla war but also the "Climate," the "Natural Resources," the "Destruction of the Environment," and the "Destruction of Culture" (The Burning of the Violins) tsunamis. According to Bergmann, all seven of these can be stopped through New Work.

All "seven tsunamis" were caused by the decimation, the degradation, and the devaluation of work, which fundamentally were brought about by three causes, namely, by (a) automation, (b) globalization, and (c) the worldwide migration from the rural land into the slums.

So far the only response to the ever more clear signs of change needed has been the frantic escalation of the concept of "economic growth." All seven of the Tsunamis have, according to Bergmann's assessment, been the result of this frenetic escalation of economic growth.

This concept of New Work puts an end to the ever more calamitous situation of the meaning vacuum of jobs, by adding two new forms of work to work and functions of the past: the work of Community Production and the deeply desired truly chosen work. By this definition, all societies would actually have an "abundance of work," and with this redefinition of work, there would be an end to the race for growth for the benefit of a few, ending the "seven tsunamis" as well.

New Work is also about creating a new culture in work and societies with educational institutions facilitating and encouraging the individual to manage the new technologies and to benefit from them for actual human flourishing. This will also bring forward and necessitate new forms of architecture with no more "brain jails" (open offices) and new ways of urban life, strengthening the community. Also, the creation of new values, and based on these, the forming of new human relationships, of new social configurations and a wholly new politics.

In this concept of New Work, the new culture will be far more intelligent (far less wasteful), far more humane (with far less poverty than we have now), and also more cheerful (for many more will be doing some work that they deeply want to do.)

An African proverb says "It takes a whole tribe to educate a single child." Visualizing this maxim, we could have a situation in which, from the time you are 5 weeks old until you die, you could be accompanied by a hive of mentors, by people who understand you, and by people who talk to you. The result would be, as Bergmann suggests, a culture that is more humane, vastly more intelligent, and more cheerful than what we observe in today's Western societies.

> The notion of having work, identifying with work, and gaining the meaning of your existence through work is more embedded in Germany than any place else. Germany is identified with its capacity to work…But this is only one side of the picture. The other side is that while in no place is one as committed to work as in Germany, in no place is the pressure to distance oneself from traditional ways of working as great. (Bergmann 1990)

14.1 New Work Best Practices

All over the world, companies, organizations, and leaders are seeking for new approaches with a sense of purpose.

The German government Federal Ministry of Labour and Social Affairs (2015 and 2017) recently launched an initiative to promote the idea of New Work in designing new ways to deal with the digital challenges in today's workplaces. Their Green (2015) and White Paper (2017) collected some questions and potential answers on "Work 4.0," regarding the fourth industrial revolution: The working world of the future will be different from today's. Will it also be better? Will we work in a more self-determined and healthy way? Will we go back to university or learn a new occupation at the age of 50? Are machines taking away our work, or are they paving the way for innovations and productivity gains, which create new jobs?

The White Paper explores the many technological potentials of the digital age together with the challenges to be "socially innovative" in using these technologies.

The human factor remains core.

Initially based on Frithjof Bergmann's works, the German approaches explained below have gone a long way of specific engagement and practice, putting personal meaning and fulfillment in the center of their activities, asking how can we encourage and empower competencies and potentials in the individual, the working and business world, and society.

14.1.1 Wala Heilmittel GmbH

Founded by Dr. Hauschka in 1935, his vision was a company where people are at the heart of all corporate activities and profit is seen only as a means to an end. Today, the approach of Wala Heilmittel is marked by the conviction that no social or economic measure in itself has any significance. The company exists to fulfill the object of the owner foundation and cannot be bought, sold, or inherited like goods. The profit is only the means to an end, not an end in itself. The end is primarily the corporate development and the development of the employees to free individuals. Wala is a member of the German Association of Companies with employee co-ownership.

> Economy must serve mankind – not the other way around. Business is about fulfilling the needs of other human beings. E. g., the production of consumer goods can be seen as a social event. Only when particular selfish interests, e.g. those of shareholders, get in the way, this process is turned to the absurd and profits are not invested for the peoples' needs. Wala benefit from our entrepreneurial freedom. We initiated a project for the production of biological mango butter, providing a sustainable and independent life for the people in this region and, at the same time, offering an excellent biological product to our cosmetics customers that had not been on the market before. The price for this activity increase to tenfold, but we are deliberately willing to pay that price – for the benefit of each and everybody in the community of our business. If more companies were willing to start this new thinking, this would serve their clients and their business. Then companies were a means for fulfilling needs of others, profit nothing but a means to be invested. (Antal Adam, press officer Wala Heilmittel)

14.1.2 *Augenhoehe: Reinventing Organizations "On an Equal Footing"*

14.1.2.1 Searching for Fair Relationships and Cooperation

While organizations and their executives increasingly feel divided, demoralized, and exhausted, they are confronted with the downside of the run for efficiency, ratings, best performance appraisals, bonus policies, etc. Actually they personally and their staff understand that they are about to waste their human potentials.

In the past, large organizations have stabilized themselves with rational, logical management (long time after their passionate, entrepreneurial start), whereas today they need to energize themselves again with leadership, professional freedom, passion, connections, face-to-face communication, trust, and mutual support that they actually are hungry for.

Sennett (2012) takes a closer look at this history of industrialization, the age of life-changing scientific findings, at the disablers for previously incorporated forms of cooperation, and the challenges of the digital revolution. While we are yearning for relationship, trust, and human encounters in work, Sennett analyzes the need for contemporary cooperation as hard work: creating working environments, where people design their own cooperative forms of working together. Sennett claims that in order to be productive on this new level, people need to be well. Sennett claims that there are some professions that can, beyond all stereotype thinking, teach us the spirit and drivers of cooperation: social reformers, artists, social workers, scientific laboratories, and surgical teams, with their forms of cooperation to be looked at "with envy" (Sennett).

Workplaces are changing. Ever more individuals are searching for new ways for shaping their working environment by participation, by developing and delivering their potentials, and by creating fair relationships in the world of business. This eye-level movement is a network of organizations where each one is searching for their individual, best way to creating a new working culture of cooperation that is successfully serving the needs of the employees, their clients, the environment, and the society.

14.1.2.2 Unfreezing Potentials on Eye Level

How can organizations unfreeze their potential? Can we change our workplaces for the better, where everyone can feel and experience their best for the benefit of all? Yes, we can, says the Augenhoehe movement.

A member of the Augenhoehe movement framed the basis of this approach by saying: "Leaving the 20th century behind, I think we are ready and hungry to feel aliveness and connectedness – at work and at home." This is the basic belief of the eye-level movement: to show that it is possible to work at "eye level" in organizations. Another stakeholder in this new approach confirmed: "The heroes of our times are those who are willing to work at eye-level."

Many persons share this vision. But managers, executives, and leaders of organizations seem hesitant to apply anything that loosens their idea of control. Augenhoehe's encouraging approach claims that every organization already has most of the resources they need to evolve – they "just" need to find them and tap into their potential.

Organizations begin to appreciate that concept, but not its application. Tapping potential may require letting go of old certainties and comfortable positions. It means reevaluating beliefs and being open to dissent, other views, and it means change, maybe chaos, and entering the unknown, along with igniting the spark.

Hamel (2012), supporting this movement, understands his publication *What Matters Now* as an agenda for building organizations that can flourish in a world of diminished hopes, relentless change, and ferocious competition.

By today, managers, executives, leaders, and supervisors from diverse branches and organizations in business, education, and public services – from telecommunication and pharmaceutical business to retail stores and clinics – have taken the courage and are actively applying the ideas of this concept to their own organizations. They dare to let go of some control and climb down the pyramid. They encourage their employees to start moving and mingling – to exchange information and energy in an equal flow and be open to what emerges.

Practicing eye-level work in an organization is addressing the individual person and is centered around their needs for autonomy, participation, and potentials. These institutions and their staff have started "reinventing their organizations" from within.

14.1.3 Resourceful Humans and Human Resources

In line with the aforementioned eye-level movement, the German consultant and entrepreneur Heiko Fischer has launched an initiative for organizational change addressing the three core values that persons are searching in their work: democracy, participation, and autonomy. Drawing on these basic motives, each individual person's freedom and this concept of "resourceful humans" build on individuals' innate wish and competencies to contribute to clients' needs. First, Fischer argues against organizations' main objective to drive their own profit, which he would define as eventually unethical: "Making profit has never been the main goal of any business. Putting profits first and last, leads into unethical waters. We must ask ourselves: What kind of meaningful added value for the clients do we want to produce and what would be the appropriate yield so that we can finance that. Business serves humans and not the other way around."

The initiative presented its vision in "HR Innovation" (2014), a reader comprising the ideas of some 25 authors on how to substantially innovate corporate culture.

Activating the human potentials and putting the positive image of resourceful humans into the center of all organizational activities on all levels in all business areas would make specific departments for human resources obsolete, because each and every individual and each manager would put resourceful humans into the center of their very business activities each day.

14.1.4 Fair Finance: Sustainable Banking

"Does your bank invest in controversial weapons, child labour or dirty energy?" Fair Finance is promoting sustainable banking globally, seeking to foster sustainable banking globally, and, ideally, a self-reinforcing process will develop in which social, environmental, and economic standards are raised continuously, ultimately resulting in sustainable credits, investments, and asset management all over the world.

Fair Finance Banks

- Promote sustainable and transparent banking. They do not see any conflict between a focus on people and the planet and a good financial return.
- Believe that these two objectives reinforce each other in the long term.
- Believe that profit does not need to be at the expense of world's most pressing environmental problems.
- Finance organizations from organic food and farming businesses and pioneering renewable energy enterprises to recycling companies and nature conservation projects.
- Give loans to enterprises in the educational and cultural sector.

According to the world's global challenges, needs, business, and private clients' search for responsible investment, fair finance banks are growing steadily.

As Peter Blom from Triodos Bank (2016) explains:

> We support positive change by and for people. We connect depositors with borrowers, investors with sustainable ventures and businesses so they in turn can create value in the real economy. We do this against a background of a low-interest environment, and much social and economic debate. Increasingly, communities and not governments take action to improve the world around them. People believe less and less in a 'global solution'. In many parts of the world they therefore choose their own solutions for dealing with renewable energy generation, access to sustainable housing and food. As a bank firmly rooted in the community and with a resilient result we are able to finance an increasing number of these initiatives and grow our positive impact.

The recently established Fair Finance Guide International (FFGI) is an international civil society network initiated by Oxfam that seeks to strengthen the commitment of banks and other financial institutions to social, environmental, and human rights standards.

FFGI builds on a pioneering model developed in the Netherlands since 2009, which was followed by a similar initiative in Brazil in 2011, both of which demonstrated leverage and potential for bringing about change. FFGI is currently active in eight countries: Belgium, Brazil, France, Germany, Indonesia, Japan, the Netherlands, and Sweden. In every country, a coalition of civil society groups, with expertise in areas relevant to monitoring and assessing the financial sector, operates under the umbrella of FFGI. FFGI coalitions often include development and human rights organizations, labor unions, environmental groups, and consumer organizations. Currently, 34 civil society organizations are running Fair Finance Guides in 8 countries.

14.2 Meeting Staff Members' Needs

Persons in twenty-first-century workplaces are trained and educated with an inclusive sense of the benefits of their human rights and global diversity.

Thomas Sattelberger (2015), international management consultant and engaged in promoting New Work, defines the five focus points that every organization is challenged by in dealing with the changing environment and the individual staff members' needs:

- Democracy in designing and managing modern workplaces – in this concept, today's members of staff are rather company citizens than employees.
- Sovereignty of the individual – acknowledging each individual person's will to freedom in defining their own lives.
- Solidarity – taking the common good into account and caring for the needy ones.
- Autonomy – of the individual person to co-create the place, time, content, and processes of their work.
- Diversity – acknowledging, accepting, and integrating each individual person's ideas, values, way of thinking and seeing the world, lifestyle, and perceptions.

Implementing this concept in organizations has just started, and it will be a challenging process that is not designed for quick wins and easy solutions but rather incorporates all the knowledge that we have by today about the human capacity to pursue a common good for the benefit of all and to be an active part of this community.

References

Augenhoehe On an Equal Footing (2015) Film. OV with English subtitles, VIMEO
Bergmann F (1977) On being free. University of Notre Dame Press, Notre Dame
Bergmann F (1990) An Interview with Frithjof Bergmann. J Int Inst 6(2), Winter 1999
Bergmann F (2004) New work new culture. Create Space Independent Publishing Platform: flow zone edition
Bergmann F (2012) New work, new culture an interview with Frithjof Bergmann, by Sarah van Gelder, boggscenter.org. Accessed July 2017

Fair Finance Guide International. https://fairfinanceguide.org. Accessed 11 Nov 2017
German Government, Federal Ministry of Labour and Social Affairs (2015/2017) White and green paper. http://www.arbeitenviernull.de
Hamel G (2012) What matters now: how to win in a world of relentless change, ferocious competition and unstoppable innovation. Jossey-Bass, San Francisco
Sattelberger Th, Welpe I, Boes A (2015) Das demokratische Unternehmen: Neue Arbeits- und Führungskulturen im Zeitalter digitaler Wirtschaft
Sennett R (2012) Together: the rituals, pleasures and politics of cooperation. Yale University Press, New Haven
TRIODOS Bank (2016) Half-year figures. TRIODOS half year report 2016. Zeist

Chapter 15
Values: A "New Surge of Responsibleness" Arising

Contents

> In an age in which the Ten Commandments are losing their unconditional validity in the eyes of many people, man must be equipped with the capacity to listen to and obey the ten thousand demands and commandments hidden in the ten thousand situations with which life is confronting him. And it is these demands that are revealed to him by an alert conscience…What leaders may give, however, is an example, the existential example of personal commitment to the search for truth…In these examples I see a growing concern with other people in a planetary level, an increased sense of worldwide solidarity...I venture to predict here and now the surge of a new sense of responsibleness. (Frankl 2000)

All current management approaches and considerations on the best roads to shape our future for positive change are addressing man's responsibility of being the core active part in this venture.

Participating in shaping one's own present and future is not only a matter of the need for some sense of coherence and of the need to control and influence one's personal life. Especially in today's world, where too many individuals feel overwhelmed, victimized rather than energized, the responsibility of integrating each individual with their own innate search for meaning is "the demand quality" of today's challenges, the task of the moment, with life questioning us and we are giving the answer.

Various values-oriented concepts are addressing and acknowledging mankind's best potentials. We need to draw public attention to these powerful resources in order "to ignite the spark" that can change the world just as much as changes have been initiated in the past by individuals, groups, and larger communities drawing on humanity's best values and competencies.

B. von Devivere, *Meaningful Work: Viktor Frankl's Legacy for the 21st Century*,
https://doi.org/10.1007/978-3-319-89791-2_15

15.1 Character Strengths and Virtues

Peterson's and Seligman's concept of global virtues and strengths is suggesting a powerful, encouraging, and resourceful look on each and every single individual person's best potentials to be acknowledged, integrated, valued, and respected in organizations and communities.

Together with positive psychology's search for drivers for human flourishing, Peterson and Seligman developed the *Character Strengths and Virtues: A Handbook and Classification* (Peterson and Seligman 2004). Their handbook represents the most ambitious project, intended for supporting and developing psychological well-being, where the *Diagnostic and Statistical Manual of Mental Disorders* (*DSM*) of the American Psychiatric Association is defining the psychological disorders, describing the disabling conditions of human beings in their search for a good life.

Peterson's and Seligman's handbook (2004) focuses on and classifies strengths and virtues that enable human thriving. Today, this handbook of each individual in the global community with the potential to shape a better world is available in more than 20 languages and the Virtues in Action (VIA) Institute on character is delivering services for human flourishing to organizations and persons throughout the global community.

These are the human potentials that Peterson and Seligman have found across cultures, incorporating their respective diverse and rich legends and myths, their cultures and values, their understanding of humanity and human capacities for becoming, what and who they are, where they come from, and where they can go at their best.

The general scheme of the character strengths and virtues (CSV) relies on six overarching virtues that almost every culture across the world endorses: wisdom, courage, humanity, justice, temperance, and transcendence.

These signature strengths include the following strengths and virtues in detail:

Appreciation of beauty and excellence [awe, wonder, elevation]: Noticing and appreciating beauty, excellence, and/or skilled performance in all domains of life, from nature to art to mathematics to science to everyday experience

Bravery [valor]: *Not* shrinking from threat, challenge, difficulty, or pain; speaking up for what is right even if there is opposition; acting on convictions even if unpopular; includes physical bravery, but is not limited to it

Citizenship [social responsibility, loyalty, teamwork]: Working well as a member of a group or team; being loyal to the group; doing one's share

Creativity [originality, ingenuity]: Thinking of novel and productive ways to do things; includes artistic achievement but is not limited to it

Curiosity [interest, novelty-seeking, openness to experience]: Taking an interest in all of ongoing experience; finding all subjects and topics fascinating; exploring and discovering

Fairness: Treating all people the same according to notions of fairness and justice; *not* letting personal feelings bias decisions about others; giving everyone a fair chance

Forgiveness and mercy: Forgiving those who have done wrong; giving people a second chance; *not* being vengeful

Gratitude: Being aware of and thankful for the good things that happen; taking time to express thanks

Hope [optimism, future-mindedness, future orientation]: Expecting the best in the future and working to achieve it; believing that a good future is something that can be brought about

Humor [playfulness]: Liking to laugh and tease; bringing smiles to other people; seeing the light side; making (not necessarily telling) jokes

Integrity [authenticity, honesty]: Speaking the truth but more broadly presenting oneself in a genuine way; being without pretense; taking responsibility for one's feelings and actions

Judgment [open-mindedness, critical thinking]: Thinking things through and examining them from all sides; *not* jumping to conclusions; being able to change one's mind in light of evidence; weighing all evidence fairly

Kindness [generosity, nurturance, care, compassion, altruistic love, "niceness"]: Doing favors and good deeds for others; helping them; taking care of them

Leadership: Encouraging a group of which one is a member to get things done and at the same time maintaining good relations within the group; organizing group activities and seeing that they happen

Love: Valuing close relations with others, in particular those in which sharing and caring are reciprocated; being close to people

Love of learning: Mastering new skills, topics, and bodies of knowledge, whether on one's own or formally; obviously related to the strength of curiosity but goes beyond it to describe the tendency to add *systematically* to what one knows

Modesty and humility: Letting one's accomplishments speak for themselves; *not* seeking the spotlight; *not* regarding oneself as more special than one is

Persistence [perseverance, industriousness]: Finishing what one starts; persisting in a course of action in spite of obstacles; "getting it out the door"; taking pleasure in completing tasks

Perspective [wisdom]: Being able to provide wise counsel to others; having ways of looking at the world that make sense to oneself and to other people

Prudence: Being careful about one's choices; *not* taking undue risks; *not* saying or doing things that might later be regretted

Self-regulation [self-control]: Regulating what one feels and does; being disciplined; controlling one's appetites and emotions

Social intelligence [emotional intelligence, personal intelligence]: Being aware of the motives and feelings of other people and oneself; knowing what to do to fit in to different social situations; knowing what makes other people tick

Spirituality [religiousness, faith, purpose]: Having coherent beliefs about the higher purpose and meaning of the universe; knowing where one fits within the larger scheme; having beliefs about the meaning of life that shape conduct and provide comfort

Zest [vitality, enthusiasm, vigor, energy]: Approaching life with excitement and energy; *not* doing things halfway or halfheartedly; living life as an adventure; feeling alive and activated

Peterson and Seligman (2004) have discovered a remarkable similarity in the relative endorsement of these 24 character strengths by adults around the world (Seligman et al. 2005). According to their research, the most commonly endorsed ("most like me") strengths, in 40 different countries around the globe and across nations, are kindness, fairness, authenticity, gratitude, and open-mindedness, and the strengths less but still consistently reported include prudence, modesty, and self-regulation. The correlations of the rankings from nation to nation are very strong and defy general cultural, ethnic, and religious differences.

The study of character strengths at work has rapidly increased in the last several years. Consultants, executives, human resource professionals, and managers are actively engaging in promoting character strengths and virtues on all levels of their organizations, i.e., executive management level, teams, and individual staff. The use of character strengths to improve their skills, performance, and health has emerged as a popular and successful avenue.

Increased attention is given to the organizational antecedents for strengths use, such as organizational support, personal initiative, autonomy, and development opportunities (Bakker and van Woerkom 2017).

Mayerson (2015) reports on studies relating to "characterizing" the workplace, using character strengths to create sustained success: human energy resources become more sustainable when work environments enable employees to experience engagement, meaning, and positive relationships in ways that don't diminish the same in others. Companies that provide employees with more of a sense of purpose far outperform the composite returns of the Standard and Poor's 500 companies. Mayerson concludes: "The time has come to humanize our organizations."

Research (reported by Mayerson) shows what organizations can do to support staff's individual sense of competence and fulfillment. It takes this systemic and systematic approach to not exploit or exhaust individual person's search for defining and experiencing their best:

- Strengths alignment – Job Sculpting Based on Character Strength: Profiles: People like to do things that they can do well. It imparts a sense of competence that feels good. But, people also like to do what they *care to* do well. Strengths of character translate into intrinsic motivation and engagement. Doing what one cares to do engenders a sense of fulfillment, while failure to take character strengths into account runs the risk of experiencing a syndrome of "success without satisfaction." This is what Frankl had diagnosed as the existential vacuum.
- Strengths appreciation – Enhancing Working Relationships: Organizations with a positive, strengths-based culture supports creativity, job satisfaction, and mutual appreciation.
- Creating a virtues-based balanced board construction.
- Systematically building an organizational culture of strengths, not as a one-off exercise, but rather as a systematic process.

- Transparently and on all levels, starting with the C-suite, establishing new habits of reflecting on the best virtues and strengths of all stakeholders is finally bringing to life "a moral compass for companies" (Mayerson), based on humanity's overarching virtues.

Defining the very personal character strengths, applying and developing them in work and private life, and getting active on the most effective interventions to strengthen and nourish these personal strengths do not only add to a personal sense of leading a meaningful life but also build the global community of a shared sense of the best virtues and strengths in mankind.

Benefiting from this handbook of *Character Strengths and Virtues* and finding out about some of the best individual competencies and values could add substantially to a sense of autonomy and to improving workplace atmosphere. At the same time, engaging in developing these individual strengths needs a workplace culture of respect and encouragement for the givers, who want to give their best and contribute to the common cause by actively introducing their own virtues and values into their daily work by the following practices:

- Using signature strengths in a new way and the daily exercise of writing down three good things that had happened, what the causes of these events were and what feelings and emotions were connected with these events, help persons to focus on their creative and experiential values.
- Another exercise, the gratitude visit, reflecting on positive events with another person's decisive support and personally saying thanks to this person, gives a powerful example of bringing meaning to the own work life and changing the workplace atmosphere for the better.

Ruch (2007) from the University of Zurich confirmed in his studies that training character strengths increases personal well-being. The largest impact was evident in training the strengths "curiosity," "gratitude," "optimism," "humor," and "enthusiasm." This manifested itself in the fact that study participants were more cheerful or more often in a good mood. People training their character strengths learned to control their actions and feelings more effectively and developed more enthusiasm.

Harzer and Ruch (2014) and Ruch and Proyer (2015) report on the positive link between character strengths, task performance, and coping with work-related stress.

Further developing positive psychology, Pennock and Alberts (2017) are defining important practitioners' skills for giving best support to their clients, among them encouraging each person's self-acceptance as the basis of all well-being. In this sense, self-acceptance is unconditional and not based on any evaluation against some type of supposed or external standard. Pennock and Alberts critically notice that some interventions refer to "the best possible self," suggesting some other, future best possible version of the self. If not introduced with care, any exercises suggested on developing character strengths or virtues could be interpreted as suggested exercises on improving the self and finally nurture lack of self-acceptance. In the end, cultivating self-acceptance is the starting point of all activities, which bring character strengths and virtues to a life of "psychological well-being" (as opposed to subjective well-being) of meaning and self-efficacy.

When implemented carefully, raising awareness about and practicing individual character strengths in the workplace, this approach may be a powerful way to bring about positive change for all stakeholders in an organization. Among a great variety of practices, training, offered by VIA (Virtues in Action) Institute, follows the three phases of aware–explore–apply. In VIA training, also offered online, Niemiec (2013) gives information about the scientific background of the character strengths approach, followed by an assessment of the individual character and signature strengths and the sensitive area of overuse and underuse of own strengths. The crucial phase relates to intentionally and mindfully applying the strengths in the workplace in joint action.

15.2 Good Work: When Meaning, Responsibility, and Conscience Meet

In his research, Gardner (2008 and 2015) is applying Frankl's concept of self-transcendence in work to the current situations and observations regarding ethical versus irresponsible, unethical behaviors in business.

Together with his fellow researchers, for more than a decade now, the developmental psychologist, scholar, and public intellectual Howard Gardner has been studying the nature of "good work." Initially, Gardner was concerned about his observations of more and more experts from all fields, going about their business in a selfish way, unconcerned with the common good. His research aim was to understand, whether one could be individually creative and humane at the same time and, if so, how.

According to Gardner et al. (2002), good work is an individual decision. Ethics are an indispensable ingredient of good work. The ethical person says "I am an X–what are my responsibilities as an X?" It is easy to claim acting responsibly when that serves the self-interest. The "acid test" for responsibility is when you do the right thing, even though it goes against your "self-interest" (Gardner). Wong (2012) also relates to the term 'good work' in his three-dimensional approach.

From these observations, Gardner is defining three E's and three M's establishing "good work."

15.2.1 *The Three E's*

When the fundamentals of good work

- Excellence
- Engagement
- Ethics

are in harmony, individuals can lead personally fulfilling and socially rewarding lives. In reality, however, this balance is never totally achieved; rather it is something that we should strive to achieve perennially. The challenge of good work is to keep all three of the E's alive, not just to be excellent technically, not just to be personally engaged, but to do both of these things while also behaving in an ethical, responsible way. As Gardner argues, this is a process involving the very human being in new, demanding situations, calling for the right and conscientious decision in the very moment: "None of us is ethical all the time, and probably none of us is as ethical as we could be. But the ethical person reflects on his mis-steps, tries to learn from them, and does his best to correct his course next time" (Gardner).

15.2.2 The Three M's

In the process of delivering good work, Gardner recommends the administration of three activities, each beginning with the letter *M:*

- Mission: What is the mission that I am trying to carry out in my work? Is it accordant with the mission of my peers, and, if not, what can I do about it?
- Model: Who are the individuals whom I admire and why? Do I turn to them effectively when I am uncertain about what to do? What lessons can I learn from antimentors, or tormentors? And if I have no single mentor, can I cobble together a viable model – a so-called frag-mentor?
- Mirror test (personal): When I hold up the mirror to my own professional work, and peer into it clearly (without squinting or distorting), am I proud of what I see? If my mother were to read in the newspaper about all that I've done, would she be pleased or ashamed? And if I do not pass the mirror test, what am I going to do about it?
- Mirror test (professional): When I hold up the mirror to my fellow professionals, am I proud or ashamed of what I see? If I am proud, am I doing my part? And if I am ashamed, what can I do to confirm the core values of the profession and, if possible, to steer it into a healthier, more aligned condition? Should I seek to become a trustee of my profession?

Whether we are 10, 50, or 100 years of age, good work is never fully achieved and never totally beyond reach. Indeed, it is better described as a continuing process of education – self-education and education by others – than as a onetime or lifetime achievement.

Ultimately, it is up to the individual, whether they strive to be seen as a good worker.

15.3 Prosocial Impact of Work and Meaningful Occupations

Across cultures, benefiting others is a deeply held, widely shared core value in life (Schwartz and Bardi 2001) and at work across jobs and industries. C. Michaelson et al. (2014) report on studies that point to the human quest for meaning and inherent self-transcendence.

Studies have examined the effects of directly connecting employees to the prosocial impact of their work. In a field experiment with pool lifeguards, those who read stories about other lifeguards rescuing drowning swimmers perceived their work as having greater impact on and value to swimmers; those who read no stories about the personal benefits of the job showed no increases in perceptions of prosocial impact and value. In another experiment, reminding patients of the consequences of hand hygiene for other patients – opposed to the benefits for themselves – increased their soap and gel usage and behavioral compliance, whereas reminding them of the personal gains did not. This evidence demonstrates how a mere story, photograph, or mention of a beneficiary can contribute to making prosocial impact more concrete and motivating the individual person in the work they are doing.

Other mindfulness exercises are drawing attention to mindfully remember and envisage all those that contributed to our daily goods, from having warm water to producing the specific shower system, to acknowledging the farmers' work in consuming the morning cereals over thinking of those workers who designed the individual car, assembled and put together the pieces up to recognizing the cleaning staff who provide for bright windows and clean desks, etc.

There is, though, a caveat to be acknowledged: those persons working in objectively "meaningful" occupations and functions in health care, education, or public service functions are highly endangered to unsustainably sacrifice their own personal needs for the greater good. Here again, the right organizational and management approaches in assuring the best prosocial impact of the services for all stakeholders, including the individual service provider, are even more important.

Along with these discussions goes increased awareness about the potential dark side of organizations demanding engagement for meaningful work, eventually rationalizing top-down manipulative and even unethical behaviors in the name of providing meaning.

Recent studies among young high potentials from Germany confirmed a "shift in awareness" (Rump and Eilers 2012) among these young professionals, wishing to take responsibility in social and societal initiatives with their search for meaning as primary motive for working. Ruch explains that this generation is very well aware that they could not cope and be productive over a lifetime span of decades of work, unless their work and the conditions were meaningful and fulfilling. Consequently, they share the common conviction that every person can make some positive contribution to society as a whole, putting meaning in work over personal status. In his study, Professor Hurrelmann (2016) from Hertie School of Governance in Berlin calls today's young professionals "the silent revolutionaries" (book title), whom he characterizes with their basic beliefs of anti-materialism, down-shifting, and a new environmental consciousness have long started to change education and the overall working culture in organizations.

15.4 Meaningful Organizations: Organizational Character

Organizational research (C. Michaelson et al. 2014) indicates that "meaningful work" is associated with products and outcomes that employees value, leading to enhanced job satisfaction, engagement, well-being, better job performance, and customer satisfaction.

There are intensive discussions and literature in business, consulting, research, and business practice about the nature and extent of the responsibility of organizations to actively foster meaning in and at work and, equally, the responsibility of individuals to continually and actively engage in work that they perceive as significant and meaningful.

In 2016, the New York-based "Academy for Management" organized a conference on "Making Meaningful Organizations." Today, the Academy has over 19,000 members from nearly 120 nations. In their call for papers, they described the present situation:

organizations occupy a central role in the ways we live our lives, for better and for worse. We often take as given that an organization's purpose is to produce economic value; and, although economic value can often add to social value, sometimes it does not. This disjuncture raises the question of what meaningful organizations actually are.

The meaningfulness of an organization is its expression of purpose, values, or worth. It involves a sense of significance that goes beyond material success or profitability; rather, it highlights how organizations can play a larger and more positive role in the world. It is an approach embraced by the next generation of workers, the millennials (in their mid-to-late 30s), who often focus on making a positive difference in the world and a contribution to society – with organizations, not in spite of them.

Interest in meaningfulness has grown, fueled in part by developments in cognitive perspectives, cultural approaches to organizational resources, positive outlooks on realizing human potential at work, institutional insights on leadership dynamics, new modes of communication that are social, digitalized and immediate, and the real-world failures of the dominant economic model. Making organizations meaningful matters, and it matters in a multitude of ways that are both immediate and far-reaching, ranging from environmental sustainability to social equality and extending across multiple levels of analysis. Meaningfulness at micro levels alerts us to engaging employees in work so as to maximize human potential, and at macro levels, it turns attention to organizational identity, culture, reputation, legitimacy, and character.

By looking across levels, we can discover mechanisms that potentially amplify or even mute meaningfulness, as well as meaninglessness. What are the mechanisms – political, economic, social, cultural, or institutional – which situate and produce organizational meaningfulness?

Organizations influence meaningfulness by:

- Engaging in meaningfulness *in* working practices that change what employees actually do.
- Engaging in meaningfulness *at* work practices that shape the context within which the work is performed. Examples of “meaningfulness in working” practices include job design, employee involvement practices, and leadership, where leaders remove obstacles from worker’s “path” and thus free them to get their work done. “Meaningfulness at work” practices include attempts to provide visionary leadership whereby leaders imbue work with greater meaningfulness by articulating an inspiring vision and linking it to shared values.

References

Academy for Management. Journal, published six times per year. Briarcliff, New York

Bakker AB, van Woerkom M (2017) Strengths use in organizations: a positive approach of occupational health. Can Psychol 59:38–46. https://doi.org/10.1037/cap0000120

Frankl VE (2000) Man’s search for ultimate meaning. Basic Books, Cambridge

Gardner H (2008) Tanner lectures on human values. University of Utah, Salt Lake City. https://tannerlectures.utah.edu/_documents/a-to-z/g/Gardner_08.pdf. Accessed 30 Apr 2017

Gardner H (2015) Good work. The focus magazine. Egon Zehnder, Frankfurt am Main

Gardner H, Csikszentmihalyi M, Damon W (2002) Good work. When excellence and ethics meet. Basic Books, New York

Harzer C, Ruch W (2014) The role of character strengths for task performance, job dedication, interpersonal facilitation, and organizational support. Hum Perform 27:183–205

Harzer C, Ruch W (2015) The relationships of character strengths with coping, work-related stress and job satisfaction. Front Psychol 6:165. https://doi.org/10.3389/fpsyg.2015.00165

Hurrelmann K (2016) Die heimlichen Revolutionäre: Wie die Generation Y unsere Welt verändert. Beltz Verlag, Weinheim

Mayerson N (2015) “Characterizing” the workplace: using character strengths to create sustained success. VIA Institute. Viacharacter.org. Accessed Dec 2017

MEP S, Steen TA, Park N, Peterson C (2005) Positive psychology in progress. Empirical validation of interventions. Am Psychol 60:410–421

Michaelson C, Pratt MG, Grant AM, Dunn CP (2014) Meaningful work: connecting business ethics and organization studies. J Bus Ethics 121:77–90

Niemiec RM (2013) VIA character strengths: research and practice (The first 10 years). In: Knoop HH, Delle Fave A (eds) Well-being and cultures: perspectives on positive psychology. Springer, New York, pp 11–30

Pennock SF Alberts H (2017) 8 positive psychology coaching skills to put on your resume in 2017. https://positivepsychologyprogram.com/positive-psychology-coaching-skills/. Accessed 20 Aug 2017

Peterson C, Seligman MEP (2004) Character strengths and virtues: a handbook and classification. Oxford University Press, New York

Ruch W (2007) The sense of humor: explorations of a personality characteristic. Mouton de Gruyter, Berlin

Ruch W, Proyer TR (2015) Mapping strengths into virtues: the relation of the 24 VIA-strengths to six ubiquitous virtues. In: Frontiers in Psychology 6:460. https://doi.org/10.3389/fpsyg.2015.00460

Rump J, Eilers S (2012) Die jüngere Generation in einer alternden Arbeitswelt – Baby Boomer versus Generation Y. Verlag Wissenschaft und Praxis, Sternenfels

Schwartz SH, Bardi A (2001) Value hierarchies across cultures: taking a similarities perspective. J Cross Cult Psychol 32(3):268–290

VIA Institute on Character. viainstitute.org

Wong PTP (2012) Spiritualilty, meaning and good work. In: Wong PTP, Wong LJC, Mc Donald MJ, Klaassen DW (eds) The positive psychology of meaning and spirituaity: selected papers from meaning conferences. Purpose Research, Alabama, pp 353–358

Chapter 16
Leadership: Taking Responsibility

Contents

> *There are two specifically human phenomena by which human existence is characterized. The first is constituted by man's capacity for self-detachment. Another capacity of man is that for self-transcendence. In fact, it is a constitutive characteristic of being human, that it always points and is directed to something other than itself…Only to the extent that someone is living out this self transcendence of human existence, is he truly human or does he become his true self.* (V. Frankl)

16.1 Addressing the Diamond in the Rough

For many decades, employees have identified meaningful work as the most important feature that they seek out in a job – ahead of income, job security, and promotions – and a primary source of purpose, of belonging to the organization, and of identity. The search for meaning in management, in leadership, in exercising

B. von Devivere, *Meaningful Work: Viktor Frankl's Legacy for the 21st Century*,
https://doi.org/10.1007/978-3-319-89791-2_16

influence top-down, and generally in the workplace has become ubiquitous. Seventy percent of the engagement employees feel at work is attributable to their manager. Frankl (1984) elaborates on the link between dedication to a task, individual conscience, and success ensuing:

> *Don't aim at success. The more you aim at it and make it a target, the more you are going to miss it. For success, like happiness, cannot be pursued; it must ensue, and it only does so as the unintended side effect of one's personal dedication to a cause greater than oneself or as the by-product of one's surrender to a person other than oneself. Happiness must happen, and the same holds for success: you have to let it happen by not caring about it. I want you to listen to what your conscience commands you to do and go on to carry it out to the best of your knowledge. Then you will live to see that in the long-run—in the long-run, I say!—success will follow you precisely because you had forgotten to think about it.* (Frankl 1984, p 16)

There are two major roads of answering twenty-first century's call for new leadership: addressing the individual person leading as the only entity for creating change and the impact that the individual person has for organizations for creating transformational change.

16.1.1 Being Directed to Someone Other Than the Self

Searching for "meaningful leadership" in Google produces 135,000 hits in just seconds.

Since decades, scientists, organizational psychologists, and practitioners from all types of organizations have been searching for what a leader and leadership is about. Over time, various models have emerged. Personality traits, behaviors, and practices of managers and leaders were assessed. Simultaneously, issues and concepts of "servant leadership," of "authentic leadership," and of "transformational leadership" were – together with the accelerated dynamics and persistency of global crisis – increasingly coming to the fore. Starting from the last century's early 1960s, there has been a clear development in the focus of awareness regarding different leadership approaches and styles to be assessed and understood more closely.

Blake and Mouton (1972) based their model more on the behaviors demonstrated by the respective leader and her staff. Their model is still being referred to until today, suggesting five different leadership styles, depending on leaders' concern for people and employees' concern for goal achievement. The integrated leadership model (Scouller 2011) claimed to bring together the more traits or behavior-oriented models of leadership by defining three levels of leadership, i.e., the public, private and personal, and inner level of leadership. The ontological-phenomenological model of leadership, defined by Werner Erhard and others (2012), suggests leaders demonstrating not only an awareness about the future but actually relating to the deep and fundamental concerns of the relevant parties. Assessing the difference between managers and leaders, John O'Leary (2016) concludes that managers' behaviors dominantly center on the manager, "doing things right."

According to these concepts, leadership behaviors focus on the staff, trusting, engaging, motivating, and empowering people, this being the crucial difference to managers, focusing on their doing the right things.

These definitions and empirical observations of demonstrated leadership are clearly indicating a self-transcending approach of individuals in exercising their respective executive function in turning their attention and dedication to others.

In a recent study of leaders' behaviors and of the academic literature, McKinsey found core leaders' behaviors, among them listening to others, seeking different perspectives, and supporting others.

In 2014, McKinsey published a series of interviews with executive managers on "Leading in the 21st century," interviewing them about their practices and behaviors to meet their current and future challenges. Leaders interviewed described these essentials for their own behaviors: awareness of the context of being "aware of all the seductions – money, sexual, praise, status – that come with taking on a leadership role," resisting these temptations, and keeping integrity, a general state of being and awareness: are you entirely present when you are present, and are you entirely away when you are away?

16.1.2 Igniting Engagement

> *How is a company responsible? Should it profit its shareholders, provide for the well-being of its employees, make excellent products, be a good force in the community, and protect nature? We think that a responsible company bears all these obligations.* (Patagonia 2012)

It was only in 1990 that William Kahn (1990) introduced the concept of employee engagement of explaining that employees unconsciously assess each situation at work and from their assessment they draw their conclusions on engaging or disengaging, asking themselves three questions that touch on three relevant areas of work life and managerial behavior:

- Psychological meaningfulness: A sense that their work was worthwhile and made a difference
- Psychological safety: A feeling that they were valued, accepted, respected, and able to perform in a positive work environment
- Availability: Routinely feeling secure and self-confident while possessing the emotional and psychological energies to perform their job

Until today, executives' understanding of what practices truly drive their employee engagement is the prerequisite for leadership, as differentiated from exercising managerial functions. For demonstrating credible leadership behavior in the organization and toward their employees, all three areas can be addressed and influenced by executives' very influence, power, and authority in the organization. It is this organizational context that executives have the best access to. Consequently, exercising leadership in these dynamic times is dealing with leaders' awareness and potential practices to influence engagement in these areas and to avoid employee disengagement.

16.1.3 Entering the Realm of Freedom

Between stimulus and response there is a space. In that space is our power to choose our response. In our response lies our growth and our freedom. (Frankl)

As a doctor, professor, scientist, and holocaust survivor, Frankl witnessed the human evidence of our unique ability to "self-detach," that is, look at ourselves from a distance. Today, self-detachment has become part of common sense management and coaching: taking a third perspective, looking at own thoughts, feelings, and behaviors from a detached perspective, has proved to discover potentials and resources unknown before, to tap into own imaginations and turn them into powerful drivers for personal encouragement and flourishing, which, as Frankl (1984) has described in *Man's Search for Meaning*, can be life-saving.

More and more leadership concepts are relating to the individual person's world views, thinking, underlying mind-sets, and beliefs: organizations do not change – people do. Executives are claiming to act as role models for their employees in supporting or driving change in the larger organizations. Accordingly, leadership approaches are focusing on the inward and only from there taking the outward perspective.

The inward-looking approach examines own modes of thinking and behaving, how reality is reflected in the heart and mind. Understanding that a person can lead a whole life without understanding their inner drivers and dynamics, the inward-looking impacts on self-understanding and the respective behaviors. This inward perspective focuses on two human capacities.

- Developing "state awareness," the real-time perception of a wide range of inner experiences, also referred to as the "inner observer." This entity may, being trained adequately, guide the individual through a state of "instinctive" internal reactions being acted out immediately, to a more conscious state of potential best behaviors. Referring to the inner observer expands the diversity of a person's potentials to be demonstrated. This is the realm of freedom each individual has access to.
- Accepting our multiplicity, from an understanding that each person is "all in one." Although many organizations are claiming to successfully assess individuals according to their types, traits, and preferences, observers from various realms of psychology, management, and those being assessed are noting that these assessments again are limiting the person and their potentials. We all possess the full range of qualities being identified in relevant tests. Actually, we show up quite differently in various contexts, situations, and roles, here exercising leadership versus there being bored out or frustrated and here being hopeful and positive versus there being reserved or overemotional. Today's leadership concepts are recognizing this individual complexity, opening up an unlimited space of self-discovery of the multifaceted, and reach personality of each individual and a new realm of freedom and responsibility to act on it.

Today, many executives are practicing meditation. There has been, until today, an evident variety of various meditation approaches and meditating practices, defined by cultural and religious background, personal and individual preferences, and also availability of respective trainings and courses. Meditation practices are definitely not limited to a specific approach.

Those executives practicing meditation have consistently reported some of the following impacts, changing their lives and their executive behaviors and perspectives likewise:

- Self-awareness and self-regulation, being described as "muscles" being trained with the effect of regaining a "mental space" and being more aware in case of slipping into old habits.
- Taking positives from the negative: This impact is dealing with first understanding own feelings of disappointment, frustration, and potential resentment of others and then taking a different attitude to these emotions, assessing them in the context of the situation rather than rejecting them. One leader described this effect: "There was more space between me and the emotional reaction that I would have had earlier. I was able to respond in a different manner and thereby not allow myself or others to be consumed by it."
- Focusing on others: Actually changing the focus from "What's in it for me?" to reflecting a situation from more angles, including more of how the situation will affect other people and the environment in which we live and of what is right or fair.

16.2 Transformational Leadership: Overcoming Self-Interest

Being human always points, and is directed, to something or someone, other than oneself--be it a meaning to fulfill or another human being to encounter. (V. Frankl)

In his approach on "leading with meaning," Adam Grant (2012) from the University of Pennsylvania puts together meaning and exercising transformational leadership by engaging, motivating, and empowering.

Together with a strong focus on values and business mission, Grant has dedicated his research on questioning how self-interest and compromising values could be overcome by an approach of "transformational leadership."

Grant (2012) conceptualizes transformational leadership by four dimensions of leader behavior demonstrated. "By engaging in these transformational behaviors, leaders seek to motivate employees to look beyond…enabling followers to view their work as more meaningful and influencing followers' perceptions through two broad sets of strategies, i. e. (i) providing messages that frame and reframe the meaning of the followers' work and (ii) actually restructuring responsibilities to change and alter the meaning of the work" (Grant p. 459f).

Leaders are engaging along these four dimensions:

- Inspirational motivation
- Idealized influence
- Intellectual stimulation
- Individualized consideration

Core behaviors of this type of leadership are, besides articulating a compelling vision and emphasizing collective identities, expressing confidence and optimism and referencing core values and ideas. Evidence suggests that when leaders engage in these behaviors, individual employees experience their work as more meaningful.

Grant concludes that "employees are most likely to perceive a transformational leader's vision as credible when it conveys behavioral integrity – a connection between words and deeds" (Grant p 460). Consequently, a leader is being understood and perceived according to her behaviors in all realms of their life.

At its core, transformational leadership strives to highlight the prosocial impact of the organization and what meaningful impact it has for others.

This prosocial impact is most tangible when employees have vivid, proximal exposure to the human beings affected by their contribution. Consequently, even when employees are responsible for a "meaningful" task as such, they gain a stronger awareness of its prosocial impact when they have direct contact with the beneficiary, enabling them to see the tangible, meaningful consequences of their action for a living, breathing person.

Research has shown that protecting and promoting the well-being of other people is the most important value to the majority of people in the majority of the world's cultures (Schwartz and Bardi, 2001).

More and more individuals are wondering what impact their work has on a global scale. So, the question is how can this direct contact with beneficiaries be achieved in this world of global business? What are the potential limitations in quality and quantity to the prosocial impact for producing specific goods and financial transactions?

So far, some research and creativity have been organized to give examples for organizing these beneficiary contacts of employees with their counter clients: call center employees responsible for acquiring university funding meet a student who in person told his life-changing story after getting a university grant; funds acquired went up. Radiologists in a clinic met their patients in an intensive face-to-face dialogue; their expert reports were much more detailed and specific.

Transformational leadership is about exercising behavioral integrity: employees are most likely to perceive a transformational leader as credible when the leaders display behavioral integrity, a connection between words and deeds, and when they provide for a credible link between the rhetoric of prosocial impact and the reality of meaningful consequences for clients, customers, children, students, patients, etc. This information highlighting the prosocial impact of work is more compelling when delivered by the beneficiaries.

Transformational leadership can organize this connectivity by redesigning company structures and the processes, so that employees can actually "make sense" of their work. While in the past, existing research has more focused on how leadership is exercised for developing self-efficacy and social identification *within* the workplace, this approach is focused on perceiving real time the social impact for the beneficiaries *outside* their very own business environment.

With the megatrends, global crisis and the existential vacuum experienced in today's workplaces, transformational leadership indeed provides for a clear road in search for meaning on the individual, the management, and the organizational level. Interpreting these findings, we find plenty of products where the international community has defined specific positive criteria for prosocial impact of products. In all areas of organizational leadership and in research, increasing attention is given for how to manage the "Copernican turn."

16.3 When People Identify with a Purpose Greater Than Themselves

> *Thus far, we have run organizations on rigid templates, fearing evolution's messy and uncontrollable nature, Perhaps we are getting ready for the big leap...Ready to open the doors of life. Ready to invite evolution...We seek wholeness beyond ego...We define a life well-lived by inner, not outer standards. We are able to transcend the either-or-thinking of modernity through the ability to reason in polarities and paradoxes. Many of us sense that the current way we run organizations is deeply limiting. We will come up with better ways, because there is too much human potential waiting to express itself.* (Fréderic Laloux)

In his globally recognized analysis of organizational development, Fréderic Laloux (2014) points out that most change projects are still referring to modernity's thinking, promising better outcomes, profit, market share, and revenue with a faster and further approach and assuring the organization of external benefits for the company and the organizations, once they would enter into some dedicated change process.

If we looked at global needs at large, the newly emerging paradigm of conscious organizations and their staff become ever more evident and urgent. Referring to Einstein's insight that we cannot solve problems with the same consciousness that created it, Laloux concludes: "We won't be able to deal with the impending crises brought by modernity (global warming, overpopulation, depletion of natural resources, collapse of ecosystems) with organizations molded in modernity's thinking" (Laloux 2014, p 287).

The new level of consciousness, which executives and their staff are striving for, is a fundamental switch to intrinsic motivation – doing what feels right in relation to inner values and assumptions. The driving force for their inventing a new organizational model stemmed from an inner imperative to make a difference, to act in accordance with their world view: "making money" for themselves or the organization was never the key motivator. With hindsight, though, they are all convinced that the new models they devised turned out to be radically more productive.

"When we are pursuing a purpose that we find deeply meaningful, we want to be effective," Laloux reconfirms and redefines Frankl's findings.

Leaders in the new organizations emerging will experience "strong headwinds," being told that their approach to rise above the usual models of leadership is risky or even foolish.

In Laloux's concept, the newly emerging pioneer organizations rest on self-management, on team decision-making, and on the distribution of responsibility to each individual person in the context of their teams. Everyone is a "leader"; hierarchies have become obsolete.

Laloux is fully aware of the great challenge that the idea of self-management might initially put on the individual person: organizations pioneering in self-organization are advised to set the right framework for their staff to follow the road of change:

- Strive to create a safe space that invites deep listening, authenticity, and vulnerability.
- Train all colleagues in interpersonal skills to enable them to deal gracefully with conflict, share life stories, start meetings with a round of check-in, and integrate peer-coaching practices.
- A clear process for conflict resolution.
- Establish a clear advice process for making decisions.

In fact, the drivers for reinventing pioneer organizations are well established and defined.

- Liberating previously unavailable energies, through:
  - Purpose: When people identify with a purpose greater than themselves.
  - Distribution of power: Self-management creates enormous motivation and energy, stopping to work for a boss, for bonus, etc. but rather working for the own inner standards.
  - Learning: Self-management is providing a strong incentive for individual and continuous learning. Learning is not limited to knowledge but rather referring to the whole realm of inner development and personal growth.
  - Better use of talent: People are not forced to take management roles that do not match with their talents; roles are defined on a fluid basis.
  - Less energy wasted in propping up the ego: Less time and energy is wasted in defending all the territories and faces that traditional organizations would offer, producing and escalating intrapersonal and interpersonal conflicts at an ever-increasing level.
  - Less energy wasted in compliance: All the control mechanisms, reporting requirements, and systematic performance appraisals, based on fear, mistrust, or mismanagement, can be slipped.
  - Less energy wasted in meetings: In pyramid structures, meetings are intervened at all levels for all kinds of reasons, for transmitting information, to resolve potential misunderstandings, for personal ambitions, and for reasons of power and individual presentation.
- Harnessing and directing energy with more clarity and wisdom.

What then would be the necessary conditions for today's organizations wishing to start creating an organization apt for the twenty-first century's challenges? Laloux suggests two necessary conditions:

- Top leadership: The top executives must have integrated a world view and psychological development consistent with the developmental level of the pioneer organizations.
- Ownership: The company's owners (the board, external owners) must understand and embrace this pioneer approach; otherwise the organization might fall back into old style mode especially in times of crisis.

16.4 The Culture You Create or the Culture You Destroy

Before the financial crisis in 2008 and after this date with heightened intensity, observers (The Conference Board 2015) have noted that companies have silently broken the "psychological contract," giving employees far fewer reasons to be loyal to their companies or walking the extra mile, after cost-cutting measures, layoffs, restructuring measures, and external shareholder value thinking have increasingly gained hold of organizations. Increasingly, employees are confronted with dysfunctional management behaviors that need to be assessed correctly and confronted in order to stop this hurtful process and create substantial change for all stakeholders involved. This assessment is hurtful to every reader and assessor alone, not to speak about those inflicted in this very environment. Research about the behaviors demonstrated in this malfunctional way has been studying various phenomena, processes, and outcomes, all of them addressing conflict management and inappropriately exercising power over subordinates.

What are managers' practices that actually "kill meaning" at work?

"Dysfunctional leadership" and the shadow sides of leadership have long been researched and addressed by Kets de Vries (2003). Starting from the distinct psychological pressures that leaders are facing, referring to loneliness of command, addiction to power, fear of envy, and the experience of a "What now?" after achieving almost all business goals, de Vries focuses on the role of narcissism of individual grown-up leaders, who were not so fortunate to experience a supporting environment in their early childhood and who, in their role as executives, become fixated on power, status, prestige, and superiority, becoming "haunted by the need to get even for real or imagined hurts." Unfortunately, in today's business world, the personality profiles of narcissist leaders are, for some organizations, understood as "socially desirable" for delivering in their objectives of "making money," resorting to "quick and dirty practices," and promising to fulfill these needs, based on their own short-term profit-driven goals. "Neurotic organizations" with a strong concentration of power might exhibit an organizational pathology with top executives exercising rigid behaviors and "sacrificing employees on their insatiable altar of their own wrath" (de Vries), and their dysfunctional leadership is mirrored in inappropriate strategies, structures, organizational cultures, and pattern of decision-making. Finally, de Vries is defining five "neurotic leadership styles," deteriorating the affected organization and their employees. The first step toward change is recognition of the danger signs. This necessitates a willingness on the part of the leaders to look within themselves and make honest (and often painful) appraisal, muting the calls of the narcissistic sirens by looking deep within. They need to develop a sense of emotional intelligence, starting with self-awareness.

Although starting with the Oracle of Delphi, Sigmund Freud, Viktor Frankl, and many others have been repeating this message, it still remains unheard for many of those, being confronted with despair and hopelessness.

According to other recent studies (Amabile and Kramer 2011), managers risk falling into four traps:

- Sending mediocrity signals: Management not "walking the talk" according to their defined mission and values and thereby negating employees' autonomy and actively driving employee engagement "to the ground" in a deeply hurting process, which is ultimately undermining employees' self-esteem and dignity.
- Strategic "attention deficit disorder": Managers focusing their attention with ever shorter spans to external developments and next steps to take, eventually missing any compass for their own decisions and communication with their internal stakeholders and each executive pushing in different directions.
- Corporate Keystone Cops: Following a famous cinema series in their early years, executives exercising their function in this way, more or less unawarely, contribute to the organization's farce and thereby creating chaotic situations for their employees. The attempts of one team moving forward or at least trying to halt the downturn of their work environment are opposed by another team, further "down" on the meaningless spiral.
- Misbegotten "big, audacious goals": Some consultants are encouraging and training organizations to engage in defining big, audacious goals for their future. While these goals read and sound "great," they often fail any reality check, because they are not aligned with the organization's actual status or capacities for delivering on these goals. While these goals suggest some kind of grandiose organizational culture, they actually might confirm hopelessness and emptiness on the employees' side, because they understand that they could, realistically, not deliver on these goals in their employee life span. This approach was actually "helping to destroy a substantial part of employees' individual sense of purpose," of their internal conviction of self-efficacy. In the end, only a few might "make it to the top," leaving behind a devastated organization, cynicism, and mistrust.

Until today, these "traps" tend to be denied and not being recognized adequately as major risks of leaders and their organizations. The cry for meaning is mirroring the dramatic and tragic effects of executives and indirectly their staff, being caught in these traps.

Amabile and Kramer (2011) are suggesting three ways to avoid these traps:

- Communicating with staff on process innovation rather than product innovation, innovating the process rather than taking the results only approach. While intensively assessing the process and looking at how things were done were widely practiced in the educational and counseling sector, it was largely disregarded in the economic sector, looking at the results with all factors driving performance were understood as cost factors that needed to be reduced. (Until today, coaching is confronted with validating their efficiency and effectiveness primarily in terms of monetary ROI indicators and costs being saved, etc.)
- Executives constantly relating to their employees' perspective, integrating their own previous experiences, and finally questioning themselves: How meaningful could this work be for someone else, if I had been in their place years ago? This approach is finally referring to a leader's humbleness in relating to employees.
- Personally having some "early warning systems" in place, signaling when the executive is losing touch with his staff, or missing pain points that have actually started sapping meaning from the people's work.

Amabile and Kramer conclude that, finally, it is the executive's responsibility for identifying and clearing systemic issues that might prevent employees to do quality work, as they would have strived to do in the very beginning.

16.5 Manifesting the Human Spirit: Exercising Meaningful Leadership

Today, the discussion about leadership in the twenty-first century is looking at the level of personal leadership, by exercising individual conscientiousness and sharing a basic belief in self-efficacy, a positive attitude toward others' competencies, and living by example.

Engaging in meaningful work leads to increases in overall employee engagement, initiative, and decreases in stress.

What then can managers do to provide for environments encouraging meaningful work? How do managers act and behave in their function to facilitate circumstances where individuals can find meaning in their work?

> *When we work creatively and productively with others, our experience of meaning can be profound....When we work directly for the good of others, meaning deepens in ways that reward us beyond measure. Some call it connection to a higher self, to God, to our own spirit, to universal consciousness, to love, to the collective good. No matter what it's called, it is deep meaning and it transforms our lives.* (Alex Pattakos)

With his approach, Alex Pattakos was one of the first experts, who, still personally inspired by Frankl, actively introduced Frankl's ideas to workplace issues, truly addressing twenty-first-century questions for leadership in persons' lives, with work claiming an ever-increasing part of them. Today, his book *Prisoners of Our Thoughts* (Pattakos 2017) sees its third edition and has been translated in 22 languages.

Alex Pattakos, cofounder of the Global Meaning Institute and member of the Innovation Group, with a broad background in medicine, law, political science, and administration, and professor, doctor, and advisor to three US presidents, has ever since been active on his "passion for exploring innovative and meaningful solutions": with his works he bridges political science, public policy, existential philosophy, psychology, innovation management, and meaning.

Pattakos expands on Frankl's psychological approach by demonstrating how Frankl's key principles can be applied to all kinds of work situations.

He encapsulates Frankl's approach in seven core principles and explains the ways in which these principles can be lived by:

- Exercising the freedom to choose your attitude: In all situations, no matter how desperate they may appear or actually be, one always has the ultimate freedom to choose the own attitude.
- Realizing the will to meaning: Commit authentically to meaningful values and goals that only the individual person can actualize and fulfill.
- Detecting the meaning of life's moments: Only the individual person can answer for their own life by detecting the meaning of any given moment and assuming responsibility for weaving the unique tapestry of existence.
- Not working against oneself: Avoid becoming so obsessed with or fixated on an intent or outcome that one actually works against the desired result.
- Looking at oneself from a distance: Only human beings possess the capacity to look at themselves out of some perspective or distance, including the uniquely human trait known as the "sense of humor."
- Shifting the focus of attention: Deflect the own attention from a problem situation to something else and build one's coping mechanisms for dealing with stress and change.
- Extending beyond oneself: Manifest the human spirit at work by relating and being directed to something more than oneself.

16.6 The Conductor as a Musical Collaborator

We could not have recorded the music (Beethoven cycle) without its environment in which we perform. Even Beethoven didn't have an especially happy childhood. This is what rings through.

One of the organizations "on the road" of supportive leadership is the German Chamber Philharmonic Orchestra Bremen, being on par with the Vienna Philharmonic or the New York Philharmonic Orchestra.

Right from the beginning, the orchestra chooses a rehearsal room in the midst of a school, surrounded by a "social hotspot." There has been no morning rehearsal without students present. From the start, the orchestra has set itself the goal of promoting individuals through the help of music. This promotion ranges from management training right through to the educational work with children.

While the average German orchestras work with a grant of up to 90 % of their budget, the Bremen orchestra needs only a third of this sum. The rest of the required funds are generated by the company. Critical to this success is the fact that those 39 musicians are not in a traditional employment relationship. For many years now, they have been the owners of their orchestra. Every musician is liable for his own personal assets if things should go bad one day (which they had experienced in the past, before they entered into this new structure).

The corporate construct of the German Chamber Philharmonic Orchestra Bremen corresponds to the inner attitude of the musicians – an attitude that reflects a high degree of creativity and motivation but also the desire for creative freedom. Each of the 35 musicians of the German Chamber Philharmonic Orchestra Bremen is also a partner in the orchestra. The members decided to get paid based on performance. Ever since then, a share of the total annual budget is calculated and a fixed salary based on performance is paid to the musicians. Those who work more days will likewise receive more money.

This requires an extraordinary atmosphere within the orchestra. External soloists and leading conductors participate. They do so even though their salaries are lower than the usual market rates. The reason is that in the German Chamber Philharmonic Orchestra Bremen, they can grow exceptionally as musicians.

Their culture is based on these five value pairs:

Need and meaning, hierarchy and democracy, perfection and adventure, energy and concentration, and success and fun.

Many business leaders would rather appreciate the classic model of the dominant leading conductor, whose direction all musicians (or their own employees) have to follow. The German Chamber Philharmonic Orchestra Bremen breaks with this image. One of the distinctive features of this orchestra is that it is one of the few orchestras worldwide performing without a regular conductor. Thus, the German Chamber Philharmonic Orchestra Bremen is not only very successful, but they are also especially confident. Their members claim that if the German Chamber Philharmonic Orchestra Bremen wants to achieve excellence, they need a constant interchange between democratic participation and functional, hierarchical structure. A hierarchical structure needs a conductor.

For example, all musicians have to know the partita. This is the document that usually is in front of the conductor and that provides an understanding of the bigger picture. It tells everyone where things are headed and what role he or she plays. Throughout the performance, musicians come to the forefront at the relevant time. If this example is transferred to the classic business model, it would look like this: Each employee knows about the corporate strategy and all its aims. However, he or she also knows when to contribute exactly what to do to help the business reach its goals.

For the hierarchical content, the orchestra still provides for a concertmaster and vocal leaders of the respective instrumental groups, who can take over management responsibilities.

In particular, when working with external artists, it becomes apparent that the German Chamber Philharmonic Orchestra Bremen has its own way of making music, which makes a big difference in the overall musical experience. In 2006, when the German Chamber Philharmonic Orchestra Bremen played with the Georgian violinist Lisa Batiashvili at the Beethoven Festival in Bonn, the conductor, Paavo Järvi, had to leave earlier for Cincinnati. His wife was about to give birth to their second child. Instead of finding a new conductor, the musicians decided to perform without one. Batiashvili, who knew Järvi, rang him, stating, "What kind of strange idea is that?" Järvi assured, "They know what they're doing!" So Batiashvili got involved in the experiment. This resulted in a standing ovation, during both the break and at the end of the concert. Batiashvili was awarded the Beethoven Ring of Bonn for this exceptional performance. She was so excited about this outstanding concert with the German Chamber Philharmonic Orchestra Bremen that she asked to play Beethoven's Concerto for Violin one more time without a conductor. Despite these experiences, the German Chamber Philharmonic Orchestra Bremen does not want to go entirely without a conductor yet.

The effort to rehearse musical pieces without a conductor is enormous. Also, a conductor offers musical inspiration through which the orchestra can develop. The type of maestro the German Chamber Philharmonic Orchestra Bremen is looking for conveys a natural authority and is open to the ideas and skills of the entire orchestra. The current conductor, Paavo Järvi, calls himself, as a logical consequence, a "musical collaborator" or "chamber musician among chamber musicians." A. Schmitt, the managing director, extracted ten value principles lived by the orchestra, sometimes contradictory: need and meaning, hierarchy and democracy, perfection and adventure, energy and concentration, and finally, success and fun.

> *It was all about the tension between opposites which needed to be upheld to ensure high performance in the long term* (Schmitt and Scholz 2011).

16.7 Integrity and Character-Based Leadership

> *We believe we each individually can inspire character-based leadership and make a positive difference in ourselves, in others, and in our communities. Character-based leadership is, each of us leading from who we are and not from our power or position.* (Mike Henry)

Character-based concepts of personality and management have gone somewhat out of fashion in the recent discussion on living values and meaning in work.

"Character" mostly is connected with a positive connotation of leading a good, responsible, and sustainable life for oneself and others: the sociologist Etzioni (1993) is defining character as "the psychological muscle," allowing a person to control his impulses, delay gratification, self-regulation, and frustration tolerance, all of which are necessary for success, achievement, and *moral behavior.*

As Mischel (2014) has demonstrated in his famous marshmallow test, all of these competencies are indeed a basic component and prerequisite of a person's capacity to live a good life and find meaning in the work they are doing.

This is what Frankl is actually referring to as a person's personality and capacity in overcoming and controlling his immediate impulses and his psychosocial or physical drivers for a certain behavior: "Man is a person and becomes a personality of his own," potentially rising above his "facticity" to the level of existentiality.

The current concepts of displaying character in organizations and leadership are mainly referring explicitly or implicitly to the positive aspect of exercising impulse control and moral behavior.

16.8 Leading from Who You Are

Ultimately, man should not ask what the meaning of his life is, but rather must recognize that it is he who is asked. In a word, each man is questioned by life; and he can only answer to life by answering for his own life; to life he can only respond by being responsible. (V. Frankl)

> The minute we take responsibility, we start to develop character. Most of the world's problems are leadership related…We can all make a positive difference. We don't need permission. We simply need to resist the inertia of our lives and do something different (Mike Henry, The Lead Change Group).

Today, the Lead Change Group is a global, virtual community dedicated to instigating nothing less than a "leadership revolution." It has become one of the most socially shared leadership blogs, and they published an anthology (Lead Change Group 2012) about character-based leadership. They define character-based leadership as "leading from who you are, not your position or power."

Their character-based leadership approach is grounded in three assumptions: leadership is influence, influence is given, and people give influence based on trust, competence, and purpose.

Working and leading from strengths and character are essential. Generally, a person can lead by position, policy, preference, participation, pandemonium, or personality, claiming that none of these are as effective as leading from individual strengths and from character. This concept of leadership includes a specific attitude – the power of humility and exercising influence through character.

16.9 Leading Abundant Organizations

In line with the salutogenesis approach, referring to a continuum of health, investigating what helps people flourish and how leaders can support a positive workplace environment, Kim Cameron (2012) has been studying leadership and organizational virtuousness and "positive organizational scholarship" (POS).

Cameron's approach is expanding to the domains of other disciplines and connecting with their approaches, including ethics, economics, peacemaking, spirituality, social movements, and sustainability.

Reframing Cameron's approach of abundant organizations, Frankl coined this "the spirit/Geistige Person" that can be observed in individuals and in organizations, capable of transcending problem orientation to a broader perspective of looking beyond the very organization to the broader context of a mission to be fulfilled, a contribution to the greater good beyond the organization.

POS focuses attention on the generative dynamics in organizations that lead to the development of human strengths, foster resilience in employees, enable healing and restoration, and cultivate extraordinary individual and organizational performance. POS is most interested in the motivations and effects associated with positive workplace phenomena – how they are facilitated, why they work, how they can be identified, and how organizations can develop on them.

Relating to an organizational continuum from deficit to abundance, Cameron is focusing his approach on virtuousness as part of a hidden and virtually given organizational abundance that needs to be deliberately developed to "heliotropic" effects on the individual and organizational level. He terms this positive approach as inherent in any human-made organization as part of the human "positive DNA," because, as he claims, there is an "inherent bias toward human virtuousness." Taking into account the evolutionary bias toward the negative, Cameron emphasizes that it takes conscious human effort to focus on the positive: the human tendency needs to be activated by leaders toward resourceful humans, fostering compassion, gratitude, kindness, forgiveness, positive regard, generosity, and gratitude in the individual and virtuous organizations indicated by integrity, optimism, forgiveness, compassion, and trust.

According to research presented by Cameron, developing "organizational virtuousness" has heliotropic effects both for the individual employee and the organization: due to hormonal, cardiovascular, and immunity responses in the body, the presence of positive relationships may be influencing individual recovery and personal health.

By today, a great variety of tools fostering abundance have been collected by Cameron and made available for organizations.

These are Cameron's "prescriptions for positive leadership," all of them referring to the given continuum, overcoming the negative bias of being focused on what does not work (Kim Cameron, 2012):

- Capitalize on the heliotropic effect – We have learned to ignore it. "Positively embarrass someone."
- Foster positive energy – Energy is four times more powerful than information and influence. Advocate for or nurture one person.
- Focus on abundance gaps – People get consumed by problems and obstacles. Use own strengths in a new way.
- Celebrate what goes right – Problems usually dominate our attention.
- Write gratitude cards and/or a personal journal.

Claiming these "positive" results, Cameron is indeed making a strong individual and business case for positive leadership.

His approach is based on driving individual and organizational well-being.

There are limitations of this concept, which is primarily based in positive psychology. He does not touch on life's existential issues of suffering and potentially coping with these existential "givens" in life, when persons are confronted with taking an attitude to their suffering as "homo patiens" and integrating this experience in their work and private lives in search for meaning, being confronted with situations, when the "abundance" approach is demonstrating its limitations in the face of adversity, fate, and suffering.

16.10 Life's Entrepreneur: From Know-How to Know Why

Doing business is working in the community for the community. (Goetz Werner)

The German entrepreneur Goetz Werner is the founder and co-owner of the German drugstore chain "dm." In 2016, dm had been awarded as "best employer" of Germany across all business branches, out of 70,000 other companies and businesses, while in the years before "dm" had been awarded for ranking the first fiver three times. Together with Glassdoor (USA), best employer (Germany) is a ranking solely according to employee satisfaction with their company. The selection criteria cover topics like leadership and vision, motivation and company dynamics, culture and communication, staff development and perspectives, family/work-life balance and demographics, and internal entrepreneurship.

Werner has led the company for 35 years. He is one of the most influential advocates for a general basic income for every one and has founded the initiative "become an entrepreneur of the future." His entrepreneurial approach and convictions are based on freedom and the ideals of the French Revolution, liberty, equality, and brotherhood. He is advocating the paradigm change from the know-how to the know why, questioning himself: Why do we produce the goods we are producing? What is the meaning of my doing this?

Werner (2007) also describes the Copernican turn from understanding humans as a means to understanding humans as an end for all production and business. So he realizes his business, providing a space for human beings, writing their personal history, and for clients, having the opportunity of fulfilling their needs in his stores. For Werner, living and strengthening this approach would mean encouraging each person to find their own meaning in work and life. In his interviews and presentations, Werner is explaining his conviction that in this sense, each and every activity in each situation has its very own meaning and that, with this definition, there can be no work which is more or less important or inferior versus superior. His approach basically includes a concept of man's general capacities of creating a world that mankind could lead a good life, relating to the human mind.

> We need to address, liberate and activate the human mind. It is through thinking that the individual person can connect their selves with their neighbor and the world…Everyone grows up with the principle of sustainability. We are born so that we can develop and grow. We search for meaning and purpose in our lives and ask ourselves how we can find it. We want to understand the world, to change it and leave our own mark on it. In order to do so we make decisions that we must at some point justify to ourselves; which brings us to the subject of sustainability. (Goetz Werner website, translation by the author)

G. Werner's reference to the "human mind" is closely related to Frankl's Geistige Person, capable of choosing one's own attitude with freedom and responsibility.

Today, G. Werner et al. (2017) has published another book on today's current societal demands for change: "Otherwise it will pop!" on controlling the financial markets and radical change of politics in order to provide for a decent living for all.

With about 100,000 employees all over Europe, dm has been elected "best employer of the year in retail" for the fifth time in a row.

16.11 Being Whole: Addressing Mind, Body, and Soul

What kind of leadership do we need to not only cope with the challenges of the twenty-first century but to actively shape the best future for all?

It is this question that Stewart Friedman et al. (1998), practice professor at Wharton Management School, is addressing in his teachings, his publications, and his research. In his globally appreciated book *Total Leadership*, Friedman (2014a) is arguing that all leadership models having been taught – on the basis of twentieth-century environments and challenges – or are still being taught to the younger generation are outdated.

There is a need for understanding the dynamic changes that have occurred during the past 20 years in all spheres of life: the social landscape, individual beliefs, world views, and life goals have changed substantially. So have the values, what humans really care about, how they understand their core beliefs, how they want to introduce their talents in work and the broader community, what legacy, and what footprint they want to leave in this world. The digital revolution is presenting each and every society, their people, and each and every individual with leading questions of how they want to benefit from these "tools" and "things" in their own life and above that. Friedman indicates that all industrial revolutions first invented new machines and tools to bring business forward with the corresponding social and psychological knowledge and common understanding of how to benefit from the inventions which were not there yet. For human development, it was not the external factors that made the final difference but rather the way societies and their individuals dealt with these externals internally, with their psychological and social knowledge.

Today, Friedman's (2014b) approach of total leadership is a recognized primary intervention in a multi-year study funded by the US National Institute of Health. These are the main assumptions on which his leadership approach is based.

Today, humanity is confronted with questions of how to live a life that is rewarding and sustainable not only individually but first and most of all on a global scale.

Leadership, as defined by Friedman, is a matter of individual consciousness, not only living in the world of business but *being* aware of all spheres of life, affecting the individual person and the individual person defining the world around them. Why, Friedman is asking the rhetorical question, care about the others spheres of life at all? Why not focus on the homo economics or enjoying the life of a homo faber? Friedman is explaining that humanity has become aware that life does not work like that, because all spheres of life are affecting the way we work. Consequently, the more a person brings in their whole person, the better leaders they are. "Total leadership" is a *modus vivendi*, a conscious consideration of all spheres of life.

Like many other leading experts, Friedman starts from scratch, giving each individual the credit and responsibility of being a leader of their own individual lives. Consequently, Friedman presents his leadership approach, which could not merely deal with business leadership but which would need to be personal leadership, addressing the individual whole life. Suggesting a four-way approach, Friedman's insights, exercises, and practices have introduced a new perspective on active leadership, embracing the potentials of each individual.

Friedman claims from the beginning that each individual person is searching for serving a larger purpose and for making this world a better place. Individuals consciously being aware of responsibility for exercising their own leadership in each realm of their lives would feel part of something bigger than their own lives and thereby find greater meaning in what they actually do in their daily work. Friedman defines four areas of a person's life that need to be assessed regarding how much importance, focus, satisfaction, and performance can be assessed in each area: work/career, home/family, community/society, and self – mind/body/spirit.

The substantial difference between common career coaching and Friedman's approach is the spirit of acting with authenticity, integrity, and creativity for the common good that Friedman is suggesting.

It is not only about the own assessment of personal satisfaction in each area but more about the effective contributions the individual person makes, according to the external stakeholders' assessment of how they feel about the other person's significant beneficence to their lives.

How can this leap to the new leadership happen? Friedman starts with addressing the self and the individual's own thinking, reflection, and communication with others, about the gap between what the person is and what the person wants to become: this is the practice of leadership addressing a person's whole life, bridging the gap between the "incomplete" leader and the "whole leader": being real, being whole, and being innovative.

Being real refers to the person's guiding values and principles, taking all aspects of the individual life and the effects of own activities on others into careful account. In this respect, Friedman's approach is an exercise in individual discovery, learning, and growth, questioning the individual person: What image do I have of myself in 20 and 30 years with respect to the question, what impact do I want to make in this world?

What legacy and what footprint do I want to leave?

Here, Friedman's approach of taking the broader perspective of the individual person's potential contribution to the life's of others is connecting to Frankl's approach that it is not us who are wondering what life holds for us but that it is life questioning us and we give the answer, and by doing so, this is Friedman's empirical findings: each individual finds ways and means to change the lives of others substantially and of ultimately finding meaning by transcending beyond the immediate yearnings of career advancement, status, and material goods.

16.12 An Awareness-Based Global Leadership Platform: Creating Transformative Change

As the intensity of disruption and conflict around strategic resources around the world increases, new leadership capacities are needed that expand leaders' understanding of the underlying causes and of taking sustainable action. Complexity and the interconnected factors of critical challenges call for "joint platforms, where leaders from around the world can come together, reflect and take action, including even those that that are not yet organized, such as future generations and children" (O. Scharmer).

16.12.1 Spaces of Global Leadership Learning

It is this understanding of global responsibility as major motivation that has developed to a worldwide movement across countries, sectors, organizations, and persons of the most various backgrounds. A global action learning platform for leaders to create societal innovation has been established by Otto Scharmer et al. (2011) and his colleagues from Massachusetts Institute of Technology. Defining the leadership challenges of the twenty-first century, Scharmer takes a global and individual perspective at the same time. He describes nine spaces of leadership and learning across the various levels of knowledge – technical knowledge, relational knowledge, and transformational self-knowledge – as well as on the degree of system level, where these changes can occur, i.e., individual, institutional, and whole system. With this approach, Scharmer connects the various areas to complex quadrant with nine distinct areas, with most common mainstream change projects addressing the individual technical knowledge area. He observes that this limited approach would miss the full complexity of the present global situation, thereby actually leaving the most important questions that "life is asking us today" (V.Frankl), as an unaddressed blind spot, and eventually failing to facilitate and "create system-wide transformative change."

16.12.2 *Open Mind, Open Heart, and Open Will*

Based on Peter Senge's systems thinking and Otto Scharmer's Theory U approach, this platform and their labs bring together leaders from a great variety of diverse organizations across the globe, learning from each other and driving change. Their practices are based on these principles:

- Co-initiating: A 2-year multi-stakeholder journey resulted in engaging more than 70 organizations in Europe, North America, and Latin America to mainstream sustainable food production practices
- Co-sensing: Practicing the competencies in seeing situations from the edges of the system, i.e., from the views of the most marginalized and from their creating a shared "whole system" understanding
- Presencing: Exercising to see one's highest future potential in their work and the effects of individual practices on those that the individual and their institution are serving
- Co-creating: Exploring the future potential by joint efforts of prototyping and quickly learn from the various stakeholders' feedback
- Co-evolving: Focusing not on the results of a change project but rather on the process and which factors facilitated and were driving the change
- Mindful systems change: Associating, aligning, and sharing compassion with the larger system being addressed, letting go of the institutional identities that are limiting human potentials, and being only focused on the here and now but rather transcending to a greater awareness
- Collective intelligence: Getting access to the three main influencing factors for global awareness projects: open mind, open heart, and open will

16.13 Leading: "The Revolution Has Begun"

> *Much of what we produce to sell to each other to earn our living is crap, either ever more luxurious, specialized goods like electronic massagers and personal oxygen bars, or cheap salty junk food and disposable clothing. Every piece of crap, because it was manufactured, contains within it something of the priceless: applied human intelligence, for one, natural capital for another - something taken from the forest or river or the soil that cannot be replaced faster than we deplete it. We're wasting our brains and our only world on the design, production, and consumption of things we don't need and that aren't good for us... In a post-consumerist world, goods are likely to become more expensive, to reflect their true social and environmental cost, prompting us to shop less as a form of entertainment... We'll be able to recover time for satisfying pleasures that derive from pursuing our deepest interests; we'll have more time with our friends and family, and more time for meaningful work.*
> (Chouniard and Stanley 2012)

Yvon Chouinard, the founder of Patagonia outdoor clothing, is an example of how exercising leadership can influence the global community in raising awareness about the global challenges humankind is facing and for impacting and creating positive change for individuals and organizations as well. With Chouinard, the company has become a leader in producing organic cotton, in recycling plastic bottles, and in putting sustainability on the political agenda. Chouinard started as a mountain climber, who just wanted to have access to better outdoor clothing when exercising his hobby. Today, his company's sales amount to about 200 million dollars and Chouinard and his wife see the company and their responsibility as a major driver for change. Chouinard's recent publication (2016) *Let My People Go Surfing* might suggest an easy-go-lucky, pleasure, and fun-oriented approach to leadership and doing business. Actually, it is all just the opposite. It is the founder's biography and a book about the core values, the culture, and the philosophies of doing good business.

"Before we are entitled to encourage other companies to act responsibly, we have to do so ourselves. There is only one way to lead and that is by being in front and leading by example," Chouinard explains. In her foreword, Naomi Klein is asking: What if we shopped to live, instead of lived to shop? and sums up this new edition as book telling the story of an attempt to change more than the single corporation but rather challenge the culture of consumption that is at the heart of the global ecological crisis.

Patagonia's business and Chouinard's leadership concept (Chouinard and Stanley 2012) are based on these philosophical principles:

- Human resource philosophy: From the start, there was no distinction between the producers of the goods and those who produced them. Today, there is an average of 900 people applying for each vacancy advertised. First functions are recruited internally to keep the culture strong. There is strong emphasis on training. The company was one of the first to offer flexible work, allowing their employees to keep connected with the company's purpose of producing the best outdoor clothing and following their personal hobbies. This is the philosophy behind the "go surfing" book title. At a very early stage of their business, the company started to provide for a company childcare facility, being directed not only to their employees' well-being with no concerns about the wellbeing of their children but also being focused on the company's responsibility of contributing to the greater good of giving their share to children's best upbringing in the community.
- Management philosophy: Patagonia's approach is managing the company by consensus, practicing an open doors management style.
- Environmental philosophy: Action is the basis of Patagonia's business. Chouinard understands his business as actively giving an example of changing the ways in which corporations and governments deal with the environmental crisis. Today, only 55 percent of Patagonia's catalogues are dealing with the products, and 45 percent are dedicated to raising environmental awareness, calling for and reporting on actions taken.

- Product design philosophy: Making the best product and at the same time not causing unnecessary harm.
- Production philosophy: Being devoted to outstanding quality and taking extra steps to make sure that all production processes are set up correctly
- Financial philosophy: Patagonia views profits as necessary, but not the end goal. It strives to balance the funding of environmental activities with the desire to continue their business for the next 100 years.

Today, Chouinard (2016) concludes that "the revolution has begun. We cannot wait for our governments, but we rather have to use our power and influence as consumers, asking for sustainable goods. The younger generation will value sustainable products. The next step will be 'green labels' in all garments, providing the consumer with information for their best decision on buying sustainable products. Actually I am a pessimist on the global ecological present and future. But in case there is rescue ahead, I want to have been a part of it" (Y. Chouinard, interview with ZEIT online, 30 June 2011, translation by the author BvD).

References

Amabile T, Kramer S (2011) The progress principle: using small wins to ignite joy, engagement and creativity at work. Harvard Business Review Press, Boston

Blake RR, Mouton JS (1972) The managerial grid. Key orientations for achieving productivity through people. Gulf Publishing Company, Houston

Cameron K (2012) Positive leadership and extraordinary organizational performance. Berrett-Koehler Publishers Inc., San Francisco

Chouinard Y (2016) Let my people go surfing. The education of a reluctant businessman. Penguin Books, New York

Chouinard Y, Stanley V (2012) The responsible company. Patagonia Books, Santa Clara

Erhard W, Jensen MC, Granger K (2012) Creating leaders: the ontological-phenomenological model of leadership. In: Snook SA, Khurana R, Noria N (eds) The handbook for teaching leadership: knowing, doing and being. Sage, Thousand Oaks

Etzioni A (1993) The moral dimension. Towards a new economics. Free Press, New York

Frankl VE (1984) Man's search for meaning, 60th edn. Pocket Books, New York

Friedman SD (2014a) Total leadership. Harvard Business School Press, Brighton

Friedman SD (2014b) Work+Home+Community+Self. In: Harvard Business Review, Sept 2014

Friedman SD, Christensen P, De Groot J (1998) Work and life: the end of the zero sum game. In: Harvard Business Review, Boston, December 1998

Grant A (2012) Leading with meaning: beneficiary contact, prosocial impact and the performance effects. Acad Manage J 55(2):458–476

Kahn W (1990) Psychological conditions of personal engagement and disengagement at work. Acad Manag J 33:4. ProQuest, pp 692–724

Kets de Vries M (2003) Dysfunctional leadership. A contribution to the encyclopedia for leadership. Sage, Great Barrington, MA, citation from: INSEAD Faculty and research, Working Paper Series 2003/58/ENT

Laloux F (2014) Reinventing organizations. Nelson Parker, Brussels

Lead Change Group (2012) The character-based leader: instigating a leadership revolution. One person at a time. Dog Ear Publishing, Indianapolis

Mischel W (2014) The marshmallow test: mastering self-control. Chevron Books, Irvine

O'Leary J (2016) Do managers and leaders really do different things? In: HBR Harvard Business Review, June 2016

Pattakos A (2017) Prisoners of our thoughts. Berrett-Koehler Publishers, Oakland

Scharmer O, Cunningham D, Kaufer K (2011) U.School: an awareness-based global leadership platform. Massachusetts Institute of Technology (MIT), Presencing Institute, Cambridge, MA

Schmitt A, Scholz C (2011) Hochleistung braucht Dissonanz: Was Teams vom 5-Sekunden-Modell der Deutschen Kammerphilharmonie Bremen lernen können. Viley-VCH Verlag, Weinheim

Schwartz SH, Bardi A (2001) Value hierarchies across cultures: taking a similarities perspective. J Cross-Cult Psychol 32(3):268–290

Scouller J (2011) The three levels of leadership. How to develop your leadership presence. Management Books, Cirencester

The Conference Board CEO Challenge (2015) Research report. http://www.conference-board.org

Werner G (2007) Einkommen für alle. Kiepenheuer & Witsch, Köln

Werner G, Weick M, Friedrich M (2017) Sonst knallt's! Bastei Luebbe, Köln

Chapter 17
The Human Potentials

Contents

17.1 The Art of Practice: Taking the Klimt Perspective[1]

If we take man as he is, we make him worse, but if we take man as he could be, we raise him to his potentials of what he can become. (Frankl, citing J. W. v. Goethe)

In 1898, the Viennese painter Gustav Klimt was requested by Baroness Sonja Knips' (1873–1959) husband, a Viennese business man, to portrait his wife. At that time, this is the Baroness' photo, as handed down (Fig. 17.1):

This is the portrait that Gustav Klimt delivered some months later, obviously showing what he saw in the Baroness (Fig. 17.2):

The portrait was exhibited at a prominent place in the Knips mansion, where the Baroness Knips, the couple, and all visitors would continually encounter this portrait – as for the Baroness many times a day, for the visitors regularly (Fig. 17.3):

Ten years later, in 1908, this photo shows Baroness Knips. She had become a very famous, dedicated activist in supporting and organizing arts events for the Viennese community (Fig. 17.4):

When he had portrayed her, Gustav Klimt actively took a positive perspective that can be coined as the "Klimt perspective":

- The art of seeing in a person what their potentials are and what they would be capable of achieving

[1] Based on the author's personal notes, B. Hadinger's findings, presentation, and lecture in her ILEX Logotherapy Training, Tuebingen/Germany, 1999, and further author's research

B. von Devivere, *Meaningful Work: Viktor Frankl's Legacy for the 21st Century*,
https://doi.org/10.1007/978-3-319-89791-2_17

Fig. 17.1 Photo of Sonja Knips in 1898 (25 years)

Fig. 17.2 Gustav Klimt 1898: Portrait of Sonja Knips (Source: https://commons.wikimedia.org/wiki/File:Klimt_-_Bildnis_Sonja_Knips.jpeg)

Fig. 17.3 The Knips mansion entrance hall with the Knips portrait by Klimt (Picture: viennatourist.at)

Fig. 17.4 Picture of Sonja Knips 1908 (viennatouristguide.at)

- The actual behavior demonstrated, raising awareness about the potentials and encouraging positive development
- The potential to actually become what a person important to us would see in us

Since then, what Gustav Klimt had intuitively seen and actively expressed with his talents in art was elaborated by Viktor Frankl's motivational theory and confirmed by diverse research studies, describing the phenomenon as "Pygmalion effect" (referring to Ovid, Shaw, and My Fair Lady) and looking at the very consequences of this effect for individual performance in the workplace: either operating in the mode of "set-up-to-fall-syndrome" or encouraging the development of "positive spirals" in the individual person.

17.2 The Good Life: The Courage to Be

There are countless definitions of the "good life" a person may lead, depending on their environment, culture, background, personality, values, and present living conditions.

Carl Rogers (1995) described the fully functioning person as a person leading a rich, full, and exciting life, experiencing joy and pain, love, and heartbreak more intensely, continually aiming at living their lives to their full potentials. Rogers defined the characteristics of this good life with:

- A growing openness to experience
- An increasingly existential lifestyle, living each moment fully
- Increasing trust in their own judgment and their ability to choose their own appropriate behavior
- Freedom of choice in choosing their own behavior, relying on their own potential for their own right and responsible behavior
- Creativity in their doing
- Reliability and constructiveness, when even potentially aggressive needs will be balanced by intrinsic goodness

Rogers defined the "good life" as a process, not a state: "This process of the good life is not, I am afraid, for the faint hearted, it involves the stretching and growing of becoming more and more of one's potentialities. It involves the courage to be. It means launching oneself fully into the stream of life" (Rogers 1995, p 186).

Wong (2015) describes his comprehensive and empirically validated approach, covering all realms of the self in this world, his integrative, meaning-centered model of a "good life": Based on his research about existential and social cognition perspectives of meaningful and good life, he found that – at least for laypeople – a meaningful life is a good life and that virtue is an indispensable dimension of the good life not only for individuals but for society as a whole. Accepting Aristotle's definition of eudaimonia, emphasizing the importance of virtue (doing good for others), Wong notes "Such a view recognizes both nature-fulfillment of human excellences as well as self-fulfillment of individual potentials." According to Wong's meaning hypothesis, meaning contributes to well-being as well as virtue. A good life is not just living well by acting well but also by connecting with people and things that matter.

In a multidimensional space of four worlds, the physical/situational world, personal world, social world, historical and cultural context, and spiritual/transcendental world, the four dimensions of existence meet in the "true self": this true self can actively live and experience well-being, virtue, and "meaning."

17.3 From Abundance to Gratitude and Giving

To lead a comfortable life with enough money and financial resources that may contribute to satisfaction in life, research has shown that above a certain level of economic and financial well-being, money does not provide for more happiness. Employees spending their yearly bonus on themselves were less happy than those who spent it for prosocial purpose (Aknin et al. 2013). Data assessed from 136 countries around the world suggest that human beings' reported elevated happiness was consistently associated with giving money to others. Prosocial spending, giving to others, is neurologically strongly related to releasing the neurotransmitter oxytocin. Nicolao et al. (2009) differentiate between "experiential purchases" and "material purchases." Relating to the community we feel as a part of is a basic human need, and it may make us "feel good," whenever we are connected with them. Connecting with the "greater good," though, does not come automatically:

> *Widening our sense of how we relate to the other inhabitants of our world helps us to contextualize ourselves, how we are fortunate in our lives and how we can help others who have not experienced the same fortune.* (Pennock 2014)

All research strongly suggest that connecting with the global community by means of digitalization and social media triggers our basic human needs, our will to meaning, and our freedom and responsibility to act on it.

17.4 Building a Culture of Purpose

> "We have placed far too much emphasis on superficial and transitory markers of success rather than enduring, life fulfilling goals." (W. Damon)

Living in paradox times, we are not only confronted with balancing all the diverse invitations and suggestions that our communities are offering to us, validating their potentials not for serving our egos but rather our search for meaning; we are constantly challenged with "making our own meanings." Purpose is a deeply individual and a social phenomenon. It is internally constructed and manifests itself in engagement with others. Purpose "is a product of inner examination and of outer exploration" (Damon 2008). Consequently, we cannot force a purpose on an individual person, but as being a part of a greater community, we are responsible for suggesting and actually living purposes and meaning potentials that may give guidance and support to others, living their fulfilled lives.

Taking young people's needs for guidance as a socially and commonly accepted basis of shared values, which their society, community, and parents are striving to demonstrate to them in the sense of "living by example," it does not require any sort of Utopian dreaming, as Damon (2008) points out:

> A culture of purpose must be built and continually be rebuilt in multiple small ways, by both individuals and institutions, that take responsibility for the values they represent…A culture of purpose cannot be enforced. Nor are there material prerequisites. People have found purpose, all through the ages, in good time and bad…Wars, epidemics, famines, hard times of every imaginable sort have served as tolerable breeding grounds for a sense of purpose for those who endured them. (Damon 2008)

People found guidance and inspiration in the larger culture of purpose that those people represented. With this perspective, there are multiple roads to take to build a culture of meaning. What Damon is elaborating on what would generally apply, not only for the younger generation, to all humans, seeking meaning and wishing to contribute to a greater purpose are:

- Community building: Providing and organizing positive activities, offering mentoring, and experiencing the impact of own engagement on other person's lives in the community with the own contribution actually making a difference for another person's life.
- Releasing the individual person's potential value for the community, the society, and the world, getting away from a deficit-oriented approach to an understanding of each individual's more or less hidden potentials for contributing to a greater cause. In this context, business coaching is finally getting away from the previous negative image of potentially "doing good in bad times" to a developmental understanding of finding, releasing, or elevating the individual best potentials, together with eliciting the values that this person finds important for her own life today and tomorrow.
- Setting the stage for a confident can-do outlook: Neither pathologizing nor overprotecting, taking neither an indifferent nor an overindulging perspective, but rather strengthening purposeful people by demonstrating strong confidence in any person's abilities to make a contribution.
- Positive role models in the public sphere: The public figures people observe must emanate a sense of purpose and transparently explain their whys and what matters to them instead of willingly delivering their stories of luxurious desires and human weaknesses to the public for further multiplied media coverage, lauding these same persons as today's most successful celebrities.

As Damon explains, we need to look past the culture of short horizons to a culture of noble purpose: Our efforts to produce higher test scores (in school for children) or KPIs (key performance indicators) for employees to be achieved have robbed us from our capacities to "instill a broader vision of the world" we want and that we would find meaningful for our global future. By focusing on constantly improving short-term-oriented measurements and highly elaborated tools for assessing individual success and performance, outcomes, and efficiency, we have, as Damon (2008) concludes, "sabotaged every possible enlightened aim that we might have" and finally *economically* are being poorly prepared to meet the challenges of this twenty-first-century globalized world. *Psychologically*, this short term, "homo economicus," understanding of human existence is seeding and feeding pessimism, uncertainty, self-doubt, a cynical world view, and materialistic craving. *Socially*, it leads to civic disengagement – in short, frustration of people's will to meaning.

Above all, this diagnosis is but the starting point for suggesting and promoting a culture of purpose, firing imaginations, encouraging highest aspirations, and empowering and rendering supportive environments for realizing the human potentials – in personal lives, in schools, in workplaces, and in all kinds of service organizations. This book has collected many examples of individuals and organizations, who have started on this journey, answering to life's questions from situation to situation, from day to day.

A culture of purpose cannot be enforced by coercive top-down decision-making. It needs to evolve over time in a complex relationship between the inner self and the world beyond the self.

Wong P. T. P (2010) describes four pillars that may establish meaningful organizations:

According to this PURE concept, meaning is the central component of a good life, individually and for organizations, and is being provided by these four sources of meaning (PURE):

- **P**urpose: Wong describes ten types of purpose being potentially elicited in organizations. To be effective, the purpose has to go beyond the bottom line: vision/mission, transcendental, societal, people, efficient process, quality products, long-term goals, short term-goals, projects, tasks.
- **U**nderstanding: Organizations need to facilitate understanding on various levels – understanding individually what is happening and also building bridges of understanding in the organization. Flat, flexible, and collaborative structures are facilitating mutual understanding.
- **R**esponsibility: Making the right decision and doing the right things. Responsibility can be demonstrated only by action: "This is where the rubber hits the road" (Wong 2010).
- **E**njoyment/Evaluation: While both extrinsic and intrinsic motivation are generally important for work satisfaction, meaningful work refers to and relies on intrinsic motivation, differentiating feeling good (extrinsic) from doing good (intrinsic), reflecting the innate moral nature of being human.

Wong is luminously describing the four options of doing wrong with the acronym CRAP: corruption, relational problems, abuse of power, and politicking to advance self-interest, all of them producing toxic environments. Again, this is only one side of the coin with plenty potentials for individual employees from all levels to engage for purpose in the organization. Wong is suggesting a list of do's and don'ts for exercising the right thing as a way of living in organizational contexts.

As for the organizational structure, Wong is suggesting four areas of responsibility: Leadership, followership, partnership, and workmanship. In organizations, each individual is accountable to his or her fellow members of staff and to his or her individual conscience. Responsible action finally shows in decision-making, accountable to stakeholders and society at large and taking pride in these activities as nay organization's common denominator.

- Enjoyment: Feeling good from doing good, reflecting the innate moral nature of humans, suggesting that, when work is meaningful, it will be reflected in high intrinsic motivational scores (opposite to extrinsic motivational sources like good compensation package, good prospects for promotion, etc.), like competency and efficacy, improvement and growth, meaning and purpose, getting along and belonging, self-esteem, actualization, and transcendence.

With their concepts, Wong, Damon, Laloux, and many others to a large extent are sharing the same ideas; integrating the human capacities for leading a good and meaningful life with a resourceful human organizational approach; bringing meaningful, purposeful, and virtuous organizations to life; and suggesting encouraging activities on the pathway to reinventing and rehumanizing organizations to their best potentials.

17.5 Human Dignity: A Transition Unfolding

> *Today's society is characterized by achievement orientation, and consequently it adores people who are successful and happy and, in particular, it adores the young. It virtually ignores the value of all those who are otherwise, and in so doing blurs the decisive difference between being valuable in the sense of dignity and being valuable in the sense of usefulness. If one is not cognizant of this difference and holds that an individual's value stems only from his present usefulness, then, believe me, one owes it only to personal inconsistency…Confounding the dignity of man with mere usefulness arises from conceptual confusion that in turn may be traced back to the contemporary nihilism…* (Frankl 1984, p 138)

Together with the global search for meaningful lives, the issue of human dignity and how to preserve it in all realms of life is gaining increased attention in business and management. Realizing the interconnectedness of humans around the globe, people are searching for meaningful work with their inherent sense of human dignity. Searching for ways to respond to the crises of continuous economic growth, depletion, and the resulting urge for global transition, the Human Dignity and Humiliation Studies Movement has emerged:

> *Particularly in a globally interconnected world, it becomes utterly clear that everybody's individual self-interest to want to live a dignified life is bound up in the common interest of all humankind to do so.* (Lindner 2017)

17.5.1 The Dignity Economy

The "Dignity Economy" envisions

> *...a world where every newborn finds space and is nurtured to unfold their highest and best, embedded in a social context of loving appreciation and connection. A world, where the carrying capacity of the planet guides the ways in which everybody's basic needs are met, a world, where we are united in respecting human dignity and celebrating diversity, where we prevent unity from being perverted into oppressive uniformity, and keep diversity from sliding into hostile division.* (Lindner 2012)

Since its foundation, this social movement has offered a new model of collaborative action based on the paradigm shift, away from the *homo economicus* to the *homo amans*. The organization currently includes around 1000 personally invited members from all continents, and their website (humiliationstudies.org) is being accessed by between 20,000 and 40,000 people from more than 180 countries per year since its inception in 2003. In 2011, the World Dignity University initiative was launched, followed by the foundation of their publishing house Dignity Press. In 2015, the organization was nominated for the Nobel Peace Prize.

"In a world in which the concept of *Homo economicus* seems to be the call of the day, our work flourishes by sharing the ego-free, renewable super-fuels of *homo amans...*." This movement claims that by today, people from all walks of life, all classes, and all countries now have the qualifications to engage in building organizations, based on self-management and self-organization. The transition being observed develops into an organizational culture of human dignity, solidarity, subsidiarity, and striving for the common good.

> *There might exist unnecessary limitations to our freedom, limitations designed by us, humankind, that can be un-designed. Why not sit together today, as humankind, liberate ourselves from all limitations that flow from human-engineered domination, while lovingly accepting and respecting only the limitations that indeed have the status of laws of nature, such as the finiteness of our planet.* (Lindner 2017)

17.5.2 Enhancing Dignity in Various Branches

Organizations from the most diverse fields and branches – schools, universities, clinics, financial institutions, banks, agriculture, and forestry – are organizing around issues of dignity, engaging in activities of responsible change, mindfully observing dignity in their specific area of activities, and defining how to observe dignity in:

- Management and exercising leadership: How can we assure that dignity is the core element in all business processes across the organization and on all levels?
- Coaching relationships and practices: How is dignity assured for all stakeholders in the relevant coaching ethics and in clients' communication?
- Finance and banking: How can money serve its function, establishing good business for the best of individual clients, society, and fulfilling global needs?
- Agriculture: How can soils, animals, and plants be cultivated in a sustainable way, ending global warming and the effects of industrialization, depletion, and exploitation of energy resources with systemic negative effects on the respective population?

- Forestry: How can the dignity of those living in and from the forests – indigenous and local population – be assured, while they are facing industrialization, land seizure, water, and other energy exploitation projects?
- Education: What are the needs of the children and of students, building the next generation, and of all citizens to assure their competencies for living a resourceful, good life, in freedom and dignity?
- Public services: How can the public services be budgeted and managed in such a way that they may meet the needs of their citizens and employees, independent of profit interests and short-term considerations on payoffs?
- Health-care systems: Which conditions do provide for healthy living conditions and what would be the best approaches for establishing healthy environments in clinics, practices, and care institutions, so that healing can happen?
- Psychiatric clinics: How can the dignity of each individual person be assured under all circumstances and patients' dignity be safeguarded in each and every part of the treatment process?
- Arts: What does assigning dignity to arts and artists imply for the society as a whole, regarding their rights and their prerequisites for exercising their role in the community?
- Sciences: How does dignity spell out in sciences, regarding testing and researching? What are the ethical guidelines or boundaries set by their respective societies, and how are these issues being negotiated among their various stakeholders?

While evolutionary in their specific activities, the initial impulse for organizational change is based on a conscious paradigm shift with the explicit leadership attitude and message to get involved in this journey.

Today, we have all the knowledge, the consulting capacity, and, more, the heart and the spirit to become engaged in this journey. Fortunately, there are so many examples of organizations, leaders, and individual persons who have started to support and actively engage in this transition that it might be called a somewhat ordinary-alternative option of how to do business in the twenty-first century. Yet, each paradigm shift is singular and needs most sensitive attention in designing the right change architecture and process. Taking the human condition on a global scale, the classic questions remain: "When, if not now? Who, if not me?"

References

Aknin LB Barrington-Leigh CP Biswas-Diener R et al (2013) Prosocial spending and well-being: cross-cultural evidence for a psychological universal. Am Psychol Assoc 104(4):635–652 0022-3514/13/. J Pers Soc Psychol. https://doi.org/10.1037/a0031578

Damon W (2008) The path to purpose. How young people find their calling in life. Simon & Schuster, New York

Frankl VE (1984) Man's search for meaning. Beacon Press, New York

Humiliationstudies. http://www.humiliationstudies.org/whoweare/whoweare.php. Accessed 13 Oct 2017

Lindner E (2012) A dignity economy: creating an economy which serves human dignity and preserves our planet. World Dignity University Press, Lake Oswego

Lindner E (2017) Honor, humiliation, and terror: an explosive mix – and how we can defuse it with dignity. Dignity Press, Lake Oswego

Nicolao L Irwin JR Goodman JK (2009) Happiness for sale: do experiential purchases make consumers happier than material purchases? J Consum Res 36:188–198

Pennock SF (2014) How spending money on others helps to promote happiness. https://positivepsychologyprogram.com/spending-money-promotes-happiness/. Accessed 25 Sept 2017

Rogers C (1995) On becoming a person. A therapist's view of psychotherapy. Houghton Mifflin, New York

Wong PTP (2010) The PURE strategy for organizational excellence. http://www.meaning.ca/PLNL/nov-2010/pure-wong.html. Accessed 12 Nov 2017

Wong PTP (2015) The meaning hypothesis of living a good life: virtue, happiness, and meaning. Paper presented at the research working group meeting for virtue, happiness, and the meaning of life project, University of South Carolina, Columbia, South Carolina. (Funded by the John Templeton Foundation) December 2015. http://www.drpaulwong.com/the-meaning-hypothesis-of-living-a-good-life-virtue-happiness-and-meaning/. Accessed 5 September 2017

Chapter 18
Meaning, Work, and Well-Being: Empirical Findings

Contents

18.1 Assessment of Meaning

More than 60 years had passed since Viktor Frankl's first "teenage" publication, when, in 1988, he concluded logotherapy has become scientifically established on the grounds of research, based on (1) tests, (2) statistics, and (3) experiments. As for the tests, Frankl (1988) was referring to Crumbaugh and Maholick's PIL Purpose in Life Test (1964), Elisabeth Lukas' Logo-Test (1981), Walter Boeckmann (1984), and others.

As for the statistics, Frankl (1988) mentions Brown, Dansart, Casciani, Sallee, and Smith et al., who gave empirical evidence that people can find and fulfill a meaning in their lives.

Nevertheless, Frankl's approach remained largely unheard, and, as Frankl observed, the basic need for meaning remained ignored and neglected. But, as he was also foreseeing, last century's crises present not only hazards but also chances: they may be "incentives to shift the accent and emphasis from mere means to meanings, from material goods to existential needs" (Frankl 1988). Considering the expeditious discussion around meaning and meaninglessness, around basic human needs not met and needs that are created for materialist reasons, one can only summarize how right he was!

B. von Devivere, *Meaningful Work: Viktor Frankl's Legacy for the 21st Century*,
https://doi.org/10.1007/978-3-319-89791-2_18

As for the meaning of work, Frankl (1985) (translation by the author BvD) explained:

- Work is a matter of experiencing own creative values and thereby finding meaning in doing this work and thereby realizing one's unique mission in life.
- The field where the unique person relates to his/her community with this relation giving meaning and value to the individual person.
- This meaning and value are always related to a specific service or work delivered (to the respective community), not to any vocation or profession in general.
- Consequently, no profession or vocation has a meaning as such, or no profession has any more meaning than the other one. It is only the concrete person, delivering his/her own specific service and work, who gives meaning to this work.
- Not the profession matters, but the way in which this profession or vocation is being exercised by the individual person.
- Each and every vocation holds the chance for the individual working person to give meaning to his/her life.
- Any person's natural relationship to his/her work as an area of potential realization of creative values and unique self-fulfillment is suffering under the current working conditions: working overtime, being occupied with routine, and unpersonal work; here, work can be understood only as a means to make money, for the worker as well as for the employer. For both earning money for living has become an end in itself. His/her money has a "what for" but his/her life has no "why."
- Subsequently, those who lose their work experience feelings of unworthiness, of no value to the community. They lack incentives to give the unique and singular meaning to their lives and lose awareness for the unique "task character of life," calling on the individual to respond to life's questions, i.e., to respond to this unique situation in a meaningful way.
- Work remains a means to achieve a meaningful living. Man's dignity forbids that man becomes a means, degrading him to a mere means of labor or production.
- Workability is not all. It is neither a sufficient nor a necessary condition to fulfill one's meaning of life. A person can be capable to work and still miss life's meaning. Another person can be incapable to work and still give meaning to his/her life.

Starting from Crumbaugh and Maholick's first empirical test of existential issues in 1964 – 3 years after Viktor Frankl had been appointed visiting professor at Harvard – until today, there is a huge volume of meaning-oriented empirical studies. Together with the widespread skepticism against a largely behavior- and drive-oriented scientific community in the 1960s, the issue of empirical testing of meaning and purpose and their effects put additional questions to those, mainly Viktor Frankl's students, who wished to present scientifically grounded, valid, and reliable insights and practices in applying Viktor Frankl's approach in their daily work in all realms of life and also to make the case for existential psychology in the interested scientific community. This continued to be an adventurous journey, because "the question of meaning is not really one question, but actually represents a cipher for a vast number of further questions"(Batthyany and Russo-Netzer 2014, p. 5).

The first wave of empirical meaning researchers concentrated on Viktor Frankl's motivation theory that man is searching for specific and concrete meaning beyond his physical, psychological, and social needs. The Crumbaugh and Maholick (1964) *The Purpose in Life Test*, being applied until today, was followed by other researches by his fellow students, cutting across mainstream psychology research. Their studies confirmed that the will to meaning is a motivation in its own right.

Today, entering "meaningful work" in Google produces 10,000,000 hits in only 40 s. Most of the research and empirical studies are referring to Viktor Frankl's "will to meaning" approach.

Most striking, until today, there seems to be a silent paradox in the academic history and reception of Frankl's meaning-oriented works: Frankl held 29 honorary doctoral degrees and received international awards and decorations; he was a frequent guest lecturer and visiting professor at universities around the world, among them President of the Austrian Medical Society of Psychotherapy, on one side; and, on the other, he noted (Frankl 1988, p 162f): "The concept of a will to meaning as the basic motivation of man is *a slap in the face of all the current motivation theories*," and he pointed out that this concept of the will to meaning is *revolutionary*, but also *breaking a taboo*, because logotherapy and existential analysis "venture to talk about life as something that always has meaning."

Taking a closer look at the latest history of empirical meaning research, we find that the academic land of work-related meaning and purpose research has largely been worked by positive psychology, organizational development research, and management research, triggered by two parallel developments, important for the rise of the meaning discussion becoming a mainstream issue of discussion: one being Maslow, at his times the most cited psychological expert for basic needs fulfillment (and the principle of homeostasis), who, in his last works, agreed with Frankl on self-transcendence as the "highest form of human development" and the other being the rise of positive psychology. With these two developments, research has rapidly focused on meaning and work, also for quite obvious reasons (accepting that search for meaning was an existential given of human beings and understanding that meaning was a constitutive element of well-being, that persons spend a substantial part of their lives at work, and that finally the work they do is strongly related to their sense of meaning), and has put meaning and work in the center of attention of all work-related discussions in the scientific and expert community.

Before continuing with some major results of this research, it must be acknowledged that logotherapy and existential analysis (LTEA) experts have, until today, not been very active in this field, for reasons to only speculate on. Until today, there are certainly too few existential psychology-related empirical studies on meaning at work (see Batthyany and Russo-Netzer 2014), continuing and updating Frankl's 1982 specific observations on meaning and work, as quoted above.

Here, the author presents findings from two academic fields – positive and existential psychology – who are increasingly acknowledging each other's diverse approaches and contributions to meaning and work, and still are working hard on their diverging language, assumptions, world views, and human image, to come to terms on what they share and where there are major differences, all this not for the sake of academic egotism but for their common purpose of supporting the human quest for meaning on the basis of their best potentials. This discussion has gained great momentum and – together with both approaches stretching all over the world – has grown in cultural and spiritual diversity being addressed in their respective studies. Existential psychologists, namely, Prof. Alexander Battyány from the Viktor Frankl Institute in Vienna and Pninit Russo-Netzer from University of Haifa, are actively leading and encouraging this dialogue, which is all too necessary to enlighten the potentials of meaning for humanity, to give answers to the cry for meaning around the globe, and to encourage the Copernican turn.

Frankl was strongly favoring collaboration with other psychotherapeutic approaches, and he remained highly interested in opening this approach "toward its own evolution as well as toward the cooperation with other schools." He had challenged the scientific community of his times with his image of humans, by, as he put it, introducing the scientific community to the layman's actual search for meaning. Frankl's question, then put in the context of discussing his motivational theory, is valid until today:

> How can we come to grips with the ills and ailments of our times, which are grounded in a frustration of the will to meaning, unless we adopt a view of man that focuses on the will to meaning as his motivation? (Frankl 1988, p. 163)

18.2 Empirical Findings of Meaning Fulfillment

Today, the substantial body of research on meaning focuses on a broad variety of diverse aspects of meaning, generally asking: To what part is meaning a motivator of human action?

The following compilation mainly refers to the latest publication by the two internationally most distinguished academic experts Batthyány and Russo-Netzer (2014), putting together the history and current research findings about meaning, fulfillment of meaning, and their multiple effects in various areas of application.

This research is focused around these questions:

What is the influence of meaning fulfillment on health?

- Lack of meaning accounts for either the causative mechanism or the level of health problems.
- There is a significant correlation between lack of meaning awareness and a general increase in neuroticism scores and, also, the severity of health and psychological symptoms.
- Psychological problems are caused or exacerbated, at least to some extent, by lack of meaning awareness.
- Awareness of meaning in life is itself a significant predictor of overall mental health.

What is the influence of meaning orientation on individual coping strategies and regaining individual resources?

- Meaning-oriented interventions significantly help clients regaining mental health. Increased sense of meaning in life has a curative effect.
- Meaning discovery played a probable or primary role in the recovery of patients.
- Meaning awareness plays a significant role in the processing of stress and traumatic life events.
- The sense of meaning significantly influences the recovery from life crises, illness, and grief.
- Activating individual meaning resources has a significant impact on the level of coping and finding access to relevant resources.
- The Reasons for Living Index (RFL), initially applied to measuring suicidal impulses, now includes an index on why patients *do not* follow their suicidal impulses.
- Meaning enables people to draw strengths and insights from their positive and negative experiences, gain perspective and distance from present situations, and point toward a worthwhile and valuable future.
- Meaning is an important component of life satisfaction.
- Meaning awareness contributes to stress reduction and post-traumatic stress adaptation.
- Meaning awareness helps us to function and flourish. It helps us to cope with uncertainty, anxiety, and existential issues in life.

Seligman's (2002) theory of authentic happiness defines meaning as one of the key components: a meaningful life is more important than a pleasant life in relating to well-being.

Meaning is also included in Seligman's five-component model of well-being: PERMA – positive emotion, engagement, relationship, meaning, and accomplishment.

Together with the rise of the positive psychology movement, a rapidly growing number of empirical tests and studies on the significance and effects of meaning for happiness, flourishing, and well-being have been published, many of them based on the *Meaning in Life Questionnaire* (Steger et al. 2006).

Until today, there is no commonly shared definition and operationalization of the construct of meaning. Various instruments have been tested and are being applied in various settings.

Purpose in Life Test (Crumbaugh and Maholick 1964), Life Regard Index (Battista and Almond 1973), Life Attitude Profile (Reker and Peacock 1981), Meaning in Life Scale (Warner and Williams 1987), Logo-Test (Lukas 1986), Sense of Coherence (Antonovsky 1987), Personal Meaning Profile (Wong 1998), Existence Scale (Laengle et al. 2003), and Sources of Meaning Questionnaire (SoMe, German: LeBe; Schnell and Becker 2007).

18.3 Meaning and Work

Many of the abovementioned findings on meaning can be easily translated into work life, operationalizing the general impact of meaning awareness for various work-related issues on all levels of person, team, management, organization, society, and the global community.

It was only over the last two decades that research has been asking what is the influence of meaning specifically relating to work? This latest research was strongly influenced and explicitly referring to Viktor Frankl's concept but still largely following its own discourse.

Studies, mostly in positive psychology and organizational development have, for very practical reasons, focused on three core areas of meaning and work (Pratt and Ashfort 2003):

- Meaningfulness *in* work: This is experienced when a person at work feels worthwhile and valuable. It is established by job design, fostering autonomy, variety and challenge, a good person-job fit, and rewarding social interactions with colleagues, managers, and clients/customers.
- Meaningfulness *at* work: Related to the self's basic need fulfillment of being part of a community and experiencing membership of the team and the organization, strengthening the individual identity. Experiencing meaningfulness at work is promoted through building strong organizational identities and transformational and visionary leadership. It is linked with higher levels of engagement, reduced absence, and better quality performance.
- Meaningfulness *and* transcendence: Here, the individual person and their work reflect an interconnection between one's identity, a feeling of contributing to the common good. It requires a safe organizational and cultural environment, encouraging employees to align themselves with "what matters" to them and to the organization.

Together with a series of empirical studies and research, Steger explored: Where does meaning in work come from? He argues that "meaningful work" can come either from the individual, bringing in some type of calling, or from the organization, offering, defining, and developing meaningful work to their employees. Steger created a Work and Meaning Inventory (WAMI), assessing three components of meaningful work:

- The degree to which people find their work to have significance and purpose
- The contribution that work makes to finding a broader meaning in life
- The desire and means for one's work to make a positive contribution for the greater good

Meaningfulness is more important to employees than any other aspects of work, including pay and rewards, opportunities for promotion, or working conditions.

Meaningful work can be highly motivational, leading to improved performance, commitment, and satisfaction.

People experiencing meaning in their work generally feel more committed to their work and to their organizations and are less hostile and less likely to be absent.

A sense of calling is linked to meaning and purpose as well as the betterment of society (Bellah et al. 1985; Dik et al. 2013; Dik and Duffy 2009; Hardy 1990).

One experiences life as meaningful when one's calling is to serve some greater good (Hunter et al. 2010; Seligman 2002; Steger et al. 2006).

A sense of calling in work is related to optimal outcome (Bellah et al. 1985; Dik et al. 2009; Hall and Chandler 2005).

Personal meaning is often linked to a sense of mission and pursuit of calling (Hall and Chandler 2005, 2001; Wrzesniewski et al. 1997). Calling is an integral part of one's self-identity (Dik and Duffy 2009; Dobrow; Hardy 1990).

Michelle McQuaid (2016) concludes: the search for meaning is not something we create within ourselves and for ourselves. Rather, meaning largely lies in others. It is only through focusing on others that we build the pillar of belonging for both ourselves and for them. And so, if we want to find meaning in our own lives, we have to begin by reaching out.

Damon et al. (2003) have found that with persons, having found their purpose of making a contribution to the world is part of an individual's search for meaning. It can be defined as the desire to make a difference in the world, to contribute to matters larger than the self. Persons having found or experienced that purpose believe that their lives are more meaningful and more satisfying.

Michaelson et al. (2014) show that meaningful work is associated with outcomes like enhanced job satisfaction, engagement, and well-being. Their studies promise increased job performance, organizational commitment, and customer satisfaction.

Grant et al. (2007) found that the single strongest predictor of meaningfulness of work is the experience that the job has a positive impact on others.

Peterson (2013) defines meaningful work, love, play, and service to be the major domains of a "good life."

People are striving to find "meaningful work," i.e., work that is significant and positive in valence, providing one with a sense of a higher purpose (Steger et al. 2012).

Littman-Ovadia and Steger (2009) examined the role of meaning in work life:

integrating character strengths at work substantially adds to experiencing meaning at work and overall life satisfaction.

Meaningful work is integral to experiencing the own sense of calling, the perception of the importance one's work has toward fulfilling one's destiny, and the opportunity of enjoying one's work while being good at it.

Schnell (2008) reported the following research findings: data reveal a relatively low prevalence of crises of meaning (4%), while being aware of own values could be partly responsible for the low frequency. One third of the sample (German-speaking participants from three countries) appears as *existentially indifferent*: a newly discovered subpopulation of people who neither experience their lives as meaningful nor suffer from a lack of meaning. For this group, relevance of sources of meaning is altogether lower than for those who experience their lives as meaningful; partially, it is even lower than for individuals who suffer from a crisis of meaning. The existentially indifferent shows very low values in *self-knowledge*, *spirituality*, *explicit religiosity*, and generativity. A multitude of sources of meaning contributes to the Germans' experience of meaningfulness in the beginning of the twenty-first century. Characteristic orientations are those toward morality, harmony, care, development, and community. Very low mean relevance is ascribed to explicit religiosity, followed by spirituality. Results show that the experience of meaningfulness increases with the degree of self-transcendence (*depth*) encompassed by characteristic sources of meaning. Meaningfulness also rises with the number of characteristic sources of meaning (*breadth*), and it is more pronounced, the more diverse these sources of meaning are (balance).

As for meaningful work, Schnell identified four aspects; when they are established, participants find that they are doing something meaningful:

- Significance
- Orientation
- Sense of coherence
- Community

Meaning and work engagement are strongly correlated with each other, with meaning as the cognitive and engagement as the motivational–emotional aspects. Here, the right balance between meaningful work and taking care of other aspects of the individual life must be carefully observed and established; otherwise, exploitation or self-exploitation is ahead.

All these studies have mainly focused on the many undeniable "positive benefits" for organizations and for employees, to target their activities on the various fields of indirectly addressing "meaning" in recruitment, job design, job control, values, social interaction with colleagues, celebrations of success, etc. In all these activities, there is an explicit link between meaning-oriented activities and alleged return on investment for the company.

18.4 Existential Approaches and Findings

It is exactly this promise of allegedly guaranteed returns on meaning-related activities, which Wong (2017) is challenging as being fundamentally opposed not only to Frankl's theoretical understanding of man's inherent will to meaning but also as being rebutted by empirical research findings, that finding meaning and well-being are not directly related, e.g., in roles such as parenthood (associated with lack of sleep, stress, deep concerns), refugee volunteer work (quarrelling with bureaucracy over migrants' fundamental needs), or participation in peace missions (potentially life-threatening).

The abovementioned studies addressing the many benefits of meaning at work also show a substantial divide between the positive psychology and the existential approach in studying meaning and work: contrary to Frankl's explicit socioeconomic engagement by clearly naming humans' fundamental frustration about dehumanization of humans by a man-machine understanding, positive psychology-oriented meaning studies are not addressing the larger societal context and environment of work in an increasingly dehumanized technological culture. Describing this divide, Wong (2014a) summarizes: "To define meaning as serving something bigger than oneself implies that a meaningful life inescapably entails transcending self-interest in order to serve a greater cause. Interestingly, most positive psychologists do not realize that to make the pursuit of happiness and well-being one's basic life orientation seems at odds with the basic orientation of meaning and self-transcendence. Positive psychology models of well-being have a limited view of meaning, which actually hinders a fuller understanding of the pervasive role of meaning in human affairs."

Over many years of research, Wong (2009) has demonstrated: Meaning is necessary for healing, resilience, optimism, and well-being.

As a result, Wong (2014a, b) has been active in developing an integrative, meaning-oriented theory, research approach, and practice, advocating bridging the gap between existential and positive psychology.

In his strive to promote a second wave "Existential Positive Psychology 2.0," Wong (2017) presents an approach, "reformulating Frankl's basic assumptions into testable hypothesis," empirical testing, and applications.

Applications of his PURE strategy in organizational development would address the following areas:

- Developing a Positive Corporate Culture: This meaning-oriented culture is defined by four types of positive cultures – (1) progressive–adaptive culture, (2) purpose-driven culture, (3) community-oriented culture, and (4) people-centered culture. These cultures contribute to intrinsically motivated high performance, because they meet people's deepest needs for meaning, community, spirituality, and agency. The ideal company should possess the attributes of all four types of healthy corporate cultures.
- Servant Leadership (Page and Wong 2000): Servant leadership emphasizes such qualities as integrity, humility, virtue, higher purpose, responsibility, and the need to develop the potentials of all workers. In terms of the identification and assessment of the construct of servant leadership, Wong and colleagues have developed two relevant instruments: a self-assessment of servant leadership and the 360-degree assessment of leadership. A detailed guide to transforming management to servant leadership is also available (Page 2009).

18.5 Linking Existential Fulfillment to Work Load and Work Engagement

Tomic (2016) reports on a study among Dutch city council members, which are assumed to be people with a particular vocation, attracted to serve the public interest. This study illustrates the usefulness of a theory-based approach, examining the association between workload and existential fulfillment on the one hand and work engagement on the other hand.

Seventy-one percent of all Dutch council members have another regular job, with their council function being executed alongside their regular job, and they do not receive appreciable financial incentives for their promoting public interest. The study assessed interrelations between council members' workload, existential fulfillment, and work engagement. Due to the many empirically proven positive effects of work engagement, the researchers were highly interested in investigating on potential links with existential issues. The study operationalized the three focus areas:

Existential fulfillment: A person who fulfills his/her existential tasks, finding life meaning and a fulfilled existence. The notions of self-acceptance, self-actualization, and self-transcendence can be interpreted as basic attitudes in pursuing existential fulfillment. This person:

- Accepts the self, his/her potentialities, and intrinsic limitations
- Actualizes the self and explores his/her possibilities and potentialities for the sake of personal growth in understanding and abilities
- Transcends the self, recognizing the otherness of reality beyond the self, searching for respectful relationships with this reality, deriving life meaning from these relationships, feeling responsible for them, feeling part of a larger whole, distinguishing interests that surpass self-interests, and being able to see the self in perspective of the outer reality

The inability to achieve existential goals may lead to burnout, whereas the achievement of these goals may result in work engagement.

Work engagement: A positive, affective–cognitive state of supreme satisfaction, to be described by vigor, dedication, and absorption. Employees displaying a high level of work engagement display:

- Vigor: high levels of energy and mental flexibility, display willingness to invest effort in their work and perseverance in the face of difficulties
- Dedication: commitment and sense of significance, meaningful experience, inspiring and challenging, with feelings of pride and enthusiasm
- Absorption: full concentration and deep immersion

Workload: The perceived level of pressure due to amount of work and task heaviness.

Findings: The study group around Tomic is cautious, yet confident about their findings, mainly their observed association between workload, existential fulfillment, and work engagement among city council members, that could be generalized for all council members in the country:

- Higher levels of perceived workload correlated significantly with lower levels of work engagement and existential fulfillment.
- The three dimensions of existential fulfillment correlated significantly positive with the three work engagement dimensions.

- High levels on self-actualization, self-acceptance, and self-transcendence corresponded with high levels on work engagement dimensions.
- The higher the score on self-transcendence, the higher the score on absorption.

18.6 The Difference Between "Why?" and "What For?"

While discussing the various constructs and scales for measuring meaning in life, specific final meaning attributions are being discussed especially in the field of primary, hospice and palliative care (Breitbart and Poppito 2014). These findings can well be translated to other fields of meaning attribution, specifically the workplace. With these definitions of meaning-related final attribution, research and practice differentiates between causal meaning attribution of an event, referring to the past, questioning the "How?" of an event, and the final meaning attribution, future related, questioning the "Why?" of an event or matter.

With this relevant differentiation, the authors' study theoretically connects with Frankl's understanding of meaning, citing Nietzsche: "He, who has a Why to live, can bear almost any How."

Research findings and practice in care and their conclusions seem extremely valuable for meaning-oriented research in work, especially in the context of coping with negative, stressful, and extreme experiences:

- While meaning has largely been defined and empirically been validated as a final attribution of general meaning constructs to a specific event, the topic of specific meaning attribution to specific events or issues has gained little attention until today.
- Positive meaning attribution to disease-related life events is clearly associated with benefits for the patients.
- Specific final meaning attribution (giving specifically defined meaning to their specific illness) correlated with higher levels of event acceptance and well-being, less perceived pressure.
- Negative meaning scores are related with negative effects regarding the illness, regardless of the severity of the illness.

18.7 Meaning Awareness and Storytelling

Persons living meaningful lives tell a specific type of stories about their lives, moving from:

- Suffering to salvation – turning a tragedy into triumph – and moving from victim to victory and from contamination to unconditional freedom
- Fatalism to growth and agency (McAdams 2013)

18.8 A Work of Service for Others

In an intergenerational study of younger and senior employees, Weeks (2017) found that participants above all age groups defined intrinsic motivation and having good relationships as most important components of meaningful work. Younger participants clearly defined "a job of service for others" to be most meaningful and rewarding. The most striking finding, though, was that every generation felt that the other one "was only in it for the money." The author argues that these findings suggest to intervene workshops where employees can experience that meaning cannot be dictated, where participants can overcome stereotypes by discussing what gives meaning to their work and life, and where individual meanings can emerge allowing for the process to develop throughout the individual work and being part of the organization.

18.9 Meaning Awareness and Sources of Meaning

Schnell has developed a comprehensive source of meaning inventory. According to this inventory, meaningfulness can be defined as a basic trust, unconsciously shaping perception, action, and goal striving.[1]

This inventory, LeBe/SoMe (Schnell 2008 and 2009), consists of 151 items, evaluating 26 different sources of meaning; identifying existential relevant cognition (personal myth), action (personal rituals), and emotion (experiences of transcending); and ultimately "evaluating the individual level of meaningfulness," as the author claims.

The 26 sources of meaning were grouped in four high-order meaning dimensions of:

- Self-transcendence: Self-transcendence is subdivided into two subcategories: vertical self-transcendence, which is related to aspects of religiosity and spirituality, and horizontal self-transcendence referring to social engagement, love of nature, self-awareness, health and generativity, and transcending self-related needs.
- Self-actualization (including challenge, individualism, power, development, achievement, freedom, knowledge, and creativity).
- Order (including tradition, practicality, morality, and reason).
- Well-being and relatedness (including community, fun, love, comfort, care, attentiveness, and harmony).

Schnell finds that sources of meaning in life come from many areas and are meaningful to different people and for different reasons. Some find meaning in religion; others find meaning in more secular ways:

[1] Interested students applying for logotherapy studies in Austria were assessed for their self-transcendance scores' and meaning orientation' with this LeBe/SoMe inventory.

- Generativity (horizontal self-transcendence) is the most powerful predictor of meaningfulness.
- Vertical self-transcendence (spirituality and religions).
- Self-actualization ranges third as giving meaning to one's life. In this context, work plays a substantial role with experiencing challenges, creativity, setting goals, and developing own knowledge.

Overall meaningfulness increases with the amount of sources of meaning (density) drawn on. Meaningfulness also increases with the diversity of sources of meaning.

Finding meaning in working for others is the strongest predictor of motivation to work.

In another study, Schnell et al. (2013) operationalized meaning in work by three interrelated levels: individual, work tasks, and organizational. Analogously to meaning in life, meaning in work is defined as a sense of coherence, direction, significance, and belonging in the working life. Against this background, meaning in work and potential predictors have been measured and tested. A survey of employees from a broad variety of professions was conducted. Predictors of meaningful work were identified in three levels:

Person: Work role fit.

Work task: Task significance.

Organizational level: Socio-moral climate and organizational self-transcendent orientation contribute positively to the sense of meaning in work.

Schnell reminds us that each work and service has some relevance for others and that, generally, work has gained too much relevance for individuals' life.

Schnell also reported that one third of the participants are "existentially indifferent." They do not believe in anything and are not interested in finding any meaning.

18.10 Work: A Broader Transcendent Life Purpose

In a most recent study by Bailey and Madden (2016), meaningful work was defined as "when an individual perceives an authentic connection between work and a broader transcendent life purpose beyond the self." This study is addressing many of the abovementioned caveats relating to empirical meaning testing. Bailey and Madden found that experiencing meaningfulness in work was:

- A personal and individual matter
- Strongly related to thoughts or memories about other family members
- Not a constant state of mind, but was rather experienced in unplanned or unexpected moments at work
- Defined and experienced independently of the respective managers but with the latter being the top destroyer of meaningfulness at work

- "A delicate flower that requires careful nurturing" (Bailey and Madden)
- A complex and profound task for organizations, supporting their employees to find their meaning in work

Specifically, five qualities of meaningful work emerged from this study:

- Self-transcendent: People talked about the impact and relevance their work had for others. A garbage collector, an academic, and a priest witnessed their work being important for others and the greater community.
- Poignant: People often found their work meaningful at moments associated with distress, suffering, or mixed or painful moments. Meaningfulness is not always a positive experience. Some scientists are observing "a tyranny of the positive," associating meaningful work with improvements of all kinds, happiness and joy. Bailey and Madden suggest that experiencing a deep sense of meaning in work is often related to cope with extremely challenging conditions or to triumph over difficult circumstances, being reported, e.g., by nurses, lawyers, drivers, and others.
- Episodic: Meaningful work was experienced not consistently, but rather in peak moments, throwing a fundamental light on the individual work and establishing a symbolic meaningfulness of the work delivered in the person's respective function.
- Reflective: Meaningfulness of work was not so much experienced in general, but was more a matter of post-reflection on the work that the person has been doing. Attributing meaning to their work was more a thoughtful, retrospective act of "finding meaning" in hindsight. For the participants of this study, this was the first time at all that they (had the opportunity of reflecting and give) thought to the potential meaning of their work.
- Personal: Meaningful work is individually understood in the context of a person's specific work function and, in addition, in the wider context of an individual person's life. Thus, meaningful work cannot be generalized by a set of definitions, valid for everybody. Actually, in this study, meaningful work was not positively associated with the team, the managers, or the organization. Again, meaningful work here goes far beyond factors of engagement and general work satisfaction findings.

Bailey and Madden also found "seven deadly sins," destroying meaning at work, among them disconnecting people from their values.

From these finding, they suggest creating a meaningful ecosystem, focusing on these four areas of meaning at work and thereby establishing holistic meaningfulness at work:

- Organizational meaningfulness: Explaining and focusing on the positive contribution of the organization to society, with no hypocrisy or manipulative activities foiling the purpose claimed.
- Job meaningfulness: Connecting individual functions with the organization's broader purpose and encouraging this personal contribution.

- Task meaningfulness: Explaining repetitive or boring work as part of the overall meaningful function, so that employees can better deal with this part without destroying the overall meaning of their work and specific task.
- Interactional meaningfulness: By definition, meaning is related to something and someone beyond the self. Employees find their work meaningful relating to the beneficiaries of their work and relating to their fellow employees. Meaningful work is connected with relationships. Past, present, and future beneficiaries of work can be imagined, giving meaning to the individual work done.

In exploring meaningful work with persons from a wide range of professions, Kössler and Scheuer found that meaningful work is not defined by the work and function as such. Contrary to other findings – suggesting higher levels of finding meaning in work with higher education and social class – their study found that there was no significant difference in finding work meaningful over various professions, with higher and lower education resp. social class. According to their findings, finding meaning in work is rather influenced by the degree of volition (sense of control) and financial and structural constraints in the workplace.

18.11 The Future of Empirical Meaning Research

Altogether, human existential and psychological needs address indicators for well-being (as defined in Seligman's PERMA-model), positive resources for coping with negative life events, and thirdly, they include issues of meaning beyond the human being in the world. This process of "collage" of ideas, perspectives, and empirical research on the human search for meaning is an ongoing process.

Above all these relevant discussions, a holistic concept of meaning and human existential and psychological needs is emerging:

- Emmons and Keortge (2003) identified five factors: personal strivings, achievement, intimacy, religion/spirituality, and generativity.
- Wong (1998) conceptualized a personal meaning profile, consisting of achievement, relationships, religion, and self-transcendence.
- Ebersole and Hess (1998) defined life narratives, life work, relationships, religious beliefs, and service as main components of leading a meaningful life.
- Schnell (2009) has developed a comprehensive Sources of Meaning and Meaning in Life Questionnaire, now available in 14 languages, for various continents, from English and Russian to Farsi.

Both, the existential and the positive psychology community, have come to find meaning and meaning awareness as central psychological and philosophical factors, relevant for human striving and coping and for understanding the individual's role and place in this world.

Is the search for meaning a means or an end of its own? What is the "true goal" of meaning motivation?

Is striving for meaning merely an instrumental matter of striving for subjective well-being or a defense mechanism, i.e., a means of motivation, or is it rather inherent in all human beings?

To which extent is striving for meaning a spiritual and philosophical question that cannot be fully captured and operationalized by empirical definitions and objective correlates?

Specifically the issue of measuring "self-transcendence" as a general component of meaning in life and, more specifically, in the workplace is an issue of substantial scientific and research with these questions, suggesting further discussion and research.

Taking Frankl's understanding of the will to meaning as the primary human motivation into account, and recognizing that this primary motivation may lie latent in the unconscious, it is spiritually rooted and remains unconditionally the very spiritual core of a person's *Geist* dimension:

- Can personal meaning be comprehensively measured?
- Can "self-transcendence, partially beyond the limits to time and space" (Wong), be empirically measured?

18.12 Discussion: Limitations of Empirical Research on Meaning

Based on a thorough theoretical framework of assessing the available meaning tests and scales and their specific constructs of meaning, Schnell T. (2009) is scientifically claiming validity and reliability for her LeBe/SoMe inventory and the according subscales, also operationalizing and measuring "horizontal and vertical self-transcendence" and advertising her meaning inventory to interested clients from all fields. Decades ago, Frankl (2000) was praising such empirical studies on meaning awareness while conceding that these studies are "deterministic" by definition. In his latest publication on "ultimate meaning," he distinctly differentiated between "meaning" and "ultimate meaning" and their empirical validation.

The author BvD would find Schnell's widely acknowledged research a valid example for the benefits and limitations of empirical meaning testing. With this interest, the author is collecting some of Schnell's and Frankl's basic findings and arguments about validation of meaning through scientific research. V. Frankl (2000, p. 142) explained:

> When setting out to discuss the meaning of meaning, I referred to meaning as something 'down to earth'. However, it cannot be denied that there is also some sort of meaning that is 'up to heaven', as it were some sort of ultimate meaning, that is; a meaning, that of the whole, of the 'universe', or at least a meaning of one's life as a whole; at any rate, a long-range meaning. I do not think that it is worthy of a psychiatrist – or, for that matter, of a scientist – to deny on a priori grounds that such a long-range meaning does exist…I am indicating that ultimate meaning would not be accessible to reason or intellect. By the same token, it necessarily would elude any strictly scientific approach.

Schnell's research (2008) – among German-speaking populations in Germany, Austria, and Switzerland (i.e., not only German nationality) – showed that one third of the sample appears as *existentially indifferent:* this newly discovered population of people neither experiences their lives as meaningful nor suffers from a lack of meaning. Schnell finds this a "surprisingly high proportion" (translation by the author BvD). Reflecting on this group's lack of meaning and lack of suffering, in her research findings, Schnell links these persons' condition to their extremely low values in self-knowledge and self-awareness. She suggests that these existentially indifferent persons might either *not realize* their indifference or *not admit* it, terming the gap between lack of meaning and perceived lack of suffering from meaninglessness as *denial* on the part of the indifferent persons, which might temporarily serve as a coping strategy.

With this argumentation, construct validity and reliability are saved at the cost of Frankl's ultimate meaning hypothesis, as Frankl had assessed the situation in his late years of work. Frankl (2000, p. 146) explained: "Small wonder that ultimate meaning is missing in the world as described by scientists. However, does this imply that the world is void of ultimate meaning. Ultimate meaning is rejected by science. However, this state of affairs does in no way entitle a scientist to deny that ultimate meaning possibly does exist. It is perfectly legitimate that the scientist as such restricts himself to a certain 'cross section' he cuts through reality, and it may well happen that within this cross section no meaning whatsoever can be found...The fact remains that not everything can be explained in meaningful terms. But what now can be explained is at least the reason why this is necessarily impossible."

Meaning, at least to its ultimate dimension, can – by definition – not be fully captured and operationalized in empirical tests and terms. Frankl himself explained: "The more comprehensive the meaning, the less comprehensible it is...Ultimate meaning necessarily is beyond comprehension" (Frankl 2000). This, however, provides for no reasons to attribute "repression" or "denial" to those, who do not match the meaning construct, limited by definition.

While Schnell (2008) is suggesting intensive further studies on this existentially indifferent population, she finds Frankl's fundamental hypothesis of man's inherent will to meaning as basically refuted by her findings, and, in addition, Schnell suggests nothing less but to subsume Frankl's will to meaning under Maslow's hierarchy of needs, which Frankl was strongly challenging throughout his work for multiple systematic reasons. Schnell (2008) explains: "... A relativization of a central assumption of meaning research can already be made on the basis of the frequency of existence of existential indifference. Thus, Frankl's postulated will to meaning is at best a growth need in the sense of Maslow (1970), but not as one deficit need, which causes a state of tension experienced as a deficiency in case of nonfulfillment ...."

Frankl (2000) "closed" the gap, equally leaving the full empirical validation question of meaning open, by arguing with the utmost philosophical, existential perspective: "...What is unknowable need not be unbelievable. True, it is not possible to find out intellectually whether everything is ultimately meaningless or whether there is ultimate meaning behind everything. But if we cannot answer the question intellectually, we may well do so existentially. Where an intellectual cognition fails, an existential decision is due."

There are two sides of the coin: Until today, homo economicus, business, and science are based on the ultimate belief – what can't be measured can't be done. All realms of life are deeply imbued, captivated, and compelled by quantities, statistics, balance sheets, and scientifically based facts and figures. On the other side, this twenty-first-century coin shows denial and repression of every other image, idea, impression, thought, and vision that cannot immediately be materialized, aligned with reductionism and increased craving for "something beyond." Together with this sociopsychological assessment, the existentially indifferent might well turn out to be the existentialists of our times, indirectly challenging the others to enter into a true dialogue about the existential givens and about what makes us human.

Batthyany's (2016) remarks favoring intensive further research over hurried conclusions seem ever more appropriate.

While Wong is dedicated to translate Frankl's approach to "testable hypothesis" and speaks for the "value of combining philosophical insights with scientific rigor," he firmly argues that, until today, positive psychology is based on an instrumental understanding of meaning-seeking and meaning-making. These are his most articulated main reservations against an instrumental definition of meaning awareness:

- Searching for meaning and making meaning may result in hyperintention and thereby actually missing what cannot be achieved directly, but only through being in the world.
- Being in the world is an open-end process. Consequently, finding meaning in one's own life and in work is an ongoing process of innumerous situations, with meanings being defined by values lived.
- Understanding the search for meaning as an ongoing process, the outcomes of "having found" meaning – be it personally, on the organizational resp. business level, in society, or globally – can only be assessed in hindsight, but it cannot be promised in advance.
- Correlations between finding meaning and various benefits oftentimes do not stand "the layman's" test, and, more seriously, their underlying assumptions might lay unethical responsibility for the negative on the individual person, who is described as not having found yet his/her true meaning in life and life satisfaction.
- Promising that meaning awareness and proactive health orientation are directly linked to health variables, among them less disorders with reduced levels of symptoms, later start of age-related memory degradation, and generally longer life expectancy, is a regression to reductionism that Frankl so consistently challenged throughout his work: Relating illness, complex issues of duration of life and potential dementia to an alleged lack of meaning orientation, immediately relates to Susan Sontag's grand essay on "Illness as Metaphor," when she revealed how the then prevailing psychophysical images of curse, punishment,

and dreadly fate, around severe conditions like cancer, do add to the patients' being stigmatized, suffering, and feeling personally responsible.

- Apparently, Frankl's approach of unconditional meaning and human dignity, relevant for the existential givens and the tragic triad of suffering and terminal conditions, needs to be rescued against the potential "terror of positivity," when meaning is advertised as saving us from actually all, that constitutes our human condition.

Suggesting further research, Wong (2017) assesses positive psychology assumptions and studies, via Frankl's main hypotheses, where he would find major differences. Just like Wong, the author BvD understands these reflections as a resource for further discussion and insight into, what he termed, Positive Psychology 2.0, best responding to individuals' twenty-first-century needs and search for meaning:

- Meaning vs. Happiness
  The major difference between pursuing happiness as an end state and pursuing meaning reflects a fundamental difference in worldview. The pursuit of meaning may entail personal sacrifice and suffering for a worthy cause; however, in terms of the larger picture, such a pursuit yields a greater good and a higher level of satisfaction.

- Being vs. Doing
  The contemporary positive psychology of meaning, strength, virtue, and well-being focuses on components of the good life that can be achieved through engaging in the proper activities (e.g., strengths-enhancing or happiness-inducing activities). In contrast to the cognitive behavioral focus of positive psychology, Viktor Frankl's spiritual approach emphasizes being rather than doing.

- Meaning-Seeking vs. Meaning-Making
  Contemporary meaning-making models (e.g., Park 2010) focus almost exclusively on the cognitive function of making sense of the world in negative situations. In contrast, Frankl's meaning-seeking model focuses more on meaning-seeking, in terms of how to live with courage, freedom, and responsibility.

Batthyany and Russo-Netzer (2014, p. 13) notes in his widely recognized publication on meaning in both positive and existential approaches that in looking at meaning research "we are constantly confronted with findings that do not seem to make much sense, if the main rationale of meaning motivation is to feel good and avoid feeling uncomfortable." The author BvD agrees with Batthyany's reflections that we almost daily witness individuals' behaviors and attitudes being directed to something beyond their "feeling good" or "happy" or needing to cope with existential life events. But rather, these persons deliberately make a decision to take a specific attitude that might substantially change their and their family's course of life, for only one reason: they wish to give meaning to their lives and dedicate their knowledge to a specific cause beyond their immediate physical and psychosocial interests.

Looking at the empirical studies and findings on meaning and work together with the current challenges and expectations this topic is facing in twenty-first-century workplaces is suggesting scientific humility and vigor at the same time. The state-of-the-art knowledge in operationalizing meaningful work "prohibit us to follow any over-simplified, exclusively 'pragmatic' perspective of meaning awareness and meaning motivation" (Batthyany 2016) while also inspiring the interested community to connect in search for meaning and existential fulfillment.

References

Antonovsky A (1987) Unraveling the mystery of health. How people manage stress and stay well. Josey-Bass Publishers, San Francisco

Bailey C, Madden A (2016) What makes work meaningful – or meaningless? MIT Sloan Manag Rev, June 01, 2016

Battista J, Almond R (1973) The development of meaning in life. Psychiatry 36(4):409–427

Batthyany A (ed) (2016) Logotherapy and existential analysis. In: Proceedings of the Viktor Frankl Institute Vienna, vol 1. Springer, Cham

Batthyany A, Russo-Netzer P (2014) Meaning in positive and existential psychology. Springer, New York

Bellah RN, Madsen R, Sullivan WM, Swidler A, Tipton SM (1985) Habits of the heart. Harper Collins, New York

Boeckmann W (1984) Wer Leistung fordert, muss Sinn bieten. Econ Verlag, Berlin

Breitbart WS, Poppito SR (2014) Individual meaning-centered psychotherapy for patients with advanced cancer. A treatment manual. Oxford University Press, Oxford

Crumbaugh JC, Maholick LT (1964) An experimental study in existentialism: the psychometric approach to Frankl's concept of Noogenic neurosis. J Clin Psychol 20:200–207

Damon W, Menon J, Cotton Bronk K (2003) The development of purpose during adolescence. Appl Dev Sci 7(3):119–128

Dik BJ, Byrne ZS, Steger MF (2013) Purpose and meaning in the workplace. American Psychological Association, Washington, DC

Dik BJ, Duffy RD, Eldridge B (2009) Calling and vocation in career counseling: recommendations for promoting meaningful work. Prof Psychol 40:625–632

Dik BJ, Duffy RD (2009) Calling and vocation at work: definitions and prospects for research and practice. Couns Psychol 37:424–450. https://doi.org/10.1177/0011000008316430

Ebersole P, Hess P (1998) Towards healthy aging. Human needs and nursing response. Mosby, Maryland

Emmons RA, Keortge SG (2003) Spiritual well-being, spiritual intelligence and work place policy. In: Giacalone RA, Jurkiewicz CA (eds) Handbook of workplace spirituality and organizational performance. ME Sharpe, Armonk, pp 123–136

Frankl VE (1985) Aerzliche Seelsorge. Grundlagen der Logotherapie und Existenzanalyse. Fischer Taschenbuch Verlag, Frankfurt am Main

Frankl VE (1988) The will to meaning. Meridian, New York

Frankl VE (2000) Man's search for ultimate meaning. Basic Books, New York

Grant AM, Campbell EM, Chen G, Cottone K, Lapedis D, Lee K (2007) Impact and the art of motivation maintenance: the effects of contact with beneficiaries on persistence behaviour. Organ Behav Hum Decis Process 103(1):53–67

Hall DT, Chandler DE (2005) Psychological success: when the career is calling. J Organ Behav 26(2):155–176

Hardy L (1990) The fabric of this world. Inquiries into calling, career choice and the design of human work. Eerdmans Publishing, Grand Rapids
Hunter I, Dik B, Banning JH (2010) College students' perceptions of calling in work and life: a qualitative analysis. J Vocat Behav 76:178–186
Laengle A, Orgler C, Kundi M (2003) The existence scale. Eur Psychother 4(1):2003
Littman-Ovadia H, Steger MF (2009) Character strengths and well-being among volunteers and employees: towards an integrative model. J Posit Psychol 5:419–430
Lukas E (1981) Validation of logotherapy. Int Forum Logother 4(2):116–125
Lukas E (1986) Logo-Test zur Messung von innerer Sinnerfuellung und existenzieller frustration. Franz Deuticke, Wien, A
McAdams DP (2013) The redemptive self: stories Americans Liebe by – revised and expanded edition. Oxford University Press, Oxford
McQuaid M (2016) Online meaning workshop. Script. http://michellemcquaid.com. Accessed May 2017
Michaelson C, Pratt MG, Grant AM, Dunn CP (2014) Meaningful work: connecting business ethics and organization studies. J Bus Ethics 121(1):77–90
Page D (2009) Servant empowered leadership: a hands-on guide to transforming you and your organization. Power to Change Ministries, Langley
Page D, Wong PTP (2000) A conceptual framework for measuring servant leadership. In: Adjibolooso S (ed) The human factor in shaping the course of history and development. University Press of America, Lanham, pp 69–110
Park CL (2010) Making sense of the meaning literature: an integrative review of meaning making and its effects on adjustment to stressful life events. Psychol Bull 136(2):257–301
Peterson C (2013) Pursuing the good life. Oxford University Press, New York
Pratt MG Ashfort BE (2003) Fostering meaningfulness in working and at work. In: Cameron KS Dutton JE Quinn RE (eds) Positive organizational scholarship: foundations of a new discipline, Berrett-Koehler Publishers, San Francisco
Reker GT, Peacock EJ (1981) The life attitude profile (LAP): a multidimensional instrument for assessing attitudes towards life. Can J Behav Sci 13:264–273
Schnell T (2008) Deutsche in der Sinnkrise? Ein Einblick in die Sinnforschung mit Daten einer repräsenativen deutschen Stichprobe. Journal für Psychologie 16(3)
Schnell T (2009) The Sources of Meaning and Meaning in Life Questionnaire (SoMe): relations to demographics and well-being. J Posit Psychol 4(6):483–499. https://doi.org/10.1080/17439760903271074
Schnell T, Becker P (2007) Der Fragebogen zu Lebensbedeutungen und Lebenssinn (LeBe). Hogrefe, Göttingen, D
Schnell T, Hoege T, Pollet E (2013) Predicting meaning in work: theory, data, implications. J Posit Psychol 8:543–554
Seligman M (2002) Authentic happiness. Using the new positive psychology to realize your potential. Simon and Schuster, New York
Steger MF, Frazier P, Oishi S, Kaler M (2006) The meaning in life questionnaire: assessing the presence of and search for meaning in life. J Couns Psychol 53:80–93
Steger MF, Dik BJ, Duffy RD (2012) Measuring meaningful work: the work and meaning inventory (WAMI). J Career Assess 00(0):1–16
Tomic M (2016) Workload, existential fulfillment and work engagement among city council members. In: Battyány A (ed) Logotherapy and existential analysis: proceedings of the Viktor Frankl Institute Vienna 1. Springer, Cham
Warner SC, Williams JI (1987) The meaning in life scale. J Chronic Dis 40(6):503–512
Weeks KP (2017, July) Every generation wants meaningful work – but thinks that other age groups are in it for the money. Harv Bus Rev. Accessed Sept 2017
Wong PTP (1998) Implicit theories of meaningful life and the development of the personal meaning profile (PMP). In: PTP W, Fry P (eds) The human quest for meaning: a handbook of psychological research and clinical applications. Erlbaum, Mahwah, pp 111–140

Wong PTP (2009) Viktor Frankl: Prophet of hope for the 21 century. In: Batthyany A, Levinson J (eds) Existential psychotherapy of meaning. Handbook of logotherapy and existential analysis. Zeig, Tucker & Theisen, Phoenix
Wong PTP (2014a) Viktor Frankl's meaning seeking model and positive psychology. In: Battyany A, Russo-Netzer P (eds) Meaning in positive and existential psychology. Springer, New York, pp 149–184
Wong PTP (2014b) Viktor Frankl's meaning seeking model and positive psychology. Retrieved from: http://www.drpaulwong.com/viktor-frankls-meaning-seeking-model-and-positive-psychology/. Accessed Aug 2017
Wong PTP (2017) Good work: the meaning centered approach. Retrieved from: http://www.drpaulwong.com/good-work-the-meaning-centered-approach-mca/. Accessed May 2017
Wrzesniewski A, McCauley C, Rozin P, Schwartz B (1997) Jobs, careers, and callings: people's relations to their work. J Res Personal 31:21–33

Chapter 19
The Human Capacity: Current Approaches in Humanities

Contents

Two specifically human phenomena, the capacity of self-transcendence and the capacity of self-detachment, are addressed and mobilized by the logotherapeutic approach.

Today, some of the most utilized and relevant approaches in the field of humanities are being applied to organizational development, human interactions, and management approaches, all of them linked to man's meaning orientation.

How do these current, diverse approaches benefit from each other and how could building on the commonalities of current research and the logotherapeutic approach be further strengthened?

19.1 New Findings in Neuroscience

The most revolutionary findings for this century are referring to how our brain with the different parts and networks functions and how we are actually inherently made to build and nourish relationships with other human beings.

As a matter of taking an attitude, we are challenged to understand our human functioning, the potentials of our intellectual capacities and our brain in all its dimensions. There is no reason for taking a deterministic attitude, of reductionism or of resigning to the digital technology. Neuroscientists are giving us abounding examples of the newly explored capacities of our "mindful networks" and of our potentials to develop on the current findings of human functioning.

B. von Devivere, *Meaningful Work: Viktor Frankl's Legacy for the 21st Century*,
https://doi.org/10.1007/978-3-319-89791-2_19

19.2 Mirror Neurons

The findings have been eliciting the meaning of initial reciprocal dyadic mirroring and resonance processes between the infant and the caretaker in the emergence of an infantile self: The neurobiological basis of interpersonal mirroring and resonance processes, whose significance extends beyond early childhood, has been termed the mirror neuron system. Beyond early childhood the mirror neuron system allows people to understand each other *intuitively*. The neurobiological basis for people's ability to *consciously* change perspective is in the frontal lobe, that is, located in the prefrontal cortex structures, where the inner conceptualization of the self and significant others is coded.

When people consciously make an effort to understand the inner world of the other, networks are always activated, where the inner image of their own person has been stored and is referred to. The frontal cortex is the location – in addition to the so-called structural neuronal networks that function as "inner self-observer" (Bauer 2016) and play a significant role for good self-care.

Mirroring and resonance processes between two persons are of relevance for any encounter, be it in work or family or private life. This has been one of the most powerful discoveries in science, reconfirming philosophers' classical approach of the utmost importance of the encounter between two persons, defined as the basic I-Thou relationship by Martin Buber (1996). What are the implications of these findings for how we live our relationships in everyday work life?

19.3 Investing in Caring Economics

Based on neuroscience's groundbreaking findings that humans are generally all interconnected, the model of *homo economicus* has finally been proved as scientifically wrong. Facing humanity's twenty-first-century problems and challenges, this still extremely powerful concept of man needs to be changed to learning strategies for sustainable behavior and prosocial activity based on the twenty-first-century knowledge.

Tania Singer, Director of the Department of Social Neuroscience at Max Planck Institute for Human Cognitive and Brain Sciences in Leipzig, has successfully challenged the homo economicus concept and created the research field of "social neuroscience." Today, she is recognized as the world expert on empathy and compassion.

Singer (2015a) explains that every person has a caring system, feeling what others feel, inside themselves. It helps us to survive, has an evolutionary basis in both men and women, and can be activated to become the future basis of our economy just as today's competition and self-interest are activated. Compassion, gratitude, and wisdom of the heart can be trained just like we are training our muscles.

Social neuroscientists are calling upon today's economists that they should start considering and acknowledging solidarity and appreciation for a common cause as another basic human trait with benefits for all. We can change the balance from egoism to altruism. The Department of Social Neuroscience at Max Planck Institute for Human Cognitive and Brain Sciences in Leipzig's partner, the Kieler Institut für Weltwirtschaft, would not claim that this approach is naive toward the ruling business. Just the opposite, as Singer (2015b) explains: "One could not seriously claim to move in the direction of more compassion for others and at the same time realize nothing but the own benefits. There is no sense in just talking about it. The leaders of the world need to make their own experience, how their awareness and conscience widens and would open their heart."

Together with an inspired interdisciplinary group, Singer et al. (2015) have created the ReSource Project, offering training for compassion for individuals. Their compassionate behavior trains and creates change for the individual, their peers and relationships, the environment, and the scientific community. The project is also aimed at bridging the gap between psychology and economics for the benefit of human mankind.

19.4 The Neuroplasticity of Our Brain

"The individual human brain is a social construct." (Huether)

Together with the mirror neuron system, neuroscientists have confirmed the discovery that the neuronal and synaptic connections in the human brain are developed from early childhood on and can be altered. The human brain has the innate ability to transcend own thoughts and intentions into larger contexts, the ability to feel what others feel, and to experience feelings of connectedness.

In neuroscientific terms, peace and love are generated by the most intricate neuronal networks. These networks and their abilities mediated by them are not preformed by an inherited genetic program. They all must be acquired, stabilized, and facilitated by experience-dependent plasticity, i.e., by education, socialization, and enculturation.

Modern brain research confirms putting on pressure and inducing fear are not only unsuitable strategies for improving performance; they also strangle curiosity and creativity in schools, businesses, and human relationships. It's high time to think about a new relationship culture. And slowly but surely, this information is starting to be implemented as a successful leadership concept everywhere. This concept is called "supportive leadership" (Huether 2006, 2016), and it aims at the promotion of the readiness to achieve through support, recognition, and encouragement. What should grow better has to be adequately watered and fertilized.

The most delicate neuronal networks of the frontal cortex are the sites where the most complex, the most sophisticated, and the most human-specific brain functions are generated: goal-oriented behavior and motivation, self-concept and self-efficacy, impulse control, consciousness, and *the ability to transcend own thoughts and intentions* into larger contexts. The ability to deal successfully with stressors is largely being influenced by the capacity to build on internal strengths and external relational support and is severely being harmed by lack of support, fear, and anxieties as they are experienced in "results-driven" working environments.

19.4.1 The Co-construction of Identity and Meaning

We all have the ability to understand the other person. Our self, our own identity, and the meaning we give to our environment and to the world are co-constructed: Our intentions are being created and modified in a shifting dialogue with the felt intentions of others. Our feelings are shaped by the intentions, thoughts, and feelings of others. And our thoughts are co-created in dialogue. In short, our conscious life is co-created. We are wired to connect with others and to build a community.

This constant process of meaning creation is a reality, and we are called to make it explicit. In Frankl's terms, we are called to consciously respond to the questions of life in freedom and responsibility.

References

Bauer J (2016) Der Beitrag der „Sozialen Neurowissenschaften" zum Verständnis der Psyche. Psychotherapie-Wissenschaft Band 6/Heft 1 /2016
Buber M (1996) I and Thou. Touchstone, New York
Huether G (2006) The compassionate brain. Trumpeter, Boston
Huether G (2016) Supportive leadership. In: Faktor A. Das Arbeitgebermagazin, June 2016
Singer T (2015a) Caring economics: conversations on altruism and compassion, between scientists, economists, and the Dalai Lama. Melia Publishing Services, Maidenhead
Singer T (2015b) Interview with ZEIT online: http://www.zeit.de/kultur/2015-08/wirtschaftspolitik-tania-singer-resource-projekt-10nach8. Accessed Oct 2017
Singer T et al (2015) The resource project. http://compassion-training.org. Accessed June 2017

Chapter 20
Meaning-Focused Approaches in Coaching, Counseling, and Psychotherapy

Contents

How can we come to grips with the ills and ailments of our time, which are grounded in a frustration of the will to meaning. ...If there is a logotherapeutic movement, it certainly belongs to the human rights movements. It focuses on the human right to a life as meaningful as possible...its combination with other techniques should be encouraged and welcome. That way, its effectiveness can be enlarged and expanded. (Frankl 1988)

B. von Devivere, *Meaningful Work: Viktor Frankl's Legacy for the 21st Century*,
https://doi.org/10.1007/978-3-319-89791-2_20

Working for an integrated, humanist, and holistic approach, the differences and borders between the professional functions in organizational management and development, human resources management, consulting, coaching, counseling, and therapeutic approaches are increasingly becoming less relevant for the active community in search for "joining their forces," in favor of a spirit of mutual cooperation and learning from each other for the benefit of everybody engaged in working for rehumanizing work.

This, of course, does not mean denying professional differences, whereas in this world of interconnections, in search for improving the situation, links between the various experts have become increasingly important and a guiding principle of cooperation beyond rather outdated borders and past limitations in thinking.

These are some of the currently most widely utilized approaches in developing human potentials in search for meaning with an integrative approach for cooperation for the best development of the human capacity in work and private life.

20.1 Coaching and Social Counseling Services in the Workplace

Each person is challenged by specific conditions. The finest of human freedoms is the ability to choose one's own attitude in this given set of circumstances. (Frankl)

More and more organizations in business and organizations are offering coaching and social counseling in the workplace. Mostly, staff may address any workplace-related or private issue affecting their work, which they want to reconsider, understand, manage, and solve.

Issues Addressed in Workplace Counseling and Coaching

Generally, staff may address any workplace-related or private issue they want to reconsider, understand, manage, and solve.

Clients bring forward all aspects relating to their work and private life, relating to:

- Individual task, function, performance
- Colleagues, team, employee–manager relationship
- Staff management, responsibility, influence
- Self-care and care for others
- Conflict and mediation
- Professional development, career, calling, meaningful work
- Questions relating to their self: self-esteem, self-identity
- Business ethics, compliance, dignity at work
- Health, stress symptoms, anxieties
- Dealing with emotions
- Clinical symptoms – depression, addiction, eating disorders, etc.
- Private, individual well-being
- Family well-being

- Existential issues
- Bereavement
- Trauma

20.1.1 Coaching Services

Coaching services are about helping coachees achieving their goals. The ICF International Coach Federation defines coaching as "...partnering with clients in a thought-provoking and creative process that inspires them to maximize their personal and professional potential, which is particularly important in today's uncertain and complex environment. Coaches honor the client as the expert in his/her life and work and believe every client is creative, resourceful and whole. Standing on this foundation, the coach's responsibility is to:

- Discover, clarify, and align with what the client wants to achieve.
- Encourage client self-discovery.
- Elicit client-generated solutions and strategies.
- Hold the client responsible and accountable. This process helps clients dramatically improve their outlook on work and life, while improving their leadership skills and unlocking their potential."

At a time, when coaching was applied and widely appreciated only in sports, it was Frankl (1988) who lucidly explained the human capacity for transcending the very self and gets new insights into the individual person's behaviors and potential other options: Referring to the human noological (spiritual, Geist-) dimension, Frankl elucidated the person's general capacity "to rise above." Here, the individual relates to their human capacity for self-detachment, not only detaching himself from a situation but also from himself. The person is actually "opening a new dimension" (Frankl), whenever he:

- Takes a stand toward his own somatic and psychic conditions and determinants
- Is reflecting upon himself
- Rejects himself
- Makes himself an object
- Makes objections to himself
- Displays his being conscious of himself
- Exhibits his being conscientious of himself
- Judges and evaluates his own deeds in moral and ethical terms
- Chooses his own attitude

In workplace social counseling settings, clients are approaching the workplace counselor on workplace-related issues: how to best achieve improved results, seeking to be more balanced, focusing on specific targets in improving their future performance. The focus of this coaching approach is on becoming aware of various options; on getting better access to individual strengths, competencies, and resources; on achieving results requested; on professional development; and on taking appropriate action. The clients want to have improved access to and strive to make the best use of their competencies. In this setting, specific objectives and outcomes are defined and are achieved in a time frame mutually agreed upon with the social counselor.

Above all either more counseling or rather coaching-related activities, counselors and certified coaches will share certain tools and techniques in their approaches. Primarily though, counselors and coaches need to be "mindful of their respective levels of expertise and practice only within their competence" (BACP, p. 06).

This actually includes accredited coaching training, in order to understand difficult conditions that cannot be adequately be treated and addressed in workplace coaching and would need further referral.

Issues of confidentiality and providing "informed consent" to the client are vitally important in workplace counseling, where a triangular contract between employer, service provider, and client employee is the most common type of service being delivered.

Above all differences of contract and service provision, workplace counselors should practice on the basis of following essential standards and personal accountability:

- Accredited coaching and, if relevant, psychotherapeutic education
- General coaching experience
- Experience of working in organizations
- Experience and understanding of short-term brief and/or solution-focused coaching

Today, professional and educated coaches as well as counselors/therapists are strongly favoring, advertising, and implementing this professionally educated approach, based on educational certificates to be transparently understood and reflected by potential clients seeking support. Due to the irrefutable demands by clients for transparent professional coaching certifications, a "Round Table Coaching" (RTC) has been established, where more than ten coaching associations around the globe have defined standards for professional coaching.

Unfortunately, there are growing concerns about intransparent and manipulating practices being applied, with clients approaching the respective professional associations of developmental trainings, education, coaching, and counseling with allegations of violation of ethical standards, harmful practices, and abuse against service providers. This has triggered the Austrian Government Ministry of Health and Education to issue a "Guideline on Esoteric Practices" (2014), banning specifically named approaches from their application in accredited counseling or coaching practices.

In 1995, at an international conference on various therapeutic approaches, Viktor Frankl was approached on a professional's "right attitude" to these growing markets of offering all types of potentially harmful practices. Once again, he reminded both sides of their responsibilities, i.e., the counselors of giving their best, professionally based support to the client with the aim of healing and the (potential) client's responsibility of taking their own action.

Above all, it needs the person's informed consent on the specific background, basic assumptions, the process, and specific interventions being applied. This framing, structuring, and case management do, however, imply specific skills on the part of the coach.

Together with professional associations, the author BvD is strongly favoring a scientifically based coaching background and education, via an initial university- and/or college-based professional development training on the art and practice of coaching, which differs from an academic counselor/therapist education.

20.1.2 Social Counseling Services

Active listening with real understanding and true empathy is one of the most potent forces for change that I know. (Carl Rogers)

Taking into account the complexity of workplace counseling issues addressed to the counselor, the very divergent content of services actually purchased by organizations, and the many potential effects of counseling services provided across the specific counseling approaches and provider's individual personality, there cannot be a one-dimensional evaluation of the return on investment regarding counseling services.

The costs of providing workplace counseling must be balanced against three dimensions, making the case for providing best workplace counseling: business, legal, and ethical.

Research (McLeod 2001) provides for good evidence that "counseling works" in all three areas.

The Business Case for Workplace Counseling

Balancing the organization's costs in terms of investment in human resources, space, and technical environment, against cost-effectiveness, cost-utility, and cost-benefit, studies (McLeod 2001) showed:

- Workplace counseling schemes and employee assistance programs cover their costs.
- Higher cost workplace counseling programs are associated with higher utilization rates implying greater cost-effects.

The legal case for providing workplace counseling:

In many industrialized countries, organizations are legally bound by national law to provide for minimum standards regarding the prevention of potentially harmful production materials and environments, stress at work, work materials and office environment, and organizational climate. Investment in employee assistance programs helps reducing organizational conflicts and the risks of legal cases.

The Ethical Case for Workplace Counseling

Counseling effects relate to all staff health- and well-being-related issues and to the employer's general duty of care and responsibility in fulfilling the psychological contract:

- Counseling helps prevent further deterioration of health and severity of conditions.
- Counseling is highly valued by staff. The majority of those who use workplace counseling say they are highly satisfied with it.
- Counseling is generally effective in alleviating psychological problems.
- Workplace counseling is effective in relieving the symptoms of both anxiety and depression.
- Counseling can reduce levels of stress in the workplace by more than 50%.
- Levels of sickness and absence fall by between 25% and 50%.
- Levels of substance abuse are reduced.
- Employees who need workplace counseling show signs of psychological distress equivalent to that found in out-patient psychiatric hospitals.
- Counseling has a moderate effect on attitudes to work.

Specific services being delivered by the workplace social counselor are defined in the respective contract agreement and the terms of reference.

According to the specific terms of reference, social counseling services in the workplace are delivered by contracted experts via:

- Short-term psychotherapy
- Counseling
- Coaching

Social counseling in the workplace is provided either by external or internal counselors to the organization via various settings.

The aims of this service are:

- To provide practical support and guidance to staff
- To raise awareness about the relevance and influence of issues and problems on employees' well-being and performance
- To relate to professionals and experts in the organization, focusing on areas of recruitment, prevention, and return to work with regard to employee health and well-being

Today's state-of-the-art standards for providing professional workplace social counseling services generally comprise six areas of quality employee assistance program (EAPA 2011):

- Contract design
- Implementation
- Direct services
- Evaluation
- Management and administration
- Cooperations and linkages

For professional, ethical, and transparency reasons, the experts providing social counseling services might cover all three types of services or only one in their social counseling services, short-term psychotherapy, counseling, and/or coaching services.

Providing business-related social counseling in the workplace imposes a special responsibility on the counselor his/her specific professional background regarding the various types of services and in clarifying the counselor–contractor and counselor–client relationship, also regarding the expectations and objectives of this "triangular" relationship.

While all three types are proving a helpful relationship with the person, there are some similarities and some differences that need to be observed.

These services are about healing, helping people address and resolve emotional problems (like anxieties, trauma, depression, addiction, eating, and all types of disorders), that make them feel bad emotionally and which hinder them from living their lives to their full potentials. Unless and until these problems are resolved, it will be difficult for the client to make substantial changes in his life and to address issues of workplace functionality and progress.

In this setting, clients are in need, confronted with light to severe, existential, emotional, and/or private issues influencing their workplace performance. For these clients social counseling services are mainly support services. Counseling services are addressing clients' emotional needs, encouraging and supporting their self-awareness and self-assertiveness, keeping them "on track," and encouraging their individual competencies in successfully dealing with a situation involving feelings of emptiness, pressure, and negative stress; and reestablishing trust in their self-efficacy. Frequently, this type of service is involving referral to a third psychotherapist with the aim of preventing further escalation and/or deterioration of health and of addressing underlying or primary client's concerns and issues that go beyond the social counselor's terms of reference or experience (i.e., dealing with own trauma or family-related issues).

Initially coined by Carl Rogers (2003), counseling helps people with physical, emotional, and mental health issues, improves their sense of well-being, alleviates feelings of distress, and resolves crises. They also provide assessment, diagnosis, and treatment of more severe psychological symptoms.

Counseling is (McLeod 2010b):

- Exploring
- Helping the client broaden perspectives
- Leading clients to embrace their own identity and life's challenges
- Guiding through

Counseling takes place "…when a counselor sees a client in a confidential setting to explore a difficulty the client is having" (BACP 2007).

Unconditional acceptance and respect for the client are essentials for a counselor. As the relationship develops, so too does trust between the counselor and client, enabling the client to look at many aspects of their life, their relationships, and themselves which they may not have considered or been able to face before. The counselor may provide a space for initial support, help the client rediscover, and get access to their own resources and to look at the options open to them, helping them to decide the best way forward.

The American Employee Assistance Professional Association EAPA (2011) is defining the purpose of providing employee assistance:

> An employee assistance program (EAP) is a set of professional services specifically designed to improve and/or maintain the productivity and healthy functioning of the workplace and to address a work organization's particular business needs through the application of specialized knowledge and expertise about human behavior and mental health.
>
> More specifically, an EAP is a workplace program designed to assist: (1) work organizations in addressing productivity issues, and (2) 'employee clients' in identifying and resolving personal concerns, including health, marital, family, financial, alcohol, drug, legal, emotional, stress, or other personal issues that may affect job performance.

According to the specific contract agreements, the roles of a social counselor in the workplace may include:

- Employee counseling – face to face, by phone, or online. A wide range of mental health topics for which short-term counseling is appropriate and concentrates on helping the individual employee client identify the skills, strengths, and resources that are already present and moving toward a solution.
- Supporting staff with any issue or challenges they may be facing, from balancing work and private time and private challenges affecting workplace performance up to children's well-being and organizing support for family care.
- Training and health education – proactive activities.
- Advising line managers on approaching troubled employees to seek.
- Advising the organization on policy matters in relation to welfare and emotional/psychological health and corresponding managerial attention and awareness.
- Facilitating organizational change.
- Critical incident support: providing immediate emotional support to staff during a crisis. The counselor will look at the current circumstances from a practical standpoint, as well as provide information that will help staff acknowledging the crisis and manage through. Here, social counseling is focusing specifically on the effects of the traumatic event and the alleviation of symptoms as needed.
- Connecting with external health providers, support services of all kinds.
- Referral to clinical support and treatment: if the initial assessment establishes that long-term specialist counseling is required, or if this is identified at an early stage of the counseling process, a referral will be made to ensure that the employee is getting the right and professional intensive support.
- Critical incident support and other trauma management.
- Advising on general staff issues like dignity at work, organizational health management, and other related employment policies and procedures.
- Monitoring effectiveness and service evaluation.
- Presenting overall outcomes and suggestions to staff and managers.
- Managing conflict situations and mediating between client and organization at work, applying own mediation and facilitation skills.

Workplace social counseling services are generally available for all staff. They provide for an opportunity, a space and a time, to talk and to be heard, confidentially, unconditionally.

Workplace counselors focus on:

- Healthy aspects and strengths of clients (individuals, couples, families, groups, or organizations)
- Environmental/situational influences (cultural, gender, and lifestyle issues shaping people's experiences and concerns)
- Dignity and diversity
- The role of career and work in peoples' lives (APA)

> Workplace counselors are expected to have an understanding of organizational cultures and workplace factors that might impact on the client and their work. They should be mindful of the different stakeholders involved. Whilst service providers can provide support to employees to increase their coping resources through counseling, stress management and various activities regarding mental health awareness training, the organization equally has a duty of care to ensure a safe and healthy working environment is provided . (BACP 2007)

Social counseling in the workplace is provided either by external or internal counselors to the organization via various settings.

The aims of this service are:

- To provide practical support and guidance to staff
- To raise awareness about the relevance and influence of issues and problems on employees' well-being and performance
- To relate to professionals and experts in the organization, focusing on areas of recruitment, prevention, and return to work with regard to employee health and well-being

Today's state-of-the-art standards for providing professional workplace social counseling services generally comprise six areas of quality employee assistance programs (EAPA 2011):

- Contract design
- Implementation
- Direct services
- Evaluation
- Management and administration
- Cooperations and linkages

20.1.3 Differences Between Coaching and Counseling Services

The primary distinction between these types of services lies in their educational requirements: counselors, interchangeably also called psychotherapists, do – with some exceptions – in almost all countries need an academic postgraduate master's degree, followed by many years of clinical practice under supervision, before they are allowed to follow their own counseling practice.

For any person, calling themselves "coaches" or offering coaching services, there are no legal requirements for any education and for practicing coaching, leaving the global coaching market complex, fragmented, and confusing. For mutual benefit, protection, and best outcomes, in many countries coaching associations have been organized on country level and/or with global affiliations, defining specific coaching educational and skills requirements, before accepting membership and credentialing on specific advanced levels of experience.

Other core differences between coaching and counseling refer to their objectives, ethics, and divergent approaches:

- Objectives: Counseling is about recovery and healing, about finding meaning; coaching is about achieving goals. Coaches are by no means trained to understand or deal with clients' potentialclinical issues.

- Another differentiation takes the client's perspective and refers to client motivations: For counseling to eliminate psychological, emotional problems or to manage a life/crisis issue and improve well-being, client's coaching motivation would be to improve performance with a distinct outcome focus.

- Relating to existential issues, and dealing with final conditions, counseling cannot be "solution-focused," brief, or goal-oriented.
- Ethics and boundaries: For counselors, there are very strict guidelines relating to confidentiality and professional boundaries in the counselor/therapist relationship (relating to adhering to the "rule of abstinence" on behalf of the therapist). In most countries, these ethics are backed by specific, legally binding ethical rules for the counselors/therapists. For coaches, mostly there are no ethical standards for their own practice, unless they are certified members of a coaching association with a specifically defined Code of Ethics. In Austria, "coaching" is legally defined as a profession with a specific framework to adhere to (education, binding chamber membership, taxing, code of conduct, etc.)
- Approaches: Counselors generally support their clients find their own answers. They do not need to have specific insight or understanding of the client's business function, the business branch, or any other issue explicitly relating to workplaces or current developments. Coaches give practical advice and recommendations, and they are explicitly expected by their coachees to do so. In workplace counseling, they are expected to be knowledgeable about the organization, management, and workplace issues. Coaches might even be active in "shadowing" their client in their daily work. Taking the client's perspective and condition would also clearly differentiate between counseling and coaching services: Counseling would imply to assess and reflect on the client's emotional and psychological level of functioning with a scientifically based, state-of-the-art counseling approach addressing the client's needs and helping the person to recover from anxieties, addiction, depression, etc. Coaching may work with a currently functioning client, having full access to their potentials.

20.2 Existential Counseling and Coaching

Existential coaching and therapy (Yalom, Viktor Frankl, Laengle, van Deurzen) start from an existential, philosophical, anthropological approach addressing issues of:

- Existence
- Trust
- Values
- Fulfillment
- Being alone/being with others, i.e., autonomy and relatedness
- Living in time
- Agency
- Meaning

Above all approaches, existential counseling and coaching:

- Explores the individual person's external and internal conditions
- Facilitates understanding and insight of the physical, social, and environmental given reality, own assumptions, thoughts, emotions, and behaviors
- Sensitizes for the perception of meaning potentialities; no specific meanings are offered. Rather, clients are guided in exploring potential meaningful goals
- Assists clients in perceiving and removing those factors that hinder them in pursuing meaningful goals in their lives
- Supports the realization of those own meaning possibilities clients have detected themselves
- Reassures on gaining access to own resources
- Encourages the client in their own meaning- and purpose-directed activities, actualizing freedom and responsibility

Specifically applying an existential approach in workplace counseling does of course not eliminate or exclude any specific, clinical assessment and treatment-related suggestions and activities, as specified by therapeutic, medical, and ethical standards. It rather adds additional understanding and depth to workplace counseling issues, addressed by members of staff.

20.2.1 The Four Worlds of Existence

> *Authentic living with courage and in humility would be a suitable existential objective. Learning to reflect for oneself and communicate effectively with others is another.* (van Deurzen)

In her existential counseling approach, Emmy van Deurzen's concept (van Deurzen 2015) can be well related to workplace counseling issues: she describes the physical, social, psychological, and spiritual realms of existence and defines four existential dimensions that each person is living in:

- "Umwelt," the physical dimension, our involvement in a physical world of objects, "where we struggle between survival or death."
- "Mitwelt," the social dimension, refers to a person's social and cultural environment, a world of other people, where we struggle with the contradictions between our need to belong and the possibility of our isolation. Problems in the "Mitwelt" center on integration vs. isolation or individuality vs. conformity. The individual is tasked with the responsibility to achieve a balance between these opposing states in order to derive existential meaning from a social group while maintaining one's autonomy.
- "Eigenwelt," the psychological dimension, where we grapple with the tension between integrity and disintegration.
- "Ueberwelt," the spiritual dimension, where we seek to find meaning against the threat of meaninglessness.

The existential approach in counseling and coaching is taking a "dialectical approach": both, the client and the counselor, understand and manage "all these tensions of human existence" (van Deurzen). On part of the counselor, this requires careful reflection and scrutiny about the client's experience and particular stance in the world, to understand their world view and his/her states of mind and to know the person's values and beliefs and the way the person makes meaning, the particular circumstances and wider contexts of the client's life.

The existential counseling and coaching process is then to elicit, clarify, and put into perspective the current issues and contradictions that might show. Counseling also involves enabling the client to come to terms with the general contradictions of human living and to help clients find a satisfactory direction for their personal lives.

From her ontological, philosophical, and psychological background, van Deurzen concludes: "The meaning of life is never given and cannot be transmitted unless a person is willing to search for it independently. Phenomenologists recognized that meaning making is one of the defining characteristics of human consciousness. It could therefore be argued that the meaning of human living is to learn to give it meaning. In order to come to a position from which we can learn to give meaning we have to first come to a point of doubt and a realization of the lack of intrinsic meaning in our lives" (van Deurzen 2015).

In the end, existential counseling may lead to a greater understanding of life "that makes everything worthwhile, ordinary, hard earned, human wisdom" (van Deurzen 2015).

20.2.2 Addressing Meaning in Workplace Services

There has not been any concept addressing workplace-related issues as philosophical and anthropological, scientifically grounded, and practically applicable like Viktor Frankl's approach. During the past decades and until today, consultants, coaches, psychotherapists, and counselors have been influenced and encouraged by

Frankl's work, publications, and life (Viktor & I film). Their theoretical background, reflections, practice, and forward-looking research are relating to Viktor Frankl's legacy in one or the other way.

The issues presented by staff can be found on the two dimensions described by Frankl (1988): the vertical dimension between the poles of meaning and despair and the horizontal dimension between success and failure. In the four quadrants established by these dimensions, the personal state of well-being might change from situation to situation, according to the triggers and questions work life raises. In social counseling, the client discovers his/her thoughts, feelings, behaviors in these situations, their resources, and their potentials, and they also discover their capabilities of taking an attitude and giving their individual answer to the demands of their present life:

Meaning

Freedom and responsibility
Conscience – right and wrong, ethics, governance
Values to live: creative, experiential, attitudinal
Sense of coherence
Achievement and success
Contributing to some greater cause

Despair

Physical, emotional, mind, behavioral
Hopelessness, demotivation
Existential vacuum
Inner void
Loss of social support
Distress
Anxieties
Depression
Loss of dignity
Manifest frustration of will to meaning
Clinical disorders
Crisis
Suicidality

Success **assessed or perceived as**

Performance
Merit
Salary
Bonus
Rewards
Position in hierarchy
Power

Influence
Number of reports
Social status
Pleasure
Luxury

Failure **assessed or perceived as**

Underperformance
Loss of self-esteem
Lack of autonomy, influence, control
Loss of effectiveness
Lack of self-efficacy
Loss of status, salary, influence, bonus
Manifest existential frustration and of will to meaning
Latent frustration and noogenic vacuum
Noetic void

20.2.3 Existential Analysis of Workplace Issues

> *The experience of meaninglessness becomes a major problem in many people's lives and it may lead to a number of concrete difficulties, which may look like personality problems or other forms of pathology. Psychotherapists are reluctant to engage in discussions with clients and patients who are seemingly disturbed, but who actually may be in search of meaning. We can only engage in such discussions if we have been willing to question our own lives and can recognize that anxieties and doubts about meaning do not have to be equated with personal pathology or mental illness.* (E. van Deurzen)

Existential analysis (Frankl 1969) explores the conditions necessary to lead a dignified and meaningful life. The aim of this analysis is to support a person to find a way of living to which the person can give his/her inner consent, and in taking own actions. "In short, to find out and live an inner yes to one's own life", i.e. still saying yes to life (Frankl 2009: Trotzdem Ja zum Leben sagen (also Laengle 2005)).

This analysis conceptualizes the individual person with their given "building blocks of existence," understood as:

- Fundamental givens of the individual person
- Remaining unconditionally and under all circumstances
- Undeniable and indivisible entity of the individual

Existential analysis sees a person as someone who can actualize and very concretely shape his own life – beyond his physical and psychosocial condition – according to those aspects that do primarily count in a person's personal life: shaping his very being, based on the individual person's:

- Undeniable dignity
- Values relating to the own conscience

- Incontestable freedom of decision
- Responsibility of relating to his being in relation to his/her specific external environment

All these building blocks establish the person's capacity of giving meaning to their individual life. Existential analysis is about studying, exploring, and searching the individual givens "toward existence" and focusing on the individual potentials of being and on what meaning (logos) the individual life can have beyond the specific circumstances of the here and now.

By definition, existential analysis is:

- Person-centered
- Presupposing the dignity of the individual person, irrespective of external, or internal conditions
- Relating to a person's conscience and values
- Supporting the person in their very being
- Acknowledging their potential suffering from external conditions or inner void
- Encouraging the individual in exploring their own freedom of decision and of taking an attitude
- Recognizing the person's taking an attitude to circumstances as an achievement (potentially the greatest)

For work life, existential analysis of a client's situation relates to the individual's objectively given noetic/Geist dimension. This dimension shows in man's quest for finding meaning in work and life, seeking understanding of own existence, and searching for something "out" there that needs devotion and that drives and pulls toward actualizing own existence.

Humans are questioning work and life, asking:

Where is the "What for?"
What is the meaning of it all?
What am I here for?

Frankl's concept is offering a grand journey of exploration into the client's potentials; redefining the person's individual meaning in work and life; reminding the person of her undeniable dignity; preventing deterioration of his health; opening up a space of hope; understanding life's "tragic triad" (Frankl) of suffering, liability, and death; and sometimes saving lives. Existential analysis facilitates the client's authentic decisions for leading a meaningful life and to bring about a truly responsible way of dealing with the individual life and the world.

Practically, applying existential analysis in workplace counseling is preventive, caring, educational, and pastoral.

Whatever circumstances, challenges, issues, hopelessness, sufferings, and, in general terms, conditions of overall perceived "lessness" the client is presenting in social counseling, facing her present situation, existential analysis of the client's issues is based on Frankl's image of humans, based on his three concepts: freedom of will, will to meaning, and meaning of life. These concepts (Battyány, Viktor Frankl Institute Website) can be actualized and explored in social counseling.

20.2.3.1 Will to Meaning

Human beings are not only *free from* specific conditions, but most importantly, they are free *to something,* namely, to actualize their very own existence in terms of understanding internal and external obstacles and defining goals and purpose that are fulfilling and that give meaning to the individual life. In Frankl's concept, this will to meaning is seen as the primary motivation of humans and as the fundamental need of humans. When a person cannot realize his/her given will to meaning in their lives, their will to meaning is being frustrated. This frustration of the existential need for meaningful goals may engender or increase psychosomatic maladies and neurotic disorders and give rise to aggression, addiction, depression, and suicidality.

20.2.3.2 Freedom of Will

> *Between trigger and response lies a space. In that space lies our freedom to act.* (Frankl)

Together with their issues presented in workplace counseling, employees may find that they cannot change any of the conditions they face: their present workplace situation in terms of defined function and tasks, fellow colleagues, team members, manager, salary and bonus structure, organizational frame, business and production purpose, office environment, the conflicts they may perceive to be trapped in, other persons' behaviors they are confronted with, and the performance indicators that are defined.

This freedom derives from the spiritual/Geist dimension of the person, which is understood as the essential human realm, the individual capacity to cope with their real physical and psychosocial conditions.

This concept of freedom of will is opening another space of understanding the very own existence in terms of personal freedom that no person and no circumstance can take from a human being: understanding and exploring the concept that humans are not fully subject to conditions but are basically free to decide and capable of taking their own stance toward all types of internal and external (biological and social) conditions open a new dimension for rethinking, for reframing, and for potentially taking another approach to the very same issues, perceived as absolute. Freedom – defined as the space of shaping one's own life within limits of the given possibilities – emerges, and the individual person "rises above" the immediate circumstances.

This notion of individual freedom touches on the core dimension of being, of being human, of becoming and realizing the very human potentials of the individual existence. With this concept of humans, any employee, questioning his own work life, is understood not as the inefficient member of staff, lacking competencies, failing to deliver the results agreed on, unwilling or resistant to change, incapable or unwilling to adapt or submit, but rather as a free and basically autonomous being, capable of actively shaping their own work and private lives.

Challenging and confronting clients with this concept fundamentally bridge the gap between potential suffering from external conditions to reconsidering own resources, capacities, potentials, and purpose for taking action. Staff members are triggered by specific circumstances to approach a workplace counselor; in counseling relating to Frankl's concept, they might find and recover their very existence and their own meaning.

Social counseling is about awareness raising for these potentials and about discovering the own dignity in individually exercising this freedom. With this concept, individuals bring forth the possible best in themselves and in the world, by perceiving and realizing the meaning of the moment in each and every situation. This meaning needs to be discovered and brought to light by the individual person, referring to the very situation the employee might be challenged by in their work or private life. Here, the social counselor and client act as two explorers searching for "the" very meaning in this specific, current situation.

20.2.3.3 Meaning of Life

According to Frankl's concept, meaning is an objective reality of human existence. On the grounds of their freedom and responsibility, humans are called to bring forth the best in themselves, by perceiving and realizing the meaning of the moment in every situation. These meaning potentials, although objective in their nature, are linked to the individual person in their ever-changing specific situation. Thus, there is no general meaning of life, no general meaning of work life or of the specific vocation, function, business, or company. This meaning needs to be detected and explored specifically, for each employee, in each company, for every individual business, and according to the very specific situation. This understanding gives room to potentially find meaning in every function and situation. There is no predetermination of meaning. Thus, while this concept of meaning presupposes basic freedom irrespective of the specific conditions, it also includes the challenge and demand to each individual in defining their own meaning and purposeful goals.

Existential analysis in workplace counseling is an integrative approach, binging together philosophical, cognitive, emotional, and behavioral facets of existence, exploring the best potentials of individual existence, and eliciting what "man can be."

The existential, logotherapeutic approach refers to the clients' existential questions raised in counseling:

Where is the "What for?"
What is the meaning of it all?
What am I here for?

Based on Frankl's explanation of critical meaning-related workplace issues, meaning-oriented counseling focuses on client's core aspects of finding meaning in his work and private life:

- Being aware and exercising creative values: What are my talents, what is my vocation and mission, what and how can I live my best potentials, and which environment and culture do I need to live my values and to experience self-efficacy, respect, and appreciation by others?
- Assessing experiential values in work and private life: What resources do I find in experiencing relationship, connection, appreciation, respect, joy, and gratitude? What is the environment, I work and live in, offering that I would find strengthening and fulfilling? What internal or external influences are blocking me from getting best access to experiential values?
- Defining potentials and options of taking an attitude: What attitude can I take to the givens of my current challenges? What can I change, what can I not change? How can I detach myself from the very moment, defining a broader meaning perspective in my work and private life challenges? What activities can I take according to this newly gained attitude? What individual freedom do I gain from taking my own attitude to circumstances I cannot change immediately?

20.3 Interventions in Workplace Counseling and Coaching: An Integrated Approach

Twenty-first-century developments and megatrends around the world have inspired experts around the globe to join in bringing together their specific approaches, based on their mutual mission of serving their clients' well-being. On conferences and in their publications, they share their engagement for the same cause, i.e., supporting the well-being of their clients. While twentieth-century psychology and psychotherapy were shaped by the distinct creation, definition, concrete application, and scientific evaluation of the various specific approaches and schools of counseling and psychotherapy, twenty-first-century counseling and psychotherapy with experts all around the globe are searching for integrative applications, which are eliciting common aspects more than what separates their schools. Latest research, publications, and applications have been strongly motivated by this search for distilling commonalities and potential benefits for the clients from the distinct approaches. This mutual search can be observed across all experts' initial approaches, be it psychoanalysis, behavioral therapy, in-depth psychotherapy, positive psychotherapy, or logotherapy. Current scientific literature published and quoted in this book is based on this integrative approach and cooperation across the various "schools."

In his foundational *Introduction to Counseling*, McLeod (2010a, b) has introduced major techniques in counseling that may be generally valid beyond cognitive behavioral counseling for meaning-oriented counseling in general: Socratic dialogue, mindfulness, behavior experiments, assertiveness training, imagery descripting, homework, and self-help learning materials. All of these specific interventions are scientifically validated and efficacious beyond the specific approach.

> Regardless of school of therapy or techniques used, ample evidence indicates that the therapist, himself or herself, is a powerful factor in the outcome of the therapy. Forging a strong therapy alliance and fostering an expectation of improvement is crucial in psychotherapy. Common factors in therapy may, indeed, account for more of the variance in therapy outcome, as compared to specific techniques. Although much can be said for actuarial decision making, it is the therapist who decides, moment to moment, when to talk and when to listen, what technique to use and why, and ...when to accept and when to encourage change. A technique or set of techniques cannot substitute for a therapist's judgment or make the therapist more empathic or caring. (Reisner 2005)

The following table of "classic" and LTEA (logotherapy and existential analysis) interventions is based on theoretical foundations, practical experiences, and this spirit of cooperation for the primary concern of counseling, i.e., supporting the client in his/her recovery and finding meaning and purpose in life. This spirit of cooperation beyond schools is also based on many scientific research results, showing that the counselor–client relationship, rapport, is one of the primary influencing factors of best counseling outcomes.

In his extensive research about the efficacy and effectiveness of psychotherapy in various approaches, Grawe (2004) has defined the following common efficacy factors of various approaches:

- Therapeutic relationship.
- Motivational clarification.
- Resource activation.
- Active support for coping with problems: Counselor actively guides and supports client toward own solving problems with the aim of strengthening self-efficacy and self-assurance.

20.3.1 Standard and Logotherapeutic Interventions

The following list of various interventions is not exhaustive, neither polar or contradictory nor generally compatible: It rather needs the specific assessment of the client's condition and selection of the specific type of interventions that best serve the person's well-being and search for meaning (Table 20.1):

Table 20.1 Workplace coaching and counseling interventions – standard and logotherapeutic existential

Standard professional	Logotherapeutic existential counseling
Primary concern: Encourage clients to get access to their own resources, find solutions, and implement according activities	Primary concern: Raising awareness about the very human capacities of the individual person in all their contexts Encourage finding meaning and consequently
• Explore clients' motivations for change and their preferred future without their problems • Define goals and solutions • Help clients gain understanding and insight of their own difficulties, emotion, stuck states, and counterproductive behaviors • SWOT analysis • Lead clients to embrace their fears and anxieties • Guide to regaining access to resources and competencies to • Implement actions based on client's self-efficacy beliefs, personal strengths, and available resources	• Consult a person's innate conscience and core values • Identify client's need for meaning and self-transcendence • Distance from the situation and habitual ways of responding • Encourage and support attitude and activities that are consistent with person's most cherished values and beliefs • Understand the tragic "triad" of life • Encourage to take a "defiant stance" toward fate and adversity • Discover the "achievement" of taking an attitude • Restore person's dignity • Socratic dialogue

20.3.2 Impact and Outcomes of Workplace Counseling and Coaching

There are direct and indirect, tangible and intangible outcomes of workplace counseling and coaching. The science and tools of quality management and evaluation of counseling and coaching services are widely researched and discussed in the respective communities and professional associations. According to the contracting organization and purchaser, the service provider, their respective professional standards and ethical guidelines and governance, counseling services are reported and evaluated in various ways (McLeod 2013). For workplace counselors, the according associations provide for helpful guidelines (BACP 2006).

20.3.2.1 General Outcomes

For reasons of transparency and accountability on part of the service provider, for the benefit of all stakeholders, namely, the purchaser and the clients, evidencing their quality and effectiveness, outcomes of workplace counseling are being evaluated via various tools and questionnaires. Evidence shows that regular evaluation of service quality goes together with distinct improvements in quality and effectiveness of the service.

In business, organizations, management, and human resources, it has become common service providers' practice to report on the effects and effectiveness of coaching and counseling services being delivered to staff. Fortunately, during the last years, substantial research (e.g., Grant 2012, 2016) and work (Schlosser et al. 2006) have been dedicated to defining the potential outcomes of coaching and counseling and to reliably report on them to respective employers, who wish to be informed, not only by their staff benefiting from these services, but by the professional experts about the staff benefits their services do provide.

Also referring to the clients' initial issues, there are direct and indirect effects of coaching and counseling. Direct effects are reported on three levels: cognitive, emotional, and behavioral. Indirect effects of coaching and counseling refer to health and well-being, self-efficacy, job satisfaction, and trust.

In some cases the purchaser provides for the specific technique of evaluation, benefiting from digital and Internet tools; sometimes there are no specific tools or processes provided. Evaluation and reporting can well be based on the counselor's own discretion. In all cases, reporting must be regular, for reasons of comparability and continuous quality management for the benefit of all stakeholders.

For reasons of general trust in the service, reporting and evaluation of counseling services must always be based on strict anonymity and confidentiality.

Reporting counseling services is structured along the three levels of quality management: structure, process, and outcomes.

Minimum structural reporting may include data about number of cases pending, which are not being further reported in the current report.

Reporting structural quality is covering aspects of confidentiality, impartiality, and accessibility, and counselor's time management refers to the cases closed during the relevant reporting period:

- Number of cases closed
- Waiting times until appointment
- Accessibility of service
- Quality of specific counseling environment
- Number of sessions
- Client gender
- Client age
- Function
- Salary band

Information on the counseling process refer to counselor/coach service quality in terms of client's satisfaction with empathy, knowledge, and communication skills.

Quality of outcomes may be reported along specific predefined items and also opens questions leaving extra room for client's additional remarks.

Based on own research and other findings on the outcomes of workplace counseling, these are the main direct outcomes reported by clients:

- Relieved from pressure
- Raised awareness about the issue the client initially addressed

- Clarified own needs, potentials, and options
- Improved self-management competencies
- Helped in dealing with staff management-related matters

Indirect outcomes of the social counseling refer to improvements regarding the various levels of workplace counseling, i.e., individual client, team atmosphere and performance, client–superior relationship, and organizational awareness raising:

- Boosting personal health and well-being
- Developing individual communication skills
- Promoting assertiveness
- Raising awareness about individual aspects of work and private life balance
- Working for an organizational, integrated health management approach
- Linking leadership approach to the specific organizational mission
- Suggesting specific training activities in specific relevant areas of dignity at work, gender diversity, intercultural awareness, business ethics, and organizational values

20.3.2.2 Evaluation of Meaning-Oriented Counseling in the Workplace

What are the specific outcomes of existential counseling and coaching and how can these results be reported and empirically be measured?

Meaning-oriented workplace counseling effects relate to the client's:

- Learning self-appreciation of own competencies that have helped in the past
- Learning to appreciate and savor what is in the external environment: supportive relationships, natural givens
- Understanding life's givens
- Activating gratitude
- Understanding the various contexts of situations above personal issues and relating to the environment beyond personal, emotional evaluation
- Becoming aware of the achievement of taking an attitude of dignity and humanity, facing limit situations outside work
- Dealing with fate
- Growing from adversity of harmful, potential target of inappropriate behavior and rising above to the human potentials beyond retaliation and victimization

According to the author's (BvD) own practice and experience with meaning-oriented workplace counseling, clients are sensitive in giving additional comments on the broader perspective of their counseling experience.

Clients' feedback to existential, meaning-oriented workplace counseling effects is strongly related to the concept of "traumatic growth" (Calhoun and Tedeschi 2001), not necessarily related to traumatic experiences in the workplace. The inventory relates to five distinct areas of growth: relating to others, new possibilities, personal strength, spiritual change, and appreciation of life.

Relating to Others

- *I have a greater sense of closeness with others.*
- *I have more compassion for others.*
- *I am more willing to express my emotions.*
- *I learned a great deal about how wonderful people are.*
- *I better accept needing others.*
- *I more clearly see that I can count on people in times of trouble.*
- *I put more effort into my relationships.*

New Possibilities

- I am more likely to try to change things which need changing.
- New opportunities are available which wouldn't have been otherwise.
- *I am more likely to try to change things which need changing.*
- *I am able to do better things with my life.*
- *I developed new interests.*
- *I established a new path for my life.*

Personal Strength

- *I have a greater feeling of self-reliance.*
- *I discovered that I'm stronger than I thought I was.*
- *I know better that I can handle difficulties.*
- *I am better able to accept the way things work out.*

Spiritual Change

- *I have a better understanding of spiritual matters.*
- *I relate to a greater power beyond human existence.*

Appreciation of Life

- *I changed my priorities about what is important in life.*
- *I have a greater appreciation for the value of my own life.*
- *I can better appreciate each day.*

General Outcomes

- *Social counseling has helped me to survive.*
- *If anybody and anything has ever helped me to understand life, it was through our encounters.*
- *My friends tell me that I am looking at my life with a completely new perspective.*
- *I am thinking about my major beliefs and values with a new awareness.*
- *I follow my inner voice and conscience with courage and self-respect.*
- *Now I have become aware of what is most important to me.*

20.4 Discussion

Specifically relating to search for meaning-oriented existential counseling and coaching interventions, the counselor cannot follow any manual. Generally, the existential approach is defined by a dilemma of reporting valid empirical data about a process and outcomes that can hardly be defined in terms of empirical facts or "positive outcomes" (e.g., in case of dealing with terminal illness, decease of staff or suicide issues). As van Deurzen notes, the existential approach resists formalization and the fabrication of a technique. Rather, existential analysis and meaning-oriented coaching and counseling are "reinvented and recreated by every therapist and with every new client" (van Deurzen 2015).

Van Deurzen (2015) notes a lack of systematic theorizing about existential psychotherapy (also applying to counseling and coaching, the author BvD) and a lack of research to demonstrate the effectiveness of this kind of work.

Considering own experience with existential counseling and coaching, the author BvD is suggesting the following assumptions and hypotheses for further research:

Referring to the counselor:

- The "existential assumptions" and hypothesis on part of the existential counselor are forming the basis of rapport and function in the process of transference and counter transference.
- The existential counselor's assumptions elicit the client's self-healing capacities.

Referring to the client:

Existential counseling and coaching:

- Refers to the incorruptible and indispensable Geist dimension of the individual
- Touches on the very dignity of the person with encounters based on the wholeness of the person, rather than the client's assumed deficiency, disorder, or illness
- Stimulates and kindles the person's individual self-healing capacities

The "effects" of existential and meaning-oriented counseling and coaching are rather long-term outcomes, guiding a person's general awareness about their own life and values and coping with the givens of life.

Since existential counseling and coaching oftentimes start with existential issues of suffering, of major life events, or of questioning life's meaning and personal meaning in general, clients are highly focused, motivated, and "hungry" for a philosophical approach, relating to life's questions.

Based on client's issues, mostly perceived by the client as "serious," "severe," or "existential" conditions, and the specific existential approach, existential counseling and coaching are highly valued and remembered by the clients, more than specific short-term interventions or behavioral therapy-related "homework." In line with these observations, many years later, clients might remember one sentence of the counseling session, "having changed the course of my life" or "having saved my life."

20.5 Psychotherapeutic Approaches

20.5.1 Third Wave Cognitive Behavioral Therapy (CBT)

"Third wave psychotherapies" (Kahl et al. 2012) comprise a heterogeneous group of treatments, including acceptance and commitment treatment, behavioral activation, cognitive behavioral analysis system of psychotherapy, dialectical behavioral therapy, metacognitive therapy, mindfulness-based cognitive therapy, and schema therapy. After more than 45 years of experience with cognitive therapy, there had been a growing awareness of its limitations. The "third wave" of behavioral therapies is characterized by themes new to behavioral psychotherapies: metacognition, cognitive fusion, emotions acceptance, mindfulness, dialectics, and spirituality.

This third wave of CBT of behavioral psychotherapies is an important arena of modern human and psychotherapy development. Their contributions to overall staff well-being and services being offered to support workplace health programs are widely acknowledged.

20.5.2 Acceptance and Commitment Treatment (ACT)

Acceptance and commitment therapy (ACT) contains psychoeducation about key mechanisms, exercises in mindfulness, and cognitive defusion. The *value orientation* of the patient is elicited and discussed, and patients are supported in *value-driven behavior* in contrast to behavior driven by emotional or experiential avoidance. ACT was associated with a reduction of depressive symptoms in men and women with subclinical depression. ACT has been shown to be effective in reducing levels of stress and burnout.

20.5.3 Mindfulness-Based Cognitive Therapy

Mindfulness-based cognitive therapy (MBCT) arose from experiences in the application of Buddhist meditation techniques in medicine. It was specifically developed to reduce the number of relapses in patients with major depression. MBCT uses psychoeducation and encourages the patients to practice mindfulness meditation. A core goal is to develop metacognitive awareness, which is the ability to experience cognitions and emotions as mental events that pass through the mind and may or may not be related to external reality. The focus is not to change allegedly "dysfunctional" thoughts but to learn to experience them as internal events separated from the self.

20.5.4 Systemic Approaches

> *Systemic therapy neither attempts a 'treatment of causes' nor of symptoms, rather it gives living systems nudges that help them to develop new patterns together, taking on a new organizational structure that allows growth.* (Von Schlippe and Schweitzer 1998)

The focus of systemic therapy has moved away from a model of linear causality and understanding of reality as objective to a postmodern understanding of reality as socially and linguistically constructed.

Systemic therapy assesses problems practically rather than analytically, i.e., it does not attempt to determine past causes as does the psychoanalytic approach, nor does it assign diagnosis (who is sick, who is a victim). Rather, systemic therapy seeks instead to identify stagnant patterns of behavior in groups of people and address those patterns directly, irrespective of analysis of cause. A key point here of this postmodern perspective is not a denial of absolutes, but a humility and recognition on the part of the therapist/facilitator that they do not hold the power to change people or systems. Instead, the systemic therapist's role is to help systems to change themselves by introducing creative "nudges."

The systemic approach is increasingly being implemented in the fields of education, politics, social work, business, consulting, counseling, and coaching. The facilitator's role is to help systems to change themselves by introducing creative "nudges," i.e., away from a modernist model of linear causality and understanding of reality as objective, to an understanding of reality as socially and linguistically constructed. Systemic approaches neither attempt a "treatment of causes" nor of symptoms; their facilitators do not categorize; rather they give living systems nudges that help them to develop new patterns together, taking on a new organizational structure that allows growth.

Initially, Maturana and Varela (1992, 1980) and systems theory researchers have first been addressing human capacity for experiencing and co-creating their selves and others. Autopoiesis, addressing the self and its creation together with others, refers to living systems capable of reproducing and maintaining themselves.

20.5.5 Hypnosystemic Concepts

Hypnotherapy is a skilled verbal communication, which helps direct a client's imagination in such a way as to bring about intended alterations in sensations, perceptions, feelings, thoughts, and behaviors, addressing and utilizing emotional impulses and blockades and getting access to own competencies.

Hypnotherapists use language, stories, and metaphors that bring about deep relaxation and an altered state of consciousness. A person in a deeply focused state is unusually responsive to new ideas, taking other perspectives and finding access to their own resources.

Hypnotherapy (Schmidt 2015) can teach people how to master their own states of awareness. By doing so they can affect their own bodily functions and psychological responses. It can be applied to a wide range of medical, dental, and psychological problems. Areas of application include anxiety and stress conditions, weight control, addictive behaviors (including smoking, alcohol, and substance misuse), and confidence issues.

Hypnotherapy is also used to enhance performance in several areas such as sports and public speaking.

> Viktor Frankl's logotherapy coincides with hypnosis in order to find means to cope with disastrous situations. His ability to 'talk himself' into a condition which enabled him to cope with his terrible situation at the Nazi concentration camp can most certainly be equated to hypnotic trance, his search for meaning is certainly a process similar to the utilization techniques of Ericksonian therapy. (Augustin Figueroa, quoted by Durbin, 2018)

20.5.6 Brief, Solution-Focused Approach

Brief therapy (de Shazer 2008) differs from other schools of therapy in that it emphasizes a focus on a specific problem and direct intervention. In brief therapy, the therapist takes responsibility for working actively with the client in order to treat clinical and subjective conditions faster. It also emphasizes precise observation, utilization of clients' natural resources and competencies, to initiate and encourage new perspectives and multiple viewpoints.

The primary approach of brief therapy is to help the client to view the present from a wider context and to utilize more functional understandings. Brief therapy is exploratory and solution-based rather than problem-oriented. It is less concerned with how a problem arose than with the current factors sustaining it and preventing change. Brief therapists do not adhere to one "correct" approach, but rather accept that there are many roads to resolution and solution, any of which may or may not in combination turn out to be ultimately beneficial for the client. This person's needs are at the core of the therapeutic encounters.

20.5.7 Strengthening Mindfulness

One of the most magnificent features of the human mind – neuroscientists are referring to the human brain – is its ability to hold past, present, future, and their imagined alternatives in constant parallel and to choose our own attitude and thinking, to detach ourselves from the very circumstances.

Wong (2012) defines seven areas of acceptance as the starting point for a process of finding meaning and of keeping hope for a better future at the same time. Achieving these levels will imply different skills, of which meditation and mindfulness exercises are only one: cognitive acceptance of what is, emotional acceptance of negative emotions, realistic acceptance of the impact of the situation, integrative acceptance of incorporating the situation in the broader context of one's own life, existential acceptance of acknowledging the event as a part of human existence, transcendental acceptance of the potential of rising above the situation, and finally transformative acceptance of "turning a tragedy into a triumph" (Frankl).

What differentiates humans from animals is exactly this ability to step mentally outside of whatever is happening to us right now and to assign it with context and significance. Instructing the distressed to be more mindful develops into "a kind of neoliberalism of the emotions."

In the worst case, the good intentions of mindfulness exercises, allegedly focused at letting go ego interests, can turn into the most self-occupied and ego-centered state of the human being and, in the end, add to the existential vacuum, nourishing feelings of void, anxiety, and depression inside rather than mindfully observing the needs of the Other, the Thou, and developing compassion for the world around the self.

Instinctive, automatic processes might be intensified by self-observation. By the same token, some mild and well-founded sensations of anxiousness or sadness will be increased and amplified by self-observation, making them more noticeable and engendering even more intense observation.

Dereflection, directing the person's attention away from the problem and toward something important to the person, and a meaning focus does two things: It opens the person's perspective up to new possibilities. Alternatively, when a person is searching for relief or assistance, it may help the person see the problem situation more clearly and find a creative solution on their own. In other situations, feeling overwhelmed, helpless or exhausted, attending mindfulness exercise classes in the workplace would rather intensify the person's feelings of helplessness, loneliness, and incapacity, adding to their suffering.

20.5.8 MBSR Mindfulness-Based Stress Reduction

MBSR is a program that incorporates mindfulness to assist people with pain and a range of conditions and life issues that were initially difficult to treat in a hospital setting. Developed by Professor Jon Kabat-Zinn, MBSR uses a combination of mindfulness meditation, body awareness, and yoga to help people become more mindful. MBSR programs have been proposed for a wide variety of conditions including stress reduction. Clinical research studies have documented physical and mental health benefits of mindfulness training programs.

Some of these studies did show that mindfulness exercises might bring some type of benefits to people in comparison with doing nothing; when mindfulness trainings are compared with any other relaxation techniques, including muscle relaxation, listening to spiritual audiotapes, or any control condition, which gives equal time and attention to the person, mindfulness exercises perform no better and, in many cases, worse (Wippmann 2016).

20.5.9 Potentials and Pitfalls of the Mindfulness Movement

Mindfulness exercises are supposed to be a defense against the pressures of modern life, but it's "starting to actually add to them. It has become a special circle of self-improvement hell" (New York Times, November 2016).

There are growing concerns over the concept of mindfulness which has actually become a multibillion-dollar "spiritual industrial complex" with Americans now spending an estimated $4 billion each year on "mindfulness products," although research has, so far, given little evidence for the assumed overwhelming benefits of this type of training: When the US Agency for Healthcare Research and Quality (2014) conducted an enormous meta-analysis of over 18,000 separate studies on meditation and mindfulness techniques. The research was aimed to determine the efficacy and safety of meditation programs on stress-related outcomes (e.g., anxiety, depression, stress, distress, well-being, positive mood, quality of life, attention, health-related behaviors affected by stress, pain, and weight) compared with an active control in diverse adult clinical populations.

They reported either low strength of evidence (SOE) of no effect or insufficient SOE of an effect of meditation programs on positive mood, attention, substance use, eating, sleep, and weight. In our comparative effectiveness analyses, we did not find any evidence to suggest that these meditation programs were superior to any specific therapies they were compared with.

20.5.10 Positive Psychology Therapy PPT

Positive psychology was defined by Martin Seligman as a new approach in psychology, the scientific study of positive human functioning and flourishing on multiple levels that include the biological, personal, relational, institutional, cultural, and global dimensions of life (Seligman and Csikszentmihalyi 2000).

Since its dynamic rise, positive psychology has been criticized in the professional field for various reasons: for overlooking the important, positive role of negativity for human flourishing, for becoming incapable of psychological growth for over focusing on flourishing, for not adequately addressing and treating signs of depression, for not providing a general theory of meaning issues beyond happiness, for denying human suffering and terminal illness, and for overlooking the human condition, when happiness and meaning cannot be harmonized.

Batthyány and Russo-Netzer (2014) published a comprehensive anthology on the similarities and differences and current research findings relating to meaning in the respective positive psychology and in Viktor Frankl's concepts.

Differentiating itself mainly from psychoanalysis, in-depth-psychology and behaviorism approaches with their problem-orientation, focusing on drives and maladaptive behaviors, positive psychology initially shaped the concept of learned helplessness and the concept of learned optimism (Seligman 1990). It builds on the humanistic movement, emphasizing human flourishing, happiness, well-being, and positivity.

Guiding theories are Seligman's concept of PERMA and Csikszentmihalyi's theory of flow. This concept addresses positive emotions, positive traits, and positive institutions.

This concept assumes that human beings are often drawn by the future more than they are driven by the past. A change in individual orientation to time can dramatically affect how people think about their own future and potentials. Positive psychology focuses on positive goals, like families and schools that allow children to grow, workplaces that aim for satisfaction and high productivity, and society teaching others about flourishing.

Fostering positive attitudes toward one's subjective experiences, individual traits, and life events, this approach is oriented toward minimizing thoughts that may arise in a hopeless mind-set and to, instead, develop a sense of optimism toward life.

Methodologically, Peterson and Seligman (2004) developed the concept of Character Strengths and Virtues. Positive psychology mainly developed and introduced ways and exercises, with which individual happiness can be developed. Positive psychology is fostering a good life, where happiness, engagement, and meaning can be lived.

Seligman and Csikszentmihalyi (2000) defined three kinds of a happy life:

Living a Pleasant Life, a "life of enjoyment," experiencing and savoring the positive feelings and emotions that are part of normal and healthy living (e.g., relationships, hobbies, interests, entertainment, etc.). Despite the attention given, Martin Seligman says this most transient element of happiness may be the least important. Today's hedonism in all its forms covers the pleasant life.

Living the Good Life or "life of engagement." It is felt by individuals when they are optimally engaged with their primary activities, experiencing the beneficial effects of immersion. Flow is experienced when there is a positive match between a person's strength and their current task, i.e., when one feels confident of accomplishing a chosen or assigned task.

Living the Meaningful life: Individuals derive a positive sense of well-being, belonging, meaning, and purpose from being part of and contributing back to something larger and more permanent than themselves (e.g., nature, social groups, organizations, movements, traditions, belief systems).

In her book *The How of Happiness*, Sonja Lyubomirsky (2007) explains that to improve happiness, individuals should create new habits; they can seek out new emotions, use variety and timing to prevent hedonic adaptation, and enlist others to motivate and support during the creation of those new habits. Lyubomirsky gives 12 happiness activities such as savoring life, learning to forgive, and living in the present, each of which could become the basis for a new habit.

20.5.11 Conclusions

Our spiritual dimension, our Geistige Person, actually allows us to transcend beyond the misery of suffering, reaching out to our own potentials or the possible help of others. It seems that this growing industry is actually denying the tragic triad of human existence, claiming that the individual person can overcome any existential givens by "living in the moment" and by being fully occupied with nothing but their own mindful living in a world being defined by their good living conditions.

The final "litmus test" for any approach supporting those in need is their application to terminal situations and potentially "giving hope in hell." Or, what good can any approach achieve, if their beneficiaries would be limited to those with fairly good living conditions or offering no support for their survival?

While all approaches discussed above might actually offer helpful support for a variety of conditions, ultimately it is Frankl's concept of the "tragic optimism," understanding and embracing life's duality and offering supportive approaches under all circumstances, which has turned out to provide for best support in all situations that can initially not be controlled or influenced by the very person. Acceptance as the basic components of tragic optimism is valid for seemingly everyday situations, in work and in private life, whenever persons feel victimized, trapped, or desperate.

References

Agency for Healthcare Research and Quality (2014) Meditation programs for psychological stress and well-being, American Psychological Association APA official website: http://www.apa.org

Batthyány A, Russo-Netzer P (eds) (2014) Meaning in positive and existential psychology. Springer, New York

British Association for Counseling and Psychotherapy BACP (2006) Research conference. http://www.bacp.co.uk/research/conf_archive/2006.php

British Association for Counseling and Psychotherapy BACP (2007) Guidelines for counseling in the workplace, written by Hughes R. Kinder A. http://www.counsellingatwork.org.uk

Calhoun LG, Tedeschi RG (2001) Posttraumatic growth: the positive lessons of loss. In: Neimeyer RA (ed) Meaning reconstruction and the experience of loss. American Psychological Association, Washington, DC, pp 157–172

De Shazer S (2008) More than miracles: the state of the art of solution-focused brief therapy. Taylor and Francis, Abingdon

Durbin PG (2018) Human trinity hypnotherapy. Website: paulguydurbin.com. Accessed January 2018

Employee Assistance Professionals Association (2011) EAPA standards and professional guidelines for employee assistance programs. Arlington

Frankl VE (1969) The will to meaning. World Publishing Press, New York

Frankl VE (1988) The will to meaning. Foundations and applications of logotherapy. Plume, New York

Frankl VE (2009) Trotzdem ja zum Leben sagen: Ein Psychologe erlebt das Konzentrationslager. In: Koesel, München D, Maturana HR, Varela FJ (eds) The tree of knowledge: the biological roots of human understanding. Shambala Publications, Boston

Grant AM (2012) ROI is a poor measure of coaching success: towards a more holistic approach using a well-being and engagement framework. Coaching Int J Theory Res Pract 2012:1–12
Grant AM (2016) What constitutes evidence-based coaching? A two-by-two framework for distinguishing strong from weak evidence for coaching. Int J Evid Based Coach Mentoring 14(1):74
Grawe K (2004) Psychological therapy. Hogrefe and Huber Publishers, Washington, D. C
Kahl KG, Winter L, Schweiger U (2012) The third wave of cognitive Behavioural therapy. Curr Opin Psychiatry 25(6):522–528
Laengle A (2005) The search for meaning in life and the existential fundamental motivations. Existent Anal 16(I):2–14
Lyubomirsky S (2007) The how of happiness. Piatkus, London
Maturana HR, Varela FJ (1980) Autopoiesis and cognition: the realization of the living. Springer, Berlin
McLeod J (2001) Counseling in the workplace. A comprehensive review of the research evidence. BACP, London
McLeod J (2010a) The effectiveness of workplace counseling. A systematic review. Couns Psychother Res 10:238–248
McLeod J (2010b) An introduction to counseling. Open University Press, Suffolk
McLeod J (2013) An introduction to research in counseling and psychotherapy. Sage, London
Peterson C, Seligman MEP (2004) Character strengths and virtues. Oxford University Press, New York
Reisner AD (2005) The common factors, empirically validated treatments, and recovery models of therapeutic change. Psychol Rec 55:377–399. Retrieved from opensiuc.lib.siu.edu/cgi/viewcontent
Rogers C (2003) Client centered therapy. Constable and Company, London
Schlosser B, Steinbrenner D, Kumata E, Hunt J (2006) The coaching impact study: measuring the value of executive leader coaching. IJCO Int J Coach Organ 3:140–161
Schmidt G (2015) Einfuehrung in die hypnosystemische Therapie und Beratung. Carl Auer Verlag, Heidelberg
Seligman M (1990) Learned optimism. Knopf, New York
Seligman MEP, Csikszentmihalyi M (2000) Positive psychology: an introduction. Am Psychol 55(1):5–14
van Deurzen E (2015) Existentialism and existential psychotherapy. Middlesex University, London. http://www.existentialanalysis.org.uk
Viktor & I, film produced by Alexander Vesely, to be internationally purchased via www.ViktorandImovie.com
Von Schlippe A, Schweitzer J (1998) Lehrbuch der Systemischen Therapie und Beratung. Vandenhoeck & Ruprecht, Goettingen
Wippmann R (2016) America the anxious: how our pursuit of happiness is creating a nation of nervous wrecks. St. Martin's Press, New York
Wong PTP (2012) From logotherapy to meaning-centered counseling and therapy. In: Wong PTP (ed) The human quest for meaning: theory, research and applications. Routledge, New York

Chapter 21
The Return of Philosophy to Every Day Life: Potentials for the Twenty-First-Century Renaissance

Contents

> *The whole universe is change and life itself is but what you deem it* (Marcus Aurelius).
> *Do not seek to have events happen as you want them to, but instead want them to happen as they do happen, and your life will go well.* (Epictetus).
> *No one can live happily who has regard to himself alone and transforms everything into a question of his own utility; you must live for your neighbor, if you would live for yourself* (Seneca).
> *All things come into being by conflict of opposites* (Heraclitus).

From ancient times until today, philosophers, researchers, and therapists have been in search for the conditions for human flourishing and for the good life. Nevertheless, for centuries, psychotherapists had neglected the study of ancient philosophy, as van Deurzen (2015) explains, although these ancient philosopher's concepts about human existence could have been a source of wisdom and insight into a well-lived human life and their practical implications. For centuries, during middle ages and then throughout modernity, the basic concepts of Greek philosophers and later of Kant, Hume, and Hegel were largely confined to separated intellectual communities, not relevant for any practical application in persons' lives.

This discourse changed, when, in the nineteenth century, Nietzsche and Kierkegaard entered the scene, followed by twentieth-century philosophers Hume, Husserl, Scheler, Jaspers, Buber, and, later, Sartre and Camus.

B. von Devivere, *Meaningful Work: Viktor Frankl's Legacy for the 21st Century*,
https://doi.org/10.1007/978-3-319-89791-2_21

21.1 Existential Philosophy and Existentialism

I leave Sisyphus at the foot of the mountain. One always finds one's burden again. But Sisyphus teaches the higher fidelity that negates the gods and raises rocks. He too concludes that all is well. This universe henceforth without a master seems to him neither sterile nor futile. Each atom of that stone, each mineral flake of that night-filled mountain, in itself, forms a world. The struggle itself toward the heights is enough to fill a man's heart. One must imagine Sisyphus happy. (Camus)

With existential philosophy and existentialism, the essence of human existence and their practical implications had been reclaimed by the public discourse.

Making sense of human existence has always been the main motive of existential philosophy, existential analysis, and existential psychotherapy.

The challenges of modernity and postmodernity for humanity, for human freedom and responsibility, for the limitations of human existence beyond all promises of technology and science, for the choices to be made, for the values to be lived by, and for the attitude to take toward the ailing and indisputable suffering of the world needed to be discussed in the open. Existential issues were, though largely separately, discussed in all spheres of life, philosophers publicly engaged in philosophic activists, and later various psychotherapists integrated existential issues in their practice. Meaning of life, existential anxiety, human freedom and responsibility, intentionality, situations in time, the self, relating to the world, existential limit situations, and the paradoxes and absurdity of existence increasingly gained professional and public attention. It is a rich foundation that the human quest for meaning can relate to. The following considerations of some major existentialist approach are not meant and cannot be exhaustive, but are rather throwing some light on major contributors to modern times existentialist approaches.

In his fundamental book *Being and Time* (published 1927), Heidegger (1962) was the first to address the basic human issue of meaning in life by asking: "Is there something rather than nothing – why and what for?". This question has been relevant to clients ever since they were approaching experts with the aim of finding an answer for their own life. Heidegger laid the foundations for existential psychotherapy, with Binswanger and Boss, later followed by Frankl, May, Yalom, van Deurzen, and others, putting life's meaning at the center of their concepts.

In 1844, Kierkegaard (1980) had been the first to philosophically address the existentially given "Angst" of all human beings: The individual person is ultimately being confronted with the existential limitations of life, with death, being alone in this world with its challenges and contradictions. This existential Angst is the trigger and basis of individual growth, of developing a concept of the self, being in the world and acting responsibly. It is through our experiencing and learning existential anxiety, not fear, that we as human beings develop our own thinking and taking an attitude to the world. In Kierkegaard's concept, existential Angst is the positive starting point for self-awareness and self-growth. Until today, Kierkegaard's concept can be interpreted as a major challenge to mainstream thinking, its denial of existential Angst, and its materialist belief in technology, terminally overcoming this existential given.

Nietzsche for the first time introduced freedom, courage, and responsibility as fundamental human basics. He encouraged people to release outdated moral and societal constraints, to reevaluate all given values, and to liberate the free will of human existence.

While Sartre and Camus both started out with the existentially given human freedom and the individual's capacity to face the absolute absurdity of life (Sartre 2007), Camus later developed his concept into the *Myth of Sisyphus* (Camus 1991), describing the human existence, fundamentally accepting and embracing mortality, and overcoming absurdity and meaninglessness of life in freedom and responsibility:

Taking the current discussion about the many facets and philosophical aspects of "happiness" into account, the author (BvD) is suggesting other translations for Sisyphus being "happy": contented, fulfilled, in peace.

Frankl has been the first neurologist, psychiatrist, and psychotherapist connecting psychology with philosophy. As he has confirmed, logotherapy – in contrast to many other therapies – is based on an explicit philosophy of life. It is Frankl's philosophical anthropology, namely, his understanding of the human condition, of man's freedom and responsibility, and of his will for meaning, that are based on philosophical considerations and explicitly referring to Greek philosophy of *logos and nous*. It was actually in critical analysis and sometimes opposition to the most influential philosophers of his time that Frankl developed his approach (Riemeyer 2007).

While during the last century, Karl Jaspers' and Martin Buber's and later Sartre's and Camus' existentialist approaches were shaping the public discourse, not any other therapeutic approach had ventured to explain its philosophical foundations like Viktor Frankl has done it.

Frankl's philosophical anthropology and psychotherapy was influenced by philosophers like Kierkegaard and Heidegger and motivated by relating to the clients in a true dialogue, aiming at "logos." In doing this, Frankl referred to Kant's demand that communication between humans be based on philosophy and Martin Buber's existentialism and philosophy of dialogue, centered on the distinction between the I and Thou relationship and the I and It relationship. Frankl shared with Buber the concept that existence is encountered between two holistic beings. This encounter is real, but it cannot be measured. Human existence is interpersonal by nature. Frankl went further by claiming that dialogue between two humans be intentionally directed toward logos: any dialogue between two humans entails a third dimension, the external world, the environment.

With this, Frankl's concept can be described as a philosophic/pedagogic/therapeutic form of dialogue approach.

The practical implications of Frankl's approach cannot be overestimated: Frankl's philosophical concept includes both, unconditional acceptance of the other person and challenging the client's thinking, beliefs, and world views. With this, Frankl's concept is not value-neutral; he rather insists on the philosophic reflection of what is being said in terms of the values attributed, reality, and responsibility to the world.

Frankl (2010) challenged the contemporary French existentialist ideas that were published by Sartre and Camus. Frankl publicly disagreed with Sartre's idea that we must accept the ultimate meaninglessness of life, arguing that "we must accept the incapacity to recognize the ultimate meaning with rational and logical terms" and rejecting Sartre's concept as an expression of modern times nihilism. He also disagreed that man creates his own essence, rather arguing that man finds his essence in transcendence.

Transcendence was defined by Frankl not in the religious or spiritual way of previous schools, but in the human capacity to detach from his somatic and psychosocial situation and condition.

Batthyany (2018) illustrates Frankl's concept of existential analysis (EA): "(It) may be understood as the philosophical and scientific basis of logotherapy as well as an essential part of a therapy proper. Basically, existential analysis means analysis with respect to existence, or 'explication of existence' with consideration of a self-responsible, self-realized, and humane life. In *general existential analysis* the pursuit of meaning is discussed and identified as a basic motivation in humans, and arguments are provided that demonstrate the fundamental possibility of finding meaning in life. On this basis the therapeutic effects of a successful search for meaning may be explained. In *special existential analysis* the specific, individual life of a person or a group is probed… Thus the therapeutic value of existential analysis lies in the elucidation of the concrete existential situation and the preparation for giving assistance in the – autonomous – search for meaning."

In this sense, the search for meaning in work is a fundamental aspect of individuals' lives. Frankl was the first psychotherapist to address the human fundamental search for meaning beyond psychotherapy, addressing dysfunctions and disorders and rather making meaning of life practically available to each individual via the explanation of existence and the concrete practical consequences of this elucidation, on the basis of each person's physical, psychosocial, and spiritual integrity.

With all his publications, explaining the implications of his concept and never hesitating to apply this concept to all spheres of life, with many of his publications selling as bestsellers not only in Europe and the United States, Frankl's approach remained unique in his connection of philosophy and existential practice. Last century's existentialism discourses remained confined to intellectual discussions largely in Europe, and the various existential psychotherapeutic approaches were being discussed in the psychotherapeutic community, addressing disorders rather than existential issues of finding meaning and how to lead a good life.

Until the turn of this millennium, philosophy at all seemed to be not much in demand, with little relevance for medical professions and for daily life. Today, the situation has turned around.

We see a renaissance of philosophy in all areas of life, across all business branches, and certainly with individual persons searching for their own path of life. Frankl has returned to current streams of professional and individual discussions about man's freedom.

In 2016, American bloggers (open source) conclude that like no other secular voice, Frankl (2006) was confident that we could find meaning and purpose in life, in spite of life's seeming chaos, through a kind of idealism that brings us closer to reality. Frankl's thesis echoes those of many sages, from Buddhists to Stoics to his twentieth-century existentialist contemporaries: "Everything can be taken from a man but one thing: the last of the human freedoms—to choose one's attitude in any given set of circumstances, to choose one's own way". Frankl turns away from the obsession with the Absurd towards actively taking an attitude.

21.2 The Rediscovery of Ancient Philosophy

In search for this public, greater good beyond individual self-actualization, Greek philosophical approaches have gained increasing attention in all spheres of life. Their practical implications are being studied by professionals and all those, searching for understanding the basics of meaning, ethics, values, and a good life. In this context, ancient philosophers have reached the C-suite; today's management and business experts communities are restudying ancient philosophy. These philosophers' concepts have reached work life. Working persons' motivation in reading ancient philosophers is based in their growing skepticism, distrust, deadlocks, and despair over the paradoxes, hardships, crises, and tragedies of current developments and their search for finding practical support in their search for meaning in their lives and their existential longing for leading their everyday life with values and contentment.

The roots of philosophy nourish finding answers to life's existential questions: in ancient times, philosophy was understood as "praxis," a therapy and cure of the soul and the site for spiritual exercises. This applied interpretation of philosophy as the art of living broke down in the middle ages and was largely forgotten by modernity with philosophy itself, retreating from any practical consequences.

It was only until positive psychology's interest in well-being, "happiness," and human flourishing that public attention started to go "back to basics" of Greek philosophers' understanding of a good life and potential human virtues, opposite to unethical behaviors.

Today, as Leontiev (2015) explains, for the vast majority of people, it is "happiness" that serves as the main goal and main reward of their life.

Until today, most people spontaneously understand "happiness" as the "hedonistic" search and their own pursuit of pleasure being the main motivation for their own life and for humans in general. Although the issue of leading a happy life has been widely researched and discussed by now, there is still little understanding of the broader concept of happiness and its foundations in Greek philosophy.

21.3 Eudaimonia: Happiness Through Living Virtues

Today's discussion about leading a good life, human virtues and human flourishing has put the Greek philosopher's approach back on the agenda to learn from what has always been the aim of practical Greek philosophy, i.e., to reflect what *eudaimonia* is and how it can be achieved. Eudaimon life is one of "virtuous activity in accordance with reason." Doing anything well requires virtue, and each characteristic activity and function has its own set of virtues.

Is there a difference between living a happy life and living a meaningful life? Does meaning and happiness naturally coincide? Can I as an individual actively pursue happiness in my personal life?

What actually is "happiness"? What is "leading a happy life"? How is "happiness" being defined and achieved? Is it an objective of its own or can it be achieved only by pursuing other goals? Is leading a happy life leading a life with pleasure or rather leading a fulfilled life? What then is the difference? Can we have a happy life, being challenged by all the predicaments, the ails, and the limitations of human existence?

From its origins, positive psychology cannot explain man's attitude toward the existential givens of life, together with the irrefutable sufferings of modern time and workplaces, and man's inherent self-transcendent directedness to meaning beyond hedonistic happiness. We are observing a world in devastating crisis with individuals and people fighting for their dignity and freedom. In these times we are currently witnessing unprecedented examples of what Frankl coined as man's will to meaning: "Man finds identity to the extent to which he commits himself to something beyond himself, to a cause greater than himself" (Frankl).

Reflecting the discussion around concepts of happiness, Martin Seligman and positive psychology have taken distinct effort in explaining their concept of happiness, differentiating their approach from the hedonistic pursuit of pleasure, and distancing from the "happy-go-lucky-smiley-Hollywood approach" (Seligman). Seligman explains that the hedonic approach has not only proved to be scientifically wrong, but, as he explains, it is "of very poor intellectual provenance." Seligman continues referring to the ancient Greek concept of eudaimonia, which was not at all associated with achieving pleasures of positive feelings or delightful things, but rather with the pleasures of thinking. In the end, though, Seligman still offers three pathways to happiness: leading a pleasant life; leading a good life by deliberately pursuing values, virtues, and individual character strengths; or leading a meaningful life. Seligman, Peterson, and Huta found (Vitterso 2016) that leading an eudemonic life was related to life satisfaction. Meaning alone can serve as a good proxy of eudemonic experiences.

The psychologist Ryff and Singer (2008) highlighted the distinction between *eudaimonia well-being*, which she identified as psychological well-being, and *hedonic well-being* or pleasure. She conceptualized modern *eudaimonia* as a six-factor structure:

- Autonomy
- Personal growth

- Self-acceptance
- Purpose in life
- Environmental mastery
- Positive relations with others.

Ryff states that the pursuit and acquisition of positive relationships is an intrinsically motivated desire that is endorsed cross-culturally as a route to leading a meaningful life.

Individuals that strive for a life defined by affiliation, intimacy, and contributing to one's community can be described as aspiring to fulfill their intrinsic psychological needs. In contrast, those individuals who aspire for wealth and material, social recognition, fame, image, or attractiveness can be described as aiming to fulfill their extrinsic psychological needs.

A study conducted in the early 1990s exploring the relationship between well-being and those aspects of positive functioning that were put forth in Ryff's model indicates that persons who aspired more for financial success than affiliation with others or their community scored lower on various measures of well-being. The strength of an individual's intrinsic (relative to extrinsic) aspirations, as indicated by rankings of importance given, correlates with an array of psychological outcomes: positive correlations have been found with indications of psychological well-being – positive affect, vitality, and self-actualization. Negative correlations have been found with indicators of psychological ill-being – negative affect, depression, and anxiety.

The Greek *eudaimonia* refers to fulfillment gained by proper development of one's highest and most human capabilities. It requires not only good character, but rational activity, reason ("logos"). The Stoics claim that the eudaimon life is the morally virtuous life. They emphasize virtues such as justice, honesty, moderation, simplicity, self-discipline, resolve, fortitude, and courage (virtues also encouraged by the Jewish and Christian tradition).

We are in the midst of a renewed and fresh interest in the very foundations of philosophy. To this extent, discussions around eudaimonia, virtues, and meaning as opposed to man's will for pleasure and hedonistic experiences all touch on man's general capacity and responsibility "to take a stand toward the conditions he is confronted with" and to be active in taking that stand, because man is ultimately free and endowed with virtues.

Greek philosophers' ethics have returned to the attention of almost all realms of life: retrieving their knowledge and wisdom has become part of a twenty-first-century renaissance and a source of strength for the modern man.

Small philosophy editions (Marc Aurel, Seneca et al.) have become gift bestsellers, managers around the world are studying the essence of philosophers' basic messages for their daily challenges, and research has been investigating and empirically testing their main topics with populations around the world.

In view of the vast literature on "happiness" in individuals, in nations, links between happiness and economic well-being as well as happiness and different cultural approaches, there is no need to overemphasize the differences between

Frankl's philosophical foundations – resting more in Scheler than in Socrates – and the current discourse around the Greek "ancestors" but to rather link to this grand history of philosophy that is being taken up by an ever-growing community and which is now gaining its own momentum.

Referring to Greek philosophy, Cederström and Spicer (2017) warns about the detrimental effects of continuous self-improvement. In a widely discussed article for The New York Times (July 2015), Carl Cederström reminded of the ancient philosophical roots of the term "happiness" and has warned about the "dangers of happiness":

> Whenever we talk about happiness, we also talk about something else: morality. We may not know what happiness itself signifies, but we do know how it has been evoked historically — to set out a template for a moral life. As we rush to make happiness the ultimate aim both for ourselves and society at large, we might want to recall some of the wonderfully rich and depressingly contradictory history of the concept. Going back to the birth of Western civilization in ancient Greece, might help us better understand our own time and the moral values we subscribe to today… We are assumed to find happiness through work and by being productive. We are required to curate our market value, manage ourselves as corporations and live according to an entrepreneurial ethos. When no sin is greater than being unemployed and no vice more despised than laziness, happiness comes only to those who work hard, have the right attitude and struggle for self-improvement. These are some of the moral values that seem to underlie happiness today: Be real, be strong, be productive — and most important, don't rely on other people to achieve these goals, because your fate is, of course, in your own hands. This is a popular message, and has been for some time… When happiness has become championed and talked about incessantly, as it is today, the best we can hope for is that it raises other universal issues — like equality, justice, truth and ethics, which we desperately need to discuss. The worst that can happen — and this is unfortunately already underway — is that happiness becomes a Trojan horse used to normalize inequality and oppression.

How then did Greek philosophers actually define a good life? What guidelines did they give to cope with the impertinences of life? What can we learn from the greatest thinkers and practitioners of their times, discussing the issues of their time with their students and followers and thereby shaping the world for all times?

21.4 Plato's Concept of "Psyche"

For both Plato and Socrates' "care for the soul" means becoming an ethically thorough human being. Plato (1997) understood the soul, "psyche," as a tripartite phenomenon, composed of the logical, the spirited, and the appetitive part with their respective functions of seeking pleasure, justice or logos, and insight. Plato argues that above all, the thinking part must finally rule above the motivation to learn or the motivation for pleasure and lust.

Plato understood the soul representing all the human mental abilities, reason, thinking, and rationality. He argued that care for the soul must be related to thinking, exploring the truth beyond mere reflections on outside experiences. Plato argues that this search for logos goes via the three pathways of exploring truth, beauty, and goodness, but definitely may not stop there, but would rather put rational thinking and search for ultimate noos beyond these three areas of attention. Plato defines the "cure for the soul" as the daily practice of searching for logos by reflecting and thinking. It is this very Platonian understanding of the cure for the soul, which was rediscovered and saved for answering to modern times' existential givens by the philosopher Michel Foucault.

21.5 Aristotle's Approach: The Good Life

Together with the ever-increasing attention for "happiness" in work and personal lives, in nations, and in the global world and how to achieve it, Aristotle's basic definition of eudaimonia has come into the center of international consideration: "eu" for good and "daimon" for spirit, together with "arete" for virtues, and eudaimonia stands for the highest human good to be achieved.

Aristotle's eudaimonia (Barnes 2001) approach contrasts to the hedonistic approach of seeking the most individual pleasure in personal life, irrespective of the effects for the other and the community, based on extrinsic motives.

It is relating to what Frankl called the innate human conscience, empowering the individual to differentiate between "right" and "wrong."

21.6 Stoicism

> Until we have begun to go without them, we fail to realize how unnecessary many things are. We've been using them not because we needed them, but because we had them. Seneca

The Stoics make a radical claim that the eudaimon life is the morally virtuous life. Everything else, such as health, honor, and riches, are merely "neutral." The Stoics therefore are committed to saying that external goods such as wealth and physical beauty are not really good at all. They emphasize virtues such as justice, honesty, moderation, simplicity, self-discipline, resolve, fortitude, and courage. For Seneca, eudaimonian virtue is the only good, immorality the only evil, and all else but a worthless mass of things, which come and go without increasing or diminishing the highest good: "A man thus grounded must, whether he wills or not, necessarily be attended by constant cheerfulness and a joy that is deep and comes from deep within, since he finds delight in his own resources, and desires no joys greater than his inner joys."

Today, being confronted with symptoms of materialism, egocentrism, and greed, with unethical and humiliating behavior, stoic philosophy has been regaining considerable attention with individuals who are searching ways of dealing with the negative antidotes to ethical standards.

And in times, when the human being is being constantly appraised and measured against his fellow next companion and when issues of self-esteem, self-worth, and self-acceptance, together with all the activities of self-optimization and self-development, are more than ubiquitous, Epicure's quote "You know yourself, what you are worth in your own eyes" is more relevant than ever.

Business coaching and some CBT experts are relating to stoic philosophers in detaching clients from the very problem situation and regaining access to the very basic assumptions of personal value.

This fundamental approach clearly relates to what Frankl claimed as life having its own and absolute meaning under all circumstances.

Marc Aurel's statement, "misfortune nobly born is good fortune," can be related to what Frankl, centuries later, termed as the attitudinal values relating to suffering and existential situations, which he termed as the highest personal achievement.

Together with the growing interest in ancient philosophy, commonalities between Frankl's approach and ancient philosophers were increasingly brought to public attention. Stephen Costello, the founder and director of the Viktor Frankl Institute in Ireland, concludes in his research about connecting Viktor Frankl's approach to ancient philosophy: "Logotherapy is a type of Socratic midwifery" (Costello 2013).

- Philosophy is both practical and therapeutic by spiritual exercises, whose aim is to form rather than inform (Stoics). Logotherapy and existential analysis is a philosophy of life, whose aim is to transform life to self-transformation.
- Frankl's attitudinal values are stoic in character.
- There is a dimension beyond soma.
- The noetic core (Frankl), the divine (stoics) transcends body and mind.
- The essence of good and evil do not determine human existence. Man decides on them by taking an attitude (Epictetus).
- Human will is unconquerable and unconditional (Socrates).
- Philosophy is daily practice (Socratic dialogue).
- Moral goodness is the end. Happiness is a by-product of virtue.
- We are disturbed not by the things, but by the view we take on them (Stoics). How we respond to things is more important than how we react to things (logotherapy).
- The sumum bonum (supreme good) is a combination of the four cardinal virtues: wisdom, courage, justice, and temperance (Stoics). The essence of human existence is ethical and spiritual self-transcendence.

21.7 Michel Foucault's Radical Demand for Care for the Self

In his late works, the French philosopher, lecturing professor and activist, Michel Foucault, put Plato's concept of self-care on the modern agenda, connecting it with a radical approach for pursuing truth and reflecting thinking. Foucault (1997) defines ethics as the intentional work of an individual on itself to subject itself to a set of moral recommendations for conduct. This happens only through practice of being in the world.

Foucault reminds us of the Delphi description to "know oneself," not aimed at continuous reflection of the self, but rather as the grounds to reflect own actions against the ethics of truth. He defines his concept of self-care as a constant search for the truth: "The care of the self is the ethical transformation of the self in light of the truth, which is to say the transformation of the self into a truthful existence."

As Foucault explained in his final lecture courses at Collège de France in 1982, his thinking is based on the ancient Greek philosophers' concept of "parrhesia," of the open and transparent dialogue between human searching for truth, because they deem it their moral, social, and political duty beyond any dangers they might face for their personal lives. Foucault understands parrhesia (Foucault 2011) as "a verbal activity in which a speaker expresses his personal relationship to truth, and risks his life because he recognizes truth-telling as a duty to improve or help other people (as well as himself). In parrhesia, the speaker uses his freedom and chooses frankness instead of persuasion, truth instead of falsehood or silence, the risk of death instead of life and security, criticism instead of flattery, and moral duty instead of self-interest and moral apathy."

Foucault combines ethics with human freedom: According to his concept, ethics is the form that freedom takes when it is informed by reflection, and freedom is exercising informed ethics. Self-care implies caring for others; the self can be found only in relating to others.

21.8 Self-Care, Self-Cult, and Self-Addiction: Differences

As explained, Foucault focuses on the ethical demand to care for oneself, referring to Plato's concept of cure of the soul. According to Foucault, self-care in ancient Greek philosophy was the starting point and the foundational principle of all activities, aimed at moral rationality. In his radical critique of modern mainstream, care for oneself' discussions, he rather finds "care without moral content."

Foucault's modern times diagnosis hits the very point of many other findings: With enlightenment, humanity has gained *freedom from* constraining beliefs and religion, but humanity has lost its way in defining what this *freedom is for*. Today, man is lost in self-optimization, suffering from "poverty of mind" (Batthyany A) amidst affluence. Not knowing their way, man has travelled the road of concentrating and rotating around the self. Foucault assesses modern psychology as "the new religion" of "self-cult," constantly being occupied with oneself. The potentialities of freedom gained once offered two roads: one road, exercising freedom by searching for the true, good, and beautiful (Plato), and the other road, leading to nothing, because "freedom – what for?" had not been searched for or been defined by enlightenment and modern societies. This, according to Foucault, holds especially true for production, technology, and science, where the self feels governed by work constraints, being deprived of his once gained freedom to decide on the course of action.

According to Foucault, humanity in modern times has gone astray, traveling the road of pursuing pleasure and joy, and now finds itself trapped by the dialectics of modernity, producing ever more things with no meaning and being suppressed by their continuous search for more, with actually finding less to nothing.

21.9 Exercising Care for the Self

How can we, according to Foucault, exercise this care for the self and how can we assess our own actions against leading a truthful existence? Here, Foucault is as radical and practical as the ancient Greek philosophers: We can do so through practicing truthful thinking, by making philosophical thinking a part of individual daily practice and by exercising parrhesia, as a truthful discourse with others. Socrates himself rigorously practiced self-care and care for others by rigorously living this rational discourse.

For many years, Foucault's critical philosophic approach was received very reluctantly, just as the other existential philosophers of the twentieth century, whose works were discussed only in specific communities. Now, Foucault's approach has gained much attention in twenty-first-century discussions and works on how to lead a life based on the ancient Greek philosophers demand, searching for truth and practicing self-reflection.

The German philosopher Wilhelm Schmid (1998) has defined specific ways of exercising self-care, philosophy, and rational thinking in everyday life, which follows Plato's understanding. All these practices are aimed at social practice and communication with others:

- Keeping a diary about own interactions and encounters
- Writing down own reflections and thoughts of the day
- Philosophic, critical reflection of the day
- Physical practice of caring for a healthy body
- Meditation
- Reading
- Broader understanding of self-care, meaning of education, and taking care of oneself
- Critical reflection of the daily practice

It is exactly this philosophically based *practice* which closely relates to Frankl's approach and legacy for application in the twenty-first-century work and private life. According to Florez et al. (2016), Frankl's definition of meaning refers to those *reasons*, tasks, experiences, and *acts* that are inherent in every situation and that *give persons a* "why" *to their existence* and, therefore, serve as motivation *to complete daily activities* as well as to set meaningful goals to fulfill. Meaning can only be achieved through the self being directed toward other beings, through encounters with others, not by self-actualization, but rather by reflecting and acting beyond self-interest.

Today's call for action to find meaning in work life largely relates to exercising human's potentials for freedom and responsibility and to experiencing creative and experiential values that resonate with the "community" around and with what ancient philosophers up to Viktor Frankl have termed the human capacity to know by conscience, and virtues, addressing the inalienable Geistige Person, intended to differentiate and bring about what is "good" with a self-transcending perspective of achieving meaning by going beyond the self.

References

Barnes J (2001) Early Greek philosophy. Penguin Classics, London

Batthyany A (2018) What is logotherapy and existential analysis? Official Website of the Viktor Frankl Institute Vienna. http://logotherapy.univie.ac.at/e/logotherapy.html. Accessed January 2018

Camus A (1991) The myth of Sisyphus and other essays. Vintage International, New York

Cederstroem C, Spicer A (2017) Desperately seeking self-improvement: a year inside the optimization movement. OP Books, New York/London

Costello SJ (2013) A sketch of the stoic influences on Viktor Frankl's logotherapy. Retrieved from http://modernstoicism.com/features-stoicism-logotherapy/

Florez IA, Schulenberg SE, Stewart T (2016) Meaning and automatic stereotyping: advancing an agenda for research. In: Batthyany A (ed) Logotherapy and existential analysis. Springer International Publishing, Basel, pp 107–119

Foucault M (1997) In: Lane A (ed) Ethics. Subjectivity and truth. Penguin Press, London

Foucault M (2011) The courage of truth: lectures at the Collège de France 1983–1984. Palgrave MacMillan, New York

Frankl VE (2006) Man's search for meaning. Beacon Press, Boston

Frankl VE (2010) In: Batthyany A (ed) The feeling of meaninglessness. A challenge to psychotherapy and philosophy. Marquette University Press, Marquette

Heidegger M (1962) Being And time. Harper and Row, London

Kierkegaard S (1980) The concept of anxiety. Princeton University Press, Princeton

Leontiev DA (2015) Experience processing as an aspect of existential psychotherapy: life enhancement methodology. J Contemp Psychother 45(1):49–58

Plato (1997) Complete works. Hackett Publishing Company Inc, Cambridge

Riemeyer J (2007) Die Logotherapie Viktor Frankls und ihre Weiterentwicklungen. Eine Einführung in die sinnorientierte Psychotherapie. Huber, Bern

Ryff CD, Singer BH (2008) Know thyself and become what you are. Journal of Happiness Studies 9:13

Sartre JP (2007) Existentialism is a humanism. Yale University Press, New Haven

Schmid W (1998) Philosophie der Lebenskunst. Suhrkamp Verlag, Frankfurt am Main

Van Deurzen E (2015) Paradox and passion in psychotherapy: an existential approach. Wiley Blackwell, Chichester

Vitterso J (ed) (2016) Handbook of eudaimonic wellbeing. Springer Nature International Publishing, Cham

Chapter 22
Optimism in the Face of Adversity

Contents

22.1 Frankl's Concept of Tragic Optimism

None of the existing models discussed above can be applied to extreme situations in which individuals can only expect bad events and have little or no control over the terrifying situation of being confronted with terminal diagnosis, with war and their aftermath, with natural or man-made traumatic events.

In these situations, it is only human to feel helpless, hopeless, and terrified, because the adversity and the terror are beyond the persons' immediate control. Here, all happiness-oriented models, all mindfulness exercises, and their widely spread research studies and findings offer no solution, no quick fixes, and no outcomes to be reported. And in this rich, industrialized Western world, there are too many individuals in extreme boundary situations, feeling desperate and lacking the most basic resources and help. When getting through each day might be a person's only true achievement, what these persons need is the same kind of "optimism" that sustained Frankl in the concentration camps.

Frankl (2006) defined his concept of tragic optimism "an optimism in the face of tragedy": all the pains inflicted on man cannot strip him of his human dignity and his abiding hope in the meaning and value of life.

This concept contradicts false illusions, escapism, and forced optimism. Even in the face of terror, Frankl claims: "Everything can be taken from a man but one thing: the last of the human freedoms – to choose one's attitude in any given set of circumstances, to choose one's own way."

This approach provides for dignity, freedom, and understanding for those who might feel victimized, devaluated, useless, worthless, and forgotten or those who are stripped by grief over a loss or traumatic event that has occurred. Frankl's "credo" has actually, until today, served as a great resource for executives, employees, experts, and coaches, coping with life's tragic events, when they want to give best support to their clients and stakeholders.

B. von Devivere, *Meaningful Work: Viktor Frankl's Legacy for the 21st Century*,
https://doi.org/10.1007/978-3-319-89791-2_22

The business coach Battista (2010) explains: "What I find comforting in Frankl's perspective is that he's *not* denying the grief and rage that spring from suffering and tragedy. He's *not* 'making the best of things.' And he's *not* blithely suggesting that 'everything happens for a reason' (which I find a particularly unhelpful expression of condolence). What Frankl *is* doing is encouraging us to acknowledge our grief and rage, *and also* to see our suffering as an experience in which it is possible to find meaning… there's something in Frankl's words, something about the search for meaning, that makes it easier. The nature of that meaning is not at all clear to me now, and perhaps it never will be. Perhaps this search for meaning is in fact the purpose of life."

Wong (2007) identifies essential components that comprise "tragic optimism":

- Affirmation of the meaning and value of life, regardless of circumstances
- Acceptance of what cannot be changed
- Faith or trust in God, in a greater power, and in others
- Courage to face adversity

Countless known and unknown individuals have been testifying this tragic optimism and have been giving hope to those being confronted with the same evils.

They actually turned their tragedy into triumph, or they spread the news that humankind cannot afford any type of reductionism or general pessimism but rather refer to the best reasons for optimism in the face of adversity, for hope in the face of hopelessness.

These persons, active in business, organizations, management, coaching, and consulting, have been serving as supporters in mind and as role models for generations and individuals, being confronted with much "smaller" every day challenges, giving them good reasons to put their perceived suffering in perspective and lifting them up to their potentials. Here, Frankl's tragic optimism serves as a monumental and realistic example of the unalienable dignity of each person in their daily challenges.

22.2 MCCT: A Holistic, Meaning-Centered Approach

Wong (2011) has defined "meaning-centered counseling and therapy" (MCCT), an integrative, meaning-centered approach, which can be seen as a blueprint for understanding and navigating through today's global challenges on all levels of business, work life, and private life.

Based on Frankl's approach, MCCT represents the "second wave of positive psychology," which recognizes both the downsides of positives and the upsides of negatives in an individual person's life. With this approach, MCCT acknowledges man's primary will to meaning and unconditional meaning of life under all circumstances. In parallel, MCCT describes a practical approach of addressing and managing meaning in work and private life.

Therefore, his MCCT approach is being quoted here in detail:

MCCT is holistic by virtue of its focus on meaning and conceptualizing humans as bio psychosocial spiritual beings. What Wong describes, does apply to all issues presented in today's workplaces and therefore Wong's reference to psychotherapy is replaced here by the general function 'facilitator': A meaning oriented facilitator approaches the individual not as a compartmentalized person, but as a person seeking wholeness in a broken world. Wong proposes that the best way to achieve a fuller understanding of the topics is to place all knowledge and findings within a meaning-centered integrative and holistic framework, that recognizes the individual as a complete human being in a specific historical and cultural context. By the same token, the best way to motivate positive change is to explore the many different modalities and avenues that resonate with this individual person.

MCCT is *existential and spiritual* by definition. Wong describes the spiritual dimension as the very core of humanness, the essence of humanity. The defiant power of the human spirit refers to the human capacity to tap into the spiritual dimension in order to transcend and cope with the challenges of life.

In today's business world, increasingly managers and executives as well as employees are searching for some type of spiritual leadership, also in the light of findings that support the importance of spiritual beliefs for personal well-being.

MCCT is relational by stressing the centrality of relationships for healing, meaning, and well-being, based on the need to belong, which is a fundamental human motivation. The phenomenal growth of social media attests to the deep-seated human needs for social connection.

MCCT is multicultural

For several reasons, MCCT is inherently multicultural in its orientation and practice: because meaning is both individually and socially constructed, one's meaning systems are inevitably shaped by one's historical and sociocultural background.

Culture has a profound and pervasive influence on people's behaviors and attitudes. We cannot understand clients' behaviors and attitudes apart from their meaning systems and cultural backgrounds. Empathy demands cultural sensitivity in working with clients from different racial, ethnic, and cultural backgrounds. All current and future approaches in workplace management stress the importance of diversity, the need for inclusive cultural empathy as an antidote to cultural biases. We cannot fully understand the meaning of behaviors unless it is viewed at all levels of the ecological context. An ecological approach enables us to understand the existential–phenomenological experiences of individuals in their interactions with the different contexts of their life circumstances.

In a multicultural society, personal meaning systems necessarily evolve through the long struggle of navigating the crosscurrents of different cultures. Therefore, sensitivity, understanding, and knowledge of such struggles are essential.

Wong emphasizes the following qualities that facilitate cross-cultural interactions: openness to new experiences, willingness to accept and tolerate differences, inclusive cultural empathy, respect for other cultures, and the humility to acknowledge one's own cultural blind spots and implicit racial biases.

Wong et al. (2016) suggests two strategies for implementing meaning orientation, integrating other current approaches:

- The PURE strategy: meaning is defined in terms of four interrelated components – defining and developing purpose, understanding, responsible action, and evaluation (PURE).
- The ABCDE strategy: the ABCDE intervention strategy is the main tool of MCCT in dealing with negative life experiences. Completely different from the ABCDE sequence involved in the rational–emotive therapy process (Ellis and Dryden 1997), this ABCDE is similar to acceptance–commitment therapy in its emphasis on action rather than thinking.
- *A* stands for acceptance, *B* for belief and affirmation, *C* for commitment to specific goals and actions, *D* for discovering the meaning and significance of the self and situations, and *E* for evaluation of outcomes and enjoying the positive results.

References

Battista E (2010) Viktor Frankl on love, suffering and the meaning of life, Post April 4, 2010, Accessed on edbatista.com

Ellis A, Dryden W (1997) The practice of rational-emotive therapy. Springer, New York

Frankl VE (2006) Man's search for meaning. Beacon Press, Boston

Wong PTP (2007) Viktor Frankl: prophet of hope for the 21st century. In: Batthyany A, Levinson J (eds) Anthology of Viktor Frankl's logotherapy. Zeig, Tucker & Theisen Inc., Phoenix

Wong PTP (2011) Meaning centered counseling and therapy MCCT: an integrative and comprehensive approach to motivational counseling and addiction treatment. In: Cox WM, Klinger E (eds) Handbook of motivational counseling: goal based approaches to assessment with addiction and other problems. Wiley-Blackwell, Chichester

Wong PTP W, Ivtzan I, Lomas T (2016) The meaning centered approach MCA. In: Oades LG, Steger MF, Delle Fave MA, Passmore J (eds) The Wiley Blackwell handbook of the psychology of positivity and strengths-based approaches at work. Wiley-Blackwell, Chichester

Chapter 23
A Meaning-Centered Integrated Approach: Viktor Frankl's Legacy for Twenty-First-Century Meaningful Work

Contents

> Ultimately, man should not ask what the meaning of his life is, but rather must recognize that it is he who is asked. In a word, each man is questioned by life; and he can only answer to life by answering for his own life; to life he can only respond by being responsible. (V. E. Frankl)

23.1 Work and Life: A Difficult Relationship

> The recognition of the other person becomes the condition of own acknowledgement. (Honneth 1995)

This is an age in which "the economy," business, and work have replaced religion, traditions, and politics as central forces in people's lives. Economic considerations of turnover, profit, and shareholder value, together with the overarching human image of the "homo economicus," are governing global business and decisions. Employees, managers, executives, and experts across various business branches are experiencing their work as meaningless, leading to demotivation, intensified negative stress, and deterioration of their health. Employees are searching

B. von Devivere, *Meaningful Work: Viktor Frankl's Legacy for the 21st Century*,
https://doi.org/10.1007/978-3-319-89791-2_23

for meaningful work, where they experience humane working conditions, personally experiencing significance, orientation, coherence, and community. Especially with the younger generation, we are observing increased self-awareness of finding the right balance between work and private life, implementing some congruity between their work and privately related values, practicing "generativity," and increasingly demanding new models and best practices of leading a good, sustainable life for themselves, their partners, their children, and future generations, being aware of global challenges. Frankl's (2006) diagnosis of the noetic crisis of last century's younger generation, lacking meaning in their work, has become an ever more current analysis for twenty-first-century workers. Working environments are insufficiently providing a framework for these expectations and for fulfilling these human needs, leading to frustration and feeling void.

Together with the ever more advancing division of labor, there are more and more tasks and functions, when the individual worker and employee can hardly recognize the meaning of his/her contribution to the end product, e.g., in many service branches, potentially being occupied with filling out excel sheets or selecting sealing caps.

Nevertheless, human beings keep searching for significance of their work, for the opportunity of taking pride in what they are doing, in experiencing a sense of self-efficacy and good relationships with their fellow workers. It is these needs that business workplaces might promise to fulfill and that critics call the "painful pawn," seducing human beings in search for meaning to fall for modernistic employers' promising pledges:

- Actualizing euphemisticly called individual freedom in work with actually ending up self-employed with almost no social standards, relating to a clear monthly income, compensation for own equipment wear or labor rights, once somehow culturally agreed upon, on the basis of shared values and convictions, after centuries of industrial disputes; e.g. taking food with own bicycle, regardless of the wind or weather, to customers, with no social security and caring for own bicycle repairs, or the ever growing 'gig-economy'
- Living with creativity and independence, constantly searching for a creative design job on Internet platforms, with the jobs advertised demanding unpaid preliminary work; these creative experts have changed their dependence on a single employer with their dependence on many platforms.
- Wishing to live their dreams and talents and bring something new to this world that they find productive and worthwhile, self-employed persons engage in startups, sharing offices in creative labs, hoping that they might experience a breakthrough like their idols in Silicon Valley. Times have changed. With their optimistic world view and personal belief, these entrepreneurs are endangered to fall prey to banks or to end up in bankruptcy, with no other option to pursue.
- Searching for balancing work and private family life, human beings are confronted with making their own choices, of either following their regular expert functions, overtime and weekend work included, or waiving their expert function and alternatively following the so called "family track," with no less than regular working hours and less salary.

- Searching for experiential values, personal development, and learning, they end up in vicious cycles of self-optimization, when finally some current knowledge is always left missing.

Following these promises, working persons are increasingly endangered to losing control of their initially well-defined purpose and goals for work, to work beyond their physical limitations, to exhaust their own resources, and to lose track of their initial best intentions for work and to always fail the goal in the race between the rabbit and the hedgehog, which they cannot win.

Here, the "self" has become the object of hidden or overt exploitation, being worded as self-actualization, self-development, self-management, self-reflection, self-awareness, etc.

In parallel, another need has emerged from the work-related experiences these human beings make in their unfulfilled search for meaning: They gather in nightly events, called "Fuck Up Nights," where thousands attend and share their stories of individual failing, crossing the taboo of success stories, letting go of their feelings of shame and insufficiency, and getting back to where they started from, their sense of human pride, and intrinsic motivation to bring their talents to the world.

In parallel, undeniably, a new paradigm for meaningful work is emerging, expanding in maturity and relevance for the overall global community of working and doing business.

Some see a new business paradigm of good business evolving, benefiting the leaders as well as employees and the greater community, with the crucial factors: trust, commitment of fostering the personal growth of their individual employees, and the dedication to create a product that helps mankind. Csikszentmihalyi (2003) calls upon "the soul" of the specific business, beyond the state-of-the-art business mission and vision statements: "The search for a life that has 'relevance or meaning' … is the primary concern of soul. This is … the need that motivates us to become part of something greater or more permanent than our selves."

Meaning is on the agenda of business and all individuals, working and exercising management functions.

Research on meaningful work (Steger et al. 2012) suggests that the concept of meaningful work includes variables such as skill variety, opportunity to complete an entire task, task significance to other people, pride, engagement, a sense of calling, and intrinsic work orientation as a matter of own identity. Nevertheless, much more research is needed, further clarifying the meaning of meaningful work and the other dimensions of work, specifically the experiential dimensions of building and empowering relationships to others in the workplace.

23.2 Meaning and Work: A Means or an End?

23.2.1 Meaning as an End of Being

Each person needs to be recognized, affirmed, and respected by the other person in all their encounters and relations, be they private or work-related.

Looking at human history, freedom, and the corresponding development of conscious and socially defined relations, and their foundations in thinking and philosophy, has been showing an ever-impressing development. Today, we are living in an era of rising attention to individual needs and their fulfillment in globally defined workplaces.

Together with all social and human rights developments and our refined mindfulness regarding the specific conditions and individual expectations regarding work, the idea and the ideal of freedom and responsibility has reentered twenty-first century's stage: throughout the ever more disastrous crises and global tragedies, largely influenced by the spheres of production and consumption, our freedom, our potentials, and our responsibilities to act on them are knocking at our door. And more: Together with all the technology providing us information from around the globe, we have come to realize that we are all part of one global community, sharing basic human conditions and needs, above all continents, specific cultures and environment we live and work in.

While "hopelessness in the face of adversity is an extravagance not be afforded" (Chief Editor of Sueddeutsche Zeitung, Germany), we are also witnesses of an unprecedented "tragic optimism," turning today's tragedies into triumph and introducing and bringing alive new ideas, approaches, and initiatives for driving the "Copernican turn," as exemplified in this book.

These new twenty-first-century entrepreneurs are thriving to make a difference in the world by introducing and activating their talents for the common good; their ventures are based on "the power of hope." Experts around the globe are observing a moral civilization of a growing movement for social development.

Up to the Declaration of Human Rights (1948), we have come to understand any person "as a being with biological, psychological, social and spiritual potentials" (newly founded Viktor Frankl Institute, Murcia).

Around the globe, we are witnessing the irrefutable and undeniable human need to live up to human potentials, to find meaning, to break through egoism, and to drive positive change.

Today, we are challenged by a task no less than making our freedom real, a freedom gained in long developments over the past centuries, and a liberty to be defined for our twenty-first-century workplaces and living conditions.

This freedom is not only a "negative liberty" from oppression – and was actually never meant as a "carte blanche" – but it is rather a potential freedom covering three areas of interaction and relating to the world: our private lives; our legal, social, and political freedom; and our freedom in working together. As human beings, in all these areas we need "recognition," binding us together by commonly shared activities toward strengthening respect, awareness, and consciousness of the other being (Honneth 1995): expressing to each other that the other person is valid in their own right and the source of legitimate claims.

The recognition of the other person becomes the condition of own acknowledgement (Honneth 1995).

What are the implications of this mutual recognition for today's workplaces?

There is a growing awareness for meaningful work. While some observers would associate this term with the Western, saturated culture of searching for meaning in an environment of saturation and pleasure, where persons could afford this quest beyond the toils and drudgeries of workplaces in distant continents, meaningful work actually refers to quite diverse, complex areas of work, addressing the potential benefits of meaningful work for individuals, organizations, societies, and the global community.

Today, business controls vast resources and has an overriding influence on the governance of nations. Excessive greed, unethical practices, and the exploitation of inequalities of workers around the globe are threatening humankind around the globe. Economic success needs to be redefined beyond short-term financial returns.

Recognizing the other person in all spheres of business and production would include exercising the ethics and morals in consumer behavior and in the workplace.

Recognition would address employers, management, and executives in workplaces, addressing issues like:

- International competition and shareholder value effectively damaging working conditions
- Layoffs and closing down of production for profits
- One-sided dismissal of the once valid psychological contract of loyalty between employer and employee
- Unethical business in dictatorships

Recognition of the other person, the Thou, would include consumers answering these concrete ethical questions:

- Which goods and services can be exchanged by money – a question specifically relevant for all health-care-related services
- Not-for-profit orientation of basic goods and services, fulfilling basic human needs
- Public discourse about the conditions and effects of luxury goods production in poor countries for consumers' hedonism in rich countries
- Special tax regulations and offers of safe havens for storing private wealth or bunkering private fortunes for private consumption from public access
- Support of consumer associations

23.2.2 Existential Analysis of the Individual Work Life

Today, we are gifted with grand opportunities of freedom. Responsibility calls on us to deliver on nothing less than the explication of our existence related to work, entailing the elucidation of a person's concrete existential situation with consideration of a self-responsible, self-realized, and humane life. Writing this individual history is work. It includes the assignment of daily striving and struggling, of effort and endeavor, of intention and industry, and of trial and error in search for finding meaning in what we create in our work and in exercising any task.

Where is the What for? Why am I doing what I do? These questions are expressing the existential search for meaningful work, which actually defines the meaning of meaning of our existence: Like Sisyphus (Powell translation of Homer, 2014), to roll the boulder up the hill only to watch it come back again, repeating this laborious action for eternity, triumphantly finding fulfillment in this endless work:

> I leave Sisyphus at the foot of the mountain. One always finds one's burden again… Each atom of that stone, each mineral flake of that night-filled mountain, in itself, forms a world. The struggle itself toward the heights is enough to fill a man's heart. One must imagine Sisyphus happy. (Camus 2005)

23.2.3 Meaning: A Terminal Value

Meaning is a terminal and indivisible value in each person.

Frankl assumes intrinsic meaning and value of life, irrespective of the specific conditions of a person's own articulate and conscious sense of meaning. This concept matches the modern concept and ideal of inviolable human dignity, valid for each human being, irrespective of where and how they live. Frankl's concept of the intrinsic value and meaning in each person's life does not only provide the basis for a potentially positive self-concept, but this approach is especially valid and beneficial for today's volatile workplaces and the dynamic changes that employees are challenged with. This approach provides for the most helpful basic assumptions on a person's indivisible integrity, dignity, worth, and talents, defining these human and individually specified qualities as givens under all circumstances, beyond feelings of failure and setbacks.

23.3 Meaning in Work: Situational Values

Meaning is also an instrumental value. By definition, meaning cannot be assigned, but is rather a matter of actively being specified only by the individual person in the course of *being.* While Frankl focuses on concrete actions in specific situations in order to experience meaningfulness, he also emphasizes that our concrete activities for finding meaning need to be linked to *logos*, which he considers the spiritual core of each person. This core needs to be continually educated, developed, and nourished toward activating goodness, truth, and beauty, linking freedom with responsibility.

According to Frankl's approach, seeking meaning is a matter of constantly searching for a responsible and equally courageous way of *being in the world.* All current leadership concepts are referring to this personal competence in terms of developing personal humility and awareness for the other.

23.3.1 Creative Meaning Values in Work

All humans wish to bring their creativity to life, to experience trustful and supportive relationships, to draw strength from the beauty and natural environment around them, and to have the strength in courageously taking an attitude to setbacks and failures, to tragic events they are facing, and to suffering and life's limitations. These areas of specifically defining and finding meaning are addressed in each and every person in each and every specific workplace. In this sense, there is no situation and no work assignment without meaning. We find meaning in living creative, experiential, and attitudinal values.

Meaning cannot be given, it can only be found. "Meaningful work" is generally being defined by the individual person. It is both significant and positive in valence for this individual person. People engaged in meaningful work seem to be more engaged and committed to their work.

Meaningful work seems important to employees' well-being, job satisfaction, and contentment: people engaged in meaningful work seem to have characteristics that are desirable for organizations, i.e., less risk of turnover, greater commitment to the organization, and greater involvement in organizational citizenship behavior.

Recently, Russo identified four main sources of meaningful work, self, others, the context, and spiritual life, defining and building on two different dimensions of individual motives in work and addressing and integrating the dynamics of perceived meaningful work, when the individual works for the self and for others.

Persons can find *meaning in work*, whenever they experience that their work matters and does make a difference, not for serving their own pleasure hedonically but for "making a difference" for others and being directed toward others, experiencing eudaimonia, growth, and purpose. Today we know that self-actualization does not serve fulfillment in the long term: living our talents and exercising our creative values for egocentric purposes do not bring gratification in the long term. It is only by giving our talents for the good of others that we experience fulfillment.

Persons can *make meaning through their work.* Here, empirical research has found innumerable examples of self-directed action, when persons introduce their talents to their workplace, potentially experiencing moments of flow, and also building and influencing their specific working conditions and the structures and environments of their workplaces, exercising leadership for others, and understanding their work in a broader sense of finding meaning by giving and experiencing their own talents. The examples also include exercising life leadership for oneself and for others and of taking responsibility not only for their own conduct but also for facilitating growth for others. Making meaning includes ideas of fairness, justice, respect, benevolence, ethical behavior, empathy, and compassion.

Both concepts understand meaningful work as work being worthwhile, important, and meaningful and a means of making meaning and fulfilling the desire to positively contribute to the greater good. The desire to make a positive impact on the greater good is consistently related to the experience of meaningful work.

23.3.2 Experiential Meaning Values in Work

There are professions specifically providing experiential values for the individual expert and for the community in all fields of art: literature; performing arts with music, dance, and theater; and visual arts with drawing, painting, sculpting, and architecture provide for many examples of connecting the creative meaning potentials of their vocation with experiential values and meaning potentials for themselves and for others. Studying and contemplating in front of a painting, listening to a piece of music, or viewing a sculpture might address a person's innate core and search for truth, beauty, and the good by following logic, aesthetics, and ethics.

Connecting the experience of flow with *logos* and *nous* is linking the individual state of being completely involved in an activity – for its own sake, when the ego falls away, when the whole being is involved – with the spiritual dimension of the person. Searching for the existential essence of being beyond self-actualization might well be initiated by this experiential meaning value.

Every person needs recognition. Our today's freedom includes our freedom from once potent traditions and religion, once claiming to know what is right or wrong for the individual. This need for personal recognition in fulfilling, loving relationships has been powerfully claimed by individuals for centuries, relating to their private spheres of choosing their partner without pressure and prejudices and external influences and publicly committing to this relationship in terms of a public and legal act.

In the area of work and production, this human need and activity of recognition has been developed and fought for with quite diverging results. Some observers are observing that the call and fundamental values for freedom, equality, and brotherhood (and sisterhood, i.e., fellowship) have been fulfilled least relating to our relations in the workplace, with the other employees sharing a sense of respect, tolerance, acceptance, community, and trust in the organization and sharing a sense of fellowship with the others around the globe, who are contributing to our lifestyle and working for products they perhaps cannot afford due to their poor living conditions or that may harm their health.

Realizing experiential values in work relates to actively shaping and following prosocial, ethical behavior to peer colleagues, in the team and in the organization. Executives are called upon to establish trust, empower others, and assure workplace relationships, governed by trust and mutual respect on eye level, understanding the other person in their own rights and persons with their intrinsic, indivisible value.

Regarding recognition of others, global consciousness is on the rise, when consumers feel shame about others paying the price for their consumer lifestyle, becoming aware of terrible working conditions in other parts of the world or feeling personal guilt for buying goods that are socially unacceptable. Initiatives for supporting fair and sustainable production, for preventing children's work, and for safeguarding better working conditions are growing substantially.

Experiential values closely relate to personal well-being by being grateful and mindful: grateful for the sacrifice that others might introduce in making our lives better, by their working shifts, by their cleaning of our apartment or parks, and by their intelligently managing their daily frustrations about insufficient working conditions or budgets in health and education, while all the same staying on board for our children's well-being and education and for our lives in hospitals and health-care institutions. Exercises of mindfulness and gratefulness for others' work contributions to our personal living and well-being can become a matter of daily routine, in the morning, under the shower, or before falling asleep: reminding each and every one of us in which way specifically our daily lives are deeply connected with others, be it the technology and luxury, of having a daily shower, enjoying coffee or tea, using a smartphone that was produced by persons living and working under devastating conditions, and up to appreciating the juicy apple that was harvested by an unknown farm worker in a warmer place on some other continent. This does not exclude engagement for facilitating improved working conditions, but on the contrary, it rather raises awareness for the global community, shared convictions and it adds encouragement for taking a meaningful attitude towards each and every work.

Personally nourishing and experiencing this thread that binds all of us together might result in other meaningful, creative values of improving and organizing this recognition for the contribution of others in the field of positive legal and social action, promoting people's recognition and their well-being, and preventing further harm.

23.3.3 Attitudinal Meaning Values in Work

> Everything can be taken from a man but one thing: the last of human freedoms to choose one's attitude in any given set of circumstances, to choose one's own way. (Viktor Frankl)

In today's workplaces understanding and practicing attitudinal values have developed into a core element of actualizing meaning.

Individual freedom and responsibility to act on it are indivisible elements of each person's life. This definitely also holds true for shaping one's work life and for taking an attitude toward the situational challenges and tasks that the individual person might be confronted with on their according levels of influence. Be it the factory worker, the executive manager, or the company owner, each individual is challenged to giving their own meaning to their work life, in the concrete way they are exercising their vocation, function, and role, in promoting others and the common good. This human capacity of taking an attitude is attached to daily routines and shows, in concrete situations, when and how the individual person relates to their selves and to other employees, how they communicate their decisions, and how their behaviors can resonate with their fellow colleagues' search for meaning in their concrete work situation. The potentials and strengths of these "positive" attitudinal meaning values are underestimated in the current discussion about meaningful work.

Mostly, finding meaning in work life through attitudinal values is being associated with existential situations in a person's life, with suffering and dealing with the tragic triad of suffering, guilt, and terminal life. Here, the knowledge and culture of attitudinal meaning values are, indeed, most desperately being articulated and most exemplifying the spiritual dimension of elevating and self-transcending the human mind.

It is only natural that we want to avoid inescapable or unavoidable suffering and that we want to keep in control of our lives, of our goals, and of our potentials for achieving these goals. In work life, these "wants" are all associated with success, performance, and functionality. For the individual employee, work is still highly related to their will to meaning, their self-esteem, and all basic feelings and emotions they might experience in the course of their work.

Today's dynamics of workplaces and the changes in specific working environments, apart from the apparent derailing practices and unethical behaviors of companies and individuals, might lead to situations in which the individual feels existentially challenged: unfair feedback, functional degradation, dismissal, forced retirement for health-related reasons, layoffs following downsizing, and closing or shifting of production sites to another country with lower standards.

This employee's will to meaning might initially be existentially frustrated by these external events, which the individual person cannot directly influence, avoid, or struggle against. These events might have diverse, direct, and sometimes dramatic implications for the employee him-/herself and for his/her family, their children, their health, their school and education, and their present and future life.

The "art of being human" is how to deal with these potentially shattering life events. Here, consciously taking an attitude might indeed – beyond the categories of visible material success – provide for the highest "achievement" in this person's life: acceptance of the situation as it is and actively searching for a road to meaningfully deal with this situation have empirically proved to restore and save the best in a person's very core. Supporting and encouraging employees in taking a defiant attitude have become a major issue in management, leadership, coaching, and consulting. Struggling for finding these attitudinal values is a challenging process for the individual in deep distress. Informing the person about the possibilities and potentials resting in themselves in taking this audacious attitude to suffering and to finding the potentially hidden message in this moment of suffering, revising one's set of individual work life goals, making the most of life in spite of suffering, and transforming the suffering into giving a heroic example to others, or transcending suffering by cultivating spirituality, are ways of strengthening and activating the person's inherent meaning of life and their will to meaning.

Taking this meaning-oriented attitude can potentially turn feelings of victimization to forthrightness, hopelessness into hope, humiliation into self-esteem, disgrace into virtue, reproach into regard, degradation into morality, and despair into meaning.

Encouraging, empowering, and actualizing meaning in a seemingly restricted situation, when decisions seem to be settled beyond the influence of the individual employee and when the die (seems to be or) is cast, Frankl's legacy remains to be recalled for dealing with the existential frustrations of twenty-first-century workplaces, mainly the inviolable individual freedom to choose one's attitude and own way in any circumstances.

23.4 Meaningful Work: A Means?

In today's business, there seems to be a silently shared understanding of the importance of meaningful workplaces. Generally there are two motivations for acknowledging this will to meaning, which are being discussed in management and research literature. These two roads might be defined, in terms of a "hard problem" dilemma (Michaelson et al. 2014), posing a systemic question.

Meaningfulness is subjective, emerging from the individual mind, in the eye of the beholder. Allowing every individual to decide what work they most wish to do, without regard for market value, would reverse the mainstream approach of capitalism.

Rather than, more or less theoretically, questioning the capitalist system as such, this notion is searching for new approaches in reinventing organizations. This understanding is based on the belief that human beings can by their own will and focused activities change mainstream thinking up to transforming business, with better business results following almost naturally. This pioneer motivation is to benevolently recognizing the individual person's intrinsic will to meaning to finding meaningful work, including the discourse about the practical, responsible consequences of this understanding. Here, we would find the innumerous examples of doing conscious business, of sustainable banking, and of substantially reinventing organizations.

Leaving everything as it is and, in parallel, trying something new "here and there" can be understood in terms of squaring the circle: focusing on meaning and staying in the system at the same time.

In search for meaning in work life, we are confronted with fundamental dilemmas, holding us internally as human beings, in the organization and beyond, which need to be transparently discussed and decided in the open:

- Autonomy vs. control by others
- Hierarchy vs. democracy
- Meaning vs. meaning indifference
- Continuity vs. agility
- Change vs. stability

23.5 Commonalities to Share

Meaning is at the heart of the human experience and well-being. Search for meaning is a natural component of work life.

Meaning is both personally construed and socially constructed. Meaning is highly sensitive to individual and cultural differences.

Informed by existential psychology, philosophy, and an understanding of the duality of human existence, current approaches recognize the dark side of the human condition as well as the bright side of fulfilling human potentials.

An integrated and meaning-centered approach not only provides for a realistic understanding of the human condition and the existential givens, but it also empowers all stakeholders to achieve human excellence and create good work to the benefit of all – the individual, the organization, and the society.

Current research is further investigating the connection between human's search for meaning, meaningful work, satisfaction in life and well-being, workplace engagement, motivation, sense of calling, stress, resilience, and experiencing flow and coping, when faced with desperate and existential situations.

The growing part of humans with total indifference toward any issues relating to meaning and to the fulfilling aspects of personally leading a meaningful life needs further attention, because they might actively and passively fall outside any area of public concern, and needs fulfillment by and in the communities they live in.

What commonalities do all the abovementioned approaches share?

Following philosophers of all times, searching for meaning and meaning-making are the meaning of life. It is through experiencing existential givens, questioning our way of being and living, that we are challenged to answer. It is through the intentionality of human existence, of human thinking, feeling, and acting being directed to something, that we are called to consciously reflect on our being in this world.

Our freedom and responsibility to act is always related to specific situations. The aims and purpose, the culture and specific ways we work, the way we produce and exercise our specific roles and functions in this work, the ways we relate to others and the world in what we are doing, and the decisions we make, relating to the conclusions we draw from what we have come to know about ourselves, our work, our environment, and the global community, are "on the table." We are not condemned to choose, but we are rather motivated to find meaning in what we choose and to make sense of what we choose.

Being confronted with the dilemmas of our times is the starting point for change. Life calls upon us to answer to the questions of these times. We are constantly reconstructing and recreating our world. Doubts are the beginning of all change. It is the tensions of human existence that provide for the space for developments and our freedom to act.

What direction do we take in acknowledging reality and the choices we can make in living an authentic life with freedom, responsibility, and courage?

Hurtful as it may be, the starting point for developments is the exploration of what is true. Distancing ourselves for a moment from our immediate involvement in our daily challenges and taking scientific reports' third perspective, what do they tell us?

They share the diagnosis of the sufferings, the ills and ailments of today's world. They see the trends to dehumanization of individuals, the still ruling man-machine thinking, the ruling concept of human mankind as a solely utilitarian, selfish *homo economicus.*

They all acknowledge the facts and data about the highly disturbing mental health situation and suicide rates in the rich countries. They all share their concern about workplaces inadequate to sustainably fulfill human needs, resulting in boredom, alienation, addiction, burnout, abuse, and existential vacuum and harming the dignity and integrity of humans.

They are airing their grievances about the culturally dominant message of fear, negativity, scarcity, mainstream scenarios of eventual destruction and, finally, man's apparent incapacities, shortcomings, sufferings, and deadly failures.

They all are actively engaged in various initiatives and activities in the field of prevention and support programs for health and well-being.

They share their will to introduce visible and effective change in whatever area they are active. They acknowledge theirfreedom not only *from* hindering circumstances but also leaving them *free enough to* take action. They are defining their freedom in a proactive, forward-looking perspective. They understand their selves as free enough to take action and to take responsibility for their influence taking.

They all have a vision of what man is positively capable of doing and can "become." Whatever function they are exercising, visibly and in executive positions or in their daily work, they bring meaning to their own lives by empowering their peers and engaging for a common cause.

They all share, directly or indirectly and outspoken or silently, Viktor Frankl's idealistic–realistic approach of acknowledging and nurturing the human capacity for virtuousness and good intentions and thereby actively rehumanizing workplaces and building sustainable relationships.

They are willing to constantly take a critical look at their selves and of changing themselves to dynamically better meet the needs of others.

They all share a systemic approach seeing the limitations of a growth strategy at the expense of others, and at the same time, they see what positive influence their own behaviors can have on their next reports, on their colleagues, on their customers and clients, and on the global community, here and now.

They are supporting all those who are struggling with the negative territories of life and who are faced with existential situations.

They encourage others in giving meaning to their lives until their very last minute, because each and every life has a meaning under all circumstances.

They all are continuously building one grand community with a sense of affluence in human virtues and strengths, because they trust in the common understanding that "life can never become short of meaning" (V. Frankl).

They all are leaving their footprints and legacy in this world, and thereby they suspend the axis of success and failure to living meaningful lives, introducing innumerous meaningful moments and thereby actually changing this world in the most dramatic sense – I dare say – they are saving lives by living the moment as if it was their one and only chance, which actually existentially holds true.

Building this community might well establish the "critical mass" that can change the general direction of global developments for establishing better workplaces.

23.6 Working Together for Finding Meaning in Today's World

Viktor E. Frankl has left us a rich legacy that we are called upon to bring to light in our time: "The world is hurt, but can be healed" (V. E. Frankl). The spiritual question comes up in poverty and in wealth alike.

We are currently observing a renaissance of the question of meaning, because meaning has become so doubtful in a historically unequalled situation of global interrelations, vast and incalculable complexity, and simple meaning offers being made to the individual, searching for an answer to the fundamental questions in their own lives and finding the right way between right and wrong.

There are some indications of turning the tragic triad of life into "justified optimism," for hope in the face of tragedy and for courage in inciting the Copernican turn.

These are some of the fundamental aspects of Frankl's legacy for the twenty-first century, explored by his student E. Lukas in her 2014 acceptance speech for Honorary Professorship bestowed from the Moscow Institute for Psychoanalysis (Lukas 2014):

- Conscience, the human organ of sense, is being refined with the progress of culture in humanity's long-term development. Supported by the means of modern communication, a great diversity of opinions and thoughts emerge. There is a glimmer of hope that resistance, self-determination, and self-confidence will rise among nations and individuals alike. Conscience is the most intimate pathfinder of the individual and of human evolution as a whole. If all the human accomplishments by peaceful conviction would go together hand in hand, progress of humaneness would be within reach.
- The power of thinking things through: there is a growing need for time and space to reflect, escaping the constant sensory overload, and getting access to the "two layers of thinking" (Frankl) – the rational, logical comprehension of things, connected to intelligence and memory, and the layer of wisdom, acceptance, freedom, consciousness, and responsibility. Leaving the sensual overload and going to the desert in order to recover own competencies and abilities to "think first – then act" are leading to the human potentials for hearing the spiritual calling of the hour and intensify a vigorous culture of reflection. This activity, however, starts with a sacrifice, self-restraint, and humility in slowing down and liberating ourselves from the inviting clutter of things.
- Digitalization, the development of computers, leads us to another aspect of hope: Mankind has created a third brain, besides his own right and left brain activities. This third brain can, if used properly, avoid false assessments and assumptions of reality. We decide if something might make sense; computers can help us in our own decision-making on taking the ethically right direction. This is an amazing technical repertoire that needs to be controlled by something meta-technical in order not to turn against its inventors.
- Globalization as an aspect of hope: Being connected with the world constantly shows us the splendid common denominators of our existence, uniting humanity around the globe on common grounds: We have learned that we will all be well or all be miserable (climate change). We are "all in this together" and are connected by this "monanthropism" (Frankl) of current challenges and common existential needs to be fulfilled.

Lukas (2014) applies Frankl's concept and engagement to twenty-first century's challenges and imagines his potential call upon us: "You are the being that always decides. With your spiritual capacities, you are the active collaborator of your fate. With your actions you are writing in a book of history, telling about the past, with an unknown number of blank pages, which, at the end, will testify on your behalf. Turn this into an epic, worthy of you."

Life is questioning us. We give the answer. Individually, as a group, as a community, each and every moment. Time and again.

Research and practice have shown the broad range of domains potentially contributive to a person's meaning in life, among them work life, implementing creative, experiential, and attitudinal values. Type of work, function, sense of control and coherence, and positive leadership are influencing the level of personal meaning in life, quality of life, personal well-being, and health.

With its general framework of defining the human condition, Frankl's approach remains an empirically tested "last call for action," based on philosophy, history, knowledge, and research in all fields.

Understanding individuals with their three-dimensional individual capacities of body, psychosocial aspects, and the spirit/Geist is providing the basis for a fresh approach in today's specifically Western world search for spiritual void and assurance.

The individual person's search for meaning can be considered as deeply rooted in one's personality and thinking. The special set of meaning constructs that a person may have access to is a matter of knowledge and general awareness about humanity's cultural heritage, the human condition as such and the rich traditions and global spiritual endowment of dealing with the duality of life.

Viktor Frankl's approach integrates learning, cognition, and awareness raising approaches by going beyond and by referring to the uniqueness of the human dimension and by therefore providing the most comprehensive approach for understanding and overcoming the present challenges and for providing the most resourceful basis for action:

The person's inherent "defiant spirit" remains the most powerful human capacity for change that cannot be destroyed and that can provide for the most unexpected changes on a global scale.

Faced with tremendous conflicts and tragic events, the individual freedom and responsibility to act on it provide for the last resort of human dignity to conscientiously contribute to a good life for all.

Overcoming the existential vacuum of our times needs answering the demands and challenges of our time with courage and openness to crossing borders in cultural and minds.

The "gift" of self-detachment and self-distancing, this awesome, specifically human capacity to take a third perspective on each situation, can be a source of creativity, contributing to the best of humanity.

Meaningful work can be a most rewarding objective to preserve and promote better and fair living conditions that support meaningful lives for their people.

Challenged by today's demands in all realms of life, we are bound to remain tragic optimists under all circumstances.

Life is questioning us; we give the answers:

What does life demand of us individually, in our function at work, and in all our private and public roles?
How is life questioning us as persons, teams, communities, and collectively?
What is our responsibility to society and humanity?
How can we as individual persons, in our respective functions, promote peace, harmony, and well-being in the workplace and in the world?
How can we empower people in their every day or existential situations and challenges to find meaning, hope, and well-being?
How can we recognize and connect with the contributions from other relevant approaches, integrating them into our common cause for improving living conditions?
How can we build on cross-cultural knowledge and awareness?
How can we strengthen hope as the ability to believe in a better future in spite of bleak reality and experience the capacity to rise in the midst of suffering?

While "we are all the same inside," we are challenged to accept the duality of negatives and positives as the essence of the human condition and to acknowledge and benefit from diverse and culturally different backgrounds and perspectives.

Our internationally shared mission as humans is to advance a servant and cooperative agenda; to enhance the well-being of all people, especially of the disadvantaged; and to alleviate their suffering. We have all the knowledge we need. We are all in this together. It is time to act, to embrace the future. We have all the knowledge, the capacities, the freedom, and the responsibility to act.

References

Camus A (2005) The myth of sisyphus. Penguin Books, New York
Csikszentmihalyi M (2003) Good business. Penguin Books, New York
Frankl VE (2006) Man's search for meaning. Beacon Press, New York
Honneth A (1995) The struggle for recognition: the moral grammar of social conflicts. Polity Press, Cambridge, MA
Lukas E (2014) Acceptance speech on the occasion of her Honorary Professorship at the Moscow University Institute of Psychoanalysis, held in Vienna, download from: https://www.elisabeth-lukas-archiv.de/welcome/elisabeth-lukas/honorary-professorship/
Michaelson C, Pratt MG, Grant AM, Dunn CP (2014) Meaningful work: connecting business ethics and organization studies. J Bus Ethics 121:77–90
Powell B (transl.) (2014) Homer's Iliad and Odyssey. The Essential Books, Oxford
Steger MF, Dik BJ, Duffy RD (2012) Measuring meaningful work: the work and meaning inventory (WAMI). J Career Assess 00(0):1–16. https://doi.org/10.1177/1069072711436160

About the Author

Beate von Devivere, M. A. and Graduate Sociologist
Owner of bvd Consult. Consulting. Coaching. Counseling.
International Practice in Frankfurt am Main, Germany.

Professional Background
For more than 20 years, Beate von Devivere has been consulting organizations and offering counseling and coaching for their staff and the international community, notably logotherapy and existential analysis. She started her professional career in technology assessment and media research, has acquired extensive management experience, and was seconded to various international OSCE peacekeeping missions. As a lecturer and trainer, she specializes in leadership trainings and management tools and has published various nonfiction books on global living conditions.

Psychotherapy Accreditation
Accreditation includes Logotherapy and Existential Analysis (accredited by Viktor Frankl Institute VFI Vienna), World Council for Psychotherapy (WCP Vienna), and Practitioner for Psychotherapy (German Government).

Academic Background
She is a graduate sociologist in Sociology, Social Psychology, and Public Law (Dipl. Soz.) from JW Goethe University in Frankfurt am Main (Germany) and received her Master of Arts in Human Resources Change Management from Technical University Kaiserslautern Center for Distance Learning.

B. von Devivere, *Meaningful Work: Viktor Frankl's Legacy for the 21st Century*,
https://doi.org/10.1007/978-3-319-89791-2

Index

B. von Devivere, *Meaningful Work: Viktor Frankl's Legacy for the 21st Century*,
https://doi.org/10.1007/978-3-319-89791-2

MIX
Papier aus verantwortungsvollen Quellen
Paper from responsible sources
FSC® C105338

If you have any concerns about our products,
you can contact us on
ProductSafety@springernature.com

In case Publisher is established outside the EU,
the EU authorized representative is:
Springer Nature Customer Service Center GmbH
Europaplatz 3, 69115 Heidelberg, Germany

Printed by Libri Plureos GmbH
in Hamburg, Germany